DISABILITY STUDIES AND THE INCLUSIVE CLASSROOM

Critical Practices for Embracing Diversity in Education

Second Edition

Susan Baglieri
with Arthur Shapiro

Routledge
Taylor & Francis Group

NEW YORK AND LONDON

Second edition published 2017
by Routledge
711 Third Avenue, New York, NY 10017

and by Routledge
2 Park Square, Milton Park, Abingdon, Oxon, OX14 4RN

Routledge is an imprint of the Taylor & Francis Group, an informa business

© 2017 Taylor & Francis

First edition published 2012 by Routledge

Library of Congress Cataloging-in-Publication Data
Names: Baglieri, Susan, author. | Shapiro, Arthur, author.
Title: Disability studies and the inclusive classroom : critical practices for embracing diversity in education / Susan Baglieri and Arthur Shapiro.
Description: Second Edition. | New York : Routledge, 2017. | "First edition published by Routledge 2012"—T.p. verso. | Includes bibliographical references.
Identifiers: LCCN 2016045463 (print) | LCCN 2016045687 (ebook) | ISBN 9781138188266 (Hardback) | ISBN 9781138188273 (Paperback) | ISBN 9781315642543 (Ebook) | ISBN 9781315642543 (eBook)
Subjects: LCSH: People with disabilities—Education. | Inclusive education.
Classification: LCC LC4019.B275 2017 (print) | LCC LC4019 (ebook) | DDC 371.9/046—dc23
LC record available at https://lccn.loc.gov/2016045463

ISBN: 978-1-138-18826-6 (hbk)
ISBN: 978-1-138-18827-3 (pbk)
ISBN: 978-1-315-64254-3 (ebk)

Typeset in Minion
by Apex CoVantage, LLC

For Lucien and Julian

CONTENTS

PREFACE

The second edition of *Disability Studies and the Inclusive Classroom* is the third iteration of work that was begun in the book by Arthur Shapiro, *Everybody Belongs*, in 1999. The newest version reflects the intersections and collaborations that are growing among inclusive education, multicultural education, and social justice education. New and revised chapters highlight the intersections between disability studies and critical multicultural studies to illustrate theories and practices that are enriched through mutual engagement. Although this book is squarely centered on disability, it characterizes inclusive education as that which accounts for and is accountable to all learners, especially those who have histories of being marginalized in schools.

The book emphasizes that to understand the issues of disability, schooling, and inclusive education we must critically examine the meanings of disability in culture. By understanding disability and disablement as produced in culture, we can better consider our beliefs and attitudes about disability as amalgamations of world histories, societal messages, and personal experiences. Rather than accepting common, often negative, stereotypes of disability and difference we can teach children to respect, appreciate, and embrace the diversities that give vibrancy to the world.

The field of disability studies is instructive in challenging traditional conceptions of disability and education. Disability studies offers an alternative to a medical model of disability. Utilizing a social model, disability is perceived in its cultural, sociological, psychological, and historical dimensions. Disability studies provides the theoretical grounding and activist spirit to move readers toward a broad, deep, and insightful understanding of disability and educational practice. The second edition includes:

- A new opening chapter that defines goals for inclusive education in connection with goals of multicultural and social justice education.
- Re-organization of Chapters 3 and 4 to provide a cultural overview of disability that illustrates the cyclical nature of orientations toward disability across the past and present.

- Chapter 7 is a new addition that illustrates commonalities across approaches to educating students who have not fit the mold laid out in schools. Situating students with disabilities in the broader context of perspectives on curriculum and education makes clear that inclusive education aims for school reform that includes but also extends beyond improvements in special education.
- Other chapters are also re-titled and re-organized to reflect clearer distinctions among instructional design, delivery of special services, and designing disability-inclusive curriculum.

The completion of the second edition is bittersweet. Arthur Shapiro passed away in 2010, as the manuscript for the first edition was near completion. A labor of love and commitment to justice, his research, wisdom, and hope for inclusive education were inscribed in the pages of the first edition. I am honored to enable his legacy to continue in the publication of the second. I offer my deepest thanks to Elly Shapiro for her support of the project. I am grateful to the team at Taylor & Francis and wish to express my sincerest appreciation for them. Lauren Frankfurt and Hannah Slater provided swift and responsive assistance and guidance toward production. I am humbled and awed by the rigorous work of editing performed by Alison Jones. I offer deepest thanks to Alex Masulis for his advice, encouragement, for not putting wheelchairs or puzzle pieces on the cover, and for the opportunity to bring this work to fruition.

S.B.

Part I

DISABILITY AND SOCIETY

1

WHAT IS INCLUSIVE EDUCATION?

Inclusion is the term used to describe school-based arrangements in which students with and without disabilities learn together in general education settings. Inclusion has been an integral step toward equity in education, the expansion of civil rights, and societal integration of young people with disabilities. Efforts to develop inclusion in schools and society have been underway for several decades. In the USA, for example, the 1975 *Education for All Handicapped Children Act* (EHA) (P.L. 94–142) first specified the right of students with disabilities to receive a free and appropriate education in the least restrictive environment. Recognized by many other nations, the 1994 adoption of the *Salamanca Statement and Framework for Action on Special Needs Education* by the United Nations Educational, Scientific and Cultural Organization (UNESCO), proclaims the fundamental right of all children to educational opportunity. With the world as its forum, work to create inclusive schools and communities is a project shared by young people, families, educators, neighbors, employers, activists, and policy makers—in short, all of us.

There is clear consensus for the value of inclusivity and the desire for communities to embrace their members and enable all to strive toward engaged and satisfying lives. Work toward creating inclusive schools and societies, however, requires us to contend with histories and beliefs about ability and disability that have long led to exclusion. Many physical structures, like buildings and developed public areas, shape a built world that does not always enable equal access for all. Community systems, like education, work environments, and other service and recreation programs, can be slow to change. Beliefs and attitudes about difference, diversity, and disability that lead to prejudice and discrimination persist through culture. The confluence of inaccessible structures in the built world, the inertia of tradition, and the persistence of prejudicial beliefs regarding disability can be understood as ableism (Campbell, 2009; Goodley, 2014). When we understand that multiple factors, which operate in a complex and intertwining manner, contribute to the continued exclusion of people with disabilities from school and society it becomes evident that seeking inclusive education is a multifaceted and equally complex endeavor. Aiming to create inclusive education means to seek understanding about ableism and take action to resist and interrupt ways of thinking and doing that are steeped within the ways schools operate. In this chapter we begin by describing what we mean by inclusive education and outlining intersecting and allied commitments across areas of educational study.

INCLUSION AND INCLUSIVE EDUCATION

In the USA, the term, **inclusion**, has become the most common to refer to practices that integrate students with and without disabilities in general education. Inclusion usually means that special educational supports, including specialized curriculum are provided in the general education setting. The Least Restrictive Environment (LRE) is a concept featured in the *Individuals with Disabilities Education Improvement Act* (IDEIA), which is the American policy that guides school practices for students with disabilities. The earliest version of the IDEIA was entered into society as Public Law 94–142 in 1975, and titled the Education for All Handicapped Children Act (EHA). The most current authorized version of the law is the IDEIA of 2004. The LRE specifies:

> To the maximum extent appropriate, children with disabilities, including children in public or private institutions or other care facilities, are educated with children who are not disabled, and special classes, separate schooling, or other removal of children with disabilities from the regular educational environment occurs only when the nature or severity of the disability of a child is such that education in regular classes with the use of supplementary aids and services cannot be achieved satisfactorily.
>
> (20 U.S.C. 1412(a)(5)(B))

The LRE clause is widely understood to indicate a preference for inclusion. It establishes the presumption that students with disabilities are educated with those who are not disabled in what are typically deemed "general" educational environments, to the maximum extent appropriate.

While inclusion nearly always refers to integrating students with and without disabilities in schools, a broader, more embracive idea of inclusive education also exists in education literature. Ballard (1999), for example, argues that inclusive education means the removal of barriers to learning for all children and works toward improving access and participation not just for students with disabilities, but for all those experiencing disadvantage in schools, whether related to "poverty, sexuality, minority ethnic status, or other characteristics assigned significance by the dominant culture in their society" (p. 2). Inclusive education strives for pluralistic teaching practices that create contexts for learning in which every student can identify with and connect to the school and to one another. The meaning and interpretation of the terms inclusion and the LRE have been the subject of contentious debate. For the purposes of this book we prioritize the language and concepts held within the broad idea of inclusive education to highlight the complex and multifaceted work of creating community and belonging in schools. Inclusive education is a concept that contains, but also transcends the emphasis on special education placement and service provision in general education. Inclusive education, in other words, encompasses the experiences of students with disabilities, but is not exclusive to them. The field of disability studies provides a useful foundation for understanding theory and practice in inclusive education.

THEORIES OF INCLUSIVE EDUCATION: INTRODUCING DISABILITY STUDIES

Disability studies is an interdisciplinary field of scholarship that seeks to expand the ways that society defines, conceptualizes, and understands the meaning of disability. Disability studies developed within and through the Disability Rights movement, which emerged during the 1960s "as a time of excitement, organizational strength, and identity exploration" through which people with disabilities, "like feminists, African Americans, and gay and lesbian activists . . . insisted that their bodies did not render them defective, [and] could even be sources of political, sexual, and artistic strength" (Nielsen, 2012, p. 160). Early and continuing efforts of disability rights activists draw attention to political, economic, and social conditions that affect the lives of disabled people as much as, or perhaps more than, the impact of impairment. With its origin in disability rights, the purposes of disability studies are markedly political. Longmore and Umansky (2001) explain, "Disability studies takes as its domain the intricate interaction among cultural values, social arrangements, public policy, and professional practice regarding 'disability'" (p. 12). They focus on contributions, experiences, and history of people with disabilities as a means to articulate past and present understandings of disability and reflect the aims of the Disability Rights movement. Through the joint missions of scholarship and activism, those aligned with disability studies underscore disability and disabled persons' experiences as distinctive and productive worldviews through which to engage in examination and critique of culture in order to pose problems and possibilities.

A significant contribution of disability studies to educational thought and practice is the articulation of the medical model and social models of disability. The medical model establishes disability to be an experience and identity belonging to the individual as a reflection of an abnormally disordered body, mind, or affect. Social models of disability, in contrast, propose disability experiences and identities as those that become embodied as people are enabled and disabled through their interactions in society. Disability, then, affects an individual, but is a reflection of how society regards and facilitates or impedes interactions among people with all kinds of bodies, minds, and affects. Disability studies involve examining the policies and practices of societies to emphasize and study the social and cultural determinants of disability, rather than the focus on physiological aspects within the medical model (Linton, 1998). Ware (2001) forwards, "the new disability studies understand disability as a way of thinking about bodies rather than as something that is wrong with bodies" (p. 110).

The medical model is the dominant perspective about disability in society and its influence in education is evident. Shea and Bauer (1997) explain that the medical model "contends that the disability should be diagnosed, prescriptive programs should be designed, and efforts should be made to remediate the disability" (p. 423). In the medical model, fixing or curing the disability can become the primary focus in the child's life and education. This perspective can lead to all other activities, including future planning, being suspended until the child is cured or remediated. Biklen, Ferguson, and Ford, at the vanguard of inclusive educational thought, in 1989, pointed out:

> Students perceived as having problems, like something broken, are sent to resource rooms, special classes, even special schools or institutions, to be repaired and later returned. Unlike a repair shop, however, many students in special education—indeed the preponderance of them never escape the special label and placement (excluding those with speech impairments that are either cured or simply disappear by the time students reach secondary level). They stay in the repair shop.
>
> (p. 8)

A significant outcome of the medical model's prevalence in education, then, is the focus on the individual as the site of problem and the development of education practices that prioritized remediation of disability. This priority, however well intended and potentially helpful, has been enacted in ways that attach special educational supports and services to particular classes that only have children with disabilities, which precludes their participation in other aspects of schools (Taylor, 1988). Disability studies offers tools for analysis that challenge the idea that "the assigned roles of people with disabilities are inevitable outcomes of their condition," which is the assumption in a medical model (Linton, as cited in Fleischer & Zames, 2001, p. 206).

The development of social models of disability within education shifts our work from a primary focus on how to remediate disability to examination of how the school environment facilitates or impedes interactions among children with all kinds of bodies, minds, and affects. Agitating for the right of children with disabilities to have equal access and opportunity in schools is a way that the Disability Rights Movement influences education, with particular emphasis on inclusion. Disability studies practitioners further point out that instruction to children with disabilities that focuses *only* on their diagnosis and remediation of impairment inequitably constrains their school experience. By framing disability in its social dimensions, attention is instead focused on how schools and curriculum may be constructed and reformed to enable students with disabilities to gain access to learning and participating with their peers.

Scholarship in disability studies with particular respect to education is burgeoning (Gabel & Danforth, 2008). Barton and Armstrong (2001) offer a view of inclusive education that prioritizes attention on removing barriers to access. In doing so, they shift the focus from the "deficient" student—as in a medical model—to the responsibility of the school and its creation of barrier-free social and organizational structures. They explain:

> From the perspectives we have adopted, inclusion is not about placement into an unchanged system of provision and practice. Also, it is not merely about the

participation of a specific group of formerly categorized individuals. . . . It is about removing *all* forms of barriers to access and learning for *all* children who are experiencing disadvantage. This approach is rooted in conceptions of democracy, citizenship, and a version of the "good" society. . . . Thus, inclusive education is not an end in itself but a means to an end—that of the realization of an inclusive society. This necessitates schools adopting a critical stance both internally and externally toward all forms of justice and discrimination.

(p. 708)

Barton and Armstrong (2001) provide a clear call for inclusive educational reform that extends beyond the right of children with disabilities to access education. Inclusive education is a process, or project, that emanates from a critique of schooling that recognizes that injustices experienced by children with disabilities are rooted in systemic problems that are also experienced by many others.

Taking a critical stance to examine education, and not just special education, characterizes the work of disability studies in education. As Tom Skrtic (1991) points out in the groundbreaking book, *Behind Special Education*, the system of special education emerged to enable schools to proceed without changing to meet the needs, goals, or expectations of children and families. Labeling struggling children as having disabilities and moving them to the parallel system of special education provided a rationale for preserving the bureaucracy of schooling. In what Skrtic deems an organizational pathology, the development of special education is the symptom of a dysfunctional educational system that does not serve its communities. In short, the foundations of a disability studies perspective on inclusive education hinges on our willingness to recognize that schools and the education system must shift to meet the diversity of communities if they are to play a productive role in seeking equity, justice, and democracy.

In imagining schools in their potential to move toward equity, justice, and democracy, disability studies finds strong allies in the fields of multicultural and social justice education. Before disability studies and before the EHA was passed in 1975, the struggle for civil rights in education, equal opportunity, and desegregation of schools was already well underway for African-American children. The extended study and works in the ongoing project to seek racial equity in education yields deep understanding of the conditions and impact of segregation and contributes a range of perspectives on how to work toward educational equity. Although movements for multicultural and social justice education have emerged along separate trajectories and with differing specific commitments, they share a perspective on schooling and education that informs inclusive education within and in partner to a disability studies framework. Each, separately and in intersection, have much to contribute to inclusive school reform.

MULTICULTURAL EDUCATION

Multicultural education is a ranging and diverse area of study and practice that challenges the dominance of White and Eurocentric curriculum and practice in schools (Banks, 1993; 2005). The racial desegregation that occurred in the 1950s in the USA is often thought of as students of color being integrated into "White" schools. The response of the education system, then, was to assimilate children of color into contexts that had been created in their absence and in the presumption of the supremacy of White culture. At the heart of multicultural education is the need to reform schools in ways that account for and are accountable to students of color. Banks (1993) identities five initiatives undertaken within multicultural education. Work toward (a) content integration strives to diversify the canon of school curriculum to increase its representation of people of color and their works. A critical perspective on processes of (b) knowledge construction requires educators to understand and engage with the impact of perspective, values, place, and time on what is presented as knowledge or truth. Efforts toward (c) prejudice reduction explicitly target racial bias and assumptions. Developing (d) equity pedagogies and (e) school cultures in which students of color are empowered aim to improve teaching practices and broader institutional structures of schools to result in increased opportunity and access to achievement toward educational equity. Over several decades of work, the umbrella of multicultural education has grown beyond a sole interest in the experiences of children of color. Work toward seeking equity for other groups at risk of marginalization in schools—including girls, young women, gender non-conforming youth, lesbian and gay students, children from non-dominant religious, ethnic, and linguistic families, and students living in poverty—is often addressed within a multicultural framework (Steinberg, 2009). Disability is also increasingly becoming part of its purview (Connor, 2012). Those in multicultural education argue that social stratification, collective experience, and shared history contribute to worldviews and ways of knowing associated with group identities that influence life in schools and interactions with curriculum.

The influence of social stratification and the opportunity gaps among students who attend poor, affluent, urban, rural, or suburban schools is well documented. Similarly, that inequitable access to educational opportunity correlates with race, disability, and language is also a persistent finding in educational research (Blanchett, 2006). Multicultural education advances work to desegregate students by race, disability, and gender, as well as equalize students' opportunities to access advanced content and high quality of teachers and facilities. Another facet of multicultural education aims to articulate the relationship between social group identity and life in schools. In the germinal work, *The Souls of Black Folk: Essays and Sketches*, published in 1903, W.E.B. Du Bois described the concept of double-consciousness. Du Bois proposed double-consciousness to capture the experience of being Black in America as negotiating "two warring ideals" between Negro and American identities. It represents the struggle between knowing the self as an American whose worth and place is perceived through a lens of White supremacy, and as a person of African descent estranged from heritage and culture by enslavement and colonialism. African-American experience, through this lens, may be understood as one of conflicted striving in a context in which being "American" is not easily compatible with or recognizable as Black identity and experience. Schools, proponents of multicultural education argue, exacerbate the distance between "American" ideals and the experiences of students of color when they do not provide equal opportunity—which is persistently the case when poorly performing urban schools serve students of color in higher proportions than in better-performing schools in other regions. The American message that education is a gateway to opportunity may ring hollow for many in the most disenfranchised locales and neighborhoods.

The movements of Pan-Africanism and Africentrism contribute to the insistence that Black experiences and histories be accounted for in the human experience. One aspect of multicultural education, then, is to offer school curriculum that reflects the world's history and diversity and does so in recognition of varied perspectives that influence the knowledge of academic disciplines. By diversifying the content and representation of people of color and other identity groups in school curriculum, the aim is to create American education through an integrative worldview—one in which Black experiences, women's experiences, and those of persons with disabilities, for example, are conceived as inextricable from the idea of a quintessentially American experience. Such work requires a shift from the Eurocentric and patriarchal paradigms that have long been privileged in school curriculum. It requires explicit reconstruction of colonial narratives that have long equated Western/European domination with manifest destiny of "progress" and White supremacy. That the histories and contributions of people of color be included in the American curriculum canon is a fairly forthright endeavor, which is not to suggest the ease of this work, simply its clarity of mission.

The concept of double-consciousness, in addition to capturing the psychic experience of occupying multiple identities and social positions, begins to draw out the development of collective and relational identities important to understand more complex concepts in multicultural education. The concepts of a Black aesthetic and the idea of the Black imagination organize the cultural histories and collective experiences that shape understanding of Black racial identity. Essential within Du Bois's (1903) idea of double-consciousness is understanding race and racialized identities as relational. What is Blackness in the absence of Whiteness, we may ask? For Du Bois, being Black in America meant seeing oneself through the lens of Whiteness, the perspective of those in power. In contemporary understandings, Du Bois's conception remains relevant to multicultural education. Being a student in an American school is to measure oneself against a curriculum lens and standard built on an image of the culture of power, which remains largely occupied by Whiteness. Simultaneous questions raised in multicultural education are, how can we provide equity in schools to enable all students access to the culture of power? And, how can we change the center of power to empower disenfranchised youth? Considerably different ideas arise in response to either or both of these questions. Some see the development of equity pedagogies and creation of empowering school cultures as the employment of strategies and culturally responsive practices that draw from students' funds of knowledge to enable achievement and upward economic mobility. Others understand the search for equity and empowerment in schools as a direct confrontation of racism, sexism, and ableism in school and society.

Critical Race Theory (CRT) and Whiteness studies are fields committed to examining and explicating how the distribution of power and privilege is mediated by and through status associated with color. CRT and Whiteness studies do not see racism as a waning artifact of history, but as active and present processes. Leonardo (2009) points out that Whiteness is a status associated with color, but experienced and expressed as power and privilege. Various groups over time—Italian, German, and Irish immigrants, for example—were not initially considered "white" in America. The recognition of these groups as "white" signified a change in their relational status, not complexion. Understanding Whiteness as a moving target directs focus away from seeing racism as the doing of "bad actors," and toward perceiving the collective experience and expression of White consciousness and White privilege that constitute, perhaps, the other side of Du Bois's lens. Those in the fields of Whiteness studies and CRT interested in multicultural education see the persistence of racial inequity in schools as a reflection of a hierarchy made convenient by history and persistently naturalized within racism.

The idea of double-consciousness is conceptually similar to, if not directly referenced in, understandings of identity and status of members of other groups considered within multicultural education. Like the relational status that Black persons experience in comparison to an image of the American as emblematic of Whiteness, other group identities have also developed as a response to collective subjugation and/ or measurement against a normate. Other groups do not seek to appropriate the identities and aims on which multicultural education for people of color are built. Rather, they build on and sharpen the construct of the normate against which many Others are valued and devalued. Within education, the normate is an abstract, symbolic representation of statistical averages and desired experiences and expectations ascribed by the culture of power.

The culture of power in education can be traced to the ideal of the public school to reflect and advance Protestant culture, the development of capitalism, and the hope for representative democracy (Kaestle, 1976). In historical context, students were separated by gender, race, and disability well into the twentieth century. It suffices to say that the school curriculum was designed to advance values and ideals modeled after the interests of White, middle class, Protestant men; neither women, nor Black people, could vote. The normative experience of education, then, was built on the image of and in service to White boys. A bit farther into the future, the educational normate increasingly became constructed in the description of achievement as statistical measure generated through testing data. For example, the normate learns to read by the average age, scores on exams and assessments within an average, and is within the range of average physical development and size. The combined influence of the archetypal school pupil with statistical measurement of achievement or intellect leads to the creation of a mythical normate against which present-day children are measured.

What the varied groups who forward multicultural education have in common is disenfranchisement within a curriculum that was created in their absence and primarily sought to assimilate them into the mores of White, patriarchal culture. For many in contemporary schools, this means being measured against a standard of color, ability, spirituality, or gender that can never actually be achieved, except in approximation of opposing identities and experiences. Multicultural education and inclusive education are invested in reforming schools and curriculum to embrace diversity as the expected and welcomed condition of education. Each are committed to presenting the unique experiences, perspectives, and contributions of Othered groups in the school curriculum to sharpen understanding of the complexity of diversity in the American and global community. Both movements aim to change the way we think about and practice education in ways that perpetuate racism, ableism, sexism, heterosexism, and colonialism. At the heart of these movements is to expose the myth and privilege of the normal child against which the experiences of children of color and children with disabilities are construed. Inclusive education, then, is social justice education.

INCLUSIVE EDUCATION AND SOCIAL JUSTICE

Social justice education refers to the family of theories and practices that recognize schools as entangled in broad networks of racism, ableism, and other injustices. Social justice educators work toward school reform aligned with aims in multicultural and inclusive education. They perceive education as a tool of societal improvement. Social justice educators work in resistance to the inequities embedded in educational practice and encourage students, through teaching and learning, to strive for positive change in their own lives and communities. Among the foundations of social justice education is the concept of critical pedagogy, often attributed to Paulo Freire (1970) and forwarded by contemporaries, Jean Anyon, Michael Apple, Antonia Darder, Henri Giroux, and Peter McLaren, to name just a few prominent contributors (Darder, Baltodano, & Torres, 2009). Practitioners of critical pedagogies in multicultural education and disability studies confront racism and ableism. They perceive systems of prejudice and discrimination that influence broad, taken-for-granted associations among poverty, race, disability, and school quality (Kozleski & Thorius, 2013). They understand how practices such as ability tracking and special education are enacted as de-facto racial segregation (Blanchett, 2006; Ferri & Connor, 2005; Losen & Orfield, 2002). Most critically, however, social justice educators work to confront trenchant problems in education and work toward school reform in partnership with individuals and communities who have been marginalized in the historical and contemporary development and practice of education. Critical pedagogies are characterized by close attention to stories, perspectives, and desires of those who are Othered in schools.

To practice critical pedagogies in disability studies and inclusive education, we pay close attention by confronting ableism and attending to the experiences of disabled people, past and present. We examine the practice and impact of disability identification and labeling practices on children and families (Harry & Klingner, 2005; Rogers, 2002). We attend to experiences of disability and special education and their impact on identity and opportunity (Clandinin & Raymond, 2006; Connor, 2008; Mooney, 2007; Valente, 2011; Wright, 1999). Most critically, educators take action in partnership with children, families, and communities to create schools in service to the expressed needs and desires of individuals and communities. Such transformative work in school reform is increasingly documented. Kozleski and Thorius (2014), with Waitoller and Kozleski (2013), describe efforts undertaken across the USA to engage in inclusive school reform partnerships. Hart, Dixon, Drummond, and McIntyre (2004) offer an account of the partnership and practice that inform the inclusive ethos of the Wroxham School in Potters Bar, England. Cammarota and Fine (2008) provide a collection of accounts of collaborations in youth participatory action research that illustrate ways that adults and youth work together in social justice education. Greenstein (2015) adds to the ways that understandings gleaned from young people characterize the course of seeking "radical inclusive pedagogy." As these authors illustrate, work toward inclusive education through social justice-oriented research and critical pedagogies is necessarily complex and often uncomfortable. To work across boundaries of profession, community, and social identity and to confront systemic expressions of prejudice and discrimination embedded in school structures, educational practices, and in the self are immense undertakings. Yet, these authors also demonstrate that change is possible. Whether considering engagement with individuals and communities, change in classroom practices, and/or systemic and societal change, roadmaps are increasingly available to guide the merger of social justice and inclusive education.

GOALS OF INCLUSIVE EDUCATION

Aligning inclusive education with social justice and critical pedagogy is a meaningful shift in how the education of students with disabilities has been perceived. More pointedly, inclusive education in disability studies is less interested in improving "special" education and more interested in improving education for all. In other words, the emphasis is on creating "general" education to be welcoming, embracive, and responsive to disability and difference. Inclusive schools aim to diversify children's knowledge, experiences, and opportunities to enable their engagement in meaningful learning and development of social relationships. Inclusive education enables children to be valued in their ways of knowing and experiencing the world and strives to engender their respect for others' knowledges and experiences. Inclusive teaching is an embrace of difference that recognizes children as beings whose identities, needs, and competencies are individually unique, yet always interwoven with varied memberships and histories held within their bodies, languages, and cultures. Inclusive learning occurs through experience with wide and varied ideas and is engaged through rigor, which Doll (2004) explains is to nurture critical thought and participation with others in intellectual pursuit. Inclusive education is to strive toward pedagogical practice that supports every teacher and learner to perceive themselves and others as capable of pursuing a path of learning that enables thoughtful and purposeful participation and action in the world around them. In this section, we offer five tenets that characterize the pursuit of inclusive schooling.

(1) Opportunities to Engage in Meaningful Learning through Diverse Experiences

Inclusive schools understand that there is value in creating opportunities for students to be with and learn alongside peers who have different identities and experiences from themselves. Diverse environments provide a context in which relationships may be formed and stereotypes and related prejudicial beliefs may be reduced. Schools and communities can adopt practices that ensure classrooms reflect the diversity in the broader community. For schools in densely populated areas or where there are many schools from which families may choose—as in urban contexts—communities can examine policies that influence how well neighborhood schools correlate with the racial, socioeconomic, language, and disability diversity present in the locale. School choice programs, the proliferation of charter schools, and the range of disability-specific schools and other independent schools available in some areas have been the topic of intense debate with regard to multiple factors, which include the degree to which various policies impact the diversity of schools. Some argue that school choice programs enable all parents to seek better education for their children, which was previously a privilege reserved for families able to afford private schools (Pedroni, 2006). Others argue that policies for charter schools and other small schools enable exclusionary practices, with particular impact on students with disabilities and English Learners, as they may decline admission to those whose needs are perceived as burdensome (Miron, Urschel, Mathis, & Tornquist, 2010; Welner, 2013). In the aim to diversify schools, there are not simple resolutions to problems that reflect a long history of social and racial stratification by neighborhoods and legacy of disability segregation in urban, suburban, and rural areas. Inclusive schools and their communities, however, engage with the complexity of the problems and seek to effect change.

On the school and classroom level, school communities may seek to examine ability or achievement tracking and grouping practices that may limit students' opportunities to learn in diverse contexts. Schools may examine the influence of achievement-based classes or tracks—different "honors" and "general" offerings of classes, for example—on the racial, gender, and disability diversity make up across the classes. Certainly, the provision of education for students with disabilities in disability-segregated self-contained and resource classes should be limited, if not eliminated. Teachers may also look closely at grouping practices within a classroom. If, for example, students only receive reading instruction with similar-ability peers, an opportunity may be missed for students to practice and perfect the basics or for all to engage in enriching discourses in which more sophisticated literacy practices may be developed. Purposeful teaching practice can emphasize interconnectedness among different people and shared responsibility for one another that moves well beyond practices of inclusion in which students share space, but not joint pursuit of learning. Inclusive education seeks to provide students with opportunities to engage in meaningful learning collaborations and develop relationships with peers through which mutual understanding and respect for each other may be nurtured.

(2) Value and Respect of Diverse Ways of Knowing

Inclusive educational practices require thoughtful and purposeful development of curriculum and teaching to honor and cultivate a diversity of perspectives and appreciation for diverse ways of knowing. The aims of multicultural and diversity education are instructive in this area. Inclusive curriculum offers learners breadth and depth of content study that enables them to recognize the contribution of diverse people to society and find value in both complementary and competing perspectives drawn from diversity of experience. We can ensure that texts and materials represent diversity in the past and present—whether in selecting literature by diverse authors or in scanning science texts to ensure images depict varied people working in the field, for example. Critical multiculturalism and diversity approaches to curriculum move beyond representation. These also require teachers and learners to reckon with traditions that prioritize perspectives that reflect a Western, Eurocentric, and colonial worldview, which emphasizes the accomplishment of Western society as a result of manifest destiny. In such an approach, perspectives of the "dominated"—largely people of color—are depicted as ancillary side notes to what was gained through being conquered or configured through a colonial lens, each of which devalue diverse perspectives even while providing representation of sorts. To nurture respect and appreciation for diverse ways of knowing, past and present, educators may take care in providing a range of perspectives, as well as engaging students in analyzing and discerning the role that power and White privilege play in, for example, depictions of societal progress, the literary and artistic canon of highly regarded works, and political and economic worldviews.

In addition to taking a purposefully critical approach to the selection of materials and topics for study with regard to multicultural and diverse curriculum, educators may also examine the ways of knowing and doing that are emphasized in what students do in school. To what extent, for example, are non-English, multiple literacies, and media literacy valued and practiced as important skills to learn and develop? As we grow our use of multi-modal approaches to teaching, including "hands-on" work, creating visual or graphic representations, and technology enhanced, we need also to ensure that these varied ways of knowing and doing are nurtured and valued alongside text and talk focused literacies. To do so requires differentiated, but equally sophisticated, ways to assess varied ways of knowing and doing. Such assessment may then guide all students toward growth and development of varied skills, rather than only being regarded as alternative methods for disability access or culturally responsive ways to learn and express. In other words, multicultural and diversity approaches to pedagogy ask that all students, regardless of their identities and experiences, consider the value and perspectives held within approaches that include, for example, Africentric curriculum (Asante, 1991), feminist approaches (Fleming, 2000; Luke & Gore, 1992), queer, or critical cripistemologies (Mitchell, Snyder, & Ware, 2014; Sumara & Davis, 1999).

(3) Embracing Difference in Self and Others

While critical approaches to multicultural and diversity curriculum are designed to ensure all students can learn and find value in diverse perspectives and ways of knowing, a related component of inclusive teaching is honoring the specific diversities of students in a school and class community. Learning communities that embrace student diversity approach differences with candor and see conflicts that may arise among varied needs and expectations as an opportunity to engage in shared problem solving. All learners have areas of strength and need, as well as characteristics or identities of which they may be proud. Students may be encouraged to share and express their particular uniqueness and curriculum can include opportunities to explore social or identity groups that can solidify belonging and pride and/or enable them to develop advocacy skills on behalf of self and others. In addition to inferring shamefulness, to be called "special needs" or identified with another disability euphemism prevents children with disabilities from participating in disability-positive or self-advocacy. Rather than downplay or hide disability, children may work toward understanding of their strengths and limits and work toward self-love. Embracing difference can be demonstrated through multicultural and diversity curriculum, but also requires attention to the particular funds of knowledge (González, Moll, & Amanti, 2006) and cultural resources (Lee, 2007) drawn upon by individuals. If we desire students to develop positive self-concepts and respect others, then classroom communities can be purposeful in supporting how children may find identity and value in themselves—through disability pride, body positive messages, LGBTQ pride, feminism, pride in heritage and language, and positive racial identity. Inclusive educators do not emphasize sameness in avoidance of the difficult, uncomfortable, or contentious political conceptualizations of race, sexuality, or disability. Instead, we take action to educate others and ourselves about the past and present experiences that inform and contribute to people's diverse social identities. In so doing, we seek to practice education to embrace difference, which preserves, rather than erases, individuality and highlights the diversities that characterize the condition of humanity and make a community enriching. Only by recognizing difference can we work toward respect and appreciation for others.

(4) Intellectual Pursuit

Inclusive learning is to engage in intellectual pursuit of knowledge and experience related to academic disciplines. It is the thoughtful and purposeful striving toward deeper understanding of the self and the world. It is not measured only by the progress gauged through educational standards, which change over time and place. One way to conceive of intellectual pursuit is in the exercise of rigor, which Doll (2004) explains is to seek various perspectives and ideas to bring new meaning and more sophisticated understanding of areas of study and interest. All children can learn and all children can engage in learning with rigor. To think inclusively about learning means to presume the competence of all children to benefit and grow from the tapestry of experiences and ideas that may be offered in academic settings (Biklen & Burke, 2006).

As we presume the competence of students, inclusive teachers employ differentiated educational approaches through an ethos of practice that strives for universal design of instruction. Such approaches aim to provide access to academic instruction that enables all to meet educational goals and to create classroom communities to which all students belong and may benefit. Inclusive learning means that all students work toward being expert learners with understanding and acceptance that such expertise develops differently for each individual (Meyer, Rose, & Gordon, 2014).

(5) Education as Agency

Inclusive education is comprised of practices that strive to position all members of a school community as teachers and learners. Such practices may enable children to perceive themselves and others as capable of pursuing a path of learning that enables thoughtful and purposeful participation and action in the world around them. Achievement and competence, in this perspective, are measured by learners' ability to set goals and courses of action that enable their life pursuits. These may be toward continued education, growth in a profession, seeking vocation, pursuing a passion, and otherwise seeking a satisfying life.

HOW DO WE PARTICIPATE IN INCLUSIVE EDUCATION?

Inclusive education is not an endpoint or even a particular destination. It is the pursuit of teaching and learning by members of educational communities who seek to understand inequity in their local contexts and strive to work against it. In critical pedagogy, conscientization is the ongoing cycle of critical reflection through which we aim to recognize injustices and examine ways that we may act against them. A key aspect of critical pedagogy is to understand it as work that is performed on the self, but that is shaped and propelled by learning from and alongside others. It is about learning what is most important and impactful on the people around us and seeking to work together toward positive change. The proposal for inclusive education, as guided by disability studies, multicultural, and social justice education, begins with the assumption that schools have been steeped in a long history marked by racism and ableism. It begins with a desire to oppose the status quo of the American public school, which historian Carl Kaestle (1976) describes, "is a gigantic standardized compromise most of us have learned to live with" (p. 396). A first step in participating in inclusive educational practice, then, is stretching beyond what has been offered to us as compromise and moving toward a critical consciousness of how children with disabilities are disabled in school, how children become disabled by school, and how we may work together to seek emancipatory experiences in education.

The project of inclusive education is a pursuit intertwined with multicultural and social justice education. The purpose of this book is to offer an introduction to the field of disability studies in order to develop an understanding of disability and ableism in schools and suggest directions for educational practices that we can employ to strive toward this facet of inclusive education. We highlight disability and disability experience, in other words, as part of an overall consciousness of the many efforts to diversify approaches to education. *Part I: Disability and Society* offers an overview of the perspectives and history through which to conceptualize the meaning of disability. *Part II: Disability in Schools* describes the policies, definitions, and common practices that guide the education of students with disabilities in American schools. *Part III: Curriculum and Inclusive Education* contains recommendations for teaching that can contribute to anti-ableist classroom communities. Our aim is to approach discussion of diversity and difference with candor and clarity. We seek to confront differences, rather than downplay or exoticize them, and to be clear in our commitments and position, while recognizing that there are many other perspectives on disability and inclusive education. We straddle the gap between the way the world of education appears and what it may become.

2

PERSPECTIVES ON DISABILITY

A paradigm is an ideology or frame of reference. It is the way one perceives, understands, or interprets a topic or issue. Individuals interpret (often unknowingly) everything they experience through paradigms, frequently without questioning their accuracy. People simply assume the way they view things is the way they really are or the way they should be. Paradigms are so ingrained in culture that they seem natural. As such, they inform beliefs and understandings that are assumed to be true and are a primary root of our attitudes and actions. When people describe understandings and interpretations of experiences that oppose dominant paradigms they are working against traditions and networks of power that benefit those working within the dominant belief structure. Awareness of the paradigms that structure our experiences and reactions to disability can enable us to identify points of conflict. As we identify conflicts between dominant and other paradigms, we can engage in critical reflection in order to locate our own understandings and beliefs and their implications for our own positions to power. Analyses undertaken in disability studies propose that in order to act against ableism, we need to shift paradigms. In this chapter we describe how culture and language reflect and construct two paradigms, or discourses, of disability—the medical model and the social model.

CULTURE AND DISCOURSE

The primary way that communities construct and express shared understandings about the world is through culture, which refers to patterns of human activity and the systems and symbols that shape the meaning of the activities. Most ideas of culture imply cohesion among groups of people and their shared understandings. Anthropologists such as McDermott and Varenne (1995), however, offer a way to understand culture as constructed through dynamic social processes:

> The coherence of any culture is not given by members being the same, nor by members knowing the same things. Instead, the coherence of a culture is crafted from

the partial and mutually dependent knowledge of each person caught in the process and depends, in the long run, on the work they do together. . . . [I]t is made of the voices of many, each one brought to life and made significant by the others, only sometimes being the same, more often by being different, more dramatically by being contradictory.

(p. 326)

As we take in the many voices and perspectives of those around us we determine which views are acceptable and those that are not; we evaluate those features of individuals that are desirable and that are not. We create structures within our social organizations to reward desirable characteristics and suppress undesirable ones. We can understand the processes through which desirability and aversion are constructed through the study of discourse. Discourse is comprised of language and the rules that govern what may be said and what is taboo to say. Consider beliefs or opinions you may hold that you would not express in most situations or actions that you perceive as improper or impolite. These behaviors and beliefs are ingrained through your interactions in the world. As McDermott and Varenne (1995) describe, however, culture is not static, but ever in the process of being created. As we adhere to the "rules" we reinforce dominant mores and ways of thinking; we create the rules in each new situation by keeping our talk and action within the range of what is considered legitimate thought and behavior. Conversely, when we resist the rules, we interrupt dominant discourses, which can contribute to shifting beliefs and assumptions that seem natural or normal within culture. We can raise ideas or act in ways that expose and make visible conflict between dominant and non-dominant discourses. There are two paradigms within which meaning about disability is made, which can be understood as sets of big ideas that inform conflicting discourses on disability. We turn, now, to describing the medical and social models of disability.

THE MEDICAL MODEL

The medical model has two dimensions: normal and pathological. Normal is defined as the absence of a biological problem. Pathological is defined as alterations in an organism caused by disease, which is a state of ill health that interferes with or destroys the organism. The medical model often referred to as the disease model, focuses primarily on biological problems and on defining the nature of the disease and its pathological effects on the individual. The model is universal and does not have values that are culturally relative. It is based on the premise that being healthy is better than being sick, regardless of the culture in which one lives.

(Hardman, Drew, & Egan, 1996, p. 18)

A medical model of disability makes meaning of disabled persons' experiences in terms of objective, innate conditions that limit their ability to participate in communities and learn in the general classroom setting. Described by Hardman, Drew, and Egan (1996), it relies on the distinction between that which is "normal" and that which is a "pathological" condition. In this view, school and society employ a discourse of scientific objectivity to position disability as a matter of fact; a law of the real (Stiker, 1997). The medical model recommends a scientific approach to disability. Diagnosing the source of deviance within the individual is the first step, followed by expert-guidance and treatment to intervene in, cure, or remedy the source of deviance. Thus, accurate diagnosis and appropriate treatment for disability are primary concerns put forth in a medical model.

Although medicine and treatment are regarded and practiced as evidence-based sciences, this does not mean that these fields of practice are immutable and rooted in an absolute truth of physiology or psychiatry. What is regarded as pathology shifts with changes in cultural norms over time and in relation to biomedical and social movements. One way of charting the interplay of culture with psychiatric practice, for example, is to consider changes in the extensively used guide for diagnosis and treatment of psychological, emotional, and behavioral problems, the *Diagnostic and Statistical Manual of Mental Disorders*, which was first published in 1918 and is now in its fifth edition (American Psychiatric Association, DSM-5, 2013). A noted change in the DSM-II in 1973 was the removal of "homosexuality" from the manual, effectively changing the way that being gay or lesbian could be regarded, both by medical professionals and in the broader society. In 1980, "alcohol abuse" and "alcohol dependence" were removed from the "personality disorder" category and to the category, "substance use disorders." The 2013 DSM-5 introduces "Hoarding Disorder," in reference to persistent difficulty and distress with discarding possessions, and "Autism Spectrum Disorder" (ASD) is a new name to incorporate previous diagnoses including "autism," "Asperger's disorder," "childhood disintegrative disorder," and "pervasive developmental disorder not otherwise specified." As diagnoses are added and removed from manuals like the DSM, identities, experiences, and/or characteristics take on changed meaning in the perception of people so-identified as clinically disordered or not, their problems rooted in aspects of character or in the biomedical realm.

The process by which an experience, identity, or set of characteristics become defined and characterized as a pathological condition is medicalization. Because of the dominance of a medical model in many cultures, medicalization can provide new legitimacy to some people's experiences of pain, anxiety, addiction, and so on, that may have been previously understood in moral terms. Medicalization serves to transform deviance from "badness" to illness, with its social response becoming therapeutic rather than punitive. Treatment for deviance in a medical model is construed, perhaps, to be more humane and hopeful than punitive measures. Medicalization can serve to remove perceived moral stigma from seeking treatment for some kinds of illness. Medicalization can focus attention to increasing social and clinical understanding toward acceptance of difference in communities.

The benefit that comes from the removal of moral stigma is to release individuals and family members from blame or shame about illness and disease. However, medicalization has also invited critique, especially related to disability. Disability is characterized by long-term and life-long experience with mental or physical impairment, which is a markedly different context than short-term illness or injury. While a medical model focused on recovery *enables* those who are likely to recover, such focus *disables* those whose lives are to be lived with impairment and disability. Making recovery a priority to enable a return to a prior state works as a temporary strategy. Making diagnosis and recovery the priority for disability, in contrast, means that a person's entire life may be defined and shaped by medicalization. Edward Tessier (1995), a disability rights activist, philanthropist, and entrepreneur, stresses, for example, how the medical model, with its emphasis on impairment, cure, or recovery, results in a narrow view of the lives of persons with disabilities:

> The medical model is a trap. It defines us simply as physical limitations, medical conditions. It is what justifies the cures, the treatments, incarcerations until you're somehow whole again. And it makes it impossible for us to be seen as full, rounded people. That's the core of our oppression.
>
> (as cited in *People in Motion*, p. 2)

The medicalization of disability leads, in Tessier's perception, to limited understanding of an individual. A medical model emphasizes the dysfunction of a body, which obscures the possibility for people with disabilities to be perceived as capable and fulfilled. Within this paradigm, a discourse of medicalization compels the desire to recover and to seek a state of wellness above all else. What is allowable for those with disabilities, then, is to desire, seek, and strive toward cure and recovery—to aim, in other words, to act, appear, or function as closely to "normal" as possible.

One feature of medicalization is the exaltation of the role of the doctor or professional in matters of diagnosis and treatment. Within the medical model, diagnosis and recovery are guided by professionals, who are typically licensed or certified in accordance with specific exams, educational degrees, and clinical experiences. The assertion of professional expertise, then, is carried out through the official process of certification or licensing, which positions the professional as an authority figure in relation to an individual or family members. People with disabilities may then be positioned in the role of a permanent patient or recipient of caregiving, through which one has limited power and dignity. In this arrangement of power, when a person with a disability disagrees with a professional opinion, resistance may be viewed as symptoms of maladjustment, depression, or denial. Parents of children with disabilities who do not comply with professional advice on recommendations are accused of being "in denial" or neglectful, in spite of the range of motivations and purposes on which families may act (Lalvani, 2012). Although everyone may benefit from seeking professional advice, most disabilities do not necessitate an individual to seek professional guidance for every life decision. The medicalization of disability, however, contributes to the perspective that professional advice is more important than infinite other factors on which people with disabilities may make decisions—quality of life, family responsibilities, career goals, and so on.

The medical model is a paradigm with varied implications. Medicalization has removed stigma from some conditions, which releases individuals from moral judgments and has enabled the development of therapy rather than punishment; understanding and empathy, rather than social judgment. Because disability refers to long-term and permanent conditions, however, persons with disabilities may be positioned as permanent patients, wherein their lives may be overly directed toward recovery. Medical accounts of disability, Michael Oliver (1990) points out, are "partial and limited and fail to take into account wider aspects of disability" (p. 5). To view disability solely as medical is analogous to viewing gender as gynecological or race as dermatological. Many people report, for example, that the embodied experiences of impaired sight, hearing, learning, or movement actually cause fewer barriers to living full lives than the loss of power, dignity, prejudice, discrimination, and intolerance that they experience in relation to others' perceptions of disability (for examples, see Linton, 1998; Gliedman, 1979; Bell & Burgdorf, 1983; Hahn, 1987; Oliver, 1996; Mackelprang & Salsgiver, 1996; Rioux, 1996). There is a need to go beyond physiological or cognitive conditions to gain a fuller understanding of disability (Rioux, 1996).

SOCIAL MODELS OF DISABILITY

Social models of disability provide another paradigm of disability that aim to move societal thinking beyond a discourse that primarily regards impairment and disability as an individual experience. Social models of disability forefront the influence our economic and social structures and central values have on the ways in which we define disability and respond to persons with them (Oliver, 1990, p. xii). They focus on the social and cultural contexts in which disability becomes meaningful as an identity and experience. Social models aim to understand disability as a total experience of complex interactions between the body and physical, social, and cultural environments. Rather than a primary emphasis on diagnosing an individual's pathology, ostensibly leading to a course of treatment toward recovery, the focus shifts to considering virtually everything else—including the social, cultural, and political environment and its influence on the meaning made about disability, life opportunities, and quality of life.

A Sociopolitical Orientation to Disability

There are a variety of theoretical approaches to social models of disability. The sociopolitical orientation is a common social model perspective applied to education and inclusion. Inspired by the Civil Rights movement of the 1960s, collective realizations of the impact of a medical model of disability led persons with disabilities to demand control and full access to society through advocacy and civil action that is known as the Disability Rights Movement (Mackelprang & Salsgiver, 1996; Fleischer & Zames, 2001). Paul Hunt founded disability rights organization, the Union of the Physically Impaired Against Segregation (UPIAS), in the United Kingdom in the early 1970s. The work of the group and its members led to the development of the social model of disability, a concept credited to Michael Oliver (1983). Paul Longmore (2005), historian and disability activist, describes the efforts of early American activists:

> Instead of attributing disabled people's social and economic marginalization to pathology, their campaign adopted a minority-group perspective. More urgent

than remedial measures to fix individuals was the instatement of equal access, reasonable accommodations, and antidiscrimination protections. Rejecting the charity approach that beseeched attention to disabled people's needs, the movement demanded civil rights enforcement to ensure their right of access to society.

(p. 507)

The demand evolved into grassroots efforts to secure improved quality of life, and which centered primarily on social and political concerns. Emerging together, the new kinds of demands and the rationale for them informed the development and naming of new paradigms through which to conceptualize disability. The "minority group", the "civil rights", the "disablism," and "independence" models are some of the names for early social models. Each purport civil rights, including access to society's spaces, places, and opportunities, and the rights to self-determination and dignity, are the central issues for persons with disabilities. We use the descriptor, *sociopolitical model of disability*, to encompass the variety of models that emphasize a civil rights perspective.

Proponents of a sociopolitical model of disability generally view variations among bodies and minds and changes in physical or cognitive function as natural parts of the human experience. Variation and impairment are anticipated and acceptable occurrences. Following this line of reason, it is not acceptable to discriminate on the basis of difference, assuming a society that espouses the equality of all its members, as in the USA. A difference becomes a *disability* when people with particular characteristics are not able to access life opportunities and experiences as a result of inaccessible contexts or other barriers related to the perceived difference. Disability, then, is a condition defined by an interaction, not only in a body.

Some theorists, such as Susan Wendell (1997), differentiate "impairment" from "disability." This emphasizes the distinction between the physical or sensory experience of a particular characteristic and sociopolitical oppression. The term, *impairment*, refers to the state of the body relative to individual function; and *disability* refers to political and economic disempowerment that results from societal barriers to people with impairments or who are perceived to be impaired. Describing characteristics as "impaired" acknowledges the limit in function that is experienced by an individual, but highlights the experience of disability as one based on context.

Simi Linton (1998), noted author of disability studies, clarifies that disabled persons "are all bound together, not by [a] list of collective symptoms but by the social and political circumstances that have forged us as a group" (p. 4). "Persons with disabilities" are a collective defined by common experiences of oppression resulting from barriers that make those with physical, cognitive, and/or sensory impairments unable to access places, information, and opportunities. In contrast to a medical model in which diagnosis and treatment of impairments are central, a sociopolitical model "views prejudice and discrimination as the major issues confronting citizens with disabilities" (Hahn, 1987, p. 184). A sociopolitical orientation to disability engages the social and political issues of persons with extraordinary bodies in ways similar to other identity groups who experience oppression on the basis of group affiliation, characteristics, or identities.

Other Orientations within the Social Model

Another approach to the social model of disability, addressed by Thomas and Corker (2002), critiques a sociopolitical model in the way that it differentiates between impairment and disability. They argue that our understandings about the nature of the body and mind as being impaired or not are produced in our social interactions, but originate and are mediated through the ways that language symbolizes our ideas about the human body. This "postmodern" orientation contends that the meaning and connotation of the word, "disability," precedes and shapes the initial meaning we make about a body. It is because we are aware of the concept that identifying people as disabled is made initially possible. The very act of assigning the label or identity of disability to someone is an act of power. Goodley (2011) discerns the minority model, cultural model, and relational models within social models.

Similar to McDermott and Varenne's (1995) view of disability *as* culture, the language we use to describe "normal" and "abnormal" bodies represent a hierarchical relationship between ability and disability. The language and concepts of exceptionality and disability, for example, communicate ideas about the way people are or "should" be. As we identify particular people or characteristics as exceptional, we simultaneously construct an idea of what is "normal." "Disability" is constructed in a hierarchical relationship with "ability." The term, "ability," is the norm and is the preferred state. "Disability" is its converse. The result is that those who become labeled or who choose to identify as disabled are positioned on the undesirable side of a dichotomy. They are fundamentally made marginal. Although norms reflect the prevalence and the usual appearance of characteristics, we can also discern value systems that favor some traits over others. Why are some characteristics chosen to be meaningful and others not? What are the value systems or systems of power in play when, referring to the earlier example, disorders are entered and removed from the DSM? The assumed neutrality or natural-ness of how we define and reward characteristics is a fallacy when we examine the many ways that the meanings and descriptions of disability and ability develop specific to culture and context and change over time.

Disability studies and the influence of the Disability Rights Movement and their ideas, products, and outcomes are increasingly perceptible in the public arena. Although disability studies are eclectic, as Gabel (2005) points out, a common tenet is their commitment to social models of disability and bringing to fore the lives, experiences, and political agendas of persons with disabilities. This commitment signifies working against histories that have presumed people with disabilities to be incompetent. The commitment is to challenge the authority granted to professionals in medical, rehabilitation, and caregiving fields, and instead enable disabled stakeholders to define and direct the course of disability experiences in society. Internationally, academic programs in interdisciplinary studies, cultural studies, the humanities, the health professions, and education with a "disability studies" orientation are increasingly available. As societies become more knowledgeable about the social and political contexts that characterize the lives and experiences of disabled persons, the influence of social models is ever more perceptible. Many international position and policy statements regarding disability demonstrate ways that the social model has gained prominence.

DISABILITY, IMPAIRMENT, AND HANDICAP

The terms, "disability," "impairment," and "handicap" are the most common English-language expressions. In general, they are used interchangeably and refer to a permanent loss in physique or functioning, relative to the average person. Professional and advocacy groups in the USA currently prefer the term, "disability." More refined distinctions among the meanings of disability, impairment, and handicap can be found in policy. One example of a national definition of disability is in the American federal law, *The Americans with Disabilities Act Amendments Act* (ADAAA) (2008). Under the ADAAA, an individual with a disability is a person who has:

(a) a physical or mental impairment that substantially limits one or more of the major life activities of such individual;
(b) a record of such impairment; or
(c) being regarded as having such an impairment.

(42 U.S.C. § 12102(2))

According to the ADAAA, an impairment must substantially limit one or more major life activities, or activities that an average person can perform with little or no difficulty. Examples of major life activities include walking, seeing, hearing, speaking, breathing, learning, performing manual tasks, caring for oneself, and working. The relationship between the terms disability and impairment is similar to the distinction made in a sociopolitical model of disability. In other words, **impairment** describes a characteristic of the body; **disability** is the resulting experience of limitation, as compared to others without impairment.

A three-fold distinction among the terms "impairment," "disability," and "handicap" is in use internationally (Wright, 1983; Johnson, 1994; Ingstad & Whyte, 1995). In 1983 the United Nations defined the terms as follows:

Impairment: Any loss or abnormality of psychological, or anatomical structure or function.

Disability: Any restriction or lack (resulting from an impairment) of ability to perform an activity in the manner or within the range considered normal for a human being.

Handicap: A disadvantage for a given individual, resulting from an impairment or disability, that limits or prevents the fulfillment of a role that is normal, depending on age, sex, social and cultural factors, for that individual.

(United Nations Decade of Disabled Persons 1983–1992, 1983)

In using all three terms, a **handicap** describes a specific disadvantage that results from the interaction of the person with a disability with a cultural environment. Thus, a person may experience some degree of individual restriction, or disability, as related to impairment, but that restriction becomes a handicap when it results in a social, political, or economic disadvantage. Those with a sociopolitical perspective on disability tend to incorporate the social and cultural environment into the overall experience of being restricted or limited, or "disabled." In other words, handicaps are not distinguishable from disabilities in that the experience of restriction results from the broader structural, social, and cultural environment. To experience disability is defined as persistently encountering handicaps.

In 2008, the *Convention on the Rights of Persons with Disabilities* was ratified by the United Nations. The Convention recognizes

> that disability is an evolving concept and that disability results from the interaction between persons with impairments and attitudinal and environmental barriers that hinders their full and effective participation in society on an equal basis with others.

It defines persons with disabilities as

> those who have long-term physical, mental, intellectual or sensory impairments which in interaction with various barriers may hinder their full and effective participation in society on an equal basis with others.
>
> (United Nations, 2007)

By describing disability as an interaction among the individual's health, personal factors, and the environment and context of daily life, the definition emphasizes the social, cultural, and economic factors that influence the degree to which a person may experience disability—as in a sociopolitical orientation. Understanding disability as interactional places greater emphasis on working toward environmental access and equity in social systems.

Is it clear that the international community recognizes that disability discrimination is a problem and that addressing physical and attitudinal barriers are ways to seek equity for and with people with disabilities. Part of the work of policy and position statements is to orient us toward clear ways of thinking and talking about problems that involve broad constituents and relate to cultural and institutional change needed in systems entrenched with unequal power, as in the problem of ableism. Like the conditions of racism and sexism, ableism is perpetuated through paradigms that apotheosize an ideal of bodily form and function and associate value, dignity, and rights with these forms. The degree of cultural and institutional change required to forge toward disability equity cannot be overstated. To move toward change, we need to be able to communicate as a society, in communities, and as individuals. Examining the language we use to communicate about disability, then, is one way that we can enter into discourse.

DISABILITY AND LANGUAGE

There are many lexicons used to communicate about disability. There is diagnostic language used by the professional community, general language proliferated by public policy and the media, and the range of descriptions utilized by individuals and social identity groups. Consideration of language practices surrounding disability in schools often boils down to finding common sets of descriptors to refer to children, which range from using diagnostic language, as in, "student with a learning disability," to general language descriptors such as, child with "special needs." Some terms, however, even when they are deemed diagnostically appropriate, are considered antiquated and offensive because of the history surrounding them, as in the term, "retarded." Other terms are rejected by people with disabilities because they are received euphemistically or are patronizing, such as "special needs," "physically challenged," or "differently abled." Recognizing the perspectives of persons with disabilities on the language used to talk about disability, while certainly complex, provides an informed outlook on the language choices we make or the terms we may hear others using.

One of the reasons for cultural discomfort with language and communication surrounding disability relates to the medical model. Because disability has been regarded as a negative experience within this framework, our language choices and changes illustrate the struggle in moving from perceiving disability as something wrong with bodies toward something simply about bodies (Ware, 2001). Awkwardness about talking about disability and fear of offending others by our talk is informed by cultural aversion to disability—we worry about talking candidly about disability for fear of highlighting an imperfection or wrongly labeling someone. We retreat to ignoring or avoiding talk about disability or to using euphemisms believed to soften conversation in reference to taboo or shameful topics. Desiring to leave behind a legacy of disability labeling and stigma and move toward language practices that capture individual and collective disabled identities inform a cultural journey to find new ways of communicating about disability.

Disability Labels

To label a person is to use a single descriptor to imply a general sense of a person. Labels tend to over-generalize or emphasize particular characteristics. They obscure other elements of personhood, which can lead to distorted perceptions of a person. In short, labeling means to classify something by naming it. Disability labels are often derived from what seem to be neutral descriptions of impairment. However, they frequently work against children and adults with disabilities. They may conjure distorted or diminished expectations and stereotyped images of what particular individuals are like. Labels are descriptions of people that take on an encompassing quality. Doug Biklen describes:

> A student who was having difficulties in learning becomes a mentally retarded student, a learning disabled student, an emotionally disturbed student, a blind student. The disability, once a suspected characteristic, then an identified quality, now becomes *the* defining factor of the student. With the label and [an educational] placement to go with it, disability achieves what sociologists call "master status." Those who interact with or observe the labeled person have trouble seeing a person; they see instead a disabled person and all of the stereotypes associated with that status.
>
> (1989, p. 13)

The label takes the place of the person's individuality, and invites others to define the essence of the person with the disability.

The concept of **social stigma**, popularized by sociologist Erving Goffman (1963), relates to labeling. Stigma is the social phenomenon by which particular traits draw severe social disapproval. Stigmatized traits include mental illness, physical disability, and being associated with particular races, religions, or other facets of identity and culture. Those who possess or are thought to possess the devalued trait are treated with aversion and excluded from society. Disability labeling is a process of categorization in which the inabilities, and the unacceptable and inferior aspects of a person are named. In turn, their exclusion from society is legitimated (Barton, 1996).

A single label does not describe a person in ways that capture who they are and how they relate to the world. For example, describing a child as "having a learning disability" does not communicate specific information about her learning needs, nor does it describe the child's achievement, competencies, personality, or interests. The term merely indicates the child's status in relation to her "abled" peers. For example, it is more useful to comment that a particular child needs help organizing ideas of writing or needs to use a computer to type than it is to simply state the existence of a learning disability. Labels are not specific enough to be useful for developing an individual education plan, but they can have long-lasting negative effects. "The power of naming is such that the labels and letters remain as an influence on social standing and self perception long after their initial judgments were made and have been subsequently modified, overturned, or rendered null and void" (Corbett, 1996, p. 47).

The use of such terms as "disabled person," implies that individuals within a disability are typically alike and that they form a distinct group that is different from the rest of society (Burgdorf, 1980). There is no such thing as a "typical blind person" however. Within the group of persons with visual impairments, there are variations in severity and types of blindness, as well as other critical factors like "time of onset." Although two individuals may currently have identical degrees of acuity, one born with blindness (congenitally blind) and one who became blind later in life (adventitiously blind), will have very different concepts of redness, the sunset, the height of the Empire State Building, or traveling ninety miles an hour. In addition, the individual born with blindness, having no memory of being a sighted person or any identity as such, would experience his or her condition as the normal, or expected, state of his or her body. In short, individuals with visual impairments cannot be grouped into the category of "the blind." The variations are too numerous to allow for a typical case. This is true for all categories of disability.

Awareness of negative language practices, especially in labeling, has increased among educators, and most agree that the title of a disability category is not equivalent to a description of the whole child and that labeling/stereotyping is detrimental to the child. Terms such as, "the disabled," "the blind," or "the learning disabled" are also fading from usage as we recognize that individuals grouped in disability categories are too diverse for such gross generalizations to be meaningful. Vash (1981), for example, argues against using terms like "the handicapped" and "the disabled," because they "carry the hidden cost of summarizing the individual(s) described as nothing more than one of their characteristics, one that conjures up a negative image in the minds of most" (p. 206). In a practical view, then, there are few situations that a disability label can aid in constructive or useful conversation about an individual. There are simply too many variables among individuals to select one as being emblematic of needs or experience. In a broader view, efforts to shift language practices to acknowledge people as multi-faceted and not defined by one aspect contribute to the argument against labeling.

Disability Euphemisms

Several euphemisms for disability are quite popular, but rather objectionable to people who may be described with them. Sutherland (1984) observed that "it is for people with disabilities to decide how we choose to define ourselves, and few of us choose to do so according to the prejudices of people who consider themselves able bodied" (p. 14). Persons with disabilities often receive terms like "physically challenged," "differently abled," "able disabled" and "handi-capable" as patronizing euphemisms. Although the terms claim to refute common stereotypes of incompetence, they are often considered defensive and reactive (Linton, 1998).

There are several reasons that euphemisms are objectionable. One is that euphemisms imply that talking directly about impairment or disability is shameful or impolite. Another is that using "nicer" language obscures the significance that impairment and disability play in a person's experiences. Smart (2001) explains:

> Euphemisms are insulting because their use implies that the reality of the disability is negative and unfortunate. Much of the language used to speak about the disability experience has been condescending, trivializing, or euphemistic. Expressions such as "physically challenged" or "mentally different" are both condescending and euphemistic, suggesting that disabilities cannot be discussed in an open and candid manner. The use of these expressions also trivializes the disability experience, suggesting that disabilities are only minor inconveniences.
>
> (p. 59)

Most persons with physical impairments do not view barriers as "challenges" that will make them stronger, more courageous, or better citizens by overcoming them and pulling themselves up by their own bootstraps. Thompson (1985) offers, for example, "It is not fun to be disabled. Being disabled is not a 'challenge' we voluntarily undertake. Nor is it that we are merely 'differently abled.' We are 'disabled'; there are just some things that we can't do, at least as quickly or easily as other people" (p. 79).

Other criticisms of terms like "physically challenged" and "differently abled" relate to the inaccuracy of the terms to describe the experience of disability and/or the ways they actually reinforce negative perceptions about persons with disabilities. Recall that in a sociopolitical perspective of disability, it is the inaccessible environment and context in which impairment becomes meaningful as disability. On the term, "physically challenged," Linton (1998) notes:

> Non-disabled people use it in conversation around disabled people with no hint of anxiety, suggesting that they believe it is a positive term. The phrase does not

make much sense to me. To say that I am physically challenged is to state that the obstacles to my participation are physical, not social, and that the barrier is my own disability.

(p. 14)

Finally, Wendell (1997), on "differently-abled," states:

I assume the point of using this term is to suggest that there is nothing wrong with being the way we are, just different. Yet to call someone "differently abled" is much like calling her "differently colored" or "differently gendered". . . . If anything, it increases the "otherness" of disabled people because it reinforces the paradigm of young, strong, and healthy body perfectly.

(pp. 271–2)

Two other common and contested euphemisms are "exceptional" and "special" because they invoke a history of segregation. When used in reference to disability, "special" and "exceptional" are instantly recognizable as connoting segregated and inferior (Smart, 2001). They are not innocuous terms because they emphasize difference and thus are polarizing. Individuals in "exceptional" or "special" programs "are then stigmatized as those who cannot 'get by' under programs designed to meet basic needs" (p. 59). Schwarz (2006) similarly observed how *special* creates a double standard:

In the name of special care, special safety, or special protection, we sometimes take the dignity of independence, choice, and freedom away from people with disabilities. We create a double standard, not letting them do things that nondisabled people take for granted, things that are often the rites of passage into maturity or adulthood.

(p. 45)

Overall, terms that attempt to veil words associated with impairment and disability and euphemisms are generally poorly received for a variety of reasons. Euphemisms communicate that the characteristics of a body or mind are too unfortunate or shameful to be talked about candidly and at worst, simply replace objectionable terms with equally problematic patronizing ones. When the occasion arises, using the terms "disabled," "disability," and "impairment" with accurate and candid descriptions of an individual's characteristics is generally preferred. It is not shameful or hurtful to describe bodies, minds, their strengths, and their limits in direct language.

People-First Language

People-first language, or **person-first language**, is one language movement whose proponents aim to resist labels and stigma by emphasizing the person and not the impairment. Phrasing in person-first language includes: "child with a disability," rather than a "disabled child;" "a child with visual impairment," rather than the "visually impaired child;" a "child with a learning disability," rather than a "learning disabled child," and so on. People-first phrasing is also preferred in the media and is often recommended for professional writing. In the majority of American school settings as well as in public discourse, "people-first" language is the preferred and recommended way to describe those with disabilities or impairments.

People-first language aims to better express the wholeness of persons with disabilities, rather than emphasize one aspect of him or her. Wright (1983), for example, stressed the importance of using the verb "have" rather than "be" with disabilities. For example, when called an "epileptic" or "stutterer," rather than "a person who has epilepsy or a stutter," an entire human being is described by just one characteristic (Shapiro & Barton, 1991). In addition, Smart (2001) argues, "every one has multiple identities, and for people with disabilities, the disability is only one aspect of their identity" (pp. 9–10). Thus, "no one likes to be referred to, or thought of, as only one aspect of his or her nature. No single label can capture the meaning on an entire person's personality and character" (p. 58). "The term 'person with disabilities,'" according to Davis (1995), "is preferred by many to 'disabled person' since the former implies a quality added to someone's personhood rather than the second term's reduction of the person to the disability" (p. xiii).

Identity-First Language

In contrast to person-first language is the preference for identity-first language. Proponents of identity-first language prefer to claim a disability identity and experience by characterizing the self as, for example, an autistic person (not a person with autism). Others seek to highlight group identity by purposefully identifying as a Disabled person (not a person with a disability). The identity-first language movement arose in response to the person-first campaign. Albrecht, Seelman, and Bury (2001) describe:

> An equally vocal group has more recently denounced people-first language as offensive, claiming that it was promoted by powerful nondisabled people, particularly advocates for persons with developmental disabilities. This second group prefers the term *disabled people*, emphasizing minority group identity politics. . . . This heated discourse struggles with expressing values that acknowledge individual difference and inclusion in a society based on civil rights.
>
> (p. 3)

Two considerations for identity-first language are highlighted. First, whether disabled people or those without a disability identity initiate a new term is a concern that reflects the role of self-chosen language to communicate a group's emerging status (Vash, 1981). Some of those preferring "disabled people" object to the use of people-first language because the origin of the form was not rooted in disabled persons' desires. The phrasing, "disabled people," may also be preferred for its grammatical construction, which emphasizes a sociopolitical perspective on disability. To describe someone as a "person with a disability" locates the disability as an attribute belonging to an individual. In contrast, placing "disabled" before "person" is read, grammatically, to indicate a position of being dis-abled, or made not-able. This emphasizes a view of disability as it is made meaningful in social contexts. In this usage, being disabled refers to an imposed social position or set of experiences, rather than a fact of an individual.

In addition to emphasizing a sociopolitical perspective on disability, some disabled people reject people-first language because it minimizes the role that impairment and/or disability plays in their lives and identities and casts it negatively. "People-first phraseology conceives of disability as a troublesome condition arbitrarily attached to some people, a condition (unlike gender, race or ethnicity) that is only significant as a remedial or managerial issue" (Titchkosky, 2001, p. 126). For some, the experience of disability offers membership in disability culture, which values the lives and expressions of diverse bodies and minds and perceives varied individual and group experiences as more complex than conditions to be managed, overcome, or tolerated. Here, identity-first language is preferred; being a "disabled person" is understood as a dynamic and significant facet of identity, a source of group membership, and/or an occasion for pride.

Another facet of group identity that pertains to language relates to the ways that oppressed groups reappropriate hurtful language or negative characterizations of their features for their own use and meaning. For an analogous example, the term, "queer," originated as an epithet for gays and lesbians and the pink triangle that is now associated with gay rights and gay pride was a symbol used in Nazi Germany to identify gay persons for discrimination and extermination. In the 1990s the declaration, "We're queer, we're here. Get used to it!" became an expression of gay pride. Adopting cruel and often jarring terms to self-identify can serve to re-value the label and disempower its effect when others use them (Galinsky, Hugenberg, Groom, & Bodenhausen, 2003). In disability rights and disability cultural movements, disabled persons sometimes refer to themselves and others in the group as "cripple" or "crip;" and "gimp." Like the term, *queer*, terms that once referred to "despised distinctiveness," now refer to "celebrated distinctiveness" (p. 231). Kriegel (1991), for example, discusses a preference for his "cripple" identity:

> I am a man who has lived all but eleven of his years here on earth as a cripple, a word I prefer to the euphemistic "handicapped" or "disabled," each of which does little more than further society's illusions about illness and accident and the effects of illness and accident. For to be "disabled" or "handicapped" is to deny oneself the rage, anger, and pride of having managed to survive as a cripple in America. If I know nothing else, I know that I have endured—and I know the price I have paid for that endurance.
>
> (p. 61)

In disability rights circles, identifying oneself as a "crip" is a testament to the struggle for rights and equity and a reminder of the damaging beliefs and attitudes still held by many.

Somewhat similar to reappropriating negative language, some groups re-cast the meaning of identifying terms or create new ones that emphasize different relational aspects of naming and identity. Differences in the language and meaning surrounding the term, "deaf," provide an example of a widely acknowledged change in words and connotation. The descriptor, *Deaf*, with a capital *D*, typically infers a cultural view of deafness and Deaf identity defined by the shared use of American Sign Language (ASL). Being *Deaf* means to share in a history and community that unite people who use ASL. Being *Deaf* is a cultural identity; being *deaf* is a label related to a degree of hearing.

DISABILITY PERSPECTIVES IN LANGUAGE

The considerable attention paid to language used to describe a person, an experience, or signal group identity indicates its importance to many. The ways we describe ourselves or are described is key to self-concept and the way others think about us. While most agree that language that invites stigma should be avoided, there is much variety in the words and terms, grammar and letter case used and preferred. Attention to language changes, particularly those sparked by Disability Rights Movements, reveals the role of language in group politics and identity. Language, then, is both descriptive and political. Words are imbued with meaning derived from history, context, and paradigms of disability. The terms, classifications, categories, and labels surrounding language used in schools and society to talk about disability relate to our policies that define disabilities and impairments, as well as to the social practices in which they become meaningful. Discerning the shifting and conflicting preferences in language practices surrounding disability provides a window into the interplay between the medical and social models of disability.

3

CULTURES OF EXCLUSION

One way to understand the construction of paradigms of disability is to examine actions, reactions, knowledge, and beliefs that seem taken-for-granted, or which persist over time. Within disability studies, two questions put forth are, How do cultures make meaning of disability and disabled persons? and How do these constructions influence responses relevant to exclusion and inclusion? In the next two chapters, we present a brief cultural history of how differences among people have been constructed as disability and the ways in which various beliefs and orientations toward disability persist and are challenged.

In 1972, Wolfensberger, Nirje, Olshansky, Perske, and Roos described varieties of typical attitudes and stereotypes made about disabilities. They enumerated typical ways in which persons with disabilities are viewed and their implications for personal, professional, and policy responses to disability. Since then, many other scholars have examined attitudes, stereotypes, and tropes that persist in the public purview (for example, see: Darke, 1998; Shakespeare, 1994; Mitchell & Snyder, 2001; Garland Thomson, 1997; Nario-Redmond, 2008; Haller, 2010). Stereotypes persist because they are reinforced in media and entertainment, they respond to the desire to simplify and organize ways to make meaning of people, and they rationalize the prejudice and discrimination that allow those in power to benefit and profit from the subordinate status of stereotyped groups (Smart, 2001, p. 185). Many of the stereotypes or tropes related to disability are discernible, nearly 45 years since Wolfensberger et al.'s work was first published.

A study of cultural histories of disability reveals that contemporary stereotypes reflect meanings made about extraordinary bodies that have echoed across time. Among the disability stereotypes that Wolfensberger et al. articulated are the following:

1. The object of pity
2. The sub-human organism
3. Sinister or evil

4. The object of dread
5. The holy innocent or the eternal child
6. The object of comedy, ridicule and curiosity
7. The burden
8. The victim of violence
9. Extraordinary Disabled, or the SuperCrip.

We situate each in history to demonstrate the persistence of particular beliefs about disability over time and place. As we work toward living and learning inclusively, awareness of the deep roots of stereotypes and their fallacies is essential to our personal and professional strategies we may use to interrupt them.

DISABILITY AS BURDEN

Throughout recorded history differences among humans have been present. Archaeologists consistently uncover evidence of persons with extraordinary bodies dating back to the Neanderthal Period (Mackelprang & Salsgiver, 1996). Most primitive societies followed the custom that individuals with disabilities had to be sacrificed for the good of the group (Funk, 1987). Early humans were hunters and foragers who lived to their early twenties. People slept on the cold ground and faced daily starvation, stress, trauma, and fear (Scheerenberger, 1983). The harshness of the environment made survival dependent on group cooperation. With the reality of hunger ever-present, each individual was vital to the band for hunting, gathering, and collective defense. Because early humans leading nomadic existences pursued their prey, those unable to work or keep up were left behind to die. The elimination of the incapacitated, old, or feeble was not only accepted but also expected. Accordingly, children who were unable to contribute to the community due to physical, sensory, or cognitive impairments were liabilities to primitive societies and infanticide was often practiced (Bowe, 1978; Scheerenberger, 1983; Morgan, 1987). For early humans, the severity of life conditions made death or abandonment the usual outcome for people with disabilities.

The environment became more accommodating to individuals with disabilities around 12,000 B.C. when humans passed from the age of itinerant hunting to growing crops, reasoning symbolically, communicating verbally, and living in communities (Scheerenberger, 1983). Yet, the view of disability as a burden to self and others persisted as a rationale for infanticide. Both the Greek and Roman cultures sought the perpetuation of physical perfection, beauty, and health. Herodotus (5th century B.C.), for example, listed freedom from deformity at the top of his criteria for happiness (Edwards, 1996). In ancient Greece infanticide was a legal right invoked by paternal decision. Any child that appeared to be or was suspected of being defective was thrown from a cliff of Mount Taygetus onto the jagged rocks below, or was left to die exposed to the elements (James, 1975; Preen, 1976; Scheerenberger, 1983). Infanticide of babies with impairments reflected the beliefs and social environment of the times. Greek religious beliefs emphasized that individuals with disabilities had immortal souls, so that their elimination from this life probably meant a more prompt reincarnation— a more pleasant prospect than lives of hardship as disabled and stigmatized individuals. This belief encouraged many parents to accept the custom as a blessing, and the best possible course of action for their children (Preen, 1976).

The laws of Sparta viewed those with disabilities as burdens to be eliminated for the betterment of their militant society. Not all impairments were construed as burdensome, however. Greece's city-state of Sparta exemplified the philosophy of "rugged individualism" and "a sound mind in a sound body," but the boundaries of who was considered disabled, however, were flexible. A soldier with an impairment—for example, a limp or the loss of an eye or even a more serious condition—but who could still fight or be of service to the military, was not considered disabled. Artemon, a man who could not walk, served in the role of military advisor and designed siege-engines and was regarded as a man of ability and prestige (Edwards, 1996). The meaning of which bodies are considered disabled, then, is dependent on context.

Eugenics and the Return of Extermination

The earliest responses to disability were abandonment, presumably leading to death. Nomadic groups abandoned impaired members to survive, while later civilizations practiced infanticide of apparently impaired newborns out of pity, tradition, religion, or superstition. Over time, communities turned toward humanism and took up care of the individual as emblematic of the social good. The advent of eugenics turned interest in the social good against the individual, notably those deemed feeble-minded. Women, especially, were targeted in an American campaign for extermination of disability.

In 1883, Francis Galton introduced the term, "eugenics," taken from the similar Greek concept meaning, "good in stock." Interested in the scientific examination of heredity, Galton proposed that preventing individuals with undesirable social traits from reproducing would better the human race. The concept was based on the assumption that biology, or any physical or psychological variation, predetermined an individual's morality and social status. Also intrinsic to this notion was the belief that the biological progress of mankind required the elimination of those considered hereditarily unfit. The eugenics movement promoted two major efforts:

> First, it sponsored research to investigate the transmission of social traits, especially undesirable ones, and undertook to classify individuals, groups, and nations on a scale of human worth. Second, it proposed biological solutions to social problems and lobbied for their implementation.
>
> (Friedlander, 1995, p. 5)

Eugenics quickly gained national and international attention, and its seemingly scientific information became translated into social policy.

Nazi Medicalization of Killing

Though touted as American science, the Third Reich, under Adolf Hitler's Nazi regime, would enact eugenic policies with tremendous impact. Having carefully studied American sterilization and institutionalization laws, the National Socialists based much of their philosophy on the "science of eugenics" (Bowe, 1978; Kuhl, 1994;

Friedlander, 1995; Pernick, 1996). With much of its rationale grounded in the American eugenics movement, the Nazis attempted to combine ethnic and eugenic racism into a comprehensive program of race improvement. Kuhl (1994) defined eugenic racism as "The demarcation of certain elements within a particular race, followed by attempts to reduce these elements through discriminatory policies" (p. 71).

Race purification and improvement as a cornerstone of Nazi ideology appeared as early as 1925, when Hitler (1925/1971) idealized the "pure" German state in *Mein Kampf*. In 1930, the Nazi Party's National Socialist German Medical Association proclaimed the "primacy of national biology" (Bleul, 1973, p. 191). Medical policies and practices became a means to enforce social hygiene. In 1933, immediately upon Hitler's assumption of power, the Nazis established special Health Courts to implement a newly enacted law requiring sterilization of those with hereditary diseases. The Nazi definition of the hereditarily sick included those with congenital mental deficiency, schizophrenia, manic-depressive insanity, inherited epilepsy, Huntington's chorea, inherited deafness or blindness, or "grave physical defect." The law, which forbade the sterilization of "normal persons," was ultimately responsible for the sterilization of between 300,000–375,000 persons perceived as defective by the state (Lifton, 1986; Finger, 1992; Gallagher, 1995). More than half (approximately 203,250) of those sterilized under the act were presumed to have congenital feeble-mindedness (Gallagher, 1995).

The Nazi policy of sterilization quickly led to a much more comprehensive and vigorous eugenics program that soon included "euthanasia" and the medical killing of approximately 200,000 disabled men, women, and children (Burleigh, 1994). The belief in euthanizing people with disabilities for the good of the individual and society was prominent in the age of eugenics. The 1920 book, *Die Freigabe der Vernichtung lebersunwerten Lebens; ihr Mass und ihre Form* (*The Release of the Destruction of Life Devoid of Value*) translated by respected professionals, Binding and Hoche (1920/1975), for example, proved influential in the Nazi regime. The work stressed the economic and social costs to society by "defective" individuals and mounted an academic argument that unworthy life included children with mental retardation, mental illness, and physical "deformities."

The Binding and Hoche book professionalized and medicalized "euthanasia" by stressing its therapeutic aspect and proposing the destruction of "life unworthy of life" as a healing process (Lifton, 1986, p. 46). The authors further pictured "euthanasia" as kind, compassionate, reasonable, moral, and economical (Wolfensberger, 1980). Binding argued that "euthanasia" was a compassionate way to dispose of the "'empty human husks' that fill our psychiatric institutions" (cited in Proctor, 1988, p. 178). Binding and Hoche's book,

> became the intellectual, social, legal, medical, and moral basis for the widespread advocacy for the destruction of handicapped and enfeebled people during the early years of World War II.
>
> (Wolfensberger, 1981, p. 2)

Many other respected eugenicists around the world shared Binding and Hoche's ideas. In 1933, Gould, an American physician, proposed in the *Journal of the American*

Institute of Homeopathy that euthanasia helped resolve economic difficulties, citing with approval, the "elimination of the unfit" in ancient Sparta (cited in Proctor, 1988). Similarly, in 1941, American psychiatrist Foster Kennedy, professor of neurology at Cornell Medical College, delineated a proposal to the American Psychiatric Association for killing "defective" and "hopelessly unfit" children, whom he labeled "those helpless ones who should never have been born—Nature's mistakes" (Proctor, 1988; Hollander, 1989; Shapiro, 1993; Gallagher, 1995). In short, the intellectual and scientific context created by eugenics made the killing of disabled persons appear compassionate, perhaps even dutiful.

Following forcible sterilization, the Nazis adopted a policy of direct medical killing of disabled persons, justified by the principle of *lebensunwertes Leben* or "life unworthy of life." The party line stressed that "[A] healthy Reich could not afford sick people because they were too expensive" (Bleul, 1973, p. 192), particularly in time of war. The Nazi rationale for such killing was to provide beds for wounded soldiers and civilians by emptying mental hospitals, foster homes, and institutions for persons with disabilities (Pross, 1992). Therefore, forcible "euthanasia" was also based on the needs of a wartime economy, or on what Proctor (1992) called "a preemptive triage to free up beds" (p. 35). The medical establishment became obsessed with how much food and resources could be saved with the killing of each defective person.

Like Binding and Hoche, and later Kennedy, Hitler, and the Nazis "medicalized" the issue of "euthanasia" for persons with disabilities, thereby giving it "scientific legitimacy." Doctors became "the guardians of national hereditary health" (Burleigh, 1994, p. 191). Once medically legitimized, "euthanasia" was then quickly and efficiently implemented by physicians, nurses, aides, technicians, and others seen as healers, who willingly dealt out death by starvation, gas, injections, and poison believed they were doing it for the "health" of their country (Wolfensberger, 1980) with "doctors [as] the highest echelon of those directly or indirectly involved in mass murder" (Burleigh, 1994, p. 154). Hitler Nazified the medical profession by redefining its goal as the "promotion and perfection of the health of the German people to ensure that the people realize the full potential of their racial and genetic endowment" (Lifton, 1986, p. 30). The role of medicine, then, was to protect the state from unwanted citizens thought to be contaminating it. Hitler allowed physicians, and especially psychiatrists, to pronounce value judgments both on individuals on medical grounds and on entire groups on medical-sociological grounds (Wertham, 1980). As Weindling (1989) observed, "The transition from medicine as care for the individual to the welfare of society and future generations attained the most extreme and brutal realization in the killing of the sick and disabled" (pp. 542–543).

While Hitler and the Nazi regime legitimized killing persons with disabilities, the medical experts assumed the crucial administrative role (Weindling, 1989). The German medical community proved itself shockingly amenable to the eradication of whole groups of people. Gallagher (1995) suggested that the reason that the doctors were so willing to comply was their own arrogance, "bred of a confidence in science and the prestige of the medical profession" (p. xvii). Part of that arrogance was based fundamentally on the medical model of viewing persons with disabilities as sick people who never get well, and therefore never live a worthy life. Under the assumption that its desire to perfect the human race justified killing, the medical profession used eugenics, genetics, and biology to provide a "rationale" for its actions (Gallagher, 1995). Not all German doctors had a direct hand in the Holocaust, however. Individual physicians did oppose the regime in various ways, even though open opposition meant certain death (Kater, 1989). Weindling (1989) stressed that not all Nazi doctors who favored sterilization, favored medical killing, and such doctors became passive onlookers rather than active participators of medical murder (p. 546). The impact of individual doctors who performed the killings, however, was far less damaging than the public and professional perception of the "science" that supported the killings.

The medical community's role helped to sell the public on the idea that Germany's "ills" were not economic or political, but were threats to the "folkish body" from the increasing number of humans who were perceived as "genetically unworthy" and "inferior." According to Müller (1991), those condemned by the government were described as "ballast to society." By making social problems medical, scientific, and genetic, the Nazis gave them an "untreatable hopeless biological cause" that justified a cure of segregation and elimination. Racial hygiene became both science and social policy governing inferiority and disability (Proctor, 1988). As a medical model, it could explain, categorize, and prescribe. The science of racial hygiene allowed the Nazis to determine the value of human beings first by mental and physical characteristics, then later by racial and social ones.

Those first killed in Germany were physically disabled children in a hospital near Wurthberg operated by the Samaritan Brothers. The SS appropriated the program under the state's policy of taking over of church-controlled asylums (Weindling, 1989). The youngsters, already victims of institutionalization and sterilization, were killed by drug overdoses (usually Luminal, a barbiturate) hidden in their food. Those who refused to eat received forced injections or suppositories filled with the poison (Conot, 1983; Smith, 1985). On August 18, 1939, the

> Committee began its work by requiring midwives, medical officers, and doctors to register all children born with serious hereditary diseases particularly "idiocy" and "mongolism" (especially when associated with blindness and deafness); microcephaly; hydrocephaly; malformations of limbs, head, and spinal column; and paralysis, including spastic conditions.
>
> (Lifton, 1986, p. 52)

Finger stated that the parents of the children selected for death were told that their children would receive "special treatments," which were in reality large doses of pneumonia-causing sedatives. Once induced, the pneumonia went untreated (cited in Johnson, 1987, p. 24). Parents were then informed by a standardized letter used at all institutions that their child had died suddenly and unexpectedly of brain edema, appendicitis, or some other fabricated cause, and that owing to the danger of an epidemic, their child's body required immediate cremation (Proctor, 1988). The condolence letters and death certificates were frequently accompanied with an urn containing ashes (Berenbaum, 1993).

Remak (1969) reported that the full official implementation of the "euthanasia" program began with Hitler's 1939 memorandum authorizing the extension of "the responsibilities of physicians still to be named in such a manner that patients whose illness, according to the most critical application of human judgment, is incurable can be granted release by euthanasia" (pp. 133–134). The signature was backdated to coincide with the invasion of Poland, and basically the beginning of World War II. A war economy sanctioned the Nazis' killing of life unworthy of life. After bombing attacks, for instance, psychiatric institutes and homes for the elderly were regularly emptied (their patients murdered) to make up for lost bed space (Proctor, 1992).

The program labeled "Aktion T-4" (named for Berlin Chancellery Tiergarten 4, which directed it) focused on chronic adult patients and "involved virtually the entire German psychiatric community and related portions of the general medical community" (Lifton, 1986, p. 65). Aktion T-4 extended the "euthanasia" project to include adults and called for the identification of all patients with more severe disabilities including schizophrenia, epilepsy, encephalitis, chronic illness, cerebral palsy, delinquency, perversion, alcoholism, antisocial behavior, and a number of others (Wolfensberger, 1981; Scheerenberger, 1983; Lifton, 1986; Proctor, 1988; Rogasky, 1988; Gallagher, 1995; Friedlander, 1995).

The first gassing of psychiatric patients occurred 45 days later at Poznán, in Poland. In Germany, itself, "euthanasia" quickly "became part of normal hospital routine" (Proctor, 1992, p. 35). Hollander (1989), in fact, noted the ease with which the program was implemented attributable in large part, to the cooperation of the "service providers" (p. 53). Because of the early success of the "euthanasia" program, it soon spread to include those less severely disabled, those with atypical characteristics, but not disabled (for example, persons with dwarfism), those reported as having behavior problems, those suspected of being racially or genetically tainted, and those who were devalued entirely for other identities including Gypsies, homosexuals, Polish prisoners of war.

"Racial hygiene" as practiced by the medical community implied that persons with mental and physical disabilities were a threat to the "body" of Germany. Hitler medically justified the Holocaust in the same way by espousing the idea that a Jewish "infection" was causing the Aryan race to be "weak and ill." The only cure was to rid the body of the infection, the Jews. The patient was neither the Jews nor the Gypsies nor any other group; it was the Aryan Race. "The way of curing the Aryan Race was to get rid of whatever had made it ill" (Lifton, 1990, p. 225). Kater (1989), in fact, emphasized that, the Nazis saw Auschwitz as a racial "clinic" and the medically logical extension of sterilization and "euthanasia" (p. 182). As Reichsfuhrer Himmler stated, "AntiSemitism is exactly the same as delousing. Getting rid of lice is not a question of ideology. It is a matter of cleanliness" (cited in Szasz, 1970, p. 214).

Euthanasia as a Prototype for the "Final Solution"

The "Euthanasia" medical killing program served, then, as a pilot scheme and training model for those who would later implement the Holocaust (Weindling, 1989). As Wolfensberger (1981) observed, "[T]he killing of the Jews evolved out of the desensitization, legitimization, personnel preparation and equipment development associated with the killing of handicapped persons" (p. 3). Conot (1983) termed the euthanasia program a "prototype" for the extermination of millions that was to follow. Berenbaum (1993) and Proctor (1992) point out the gas chambers, method of transport of "patients," and even process for disposing bodies were developed at the killing centers for disabled people.

> The ultimate decision to gas Jews emerged from the fact that the technical apparatus already existed for the destruction of the mentally ill. In the fall of 1941, with the completion of the bulk of the euthanasia operation, the gas chambers at psychiatric hospitals were dismantled and shipped east, where they were reinstalled at Majdanek, Auschwitz, and Treblinka. The same doctors, technicians, and nurses often followed the equipment.
>
> (Proctor, 1992, p. 37)

Dr. Andrew Ivy, who helped prosecute the Nazi physicians at Nuremburg concluded, "Had the [medical] profession taken a strong stand again the mass killing of sick Germans before the war, it is conceivable that the entire idea and technique of death factories for genocide would not have materialized" (cited in Gallagher, 1995, pp. 31–32). Gallagher added that "had the doctors acted differently, had they said no, things would have been different. An early link in the chain of events leading to the Holocaust would have been broken" (p.32). As Fiedler (1996) wrote of the link between euthanasia and the "final solution": "It is a development which should make us aware of just how dangerous enforced physiological normality is when the definition of its parameters falls into the hands of politicians and bureaucrats" (p. 150). The horror of the Holocaust exposed, human rights took on new importance, leading to changes in policy and attitudes, which would shape contemporary life for persons with disabilities.

The New Eugenics?

In contemporary society, prenatal screening positions disability to be a feature on which life and death may be decided (Parens & Asch, 2000). Proponents of assisted suicide, which many argue would disproportionately impact treatment decisions for people with disabilities, emphasizes the "right to die" at cost to efforts supporting the "right to live" (Gill & Voss, 2005). In entertainment, films that garner highly publicized releases, like *Me Before You* (Owen, Rosenfelt, & Sharrock, 2016) and *Million Dollar Baby* (Haggis, Rosenberg, Ruddy, & Eastwood, 2004) perpetuate the beliefs that severely disabled individuals desire death. In *Me Before You*, assisted suicide, as desired by a disabled man, is portrayed as an act of love. *Million Dollar Baby*, winner of multiple Academy Awards, depicts the story of a boxer who becomes quadriplegic in a match. Her trainer honors her wishes to end her life, delivering the message that life is not worth living as a disabled person, and that euthanizing/murdering a person with a disability is a merciful response. The disability rights group, Not Dead Yet, organized national demonstrations at the theatres screening *Million Dollar Baby* and *Me Before You* and sparked a lively debate in the press and media (Dolmage & DeGenaro, 2005). While the group does not advocate for censorship, they seek to ensure that the general public realizes not all disabled people see euthanasia as a reasonable response to disability.

In a *New York Times Magazine* piece, Harriet McBryde Johnson (2003), a Disability Rights activist and attorney, described her reaction to philosopher Peter Singer's argument for a utilitarian perspective that could justify infanticide by withholding of treatment for newborns with significant impairments.

> He insists he doesn't want to kill me. He simply thinks it would have been better, all things considered, to have given my parents the option of killing the baby I once was, and to let other parents kill similar babies as they come along and thereby avoid the suffering that comes with lives like mine and satisfy the reasonable preferences of parents for a different kind of child. It has nothing to do with me. I should not feel threatened.
>
> (Johnson, 2003)

Prenatal tests, amniocentesis, and chorionic villus sampling (CVS), are regularly performed on women during early pregnancy. Both tests can indicate whether the fetus has or is at risk of having certain disabilities indicated in chromosomes, notably Down syndrome. Because the prenatal tests solely target disability as the basis for a potential decision to terminate a pregnancy, they may be considered discriminatory from a disability rights perspective (Asch, 2000).

While the ancient practices of ritual infanticide are not likely to return, Zoe Gross (2014), through the Autistic Self Advocacy Network, issued an Anti-Filicide Toolkit in response to the features of media coverage on a spate of autistic people being killed by family members and caregivers.

> when parents normalize murder by saying that all special-needs parents have murderous thoughts, the result is an environment in which these murders are seen as acceptable. Media coverage like this sends a message that homicide is a normal, understandable response to any discomfort one might experience while parenting a disabled child, and we can't pretend that other parents of disabled kids aren't hearing that message.
>
> (Gross, 2014, p. 3)

She continues:

> When parents of kids without disabilities murder their children, we are universally united in condemnation. It is only when the victim is disabled that we pause. It is only when the victim is disabled that we are encouraged to understand. This is a double standard, and it reveals dangerous things about our beliefs.
>
> (Gross, 2014, p. 6)

Gross, first, brings attention to the number of children with disabilities that are killed by their caregivers for reasons typically described as mercy. Second, she points out that media coverage of these crimes has focused on the parents and the burden of raising disabled children, which elicits public sentiment not entirely removed from those beliefs and contexts in which infanticide was practiced in the ancient world and throughout earlier history.

DISABILITY AS OBJECT OF DREAD

In addition to posing apparent burdens to the survival or fitness of communities, disability has been perceived as signifiers of the divine and/or omens, often a sign of divine wrath and providence that presaged evil (Fiedler, 1978; Monestier, 1987; Bogdan, 1988; Thompson, 1994; Garland, 1995). A striking difference or impairment was perceived as evil, ominous, or unlucky, with a strong "demonological conception of a power that controlled behavior" (Ross, 1978, p. 8). The early Mesopotamians, for example, viewed diseases and mental disorders as punishment from God or as possession by the devil or evil spirits. Mental and physical diseases were considered impure, taboo, and the result of sin. Children born with facial differences were treated with hostility and accused of being evil, as were their parents (Charkins, 1996, p. 38). The ancient Assyrians assumed that children with disabilities or physical differences were omens (Monestier, 1987), and like the Babylonians, divined the future based on features of the abnormal birth or body (Thompson, 1994). In ancient Greece and Rome, children with unexpected facial features were believed created by the gods for their own amusement and sent to warn, admonish, or threaten humans (Charkins, 1996, p. 38). The birth of a deformed child was seen as a punishment inflicted upon its parents by the gods (Garland, 1995). Blindness was considered a Divine punishment for sin, though supernatural powers were believed granted to blind persons and viewed as compensatory gifts of the gods (Hewett & Forness, 1977). Infanticide of children presumed evil or magical because of disability or deformity was widely practiced in the ancient world. The East African Wanika tribe, Aztec American Indians, ancient Melanesians, Indians, South African Kaffir tribe, and the aforementioned Greek and Roman traditions all exterminated infants and sometimes the birthing mothers, as well (Ross, 1978; Van Riper & Emerick, 1984).

The Abrahamic traditions, of Judaism, Christianity, and Islam, prevalent during and after the Middle Ages, taught that people with disabilities were expressions of God's displeasure (Mackelprang & Salsgiver, 1996). Disability signified "sinner" to the ancient Hebrews, and people with disabilities were thought to be possessed by evil demons. They viewed madness as retribution afflicted by an angry God and believed it to be supernaturally inflicted on those who sinned. For example, the first book of Samuel describes the details of King Saul's paranoia. As early as the 7th century B.C., Moses told his people in the book of Deuteronomy (28:15,28) "[I]f you do not obey the Lord your God and do not carefully follow all his commands and decrees . . . the Lord will afflict you with madness, blindness and confusion of the mind" (Bullock & Mahon, 1997, p. 32). Similarly, the Qur'an, the book of Islam, includes parables in which non-believers or those who act against Allah are made blind, deaf, or mute. Also like other traditions, some impairment is viewed as divine punishment. The Sura Muhammed states, for example, "Those it is whom Allah has cursed so He has made them deaf and blinded their eyes" (47.23). Haj (1970) notes that visual impairments are by far the most common type of disability mentioned in the Qur'an.

Despite the later tenet of Christianity to protect and provide for disabled individuals, religious leaders of the Reformation often promulgated strong convictions about the linkage of sin and disability. Both Luther and Calvin, for instance, considered persons with intellectual impairment to be essentially evil, possessed, and filled with Satan. According to Monestier (1987), such beliefs were based on early Christianity's strict notions of good and evil and its interpretation of natural phenomena as attributable to the intervention of either God or Satan. Good and evil were thought to be in constant conflict. Since, according to the Scriptures, God created man in His own image, monsters and "the deformed" had to be creations of the Devil. Similarly, the basic theological attitude toward individuals with mental illness was that such persons were demonically possessed, dangerously inferior, and, therefore, not deserving of Christian charity. The most common treatments for mental disorders were torture on the rack and death at the stake or gallows.

Reponses of societies to disability as signifying of spiritual, moral, or religious impurity typically led to violence toward or exclusion of children and families. The fear and aversion toward disability as a symbol and signifier of dread has woven its way into more contemporary and persisting narratives, especially in literature. Disablement— like being made blind or deaf or through making of a monstrous figure has been used as a symbol of retribution for sins. Longmore (1987) described this trope as monster or predator or "one reviled by society as repulsive to behold and dangerous to its well-being." Characters also have a "violent loss of self-control, living in a moral vacuum where life holds little value" (p. 68). This trope appears in classic horror stories like *The Phantom of the Opera* (Leroux, 1910; film: Webber & Schumacher, 2004), *Dr. Jekyll and Mr. Hyde* (Stevenson, 1886; film: Saville & Fleming, 1941), and *The Hunchback of Notre Dame* (Hugo, 1831; Berman & Dieterle, 1939; Hahn, 1996).

Closely related to aversion to disability based on its association with sin or spiritual impurity is Wolfensberger et al.'s conceptualization of disability as representing a sinister or evil personality. Longmore (1987) found that the most common association of disability is with malevolence. "Deformity of the body symbolizes deformity of the soul. Physical handicaps are made the emblems of evil" (p. 66). Fiedler (1996) similarly stated, "[I]n the throes of our paranoia and projection, we convince ourselves that the crippledness of the cripple is an outward and visible sign of an inward state" (p. 41). Bogdan (1988) illustrated how such stereotypes are internalized. He described watching *Treasure Island* on television one evening with his ten-year-old son and his friend:

> Near the beginning of the film my son's friend, Jeremy, who was confused about the plot asked: "Who's the bad guy?" My son replied: "If they look bad, they are bad".
>
> (p. vii)

Bogdan, struck by his son's insight, continued:

> In the film, part of being bad is looking bad, and villains were marked by various disfigurements and disabilities, such as missing limbs and eyes. Horror film monsters are scarred, deformed, disproportionately built, hunched over, exceptionally large, exceptionally small, deaf, speech impaired, visually impaired, mentally ill, or mentally subnormal. In fact, the word monster is standard medical terminology for infants born with blatant defects.
>
> (p. vii)

Kiger (1989) found the messages regarding disability in film are often derogatory, victimize or degrade persons with impairments, and add up over time to "establish distinct patterns of imagery" (p. 155). Garland Thomson (1997) confirms similar patterns in literature, and Darke's 1998 analysis of film supports Kiger's claim that there are distinct patterns of imagery associated with disability. Images that enforce a relationship between monsters and villains and characteristics of disability can be found in innumerable cultural products.

In fairy tales, the evil ones are most often giants, as in *Jack and the Beanstalk*, or dwarfs like *Rumpelstiltskin*. Often, they are also toothless witches with humps on their backs and eye patches. Remember the crooked man who lived in a crooked house? The relationship between outer physique and evilness is exemplified by the characterization of *Peter Pan*'s "Captain Hook" (Barrie, 1904, 1911; Kennedy, Marshall, & Molen & Spielberg, 1991; McCormic, Fisher, Wick & Hogan, 2003), named for his prosthesis. Similarly, one of the most popular classical literary devices for conveying evil or disparagement is "the twisted mind in the twisted body" (Margolis & Shapiro, 1987). According to Mitchell and Snyder (2001), it is common for authors to use the device of the "deformed" outer body to reflect the "deformed" inner qualities of their characters. Similarly, Davis (1997) found, "If disability appears in a novel, it is rarely centrally represented. . . . [S]ufficient research has shown, more often than not villains tend to be physically abnormal, scarred, deformed or mutilated" (p. 19).

Fairy tales and classic works of literature that rely on disability tropes to underline villainy are still widely in use. Contemporary stories that depict impairment and difference as relevant for a range of characterizations are increasing. Emblematic of shifts in mainstream depictions of disability are the 2003 Disney blockbuster film, *Finding Nemo*, and its sequel, *Finding Dory* (Collins, Stanton, & MacLane, 2016). Both movies depict a host of anthropomorphic sea creatures who are introduced to audiences as, for example, having allergies and intolerances, Obsessive Compulsive Disorder, memory loss, and eating disorders. Nemo's story provides an origin sequence to introduce the damaged egg to which his disproportionate "lucky fin" is attributed, as well as the loss and fear that explains his father's overprotection. The characters in *Finding Nemo*, as well as in many other contemporary works, certainly depart from the classic use of disability as portent of dread and signifier of evil.

DISABILITY AS OBJECT OF PITY

Many religious traditions in early societies considered congenital disability and difference as "an example of the capacity of the divine to violate natural law" (Garland, 1995, p. 59). The birth of a disabled or deformed child was treated as retribution against the tribe or parents for angering the gods, and although seen as an innocent victim of its parents' sinfulness, the child served as a reminder of general human evilness. The view of disability as a moral judgment and punishment persists, perhaps, because it is difficult to tolerate a world where punishment is dispensed "with an even hand" to both the guilty and innocent alike (Gallagher, 1995). Not all cultures interpreted the spiritual or religious occurrence of disability as ominous, however. The early Egyptians were among the first to display an interest in the causes and cures of atypical characteristics, as well as the personal and social well-being of individuals with disabilities, especially those with visual impairments. Confucius (551–479 B.C.) taught that fundamental to a just and peaceful world was the decent behavior of the individual. His beliefs were rooted in the concept of a moral sense of responsibility toward others, which included kindness, gentleness, and service to those of weak mind (Scheerenberger, 1983). Confucius taught that the "weak minded" had a claim on society which had a responsibility to care for those who could not care for themselves (L'Abate & Curtis, 1975). Family loyalty was an important value and "Everyone calls his son his son, whether he has talents or not." Every individual was regarded as an integral member of the family even if he or she differed mentally or physically (Ross & Freelander, 1977). Buddhism, originated in approximately 400 B.C., taught that all other forms of righteousness" are not worth the sixteenth part of the emancipation of the heart through charity" (Trattner, 1994, p. 1). Buddha taught that love was expressed through helpfulness, charity, and generosity (Scheerenberger, 1983). A result of that philosophy was the early establishment of a ministry, in approximately 200 B.C. by Asoka, a Buddhist monk, for the care and treatment of persons with disabilities, which included appointed officials to oversee "charitable works" (Van Riper & Emerick, 1984, p. 19).

Awareness of and compassion for persons with disabilities was further ushered into world cultures through Judaism. The early Hebrews made the practice of giving alms a religious requirement. Judaism prohibited infanticide of newborn children with disabilities and emphasized the importance of charity to "the sick, the old, the handicapped, and the poor" (Barnes, Mercer, & Shakespeare, 1999; Trattner, 1994). Between 400 and 500 B.C., as the Hebrews began codifying their laws, they explicitly forbade taking advantage of an individual's disability for sadistic, economic, or other reasons. The Torah, for example, specifically states:

- Thou shalt not curse the deaf, nor put a stumbling block before the blind (Leviticus 14:14).
- Cursed be he that maketh the blind to wander out of the way (Deuteronomy 27:18).

Islam also directed its followers to more humane treatment of people with disabilities in comparison to Greco-Roman traditions (Scheerenberger, 1983). The Qur'an views infanticide as a sin: "Kill not the old man who can not fight, nor the young children nor the women." It also considers persons with intellectual and psychiatric disabilities to be Allah's innocents:

Give not unto those who are weak of understanding the substance which God hath appointed you to preserve for them; but maintain them there out, and clothe them, and speak kindly to them.

In Christianity, though impairments were considered punishments for sin, people with disabilities were regarded as needing healing and general support (Barnes, Mercer, & Shakespeare, 1999). As in Judaism and Islam, the Gospel stressed the notion of showing charity, sympathy, and pity to those with physical and mental impairments and recognizing them as children of God (Preen, 1976). Jesus Christ, who preached a way of life based on love and mercy, is depicted as particularly concerned with the well being of children (Scheerenberger, 1983). He cured their impairments by miraculous healing, drawing upon their faith to achieve the exorcism of demonic influences (Scheerenberger, 1983).

The healing acts Jesus performed served as object lessons to glorify God or to vilify the unbelievers. Disabled people existed "in order that the works of God might be magnified in him" (Paré, 1840/1982, p. 4). Underlying these healing miracles was an assumption that disability symbolized impurity and evidenced a soul to be saved (Bowe, 1978; Ross, 1978).

Forgiveness of sin and physical healing are represented as equivalent (Eiseland, 1994, p. 71). The healing miracles of Jesus had an enormous influence on future attitudes. Although the laws of the early Hebrews displayed sensitivity toward those with disabilities by forbidding their exploitation or humiliation, certain common presuppositions associating one's purity with one's outer appearance nevertheless arose, producing restricted religious and social roles. The Hebrews required their practicing priests (Koheins) to be without blemish. Such restrictions resemble those imposed by the early Greeks who had a propensity for physical perfection in their religious ceremonies: "Not only did the victims which were offered in sacrifice have to be without blemish, but the priests, too, were required to be physically perfect" (Garland, 1995, p. 64). The Romans, as well, prohibited men with disabilities from the priesthood of their pagan temples, "a practice embraced by the Roman Catholic Church, which continued until recently, to bar disabled men from its priesthood" (Gallagher, 1995, p. 248). While the biblical attitude toward persons with disability is generally one of acceptance (Astor, 1985, p. 40), many of the world's most popular religions favored protectiveness and charity, rather than entry into the full privileges of worship and society. The Abrahamic traditions collectively preached sympathy and pity; and the faith or Church assumed the role of provider for the less fortunate by furnishing food, protection, and shelter. While arguably placed in a better position than being killed or exiled, people with disabilities were characterized as objects of pity in need of charity.

As the Renaissance began, the Roman Catholic Church began accepting persons with disabilities into monasteries and asylums for protection and care as wards of the church, thereby removing them from society. Disability became hidden, the prevailing attitude being "out of sight–out of mind." Persons deemed mentally retarded and mentally ill were housed in monasteries, hospitals, charitable facilities, prisons, almshouses, pesthouses, workhouses, warehouses, and other available buildings (Scheerenberger, 1983, p. 34). Far from offering protection and care, however, many asylums became places of horror.

A typical example of the horrors of asylums emerges from the history of Bethlehem Hospital in London. Later known as "Bedlam," the hospital was founded in 1247, when the sheriff of London gave his estate and land to the Bishop and Church of Bethlehem to build a hospital for the Order of St. Mary of Bethlehem. In 1377 a few patients with mental illness were transferred there from a storehouse thought to be too close to the royal palace (Scheerenberger, 1983). The number of people with mental illnesses at Bedlam grew, and in 1547, King Henry VIII gave the hospital to the City of London as a hospital for "poor lunatics" (Arieno, 1989, pp. 16–17). An investigation in 1815 found that the patients were often chained and manacled to the walls and slept on piles of hay soiled with human waste (Metcalf, 1818).

Early American Practices

The American colonists brought with them from Europe many religious customs, ideas, and attitudes. The prejudices toward persons with physical and mental disabilities that existed in Europe likely followed settlers to colonial America. The major concern within the colonies, however, focused on the problem of dependency and disorder in the developing communities, rather than on impairment or public spectacle (Ferguson, 1994). Throughout the seventeenth and eighteenth centuries, most cases involving those deemed disabled concerned their poverty, unemployment, or vagrancy (Grob, 1994).

> Whether it was because you could not walk or talk, or were old or orphaned, widowed or homeless, the etiology of your indigence was seldom an urgent question. What mattered to the community was, first, whether you were a resident or not; second, who would care for you; and third, how the provisions for care were to be handled.
>
> (Ferguson, 1994, p. 24)

During the colonial period the emphasis was on the social and economic impact of impairment, rather than medical cause.

It was the custom of colonial families with means to care for their own members with disabilities—often out of concern for the preservation of the individual's property rights. The care of persons with impairments remained a family responsibility, so long as family members could provide the basic necessities for life. If, however, the effects of the disability spilled outside the family, care of the individual fell under the jurisdiction of the local community, which, in turn, was required to assist the individual or his or her family.

Gradually, laws codified the process for the public care and treatment of persons with disabilities. The first such law was enacted by the Massachusetts legislature in 1614. Most of the laws described the requirements for receiving public assistance and emphasized the criteria for residency. For example, an individual or family was required to live and work for a period of three months to one year before legal residence could be established. Determining the residency of a pauper was important because residency created a responsibility for his or her care. A stranger, by contrast, who could not support himself or herself was banished, unless a resident assumed responsibility (Bowe, 1978; Rothman, 1990; Trattner, 1994). Early American guidelines for handling unemployed persons—a category into which those with disabilities often fell—were generally concerned with where to place the financial burden of care. Thus, they served to both "relieve the needy resident while cutting off and excluding the dependent outsider" (Rothman, 1990, p. 20).

Disabled colonists without families or those whose families could not or would not support them were "placed out" or "farmed out" to other families who received public assistance for providing them with room, board, shelter, and care. Many times, the agreement included indentured service akin to slavery. In fact, until the latter half of the nineteenth century many communities "auctioned off" those with physical or mental disabilities to whomever made the lowest bid, and were then free to demand manual labor services from the persons bought during their period of retention, support, room, and board (Baumeister & Butterfield, 1970; Funk, 1987; Obermann, 1965; Trattner, 1994).

Different from the infrastructure in European cities, colonial America initially had few systematic approaches to deal with people with disabilities. Those who were not perceived as a threat to public safety were often afforded the opportunity to work. Newcomers to a community believed to have the potential of becoming public charges were often "warned out"; that is, strongly encouraged to leave. It was not uncommon for local officials to force the return of persons deemed insane to the community in which they were legal residents (Grob, 1994, p. 16). Another practice was "passing on." This consisted of a community kidnapping their own "feeble-minded" and "insane" inhabitants at night and leaving them on the outskirts of strange, far away towns, with the hope that their inability to communicate would effectively preclude their return (Burgdorf & Burgdorf, 1975). Beyond the family, care and treatment was largely up to local officials who minimized the town's burden by keeping insane, destitute, and disabled persons out.

The Growth of Residential Placements

As American infrastructure grew, the colonists were able to enact ideas brought with them from England and Holland regarding the treatment of poor, ill, and disabled persons. Storing society's unwanted in almshouses, poorhouses, and hospitals was a European practice dating back to at least the tenth century (James, 1975). The first almshouse in America was built in Boston in 1660, and others across the colonies shortly followed. The presence of other residential facilities including jails, insane asylums, and poorhouses would also grow over the next hundred years (Baumeister & Butterfield, 1970; Crissey & Rosen, 1986; Rothman, 1990; Ferguson, 1994). All of these became places to house colonists with disabilities whose care was charged to the public.

The choice of residential placement usually depended on how the individual with the disability became known to authorities. Those able to work were sent to workhouses or almshouses where rehabilitation into hardworking, useful citizens was the aim. If the offender exhibited behavior deemed disturbed, they were sent to hospitals for the insane; and if caught breaking the law, they were sent to prison (Crissey & Rosen, 1986). The growth of residential placements replaced the need for practices like banishment and passing on, but placement in them usually resulted in physical and mental abuse and torture. As in Europe, the facilities ultimately became known for their deplorable conditions, mistreatment, and neglect (Funk, 1987, p. 9).

The Growth of Residential Facilities

In 1773, the Publik [sic] Hospital for Persons of Insane and Disordered Minds opened in Williamsburg, Virginia, marking the first American public facility designated to house those deemed mentally ill. Over the next 100 years, other large asylums, as well as small, private facilities with similar purpose grew in number. The majority of colonial Americans deemed poor, sick, feeble-minded, and insane, however, were grouped together under the label of "pauper" and were held in jails or almshouses (James, 1975; Scheerenberger, 1983, Trattner, 1994). As early as 1729, officials in Boston sought authorization for a separate facility to keep "Distracted Persons Separate from the Poor." It never happened. In 1764, Thomas Hancock, a wealthy Bostonian, bequeathed £600 for the establishment of a facility exclusively for insane persons. The bequest was never used for the purpose. It was not until the mid-nineteenth century that comprehensive reform would target the care of persons now deemed disabled.

Concern over the appalling conditions found in the alms house system roused reformers like Dorothea Dix and Samuel Gridley Howe to crusade for state supervision of institutionalized facilities and for the establishment of state institutions that would provide specialization of care (Bell & Burgdorf, 1983). While teaching a Sunday school program in the East Cambridge House of Corrections, Dix found conditions there abominable—for example, insane women kept in unheated rooms. This discovery inspired her to visit, during 1840–1841, almshouses, jails, and houses of correction throughout Massachusetts, recording lengthy, detailed descriptions of the squalid conditions she observed. Shortly after, Dix argued her case before Massachusetts State and federal legislators. She agitated for State supervision of institutional facilities as well as for specialized care facilities, like hospitals, to serve those deemed insane, demented, and imbecilic. Her enormous influence resulted in a growth of state psychiatric hospitals and the reform of existing ones over the next forty years (Burgdorf & Burgdorf, 1975; President's Committee on the Employment of the Handicapped, 1977; Bell & Burgdorf, 1983; Scheerenberger, 1983; Shapiro, 1993; Ferguson, 1994).

Responding to the influence of reformers like Dix, State Legislative Committees began to attack the almshouse relief system as inefficient, wasteful, and ineffective. They began pressing for a shift of public programs for poor and disabled people to those providing more structure and organization with indoor institutional care. In 1846, Massachusetts enacted the first legislation providing for a public facility for persons with feeble-mindedness [sic], part of which required an inquiry into the "condition of the idiots on the commonwealth [and] to ascertain their number and whether anything could be done for their relief" (Baumeister & Butterfield, 1970, p. 5). Samuel Gridley Howe, director of the Perkins Institute and Massachusetts School for the Blind, was appointed head of the commission.

Howe's institute was home to one of many residential educational programs for persons with disabilities that had been established in America. The Massachusetts Asylum for the Blind (later the Perkins Institute) had been established in 1832; The American Asylum for the Deaf was established in Hartford, Connecticut, by Thomas Gallaudet in 1817, followed by the New York Institution for the Deaf and Dumb in 1818; and public programs for deaf individuals followed in many states, with Gallaudet College founded in Washington, D.C. three years later. Howe's 1848 findings emphasized the success of these programs and advocated that Massachusetts develop schools, rather than institutions more concerned with restraint and containment of "idiots." Though skeptical, the Massachusetts legislature provided funding to establish an experimental school for the feeble-minded. On October 1, 1848, a wing of Perkins Institute became the first permanent institution in the United States, as it accepted ten children into its new program. Three years later, having been declared a huge success, the school was incorporated by the state and officially named the Massachusetts' School for Idiotic and Feebleminded Youth.

The efforts of Dix, Howe, and other reformers of this era, resulted in the distinction of disability from criminality. The subsequent proliferation of residential institutions for individuals with disabilities offered a public alternative to jails and hospitals. The founders of these early institutions saw as the primary goal of their education and treatment programs, the ultimate return of persons with mental retardation to their own homes and communities (Bell & Burgdorf, 1983, p. 19). It was believed that with proper perseverance, persistence, and skill, such minds might be trained. Howe fought to have each new institution considered a school with education its primary function, rather than as an asylum, with implications of custody being primary. To enhance their success, these first institutions accepted very few students and only those who offered a reasonable prognosis for achievement. Over time, however, developing small-scale educational facilities was replaced with larger projects.

The Rise of Institutions

Between 1870 and 1890 construction on large facilities proliferated. The role of institutions to provide education and vocational training was replaced by the notion that residential facilities best provided protection for a population needing to be sheltered from the demands of the outside world (Burgdorf & Burgdorf, 1975). Increasingly, the institutions, now developed for adults, were characterized as "benevolent shelters." Institutions were now characterized as charitable housing. The result was the development of many large institutions housing great numbers of disabled people far from population centers, which provided no training that might enable their residents to return home. Some residents were taught some basic skills like farming and gardening to help defray institutional costs (Bell & Burgdorf, 1983, p. 19). The view of the institution as a school faded and housing for short-term training was replaced with comprehensive care for long periods of time—sometimes even for life (Baumeister & Butterfield, 1970, p. 9).

As late as the 1960s, disabled children and adults were subject to the dehumanizing conditions in large-scale residential facilities, such as state hospitals and institutions. Virtually all decisions, from choice of food and activities to the schedule for sleeping and bathing, were imposed by the structure of the facility. The daily routines of institutions were humiliating. Shapiro (1993) described, "it remained common for inmates at state hospitals to be bathed by stripping off their clothes, forming them into a line, and spraying them with water from a garden hose" (p. 160). Blatt (1970, 1981), while observing four state institutions for persons with intellectual disabilities in four eastern states during the Christmas season of 1965, found remarkably similar conditions to those described over 150 years earlier in the Bedlam and York asylums. He related the following first hand account:

As I entered this dormitory, housing severely mentally retarded adolescents and adults . . . an overwhelming stench enveloped me. It was the sickening, suffocating smell of feces and urine, decay, dirt and filth, of such strength as to hang in the air and, I thought then and still am not dissuaded, solid enough to be cut or shoveled away. But, as things turned out, the odors were among the gentlest assaults on our sensibilities. I was soon to learn about the decaying humanity that caused them.

(1981, p. 142)

Like conditions at the Bedlam and York asylums, Blatt encountered filth, cruel, inhuman treatment, including the common use of restraints and solitary confinement:

Many dormitories for the severely and moderately retarded ambulatory residents have solitary confinement cells or what is officially referred to, and is jokingly called by many attendants, "therapeutic isolation." Therapeutic isolation means solitary confinement—in its most punitive and inhumane form. These cells are located on an upper floor, off to the side and away from the casual or official visitor's scrutiny. . . . Isolation cells are generally tiny rooms, approximately seven feet by seven feet.

(pp. 143–144)

Neglect and cruelty were characteristic of conditions in many institutions.

Throughout the latter half of the twentieth century, the doors were closed on many large-scale institutions as the egregious conditions were exposed to the public. The idea that containment and state control of the activities of people with disabilities is in the interest of self-protection, however, persists. Public financial support provided for people with disabilities, for example, is often perceived as a charitable gesture. This construction of care positions people as vulnerable and fearful of loss of benefit or housing, which imposes limits on speaking out on maltreatment and injustice.

The Problem with Pity

A lasting influence of religious and moral traditions of pity, care, and protection for persons with disabilities was the creation of the provider–receiver relationship. Wolfensberger et al. listed four views associated with the view of persons with disabilities as objects of pity: First, the person with a disability is seen as suffering from his or her condition. Second, although the person may be seen as suffering, he or she may also be believed to be unaware of his or her deviance. Third, the person is seen as an eternal child who never grows. Fourth, being held blameless for his or her condition, the person is seen as not accountable for his or her behavior.

Characters like Tiny Tim in Charles Dickens's (1843) work, *A Christmas Carol*, exemplify this pitiable characterization. Authors often use the stereotype as a device for revealing another character's goodness and sensitivity. For example, disabled characters offer the possibility for spiritual or moral redemption, as Scrooge becomes the savior to Tiny Tim. Disability becomes a device of characterization in order to propel the plot of the story or add dimension to non-disabled characters (Mitchell & Snyder, 2001; Garland Thomson, 1997). Characterizations as objects of pity are also useful to elicit emotional responses, not only in works of art, but also in media events such as tele-thons. According to Longmore (2005), Tiny Tim was the model for the infantilized image of poster children. The image of the pitiable disabled person serves as "vehicle of others' redemption, existing not for himself or herself, not as a human being in his or her own right, but to provide the occasion for non-disabled people to renew their humanity" (pp. 505–506).

DISABILITY AS SUB-HUMAN

As views of people with disabilities were shaped by pity giving rise to charitable works in their care and protection, a coinciding image of disability lurking within was their characterization as sub-human. The inhumane conditions of early and more contemporary residential facilities for people with intellectual disabilities, especially, reflected this belief. An upswing in improvements to care and facilities and aims to educate people with disabilities were replaced with a focus on long-term custodial care. Shifts in the attitudes toward disability and mental illness occurred in the latter parts of the nineteenth century. The belief that containment in institutions was for the protection of those with disabilities also began to change. The sentiment that society needed protection *from* disabled people grew in the late 1800s and early 1900s (United States Commission on Civil Rights, cited in Bell & Burgdorf, 1983, p. 19).

The Making of a Social Menace

In 1912, Henry Herbert Goddard, then Director of research at the Training School at Vineland, New Jersey, for Feeble-Minded Girls and Boys, published the famous study, *The Kallikak Family: A Study in the Heredity of Feeble-Mindedness.* Goddard began his case study with a woman in his institution, whom he named Deborah Kallikak. He proceeded to trace her genealogy through many generations. Goddard described two branches of the Kallikak family born of a single progenitor. Deborah Kallikak and her ancestors—mostly poor and feeble-minded—"demonstrated" the outcome of the progenitor's one-time affair with a barmaid. The progenitor's other children, who were born in marriage to a woman of "good stock," were successful and moral. The different outcomes in the familial branches, Goddard thought, demonstrated the pas-sage of particular traits through a family's lineage. Ultimately, he proposed the hered-ity of intelligence, mental health, and morality. Thus, feeble-mindedness became closely linked with poverty, crime, and illegitimacy.

In his study, Goddard also coined the term, "moron," which became widely accepted for those considered to be "high grade defectives." They evinced the typical characteristics of intellectual denseness, social dullness and inadequacy, and moral deficiency. The fear, however, was that morons were not afflicted to a degree obvi-ous to the casual observer nor were impaired by such adventitious means as brain injury, disease, or other injury. The next-door neighbor could be a family of poor lineage, perhaps hiding a recessive gene predicting feeble-mindedness. Eventually, feeble-mindedness changed from being merely associated with social vices to being their fundamental cause (Trent, 1994; Haller, 1963). The myth of the "menace of the feeble-minded" and the figure of the moron became an icon and force in American social thought. A social response followed. During the early 1900s cautionary pamphlets and enactments incorporating the principles of eugenics began to appear in states throughout the nation. Titles of the pamphlets include, for example, *The Menace of the Feebleminded in Pennsylvania* (1913), *The Menace of the Feebleminded in Connecticut* (1915), *The Burden of the Feeble-Minded* (1912) in Massachusetts, and *The Feeble-Minded, Or, The Hub to Our Wheel of Vice* (1913) in Ohio (cited in Gilhool, 1997, p. 269). The materials described plans to segregate the "unfortunates" in remote areas, hence protecting "normal" residents from social ills, as well as grouping people of the same "kind" to prevent undesirable traits from polluting upstanding family lineages. Beyond fear mongering, more dramatic social responses to "the menace" were also on the horizon.

Controlling Feeble-Mindedness and the Unfit

The eugenics movement highlighted studies such as Goddard's to raise the fear that the prevalence of congenital physical disability and feeble-mindedness would undermine society (Smith, 1985). The public became afraid that the occurrence of such disabilities was increasing rapidly in modern civilization and that "the spreading of handicapping conditions through heredity was the single most important problem facing American Society" (Burgdorf & Burgdorf, 1977, p. 998). The eugenics movement had all the fervor of a religious crusade, of which American science was at the forefront (Smith, 1985). The early eugenic aim of eliminating unwanted inherited disorders from human populations by selective marriage practices soon evolved into laws enforcing compulsory sterilization, restricted immigration, restricted marriage, and custodial care (institutionalization) to halt the perceived menace of mental disease and delinquency.

The expanding interest in genetics, at the beginning of the century, led to the establishment of the first organization of the eugenics movement, the American Breeders Association. Organized in 1903 by leading agricultural breeders, renowned university biologists, and others including Dr. Charles Davenport of Harvard and Alexander Graham Bell, the organization established in 1906 several committees to research specific breeding problems. One of their primary committees, the Committee on Eugenics set out "to investigate and report on heredity in the human race" [and] "to emphasize the value of superior blood and the menace to society of inferior blood" (Haller, 1963, p. 62). In 1911, the American Breeders Association, wanting to "purge from the blood of the race innately defective strains," recommended the following procedures: selective scientific breeding to remove defective traits, restrictive marriage laws, euthanasia, sterilization, and life segregation for all handicapped persons (Burgdorf & Burgdorf, 1975, p. 887). Two years later, the Association defined as socially unfit "the feeble-minded," "paupers," "criminaloids," "epileptics," "the insane," "the constitutionally weak," "those predisposed to specific diseases," "the congenitally deformed," and "those having defective sense organs." They further advocated that such humans should, if possible, be eliminated from the human stock if we would maintain or raise the level of quality essential to the progress of the nation and our race (cited in Scheerenberger, 1983, p. 154). Society would have to be saved from the burdens imposed upon it by these defectives by such methods as marriage restriction, sexual sterilization, and permanent institutionalization.

Already by the mid-1890s approximately half of the states had passed laws declaring null and void the marriages of insane or feeble-minded persons on the grounds that such persons were not capable of making contracts (Haller, 1963). By the late 1970s, most states carried statutory prohibitions of marriages where one of the partners was mentally ill or mentally retarded (Burgdorf & Burgdorf, 1977). In addition, while some states restricted marriage among persons considered physically handicapped, at least 17 extended such prohibitions to persons with epilepsy. A number of states also restricted or denied the right of persons with mental retardation and those considered "deaf mutes" from entering into any sort of legal contract. Such restrictions also served to control marriages, which are contractual agreements at law.

Sterilization

Compulsory sterilization became practically feasible in the late nineteenth century when safe, effective, and morally acceptable surgical methods were developed. Up to the 1890s the only surgical procedure available for producing sterility was castration, considered extremely radical because it was medically dangerous, caused undesirable changes in secondary sexual characteristics, and was widely considered morally unacceptable. Such thoughts, however, did not stop some institution administrators. During the 1890s, Dr. F. Pilcher, Superintendent of the Kansas State Asylum for Idiotic and Imbecile Youth, castrated 44 older boys and men for masturbating (Trent, 1994, p. 193). He also had 14 girls clitorectomized until public outrage forced him to stop (Burgdorf & Burgdorf, 1977, p. 999). Martin Barr, a contemporary of Pilcher's, stated in an 1899 journal article, that one of the benefits of castration was the fact that "some nice male soprano voices could be obtained for the institutional choir" (cited in Baumeister & Butterfield, 1970, p. 12).

By the end of the nineteenth century, the vasectomy (severing the vas deferens) for men and the salpingectomy (the cutting or removing of the fallopian tubes) for women, were developed. Seen as safe and morally acceptable surgical procedures, sterilizations of those deemed feeble-minded increased, especially in institutions, despite the fact that no state had enacted legislation authorizing them (Burgdorf & Burgdorf, 1977). In 1907, however, Indiana passed the nation's first sterilization law, which applied to "inmates of state institutions who were confirmed criminals, idiots, imbeciles, or rapists" (Burgdorf & Burgdorf, 1977, p. 1000). By 1930, 28 states had enacted compulsory laws that authorized the sterilization of "inmates of mental institutions, persons convicted more than once of sex crimes, those deemed to be feebleminded by IQ tests, 'moral degenerate persons' and epileptics" (Friedlander, 1995, p. 8). By 1938, more than 27,000 forced sterilizations had been performed in the United States (Smith, 1985).

The flood of state statutes authorizing eugenic sterilizations met occasional obstacles in those courts that found such procedures unconstitutional, until 1925 when the Supreme Court of Virginia made its ruling in the landmark case of *Buck v. Bell* (1925) reinforcing the state's right to force unwanted sterilizations. In 1924, Carrie Buck had been committed to the State Colony for Epileptics and Feebleminded at

Lynchberg. Under the authority of the *Virginia Sterilization Act* (1924), which provided for the sterilization of "mental defectives" confined to state institutions when, in the judgment of the superintendents of those institutions, "the best interests of the patients and society would be served by their being rendered incapable of producing offspring" (White, 1993, p. 404), the superintendent presented to the Colony's Board of Directors, a petition for an order to sterilize Carrie by salpingectomy. The superintendent alleged that she had the mind of a nine-year-old, was the mother of a mentally defective child, and was the daughter of a woman previously committed to that same institution. The petition was granted.

Carrie's state appointed guardian appealed the decision up to the United States Supreme Court (Burgdorf & Burgdorf, 1977, pp. 1000–1005). Justice Oliver Wendell Holmes, writing for the eight-person majority of the Court held that the Virginia Statute was legal and did not violate Carrie's rights under Due Process or the Equal Protection Clause of the Fourteenth Amendment (Friedlander, 1995, p. 8). Thus, the Court endorsed the eugenic justifications for the state's sterilizing the unfit and the often quoted excerpts of Holmes' opinion entered the language:

> It is better for all the world, if instead of waiting to execute degenerate offspring for crime, or to let them starve for their imbecility, society can prevent those who are manifestly unfit from continuing their kind. The principle that sustains compulsory vaccination is broad enough to cover cutting the fallopian tubes. . . . Three generations of imbeciles are enough.
>
> (cited in Burgdorf & Burgdorf, 1977, p. 1004)

Holmes' decision opened the floodgates for sterilizations in the United States. In 1927, Carrie Buck was sterilized. Ironically, "Carrie's child, alleged to represent a 'third generation of imbeciles,' actually grew to be an honor student" (Smith, 1994, p. 234). In fact, Carrie herself left the institution after she was sterilized, married a deputy sheriff and lived a modest, productive, and respectable life. It was later proven that she did not have mental retardation, and careful examination of her family tree would have revealed she was actually descended from a prominent Virginia family (Smith, 1994). Smith (1994) estimated conservatively that 50,000 people had been sterilized in the United States under that authority. More than 4,000 had been sterilized at the Lynchburg Training School alone.

The image of the intellectually disabled person as sub-human enabled containment and sterilization for their own and others' protection. Other violations of human rights were also evident during the mid-century in residential facilities. At the Fernald School, during the 1950s, government-sponsored research was conducted on children with intellectual disabilities without their knowledge or guardian consent. The Advisory Committee on Human Radiation Experiments (ACHRE) (1996) found that groups considered powerless and dependent were targeted for experimentation. These groups included infants, children, minorities, the terminally ill, persons with cognitive disabilities, and those in institutions. Thus, the institutionalization of the nation's most vulnerable members offered a population of people who could be used at scientists' disposal.

In the Fernald School experiments children were told they were participating in a science club activity and fed oatmeal breakfasts with small doses of radioactive isotopes. Through the response of children to ingredients given in milk and cereal, researchers hoped to ascertain if a chemical in oatmeal would interfere with the body's ability to absorb iron and calcium. (Advisory Committee on Human Radiation Experiments, 1994; "Retarded school alumni," 1994). Such experimentation on "vulnerable populations" occurred between World War II and the mid-1970s on over 16,000 humans with the Atomic Energy Commission's express approval or financial support. For example, during the 1960s at the University of Arkansas Medical Center in Little Rock, children with mental retardation (some as young as 13) who were wards of the Arkansas Children's Colony, a state institution, received "iodine-131" in a thyroid study. In a similar University of Arkansas study experiments involved infants as young as nine months. A study completed at the University of Washington between 1954 and 1958 used "mental patients" from the Northern State Hospital in Sedro-Woolley as unknowing subjects (Burns, 1995; Hoversten, 1995a, 1995b).

Contemporary Views

In 1972 Wolfensberger et al. wrote that a common stereotype was of persons with disabilities as being sub-human. People with intellectual disabilities are "particularly apt to be unconsciously perceived or even consciously labeled as subhuman, as animal-like, even as 'vegetables' or 'vegetative.'" He recalled the public statement of a state institution's superintendent who referred to some of the residents as "so called human beings below what we might call an animal level of functioning" (pp. 16–17). This imagery is found in literature by writers like Steinbeck (1937) who, in his widely-read novel, *Of Mice and Men*, describes Lennie, an intellectually disabled adult, walking "heavily, dragging his feet a little, the way a bear drags his paws" (p. 10). Steinbeck then describes Lennie drinking from a stream "with long gulps, snorting into the water like a horse" (p. 10). The book ends with Lennie being "disposed of" by a shot to the back of his head similar to the way an old sick dog had been "disposed of" earlier in the story. The killing by his companion and caretaker, George, is typically interpreted as a humane end to Lennie's life.

In 2007, the Ashley X story (Kirschner, Brashler, & Savage, 2007) brought "growth attenuation therapy" to the public purview. Ashley X was 7-year-old girl who required intensive care related to disabling conditions. Her family and doctor sought growth attenuation therapy to limit her further growth and maturation. This course of treatment included the surgical removal of Ashley's uterus and breast buds to prevent puberty, which her parents claimed would make homecare for her impossible, thus reducing her quality of life. Although the procedure was eventually deemed unethical, reports of therapies seeking similar results through hormone regimens have appeared over the last years. The public course of commentary revealed that beliefs about disabled people as less-human and the priorities of caregivers over the individuals for whom they care continue to persist in modern discourse. Care is still seen as charity, the quality of which may be determined by the provider. The bodies of persons with disabilities continue to be ravaged in the name of "their own good."

An ongoing subject of interest among the disability community is research into the human genome. While not inherently problematic, a concern is that a genetic map of the human can be potentially misinterpreted to denote an ideal human form or chemistry. Because science is generally considered the arbiter of truth in contemporary America, disabled activists and scholars are acting as harbingers, warning of the slippery slope in genetic engineering that can lead us to a new era of eugenics.

CONCLUSION

In this chapter we have juxtaposed persisting tropes about disability and disabled persons with historical accounts and contemporary issues. This historical examination of the treatment and segregation of persons with disabilities provides insight and perspective for understanding the origins of our more familiar current common beliefs and attitudes. Throughout time and across contexts, extraordinary characteristics and impairments have been an occasion for meaning. Whether perceived as divine punishment or reward; considered sin or blessing; or deemed pathological by science, culture's discernment of difference has played a role in the lives of those deemed disabled. In tracing the treatment of disabled persons, we see the origins of paternalism in Greco-Roman times; the benevolent and charitable response in Judeo-Christian traditions; and the response to rid society of its undesirables in the eugenics movement and under the Third Reich.

The concept of normalcy has been used to justify the differential treatment of society's "undesirables" throughout history. Deeming differences to be pathologies once made allowable the segregation, abuse, and murder of particular people and groups of people. The specific characteristics that have signified a rationale for differential treatment vary according to place and time; religion and culture. To account for this diversity, we must understand how the idea of pathology can be applied to almost any trait, with the resulting position of being "disabled," or made unable to participate and benefit from society's opportunities. Gordon and Rosenblum (2001) make a strong case, in fact, that disability shares many characteristics with American constructions of race, gender, and sexual orientation. They consider how each status is constructed through unceasing social processes in which people are named, aggregated and disaggregated, dichotomized and stigmatized, and deprived of attributes valued in our culture. Innumerable parallels between the treatment of people with disabilities and other subjugated groups through history should be evident— from other groups targeted in Nazi Germany to justifications for the enslavement of people of color to the Tuskegee syphilis experiment that withheld treatment from African-American men in the name of research. The world's history is marked by histories of extermination and segregation justified by religion, moral order, public health, and science. Beliefs and understandings about the nature of disability and the personhood of disabled people have more often led to disempowered positions. Perceptions of disability as evil, dreadful, pitiable, menacing, and sub-human have each reverberated throughout time and context enabling practices as dramatic as euthanasia and forced sterilization and as persistent as containment and segregation. Persisting stereotypes and tropes about disability are reflections of histories and beliefs that run deep into human consciousness. They are created and circulated over time and reinforce the paradigms on which they were built. In the next chapter we move from emphasis on cultural beliefs, attitudes, and histories that undergird exclusion to those that inform inclusion and integration.

4

MOVING TOWARD CULTURES OF INCLUSION

Bullock and Mahon (1997) state, "Two basic views in the ancient world existed regarding the etiology of disability. One attributed illness to supernatural or divine intervention, and the other view was that illness and disability were due to natural causes" (pp. 19–20). Many religious traditions characterized particular physical and sensory differences as inhuman or reflective of sin, and therefore "justifiably" barred particular people from equal participation in worship and other facets of public life (Shapiro, 1999; Stiker, 1997). Not all early cultures interpreted disability as occasions for extermination or exclusion, however. Many American Indian cultures valued rather than devalued those with physical and mental differences. The North American plains tribes, for example, admired deaf children because of their skillful use of signed languages (Moores, 1996). According to Moores (1996), "The priests of Karnak trained the blind in music, the arts, and massage. Blind people participated in religious ceremonies and, during some periods, represented a large proportion of the poets and musicians of ancient Egypt" (p. 32). As early as 850 A.D., Japan reserved membership in masseuse guilds for blind individuals, which guaranteed a source of work. In ancient China, it was not uncommon to find blind scholars, soothsayers, storytellers, and musicians (Hewett & Forness, 1977, p. 15). Rather than exterminate or contain people with disabilities, many early cultures found ways to weave worlds that enabled people with some kinds of impairments into their communities and economies. In this chapter, we describe the ways that people with disabilities have been present in public life through discussion of contemporary policy and popular culture throughout time.

THE DISABILITY RIGHTS MOVEMENT

The first half of the twentieth century was an internationally tumultuous era, characterized by two World Wars and The Great Depression. While disabled people were still subject to horrific treatment rationalized by the pseudoscience of eugenics, innovation, humanism, and a new face of disability seen in returning war veterans also marked this period of history. As early as 1914, federal policies including The War Risk Insurance Act (1914) and The Smith-Sears Veterans Rehabilitation Act (1918) were established to address the concerns of disabled veterans. The Disabled American Veterans organization was eventually formed in 1920, and the National Easter Seal Society was established in 1922. Although these organizations and policies did not reflect the contemporary initiatives posed by disabled persons (veterans and others, alike), their emergence signified increasing public interest and organization around disability issues. In 1932, Harry Jennings built the first tubular, folding wheelchair, which became the prototype for those in use today. The League of the Physically Handicapped (1935–1938) formed as one of the first disability organizations to make discrimination in policy and employment its primary issue. President Franklin D. Roosevelt, along with Eleanor Roosevelt, advanced the concerns of people with disabilities through supporting the March of Dimes (1937) and other policy initiatives, respectively. A confluence of scientific, social, and political factors paved the way for a new era of disability rights to emerge.

By the end of the 1950s disability policy had begun to adopt a civil rights orientation. There was increasing humanization of disabled people based on qualities of deservedness, normality, and employability. There was also a move from societal indifference to recognition that the remaining "unfortunates" must receive some minimum level of care (Funk, 1987). The National Association for the Deaf (NAD) had been founded in 1864, and the American Foundation for the Blind (AFB) in 1921. Noted previously, veterans and those with physical disabilities had broken into the "mainstream," and awareness of intellectual disability was growing. For example, Rose Kennedy, the intellectually disabled sister of President John F. Kennedy, gave a new face to "retardation" in 1960. In 1972, a series of exposés on the Willowbrook State School in New York City aired on television and brought unprecedented public attention to the conditions in institutions that visitors like Blatt had described. The result of the exposure was a class-action lawsuit that mandated reforms to the facility. More importantly, however, the publicity generated by the case brought attention to the civil rights of people with disabilities. Rather than merely seek reform of facilities, reform in the systems that placed people in institutions also became a focus. The idea of independent living for people with intellectual and developmental disabilities was brought to the fore. The independent living movement offered a notable shift from the attitudes before then, which Funk describes as tolerant of retaining persons with disabilities in a caste status and assuming that most would always require segregated care and protection.

Independent Living

The idea of independent living was not a new one in the 1970s. A trend in deinstitutionalization through the 1950s–1960s had burgeoned from the efforts and activism of physically disabled persons. In 1958, for example, Anne Emerman, who was living at the Goldwater Memorial Hospital in New York City, was selected as a test case in independent living. The 21-year-old, quadriplegic, wheelchair user entered the "mainstream" and ultimately completed college and a master's degree, worked as a psychiatric social worker, served as the director of the Mayor's Office for People with Disabilities in New York City, and became a wife and mother (Fleischer & Zames, 2001). This "test case," and others like it, fueled an era of activism in independent living that those with developmental and intellectual disabilities would eventually also benefit from.

Prior even to the test cases in New York, some of the first college programs for persons with disabilities had been established in what are now the Kansas State Teachers College and the University of Illinois (Fleischer & Zames, 2001). Catering to disabled veterans, these schools capitalized on their relatively compact and flat geography to welcome wheelchair users. Subsequently, they developed assistance centers, sports programs, and accessible transportation options as part of the college experience. The National Deaf-Mute College, which changed its name to Gallaudet College in 1954, had been serving students using an array of communication modes since 1880. The successes that came out of these programs offered promising possibilities for people once deemed unable to work or live full lives. These examples aside, although early pioneers like Emerman and Marilyn Saviola, the first resident of Goldwater to attend college while living there, were quite ready to enter the world, the world was not as ready for them. Getting into and getting funding for college, securing an accessible place to live, getting financial and medical assistance, gaining employment, and negotiating a physical environment that was more often not friendly to wheelchair users were all barriers to independent living. Most of society had not taken a lead from the efforts of those at Gallaudet, Kansas State Teachers College, the University of Illinois, and a handful of others.

The issue of containment posed by institutions and nursing homes quickly shifted to one of restriction posed by the barriers in most of the world outside of them. It was not enough that a few programs had been established as "disability-friendly." Disabled persons deserved access to the society at large. In 1962, Edward Roberts, a quadriplegic polio survivor who spent most of his life in an iron lung, successfully sued the University of California (UC) to gain admission, insisting that he had an equal right to education. Roberts' enrollment at UC-Berkeley, however, also meant that appropriate housing would need to be provided. As other quadriplegics joined Roberts on the campus, organizing for better services, housing, and assistance for living became possible. They formed a political group called The Rolling Quads and worked on getting services such as wheelchair repair, accessible housing, and attendant care (Fleischer & Zames, 2001, p. 39).

In 1969, the Physically Disabled Students Program was funded as part of a national initiative for minority students. The blueprint for the independent living movement was born, rooted in a new way of conceptualizing the needs and issues central to the lives of disabled people. Shapiro (1993) captures the change:

> The medical model of disability measured independence by how far one could walk after an illness or how far one could bend his legs after an accident. But Roberts redefined independence as the control a disabled person had over his life. Independence was measured not by the tasks one could perform without assistance but by the quality of one's life with help.

(p. 51)

In 1972, the Center for Independent Living at Berkeley was formed as an agency governed by and for people with disabilities. Its founder, Ed Roberts, became a new kind of "poster-child," symbolizing not charity or pity, but self-determination and the fight for civil rights of disabled people. The recognition of disabled people's agendas as centered on rights and access emerged, and the Disability Rights Movement was ushered in, only slightly after the more frequently honored Civil Rights and Women's Rights Movements of the time.

Organizing for Action

By the 1960s, the USA entered a time when formal organizations and coalitions of persons with disabilities could, by analogy to other oppressed groups, focus their efforts on civil rights issues pertinent to *all* categorized "disabled." Prior to the Disability Rights Movement, most organized efforts to improve the quality of life for persons with disabilities were specific to a particular impairment—as in the NAD and AFB—or characterized as charity. Leadership and strategic planning for the latter involved, at best, only marginal participation of their intended stakeholders (disabled persons). The upwell of anti-discrimination action surrounding race and gender led disabled people to also challenge their limited employment and housing options and other exclusions. Like leaders of other movements, disability rights activists believed that self-advocacy and grassroots strategies would promise change more aligned with their agendas. In addition, the idea of defining disabled persons as a group brought together by common oppression, rather than defined by specific impairments, emerged (Linton, 1998).

In the wake of early pioneers in independent living, Judith E. Heumann organized the group, Disabled in Action (DIA), in 1970, whose legacy of demonstrations and lawsuits for disability rights began with demands for accessible public transportation in New York City. Eventually growing into the national group, Self Advocates Becoming Empowered (S.A.B.E.), the *People First* movement took cues from organizations in Sweden, Canada, and the United Kingdom, and began advancing the self-advocacy of persons with intellectual disabilities in 1974. The Union of Physically Impaired Against Segregation (UPIAS) organized to issue a proclamation in 1972, which would ignite the Disabled People's Movement in the United Kingdom. Thus, grassroots organizations formed the basis of the Disability Rights Movement in the USA and internationally.

PUBLIC POLICY FOR INTEGRATION

Among the first areas of business for the new activists were exposing the undignified, at best, and deplorable conditions, at worst, of the institutions, hospitals, and nursing homes in which many adults and children with disabilities were living. To that point, the architecture of most buildings and streets prohibited the free movement of a new generation of wheelchair users. Societal attitudes had accepted the "wheelchair-bound" images of "crippled" people as an unfortunate, but understandably restrictive condition. Children and adults identified with developmental and intellectual disabilities had long been warehoused in institutions. In a dawning era of disability rights, medical researchers, charitable organizations, and rights groups turned attention on improving the living conditions of children and adults with disabilities, although researching and curing impairments remained a focus for many. Several federal policies reflected these new interests.

Section 504 of the Vocational Rehabilitation Act

Although earlier legislation and policies in the USA had reflected some of the concerns of disabled people, the *Vocational Rehabilitation Act of 1973 (PL 93–112)* is regarded as the first civil rights act specific to the group. When, in 1972, President Nixon vetoed early versions of the act, disability rights activists emerged with force. DIA members, including Heumann and eighty others, halted traffic with a sit-in on one of New York City's main thoroughfares. When the act was brought to vote in 1973, a march and rally on the Capitol ensured that the attention of policy makers and the public would be captured to guarantee its passage.

The *Vocational Rehabilitation Act of 1973* was passed into federal law on September 26, 1973. The original act barred employment discrimination, mandated affirmative action in employment, and established the Architectural and Transportation Compliance Board (now named the Access Board). Most significant to solidifying disability rights, however, *Section 504* of the act barred discrimination in all programs receiving federal financial assistance. Thus, the mass of social systems—unemployment, social security, state courts and agencies, schools, hospitals, and more—were now charged with upholding disabled persons' civil rights. *Section 504* stated:

> No otherwise qualified handicapped individual in the United States, as defined by section 7(6), shall, solely by reason of his handicap, be excluded from the participation in, be denied the benefits of, or be subjected to discrimination under any program or activity receiving Federal financial assistance.
>
> (U.S. Congress, 1973)

The wording in *Section 504* matched the *Civil Rights Act of 1964*, which abolished discrimination in federally funded programs on the basis of race, color, or national origin.

As thrilling as the passage of the Act was, however, regulations were not in place to specify situations constituting discrimination, nor their remedies. When Howard University law student, James Cherry, was denied the use of a building's elevator and a request for a closer parking space, it became clear that the impact of *Section 504* was limited without specific direction. He initiated a lawsuit demanding that the Department of Health, Education, and Welfare (HEW) develop and enforce regulations for *Section 504*. In July of 1976, Cherry won his case (*Cherry v. Mathews*, 1976). Pushing the government to develop and pass the forthcoming regulations became a cause around which more local organizations of disability rights could join together and rally. "Until this point," Fleischer and Zames (2001) point out, "the disability rights movement had been local and disparate. With this concerted endeavor to obtain implementation of the Section 504 regulations, the movement became national and focused" (p. 52).

The American Coalition of Citizens with Disabilities (ACCD) had been founded through a Rehabilitation Services Agency grant in 1975, and included members such as Judith E. Heumann, Fred Fay, Ralf D. Hotchkiss, Sharon Mistler, Roger Peterson, Al Pimentel, and Eunice Fiorito—all people with disabilities (Fleischer & Zames, 2001). After Cherry's lawsuit, the group exerted pressure on HEW and congress to issue and amend *Section 504*. When HEW did not meet the ACCD's deadline on April 4, 1977, April 5th dawned with disability rights activists demonstrating at most of HEW's offices in ten federal regions and the nation's capital. Coverage of the longest sit-ins in San Francisco and Washington, D.C. garnered national attention. The regulations were issued and signed on April 28th, alongside those issued to amend another disability rights act—the *Education for All Handicapped Children Act.*

The Education for All Handicapped Children Act

At the same time adults with disabilities were organizing for access to employment and independent living, parents were also agitating for the rights of their children with disabilities to access public education. Advocacy and parent organizations such as the ARC and the United Cerebral Palsy Association had been fighting for deinstitutionalization at the same time as others. Parent organizations had also successfully lobbied Congress to establish a federal bureau for "handicapped children" and to provide funds for training special education teachers and developing appropriate curricula (Shapiro, 1993). However, access to *public* schools, rather than special, segregated programs was a right yet to be solidified. Children with disabilities could be denied entry to a school, and there were no provisions to guide the implementation of appropriate curriculum and facilities. In the early 1970s two lawsuits were brought to argue the right to education of *all* children.

In 1971, the Pennsylvania Association for Retarded Children (PARC) won a class-action suit against the Commonwealth of Pennsylvania claiming the right of all children to enter public schools. To that point children with disabilities could be denied entry to school. Shortly after, the decision in *Mills v. Board of Education of the District of Columbia* (1972) extended the ruling in *PARC v. Pennsylvania* to include, "a presumption that among the alternative programs of education, placement in a regular public school class with appropriate ancillary services is preferable to placement in a special school class." With both Courts acknowledging the overdue right of all children's access to schools—granted in 1954 to African-American children in *Brown v. Board of Education of Topeka*—and, alongside the passage of the Rehabilitation Act, legislation specific to education was on the horizon.

In 1975, Congress passed legislation that guaranteed a free and appropriate education for all of the nation's approximately eight million children with disabilities—namely, *Public Law 94–142*, the *Education for All Handicapped Children Act* (EHA), which is now IDEIA. The act included six major provisions to ensure disabled youngsters an education appropriate to their individual special education needs:

1) "Zero reject" requires that all children receive a free, appropriate education. No child may be denied an education because of the severity of his or her disability.
2) A non-discriminatory evaluation means that the required assessment of a youngster's handicap is conducted by a multidisciplinary team, is not culturally biased and is individually administered (no group testing).

3) An individualized education program (IEP) ensures that the educational program is tailored individually to meet the needs of each child.
4) Parent and student participation in decision-making.
5) Access to the Least Restrictive Environment (LRE).
6) Right to Due Process, or procedures that guide resolutions of conflict between the parent/student and the school.

Children with disabilities are protected under *Section 504*, which guarantees that they receive educational services and opportunities equal to those provided to their peers. The EHA, however, specified that children were also entitled to receive additional special education supports and services to ensure their *benefit* from the learning experiences provided. In other words, *Section 504* guarantees equal access and non-discrimination to public schools and their curriculum, but the EHA required schools to ensure that children are benefiting from the educational program. It is not enough, for example, for a child to simply be in a classroom with others; the curriculum must be catered to the unique needs of each child.

Post-Legislation Activism

With the passage of two historical acts, disability activists were able to capitalize on their newfound recognition, and continued pushing for refinement in the provisions and regulations in the courts and the streets. Disability rights had gained an attentive audience and many disability organizations focused on civil rights and access to public society emerged. *Guide Dog Users* was organized in New York City; the first convention of *People First*, organized nationally as Self Advocates Becoming Empowered, was held; and *Black Deaf Advocates* was established. Disabled in Action mounted several lawsuits and demonstrations focused on securing accessible public transit—most notably in the 1976 Transbus lawsuit (*Disabled in Action of Pennsylvania v. Coleman*, 1976). Following the success of 1982 demonstrations for accessible busses in Denver, Colorado, Wade Blank and residents of the Atlantis Community founded ADAPT, an influential and radical disability rights group. The group organized local events, but sought national influence and took on the federal government in mounting the suit, *ADAPT v. Skinner* (1989). The court ruled that federal regulations requiring that transit authorities spend only a small percentage of their budgets on access were arbitrary and discriminatory. A smaller profit margin, in other words, is not a rationale for denying people access to public transportation.

The Americans with Disabilities Act (ADA)

Although *Section 504* and the *EHA* provided non-discrimination guidelines for people with disabilities, it would take a more comprehensive law to ensure their full civil rights. As member and chair of the Texas Task Force for Long Range Policy for People with Disabilities during the 1980s, Justin Dart, polio survivor, activist, and businessman had begun work on the legislation that would become the *Americans with Disabilities Act* (ADA). The ADA would eventually pass the Senate and the House of Representatives by a wide margin. The concerns about the new legislation related not to its passage, but to who would be included in its coverage, and whether inclusion in the *Civil Rights Act of 1964* would be adequate and even favorable. Having a specific, possibly weaker, civil rights law for people with disabilities could lead to differentiating the rights of those protected in the *Civil Rights Act* from those specified in the ADA. The National Council on Disability, under President Ronald Reagan, determined that disability discrimination is distinctive and substantially different from other kinds of prejudice, therefore requiring its own law. The new law maintained the definition of disability in *Section 504*, and made more specific the protection of individuals discriminated on the *perception* of disability, even where the individual's "impairment" does not affect one's abilities. In particular, those with AIDS or HIV, learning disabilities, those recovering from cancer or mental illness, and those with facial disfigurement were now explicitly protected by disability law.

President George H.W. Bush signed the *Americans with Disabilities Act (PL 101–336)* on July 26, 1990. More comprehensive than the *Rehabilitation Act*, the ADA extended rights provisions and non-discrimination to the private sector. All public services and facilities, not only those that received federal funding, would be held to comply with a standard for access and equality. Each part of the law was designed to end discrimination toward persons with disabilities and is thought to be the most significant piece of federal civil rights legislation since the *Civil Rights Act of 1964*.

The ADA prohibits discrimination in both the private and public sectors in employment, public services, transportation, and communication. It also provides a comprehensive mandate to bring persons with disabilities into the economic and social mainstream of American life. The ADA contains strong standards and provides that the federal government play a central role in their enforcement. Basically, the law prohibits discrimination on the basis of disability or impairment and provides civil rights protection similar to that guaranteed to individuals on the basis of race, sex, sexuality, national origin, age, and religion. The legislation answers the following persistent questions in the five titles of the ADA of 1990, which are paraphrased below.

Title I. Who is considered disabled? A firm definition of "disability" underlies the authority of the ADA, which defines "individual with a disability" rather broadly. A person may be considered disabled if he or she (a) has a physical or mental condition that substantially limits one or more of the major life functions, (b) has a record of such impairment, or (c) is perceived as having such an impairment. Even if the impairment is no longer present, the individual may still be considered disabled. Therefore, if an employer fails to hire,

> [an] individual who was once known to have alcoholism, cancer, or mental illness, or may still have a severe disfigurement, that employer may be guilty of discrimination. Not covered under the definition are those with minor, non-chronic conditions that last a short time like sprains, infections or broken limbs.

Title II. How are public accommodations affected? ADA's public accommodations requirements which became effective on January 26, 1992, define public accommodations as "private entities that affect commerce." Thus, the requirements extend to hotels, restaurants, theaters (how many times have you seen wheelchair users at the movies?), doctors' offices, pharmacies, retail stores, museums, libraries, parks, private schools, and day care centers. Not covered under the ADA are private clubs and religious organizations including churches, mosques, and synagogues.

The ADA also affects ways in which public accommodations determine who may receive their services. For example, a business that requires a driver's license as the only acceptable identification for cashing a check, could be considered discriminatory toward persons with blindness. In addition, the ADA requires appropriate auxiliary aids and services to ensure effective communication with those with hearing and visual impairments. These may include qualified interpreters, assistive listening devices, note takers, large print or Braille materials, or taped texts. The law does not require such aids if they cause an undue burden or basic alteration in the nature of the goods and services provided. The public accommodation must still provide an alternative auxiliary aid. For example, restaurants are not required to have Braille menus if waiters or other employees are available to read the menu to a customer with blindness. Similarly, stores need not provide Braille price tags if such information is available orally from sales personnel on request. They need not provide sign language interpreters if their sales employees are willing to communicate in writing when necessary. Physical barriers need to be removed only when it is "readily achievable,"—that is, carried out without much difficulty or expense. Examples of readily achievable modifications include providing ramps, lowered telephones and urinals, or spaces for wheelchair users in theaters.

Title III. How are transportation services affected? The ADA requires the Department of Transportation to issue regulations mandating accessible public transit vehicles and facilities, and all public transit buses and rail cars ordered after August 26, 1990, must be accessible to individuals with disabilities, including wheelchair users. In addition, transit authorities must provide comparable paratransit or other special transportation services. As of July 26, 1993, all existing rail systems must have one accessible car per train and all new bus and train stations must be accessible. Finally, all existing Amtrak stations were to be accessible by July 26, 2010.

Title IV. How are communications affected? Companies offering telephone services to the general public must offer telephone relay services to people who use telecommunications devices for deaf persons (TDDs) or similar devices.

Title V. How is employment affected? The ADA employment provisions apply to private employers, state and local governments, employment agencies, and labor unions. Specifically, the ADA prohibits discrimination in all employment practices including job application procedures, hiring, firing, advancement, compensation, training, and other terms, conditions, and privileges of employment. It applies to recruitment advertising, tenure, layoff and leave procedures, fringe benefits, and all other job activities.

Since the ADA

The ADA is a landmark specifying the rights of people with disabilities to an accessible and non-discriminatory society. The provision of rights, however, does not erase a history of prejudice, misunderstanding, and long-lasting negative attitudes toward disability. Disabled individuals and activists continue to experience institutional and individual prejudice and discrimination (O'Brien, 2004), and regularly point out that this "largest minority" is the group with the highest rates of unemployment and poverty—almost 30 years after the passage of the ADA. Patterns in high proportions of poverty among African-Americans similarly persist more than 50 years after the *Civil Rights Act*. Advances in transportation and building accessibility are too often stymied by businesses and service providers who claim that the cost of renovating existing structures to be accessible outweighs the benefit. Additionally, the courts have heard many employment suits brought under the ADA, with the majority decisions neutralizing the impact of the ADA. Infamously, the rulings in *Sutton v. United Airlines* (1999) and *Toyota Motor Manufacturing v. Williams* (2002) demonstrate situations in which one can be "too disabled" to work, but not "disabled enough" to be protected under the ADA. The ADA has protected businesses, employers, and agencies more readily than disabled people (Russell, 1998). The hearts and minds of many, unfortunately, have not caught up to the ideals forwarded in the spirit of much civil rights legislation. The ADA was reauthorized as *The Americans With Disabilities Act Amendments Act* (ADAAA) in 2008. The changes aim to clarify what the law covers by broadening its description of disability. The intent is to focus employers on their responsibility to anti-discrimination and accommodation, rather than on analyzing what constitutes disability under the law, as turned out to be key in many lawsuits. In a 2013 analysis of ADAAA cases brought to the Supreme Court, Befort argues that the amended Act has, in fact, enabled more cases to be heard in court, rather than resolved by summary judgement hinging on the disability status of claimants.

Disability Rights and Education

The relationship of litigation to legislation is provided in the U.S. Constitution. Cases decided in the Court system set national and state precedents for similar situations to follow. Therefore, Court decisions in one case actually clarify and refine understandings of legislative dictates that ultimately apply to the interpretation of the laws at large. *Sutton v. United Airlines*, for example, clarified the definition of disability in the ADA. In education, several landmark cases were brought to the Court seeking refinement in the interpretation of the EHA/IDEIA. In 1985, some United States Government officials still resisted all assistance to persons with disabilities, and advocated the repeal of *PL 94–142* based on stereotyped ideology. Then Secretary of Education, William J. Bennett, appointed as a special assistant for the Office of Educational Philosophy and Practice, Eileen Marie Gardner, who had written for the American Heritage Foundation that "the handicapped constituency displays a strange lack of concern for the effects of their regulations upon the welfare of the general population" and that regulations enacted to aid children with disabilities "probably weakened the quality of teaching and falsely labeled normal children" (cited in Friedberg, Mullins, & Sukiennik, 1992, p. 10). Gardner is also quoted as stating that,

> [Disabled children] and their parents are selfish. They are draining badly needed resources from the normal school population [to the extent of $1.2 billion]. . . . Children and all who suffer affliction were made that way to help them grow toward spiritual perfection and . . . we are violating the "order of the universe" by trying to help these people.
>
> (p. 10)

In response to opposition, Gardner resigned in 1985 and, in 1986, Congress enacted further amendments to *PL 94–142* enlarging the responsibilities of states and school districts regarding the education of children with disabilities. The complaints raised by Gardner, however, that (1) children with disabilities cannot benefit from education, (2) that the cost of education for children with disabilities is a financial burden, and (3) that children with disabilities have negative impact on their peers, would be tested in the courts. Among the tenets of IDEIA that relate to inclusive education and have been tested in the courts are Free Appropriate Public Education, and Least Restrictive Environment.

Free Appropriate Public Education (FAPE)

In *Board of Education v. Rowley* (1982), the definition of Free Appropriate Public Education (FAPE) was interpreted. At the time, Amy Rowley was a Deaf first-grade student who could access about half of the classroom instruction through lip-reading, but whose parents believed she would progress further with the provision of an ASL interpreter. After a series of appeals, the Supreme Court accepted the case. It found— by a one-vote margin—that FAPE did not specify that a child be entitled to services seeking a *maximum* or potential benefit. Because Rowley was making progress comparable to her peers, the law did not require providing instruction in ASL. The decision in the case upheld the right of a school—over parents—to determine the special education supports and services provided to a child, and also interpreted the provision of FAPE to specify a minimum, rather than maximum standard for academic progress. In subsequent versions of IDEIA, however, ASL is included as a Native Language, which protects Deaf students' rights to be instructed and assessed with it. There has not been further clarification, however, to the interpretation of FAPE as meaning a student with a disability has the right to an adequate, not necessarily optimal, education, under IDEIA.

Least Restrictive Environment (LRE)

Given the history of segregation of students with disabilities in schools and the beliefs of figureheads like Gardner, however, it is not a surprise that many cases have been brought to the courts to clarify the meaning of the LRE, with implications to FAPE. In *Daniel R.R. v State Board of Education* (1989), a suit was brought to contest the removal of Daniel from a "mainstream" pre-kindergarten class into a special education program. Daniel's teacher had modified the general curriculum for the child diagnosed with Down syndrome and cognitive and speech impairments, but objected to the amount of support he required. The school changed his program to one in which he could eat lunch in the mainstream some days and only if his mother accompanied him, and he attended class in a segregated program. The court established a two-prong test to determine whether the LRE was being met: (1) Can education in the regular classroom with the use of supplemental aids and services be achieved satisfactorily? And, (2) if it cannot, has the school mainstreamed the child to the maximum extent appropriate? The court decided in favor of the school by determining that Daniel's need for support detracted from the education of other children in the mainstream class, and that the school was providing other opportunities for him to interact with non-labeled children. Although the decision was not what some disability rights advocates might have hoped, it provided a test for mainstreaming, and specified that the benefits of mainstreaming need not only relate to academic instruction. Social integration was also a goal of the LRE specification.

Undoubtedly the most contentious element in the law, the provision of the LRE was again clarified in *Oberti vs. Board of Education of the Borough of Clementon School District* (1993). *Oberti* refined the relationship between FAPE and LRE raised in *Daniel R.R.*, and also stated that the burden of proof was on the school to demonstrate compliance with IDEIA and the need for a segregated placement, rather than on the parents to argue that the school was not in compliance and that inclusion was possible. In response to Rafael Oberti, a boy with Down syndrome, the Court determined, "Inclusion is a right, not a special privilege for a select few". In addition, it specified, "education law requires school systems to supplement and realign their resources to move beyond those systems, structures and practices which tend to result in unnecessary segregation of children with disabilities." In other words, the school is compelled to alter its structures and curriculum to respond to children and an inclusion initiative, rather than place students according to the existing, problematic school design.

Inclusion and inclusive education, continues, indeed, to be a most pressing concern in education for students labeled disabled. The medical model clearly informs IDEIA and each of the court decisions that have interpreted the meaning and practice of LRE and FAPE. Developing a school program around a child's impairment emphasizes one aspect of him or her above all others. Additionally, cost-benefit analysis or discussion of the impact a student's presence has on others, while deceptively pragmatic, detracts from attention to the *civil rights* of children labeled disabled (and ignores the benefit to all of gaining familiarity with children who have many unique identities, characteristics, and experiences). Schools are charged with ensuring the academic progress of all children, but they do much more than that. As a massive social system in which all children are compelled to participate, schools' actions must reflect, and even advance, the broader goal of an integrated society. Rationalizing segregation in education based on the perceived "benefit" of separation to address impairment denigrates the intended spirit of the ADA and disability rights. It reflects the tropes Wolfensberger et al. (1972) posed of disability as pity and menace or of education as a charity, rather than a right.

INFLUENCE OF PARADIGMS ON PUBLIC POLICY

Many have discerned the relationship of paradigms of disability to social policy. Hahn (1987) elaborates on the limitations of the paradigm that defined disability almost exclusively from a medical viewpoint:

> Disability was considered a "defect" or "deficiency" that could be located within the individual. From the clinical perspective of medicine, efforts to improve the functional capabilities of individuals were regarded as the exclusive solution to

disability, and policy changes were essentially excluded from consideration as a possible remedy for the difficulties confronting the disabled.

(p. 181)

Similarly, Pope and Tarlov (1991) stress, the problems that disability related programs seek to address are often viewed as inherent to the individual and as independent of society (p. 244). The emphasis on pathology in the individual detracts attention from issues of equity, which many persons with disabilities find to be the more pressing.

In contrast to the influence of a medical model, Oliver (1990) discusses the benefit of conceptualizing disability policy through a social model. He contends that if disability were defined as social oppression, social policies geared towards alleviating oppression, rather than compensating individuals, would be developed. The most important policy issue would become designing and modifying the environment—including attitudes and social arrangements—to permit access to opportunity for all (Kirchner, 1996).

Changing paradigms from the medical model to social models is a challenge posed to both individuals and societies. Resisting stereotypes, prejudice, and discrimination are important to changing attitudes and correcting misperceptions about persons with disabilities. It is certainly possible to develop more positive attitudes toward persons with disabilities by identifying and then resisting problematic assumptions. John Hockenberry (1995), noted journalist and disability rights figure, states:

Each stereotype thrives in direct proportion to the distance from each class of persons it claims to describe. Get close to the real people and these pretend images begin to break up, but they don't go easily. Losing a stereotype is about being wrong retroactively. For a person to confront such assumptions they must admit an open-ended wrong for as long as those assumptions have been inside them. There is a temptation to hold on to why you believed those stereotypes. "I was once frightened and disgusted by a person in a wheelchair." To relinquish such a stereotype is to lose face by giving up a mask.

(p. 89)

The process of identifying and changing deep-seated attitudes and beliefs is not an easy or comfortable one. In his theory of transformative learning, Mezirow (1991, 1998) describes a way to conceptualize learning processes involved in shifting paradigms. Briefly, transformation begins when a person experiences a dilemma between what they believe and new information. Learners then engage in a process of *critical reflection*, which requires thinking about the nature of their thoughts, the process through which thoughts are formed, and the meanings that their thoughts purport in order to examine or pose possibilities for change (i.e., learning). Through critical reflection, learners question and possibly re-shape their paradigms, which constitutes the experience of transformative learning.

Although transforming seems like a straightforward process, our beliefs, emotions, and reactions to disability may feel quite uncontrollable. People may feel uncomfortable because they are unsure of how to act with persons with disabilities. There is fear about saying the wrong thing or using the wrong word, of not doing something that would be appreciated, or of doing something unwelcome (Cohen, 1977). Discomfort can result from the lack of knowledge and experience many people have with disability. Additionally, researchers have linked feelings of discomfort and guilt to an "existential anxiety" experienced by non-disabled persons when encountering disability (Hahn, 1988). Existential anxiety occurs when facing someone with a disability leads one to imagine the potential loss of functional capabilities. Zola (1982) illustrates, "when the able bodied confront the disabled they often think with a shudder, 'I'm glad it's not me.' But the relief is often followed by guilt for thinking such a thought" (p. 202). Other aversions to disability may relate to a fear of human vulnerability that images of impairment may invoke.

Emotions that relate to innermost anxieties are difficult to transform. But many aversive reactions reflect a general lack of experience with persons with disabilities. The situation is exacerbated by the prevalence of stereotypes. Further, knowledge generated in the medical model emphasizes dysfunction and hardship. Linton (1998) calls upon people with disabilities to take charge of developing different knowledge about disabled lives and experiences. She writes:

> The cultural narrative of [the disability] community incorporates a fair share of adversity and struggle, but it is also, and significantly, an account of a world negotiated *from the vantage point of the atypical* [emphasis in original]. Although the dominant culture describes that atypical experience as deficit and loss, the disabled community's narrative recounts it in more complex ways.
>
> (p. 5)

Increasing the number of rich and authentic accounts of the lives of persons with disabilities available in literature and media can expand the public's knowledge. In turn, increased visibility and interaction with persons with disabilities can help people feel more comfortable with ways of interacting with others in our world. As the number and variety of images of people with disabilities increase, we become more able to resist "group" stereotypes, since the images of disability we might imagine would be diverse.

The paradigm through which we understand disability informs the way we create our environment. If a culture perceives the experiences of persons with impairments only as those of loss and tragedy, and if we understand disability only as an individual's need for cure, we deny people the fullness of their lives. Emphasis on intervention for the individual's body or mind detracts from efforts to remove barriers and increase access to the community, its services, and its opportunities. Social models of disability provide a paradigm that places the physical, social, and political environment as the crucial focus of intervention. Some elements of legislation indicate a sociopolitical approach. The Americans with Disabilities Act mandates accessibility in many public places and services; The Individuals with Disabilities Education Improvement Act favors the Least Restrictive Environment, which indicates a preference for special education services provided in general education settings. International collaboration has similarly brought attention to the injustices around the world. In 2007, the United Nations (UN) adopted the *Convention on the Rights of Persons with Disabilities*, which adds to the UN's *Universal Declaration on Human Rights* (1948) and specifies particular protections for disabled persons. The adoption of the *Salamanca Statement and Framework for Action on Special Needs Education* by the United Nations Educational, Scientific and Cultural Organization (UNESCO) in 1994 advances children's right to education, as well as to inclusive environments. Disability issues have been viewed through the civil rights and minority group paradigm only recently. Continued education about these perspectives can raise awareness about physical and attitudinal barriers to persons with disabilities. Greater understanding can broaden the focus on medical intervention to include, if not prioritize, environmental alterations. In turn, the responsibility for creating an inclusive environment may be shared by everyone in society. One way that nearly everyone is touched by disability is in the production and consumption of popular culture, media, arts, and entertainment.

DISABILITY AND POPULAR CULTURE

The message of disability rights is really quite simple: People with disabilities should direct the course of their lives. When unable to advocate for themselves, decision-making should be done according to the individual's best interests, which would protect his or her dignity, civil rights, and quality of life with support—noting that such interests are not necessarily the same shared by their caretakers, health professionals, educators, or other systems through which they are served. Enduring stereotypes and prejudice prevent the wide acknowledgement of these values, which, in turn, maintain the hold that a medical model and the inertia of history and culture has on disabled people. It may seem odd to discuss issues of disability representation in the media, arts, and entertainment alongside matters of policy, science, medicine, and research. However, the two facets of contemporary life interplay in unexpected ways. What is acceptable in public policy, science, and medicine is informed by the beliefs and attitudes professed by the cultures in which the disciplines are practiced. We turn to a focus on disability in the arts and entertainment.

The Object of Comedy, Ridicule, and Curiosity

People with extraordinary, unexpected physical features have long been a source of fascination. Some cultures marveled at and prophesized according to disability, others saw people with disabilities as sources of entertainment. Aristotle, for example, deemed persons with disabilities *lusus naturae* or "jokes of nature," which, in turn, made them appropriate sources of amusement or pets in the households of the wealthy (Fiedler, 1978). As early as 1000 B.C. disabled individuals were used to provide entertainment and amusement in Egyptian, Greek, and Roman cultures. An enduring image of the Middle Ages is the court fool, or jester, who were often little people. "Freak shows" of the nineteenth century featured individuals with extraordinary characteristics for the purpose of entertainment. One might argue that the proliferation of contemporary documentaries about medical mysteries and rare conditions illustrates continuing fascination with disability. The use of disability as an object of comedy, ridicule, and curiosity, then, is another of Wolfensberger et al.'s (1972) tropes that persists in the present day.

Entertaining the Aristocracy

The earliest use of little persons as court fools was among the Egyptian pharaohs who chose members of the Danga pygmy tribe as mainly a curiosity, but also for amusement (Bullock & Mahon, 1997). It was customary for wealthy men in the Roman Empire to keep half-witted and "deformed" slaves in their houses for purposes of entertainment; further, females were known to keep "physically stunted" and "mentally deficient" slaves as substitutes for "lap dogs and teddy bears" (p. 21). Deformed slaves were used for entertainment in the court of Attila around A.D. 500 (Bullock & Mahon, 1997). The Spaniards under Cortez, invading Mexico in 1519, entered the city of Tenochtitlan (now Mexico City), where they were shown the Aztec Emperor Montezuma's extensive royal zoo. The Spaniards were amazed to see that alongside the many rare wild animals on display, were persons with dwarfism or albinism, bearded women, and other "deformed" humans (Van Riper & Emerick, 1984). During the Hellenistic Period, little people were highly prized as pets and often given as gifts.

By the second century A.D., persons with extraordinary physical traits were commonly found in homes of wealthy Romans to provide household entertainment. The fool or buffoon became a part of entertainment and feasts—making the guests laugh with his so-called "idiocy" or "deformity." "The popularity of statuettes and vase-paintings depicting deformed dwarfs, hunchbacks and obese women strongly suggests that people of this sort were in high demand as singers, dancers, musicians, jugglers and clowns" (Garland, 1995, pp. 32–33). In fact, the Romans established a special market, called the "teraton agora," where legless and armless humans could be purchased along with giants, dwarfs, and hermaphrodites (Durant, 1944).

The ridicule of persons with disabilities continued apace during the Middle Ages. Most individuals with physical or intellectual disabilities were imprisoned or driven from cities into the rural areas to fend for themselves. The nobility, however, boarded some people in return for being on display as curiosities, objects of ridicule, or performers (Snow, 2001). Charles V of France gave exclusive rights to the province of Champagne to supply his court with fools. Ownership of little people was a high status symbol among the Russian aristocracy.

During the twelfth century, English kings began to make the care and treatment of "idiots" a matter of royal concern and, therefore, their wards. Philip IV of Spain gathered intellectually disabled persons into his court where they were well fed and well clothed and had the freedom to do as they pleased. In 1490, King James IV of Scotland, brought to his court the Scottish Brothers, twins joined in the upper part of the body and having four arms and two legs. The king ordered that the brothers be carefully raised and well educated. Under his patronage and protection, the brothers learned to play musical instruments, sing in harmony, and read Latin, French, Italian, Spanish, Dutch, Danish, and Irish (Thompson, 1968, 1994).

Though little people gained entry to royal homes as objects of curiosity and ridicule, some "court dwarfs" worked themselves into positions of great power (Fiedler, 1978). They gained charge over the master's treasury, under the assumption that a dwarf would be easier to find and catch should he attempt to abscond with the funds. In fact, several court dwarfs became quite influential and found themselves in positions of total trust within the court and noble households. They were given unlimited license of speech, and often became the pets and favorites of their Royal or Court ladies of the time (Thompson, 1994, p. 188). Once trusted by a king or noble, they often proved capable of moving up from the status of joker to counselor. Emperors Augustus and Tiberius had court dwarves by their sides for consultation on matters of state. In the late Middle Ages, Bertholde, a court dwarf known for his cleverness, became the King of Lombardy's prime minister. Both little people, Jacof Ris became an ex-officio counselor to the Imperial court of The Emperor Charles VI of Vienna, and Godeau was appointed Archbishop of Grasse in 1672, by Richelieu (Fiedler, 1978). However, though there were such exceptions, in the Middle Ages most people with disabilities were regarded as playthings of the aristocracy and often subject to harsh abuse and ridicule.

Even so, the spectacle of disability was received in various ways and was largely dependent on context. Outside of the royal court, some persons with disabilities would beg from the lower classes to make a living. The art of begging, highly lucrative and remunerative, sometimes resulted in self-mutilation and children being purposefully deformed for the purpose—a practice dating back to ancient Rome. From the fourteenth to the seventeenth centuries, people with psychiatric and cognitive disabilities were systematically removed from the streets and into hospitals, almshouses, and institutions. For a small sum, the public could visit some hospitals to view the "patients" who were displayed as exhibits. Most famous were the "antics of the lunatics" at London's Bethlehem Hospital. There, visitors would stare and laugh at the writhing and screaming of the chained inmates. Certain attendants would beat, prod, and agitate inmates with clubs, sticks, or whips to get them to perform dances and acrobatics to ensure the visitors a good show (Evans, 1983). No longer the privilege of the upper classes, lower classes could also find amusement in the spectacle made of abusing people with disabilities.

Toward Modernity: Medical Curiosities and Freak Shows

The movement of people into hospitals was predicated by a new way of thinking about extraordinary attributes. Non-desirable ways of thinking and behaving became attributable to mental disease or defect, rather than to moral failings or spiritual signs (Foucault, 1965). Physical disabilities were viewed as medical anomalies rather than as evil omens, the results of witchcraft, or parental punishments for past sins (Bogdan, 1988). By the late 1800s, persons with disabilities began to be viewed as medical anomalies, which subjected them to scientific study and classification.

Heightened scientific interest paralleled and furthered the public's fascination with extraordinary and foreign physical features, which fueled the popularity of the so-called "freak show," most popular between 1840 and 1940 in the USA. Called a variety of terms, including Sideshows, Ten in One, Odditorium, and Museum of Nature's Mistakes, these shows put people with extraordinary characteristics (some of them false) on display (Bogdan, 1988, pp. 2–3). The comments of physicians and natural scientists who visited the "human curiosities" served to fan widespread interest and debates as to the nature and origin of the "creatures," who were often presented to the public in ways to parallel then-new scientific theories about human variation (Bogdan, 1986, 1988).

The fascination with "human oddities" and even their manufacture was not just a Western phenomenon. China, for example, also has a history of producing curiosities. The following describes a method used during the nineteenth century:

> Young children are bought or stolen at a tender age and placed in a *Ch'ing*, or vase with a narrow neck, and having in this case a movable bottom. In this receptacle the unfortunate little wretches are kept for years in a sitting posture their heads outside being all the while carefully tended and fed. When the child reached the age of twenty or over, he or she is taken away to some distant place and *discovered* in the woods as a wild man or woman.
>
> (*China Mail*, May 15, 1878, cited in Fiedler, 1978, p. 50).

The freak show continued earlier practices that made disability into spectacle. Bogdan (1988) explained, the idea of the "freak" is a created perspective comprised of a set of social practices that create a stage for making features fascinating and exotic. The juggling, dancing, acrobatics, and side-show set and stage created the characterization of disability as curiosity. The famed circus entrepreneur, P. T. Barnum, for example, once reportedly approached an extremely tall man and asked him if he had any interest in becoming a giant. Thus, framing people with unexpected and extraordinary features for entertainment in staged contexts *made* disability into freakery. Making persons with disabilities into objects of fascination has been one enduring response to difference.

Disability in Entertainment

The entertainment industry has a long history of its use of images and representations of disability. In many cases, television, film, and books have expanded their inclusion of disabled characters, which has resulted in more diverse depictions of disability. Offering a variety of depictions of disability lessens the impact that one type of image may have in constructing or perpetuating stereotypes, and is therefore, a favorable phenomenon. Stereotypes, however, have been a topic worthy of public attention. In 1991, for example, members of the National Federation of the Blind protested outside of the ABC network offices around the country in objection to the depiction of a blind character in the sitcom *Good and Evil*, who destroys a chemistry laboratory by clumsily wielding his long white cane, and then attempts to solicit a date with a fur coat on a coat rack, mistaking it for a woman (Shapiro, 1993, p. 37). Similarly, in 1997, after learning that the Walt Disney Company was reviving Mr. Magoo for a film starring Leslie Nielsen, the National Federation passed a resolution to "take whatever action appropriate to protest" because, "The message is that lack of sight means incompetence" ("Mr. Snafoo," 1997, p. 21).

Recent foci of disability rights groups have been the films, *Million Dollar Baby* (Haggis et al., 2004), *Tropic Thunder* (Cornfeld, McLeod, & Stiller, 2008), and *Me Before You* (Owen et al., 2016). The disability rights group, Not Dead Yet, organized demonstrations at both *Me Before You* and *Million Dollar Baby* screenings to raise awareness about objections to the connection between disability and euthanasia depicted in the films. *Tropic Thunder* depicts actors behind the scenes of a film shoot and features dialogue between characters as they discuss one of the actor's previous roles playing a man with an intellectual disability. The protests surrounding *Tropic Thunder* garnered public debate and commentary, bringing the "R-word" to center stage. The advice, "Everybody knows you don't go full retard," is part of the dialogue addressed to an actor, played by Ben Stiller, as he is reflecting on his work playing a character named "Simple Jack"—an experience woven through the film. Co-writer Etan Cohen claimed, "Some people have taken this as making fun of handicapped people, but we're really trying to make fun of the actors who use this material as fodder for acclaim" (Adler, Richard, & Horowitz, 2008). In spite of the filmmaker's ironic intent, activists strongly objected to the frequent use of the "R-word" and the depictions of "Simple Jack" and took the opportunity to bring the public into the argument. The production company, DreamWorks, took down a promotional website featuring "Simple Jack," and later, added an announcement discouraging the use of the word, "retarded," on the DVD. Not only do these examples attest to the liveliness of the disability activism today, but also demonstrate that the public is interested, and the press responsive.

Two other tropes related to disability that persist in media and entertainment are those of the "supercrip" (Haller, 2010) or the extraordinary disabled and of the holy innocent or the eternal child (Wolfensberger et al., 1972).

The Supercrip

The extraordinary disabled is the romantic, idealized, and overstated super-disabled figure, often called the "supercrip." Media scholar John Clogston (as cited in Haller, 2000) defined the supercrip as:

> The disabled person is portrayed as deviant because of "superhuman" feats (i.e., an ocean-sailing blind man), or as "special" because they have regular lives "in spite of" disability, (i.e., a deaf high school student who plays softball). This portrayal reinforces the idea that disabled people are deviant—and so, for someone who is less than "complete" the accomplishment is "amazing."
>
> (Haller, 2000, p. 7)

Such stories appearing in the media are often received as inspirational stories. Extraordinary fictional characters with disabilities are found largely on television shows, films, and in comic books. The character, "Joe," in *Family Guy* (MacFarlane, 1999) and the depiction of Christy Brown in *My Left Foot* (Pearson & Sheridan, 1989) are two examples of media deploying the supercrip stereotype. The characterizations alternately rely on incredulity of people with disabilities accomplishing typical activities and hyperbolic representations of accomplishment that gain meaning in the juxtaposition of dysfunction with hyper-function.

The idea of the extraordinary disabled person can be connected to long histories of association of disability with divinity, especially with regard to blindness. The Zuni, a Native American tribe, for example, believed that those with intellectual disabilities had intimacy with good spirits and often regarded their words and sayings as divine (Ross, 1978). In ancient China, blind persons often received training as fortune-tellers (French, 1932). The association with blindness and divinity is particularly carried on in literature. Disability in literature, Mitchell and Snyder (2001) suggest, is both a "stock feature of characterization and [employed as] an opportunistic metaphorical device" (p. 47). Kelley (2013) points out that blindness simultaneously signified different meanings in ancient Greece and Rome. Being blinded was punishment and consequence for an individual's guilt, as in the examples of the Cyclops, who is blinded by Odysseus after having eaten his men; and Oedipus, who blinds himself once the truth about his relationship to Iocaste is revealed. In the same context, familiar in the figure of Tiresias from Greek tradition, blindness may be a punishment of the gods, but subsequently implies a connection to the gods.

Jernigan (1983), comments on misconceptions about blindness "that go to the very root of our culture and permeate every aspect of social behavior and thinking":

> These misconceptions go back to the days when a blind person could not dodge a spear. In today's society, dodging a spear is not an essential ability but the stereotype of helplessness has remained intact, surrounded by a host of other stereotypes: The blind are simple, spiritual, musical; they have a special sixth sense; their other senses are more acute—in short, they are different and apart from the rest of society.
>
> (pp. 58–59)

Contemporary comic books, many which are turned into movies and animated series, have also spawned a number of heroes with disabilities, each possessing extraordinary skills that over-compensate for disability. For example, the title character of *Daredevil* (Arad, Foster, & Milchan, 2003; Lee, Everett, & Rosen, 1964), whose exposure to a radioactive substance simultaneously renders him blind and imbued with other heightened senses, including "radar sense." Like other tropes on disability the super-crip image is present in media, arts, and entertainment, which exemplify, perhaps, the continuation of persons with disability as objects of curiosity and fascination.

The Holy Innocent or The Eternal Child

In many and various cultures, individuals with disabilities—particularly those with intellectual disabilities—have been viewed as the "special children of God." They are anointed by grace, or portrayed as "'gee-golly,' happy-go-lucky simpletons" (Biklen, 1981, p. 5). As such, they are usually seen as incapable of committing evil voluntarily, and consequently may be considered living saints. It may also be believed that they have been sent by a higher power for some special purpose. The role of intellectual disability to signify holiness or eternal innocence has been recognized in a number of cultures and eras, and is reflected in films including *Forrest Gump* (Finerman, Starkey, Tisch, & Zemeckis, 1994), *I Am Sam* (Herskovitz, Solomon, Zwick, & Nelson, 2001), and *Rainman* (Johnson & Levinson, 1988). In each, the eternal innocence of the disabled protagonists is a device used to reveal the flaws and foibles of their "normal" adult peers, and often poses situations in which *other* characters can find redemption through their experiences with the protagonist.

Disabled individuals seen as holy innocents were generally considered to be "harmless children" no matter their chronological ages. As a result, families, caregivers, and professionals who work with disabled persons frequently acquire the "Albert

Schweitzer" or "Mother Teresa" syndrome, and characteristics such as having outstanding patience and are "doing God's work" are attributed to them. A major effect of the Holy Innocent stereotype is the juvenilization of adults with disabilities. Biklen (1981) believes the important point to be made is that adults with intellectual disabilities "experience the same emotions as non-disabled people, are capable of a broad range of behaviors, and possess individual and complex personalities" (p. 5). Images that depict disabled persons as eternally innocent and child-like contributes to paternalism and a denial of adult rights.

The representations and presence of disability and disabled persons in the media, entertainment, and culture are certainly shifting. While many tropes and stereotypes persist, they are joined by the variety offered in proliferation of social media through which disability activists and advocates pose other depictions of life and perspectives on disability. In addition, introduction of complex disabled characters such as Tyrion and Jaime Lannister in the lauded television series and book, *Game of Thrones* (Benioff & Weiss, 2011) and the series, *A Song of Ice and Fire* (Martin, 1996), respectively, shift disabled characters from object to subject. The acclaimed *Breaking Bad* (Gilligan, 2008) television series, and ABC's *Speechless* (Silveri, 2016), have garnered support for their casting of disabled actors in roles depicting disability. A central argument about disability in media and entertainment is not that disability should be depicted in only "positive" ways, but that variety in the narratives and depictions of disability would better represent and reflect the experiences of this large minority group.

The Continued Impact of Stereotypes

Wolfensberger et al. proposed several stereotypes gleaned from the cultural and social context in 1972. They argued that stereotypes and their related prejudices can lead to discrimination in everyday interactions, as well as operate within oppressive social structures and systems. The observations are still relevant several decades after their work. Henderson and Bryan (1997) document that the five most common forms of prejudice and beliefs toward people with disabilities include that they (1) are inferior, (2) are totally impaired, (3) are less intelligent, (4) need charity, and (5) prefer the company of others with disabilities (pp. 70–75). Mackelprang and Salsgiver (1996) describe one of the prevailing beliefs rooted in our culture:

> [P]eople with disabilities can not and should not work or otherwise be productive. Contributing to the belief that people with disabilities should not work is the role of sick people in Western culture. People with disabilities, whom society assumes are "sick," are expected to fill this role even when they are perfectly healthy. As with those who are sick, people with disabilities are to be taken care of and to be provided for. Their only obligation is to be grateful for the help given them, thus subjecting them to a form of benevolent oppression.
>
> (p. 10)

Nario-Redmond (2008) confirms that the stereotype of disabled persons as unemployed and non-productive persists. Such stereotypes may influence the opportunities one is privy to, as well as one's self-concept. Sutherland (1984) points out, "Someone who is assumed to be stupid is unlikely to receive much intellectual stimulation" (p. 59). Stereotypes lead to behaviors and actions that limit and reduce opportunities for people in that category (Smart, 2001, p. 185). Disability activists and increasingly shifting understandings about disability draw attention to cultural products that purport beliefs antithetical to the goals of disability rights. Work to instantiate disability as a valued and valuable perspective and experience is burgeoning in disability arts and disability culture.

DISABILITY CULTURE AND THE ARTS

The Disability Rights Movement is marked by local and national organization of groups dedicated to the social, political, and increasingly, cultural issues that affect people with disabilities. Deaf culture has a long and rich history rooted in its members' shared language and concretized in its well-documented community histories (Padden & Humphries, 1988). The concept of *disability culture* is relatively new, by contrast, and debates on its meaning and existence ensue. Mitchell and Snyder's (1995) film, *Vital Signs: Crip Culture Talks Back*, documents participants at a national conference in disability and the arts. Performances and interviews offer a glimpse into many impressions of disability espoused by conference attendees, as well as the variety of expressions of disability available in art and performance. The filmmakers offer, in a later work, "The point of the film is not merely to present a chorus of voices but to capture the diversity, originality, and vitality of vantage points that characterize contemporary disability communities" (Snyder & Mitchell, 2006, p. 176). Present among the commentaries, however, are aspects indicating beliefs, ideas, and traditions shared among those who subscribe to an idea of disability culture. These include recognition of a shared history of oppression, a social and political approach to disability rights, and group pride.

Peters (2000) makes an argument for disability culture by examining three approaches to understanding the meaning of culture—historical/linguistic; social/political; and personal/aesthetic. We have, within the scope of this chapter, demonstrated the historical lineage of disability rights, including its "heroes" who are frequent reference points to tell its legacy. Organizations and groups arising out of the rights movement serve as locations for social cohesion, which are also found in communities like Berkeley, California, known as a "mecca" for people with disabilities, due to the efforts of Ed Roberts (Fleischer & Zames, 2001). A general orientation to sociopolitical perspectives on disability constitutes a basis for shared understanding around individual experiences of group oppression, which are solidified in community publications such as *Ragged Edge*, an online magazine dedicated to disability activism and rights that originated as the print publication, *The Disability Rag*, in 1980.

Considered through its personal/aesthetic components, disability culture is noticeable in declarations of pride in the form of one's body. Peters (2000) writes,

> When I say I am 25 years old, I am not referring to my chronological age, but the age at which I became physically disabled and could proudly assert "I am disabled".

For those who subscribe to the view of culture as personal/aesthetic, the ability to assert an aesthetic pride in the disabled body is a necessary prerequisite to political identity and is the source of empowerment.

(p. 596)

Nowhere is pride in the disabled body more evident than in disability arts. Disability arts encompass the wide variety of authors, poets, playwrights, actors, sculptors, painters, musicians, and performers whose work emanates from experiences of disability. A defining point, *disability art* is specific to works of disabled artists, whose experiences with disability are recognized as an integral force underlying the artistic process. Painter Riva Lehrer, for example, offers dynamic—both in style and content— portraits of disabled figures, taking her cues from the desires of her models/subjects (Snyder & Mitchell, 2005). The works of late playwright, John Belluso, offer stories told from a disabled, personal point of view (Schou, 2006). Collections including *Staring Back: The Disability Experience from the Inside Out* (Fries, 1997) and *Points of Contact* (Crutchfield & Epstein, 2000) anthologize contributions of disabled writers and essayists to poetry, fiction, and social commentary.

Simi Linton (2008), founder of Disability/Arts, notes the aim of her work, which is "to increase the scope and visibility of the vibrant arts movement emerging from the disability community, and increase the participation of disabled people in all areas of the arts" (http://www.similinton.com/dac.htm). The spread of disability art is a strong indication of the liveliness of disability culture. In addition, pride events, such as the Disability Pride Parade, an annual event in Chicago, demonstrate the celebratory cohesion of disabled people. No longer useful only for political action, the idea of a disability culture emerges in joined celebration of its history, art, and its pride.

The concept of disability culture, as noted previously, is debated among those abled and disabled alike. Like any culture, its centrality for some does not mean that all people who might identify as disabled adopt it. Developing pride specific to disability can be difficult to grasp. As Gliedman and Roth (1980) once stated, "No one argues that mental retardation is good, blindness is beautiful, that doctors should stop research into the causes of cerebral palsy" (p. 23). Even Irving Zola (1982), a founding figure in disability studies, made this observation:

As the melting pot theory of America was finally buried, people could once again say, even though they were three generations removed from the immigrants, that they were proud to be Greek, Italian, Hungarian, or Polish. With the rise of Black power, a derogatory label became a rallying cry, Black is beautiful! And when female liberationists saw their strength in numbers, they shouted, Sisterhood is powerful! But what about the chronically ill and disabled? Can we yell, Long live cancer! Up with multiple sclerosis! I'm glad I had polio! Clearly a basis of a common positive identity is not readily available.

(p. 208)

The reservations of Zola and Gliedman and Roth, written over 25 years ago, capture complexities in the movement for disability culture and disability pride. We believe, however, that the proliferation of disability arts, recognition of the Disability Rights Movement, and attention to ongoing activism can contribute to reshaping a view of disability that centers on a value for diversity, appreciation of its history, and a source of positive identity and pride.

CONCLUSION

The modern era of disability is hailed as a period in which disability rights gained recognition and had an impact on policies, law, and social practices, which were influenced by disabled people as never before in history. Simultaneously, the time period is peppered with contradictions. It has been a long difficult trek from the time persons with disabilities were left to die or thrown off cliffs as babies to the *Americans with Disabilities Act*, yet eugenic medical practices and the ideologies of some "right to die" proponents should give us pause in what may be premature celebration. The ideas of deinstitutionalization and independent living have influenced many nations and cultures, but not all; and the depictions of disability in the media, arts, and popular culture have improved through diversification, though the occasion for protest still arises.

This chapter depicts an evolutionary progression suggesting the distance society has come in its acceptance, treatment, and integration of persons with disabilities. However, the influence of a medical model and the prejudices embedded in it continues to overshadow the self-determination many disabled people seek. As Rioux (1996) points out, "Rehabilitation in itself, no matter how effective, will not lead to fulfilling the goals of human rights" (p. 9). The stigma of disability remains a common reality, and persons with disabilities continue to be denied equal opportunity as a result of stereotyped and prejudiced images based on myths and earlier attitudes. Of the continued fight, Russell (1998) writes,

> We must retain enough optimism so vital to ensuring a just society that we can consciousness-raise, educate ourselves and others, and join in public debate through town hall meetings, the internet and local and national referendums that can result in more participation and justice worldwide.
>
> (p. 235)

With significant rights now won in policy and law, the remaining work is largely cultural, which Russell captures in the idea of consciousness-raising. What better way to raise consciousness than in work with children and schools? Informed with knowledge of history, language, disability rights, and disability studies, we believe that educators can play integral roles in advancing the self-determination of disabled people. Educators can both advance integration through implementing inclusive practices for children labeled with disability, and develop curriculum and content that offer views of disability and disabled people in social, political, and cultural contexts. In the next chapters, we provide concepts and practices to guide educational work that honors disability rights and its legacy, and seeks further realization of its goals.

Part II

DISABILITY IN SCHOOLS

5

CONCEPTUALIZING DISABILITY IN SCHOOLS

National and international attention to disability has provided some ways to conceptualize and define disability in a broad sense. The ADAAA, for example, distinguishes impairment from disability to define which persons are covered by its policies. The UN *Convention on the Rights of Persons with Disabilities* defines persons with disabilities in order to appropriately direct a human rights agenda. In education, the *Individuals with Disabilities Education Improvement Act* (IDEIA) provides the vocabulary used to define disability. Greatly influenced by the medical model of disability, thirteen categories of impairment are defined, which describe the students who may receive special education services. The previous chapter provided discussion of many ways that disability language and labels are contested and perceived differently by various stakeholders. Language and labels used in education are similarly subject to the same variety of perspectives. This chapter offers an overview of the definitions of disability described in IDEIA. In addition, it provides discussion on aspects of the labels that have been contested, especially in the Disability Studies in Education field. The aim is to provide candid information about the influential educational policy, IDEIA, while also offering critical examination of the language practices contained in it.

IDEIA DEFINITIONS
(1) Visual Impairments (including blindness)
A visual impairment is a limitation in vision that, even with correction, adversely affects sight. Visual impairments that require special educational services occurs rarely in children—in less than .10 percent of the population between the ages of 6 through 17 (NCES, 2015). The term, "Blindness," carries various definitions and despite its common use to connote a total absence of sight, the vast majority of people with visual impairments do perceive some degree of visual information. Rather than emphasize dysfunction, the descriptors, "partially sighted" or having "low-vision" are sometimes preferred.

(2) Hearing Impairments and (3) Deafness

Hearing impairment is a general term indicating a hearing loss that may range in severity from mild to profound. Discussed in earlier chapters, some Deaf persons who use American Sign Language identify themselves by the language they use, rather than by their degree of hearing, and consider themselves to be part of a linguistic minority. Only .20 percent of children in schools receive special educational services for hearing impairment (NCES, 2015).

(4) Deaf-Blindness

Deaf-blindness is the third sensory impairment specified by IDEIA and means concomitant hearing and visual impairments. Educational approaches for children who are blind often capitalize on providing auditory information, and visual information for those who are hard of hearing or deaf. Because children with deaf-blindness do not have sufficient access to visual or auditory information, educational approaches require an educational plan or program that attends to the combination of these relatively rare characteristics. Only 1,000 children received special educational services under this category in the USA in 2013 (NCES, 2015).

(5) Speech or Language Impairments

According to IDEIA, "Speech or language impairment means a communication disorder, such as stuttering, impaired articulation, a language impairment, or a voice impairment, that adversely affects a child's educational performance" (IDEIA, 2004, Sec. 300.8). Van Riper and Emerick (1984) defined speech as "defective" when "it deviates so far from the speech of other people that it calls attention to itself, interferes with communication, or causes the speaker or his listeners to be distressed" (p. 34). In other words, speech is considered defective when, relative to others, it is conspicuous, unintelligible, or unpleasant. Approximately 20 percent of children receiving special services do so for speech or language (NCES, 2015).

(6) Orthopedic Impairments

Orthopedic impairments are related to the function of the muscles and/or skeleton and may affect mobility, range of motion, and/or reliable control over one's movements. An orthopedic impairment does not necessarily indicate disability. If the individual is able to move on her or his own or to use a mobility device to negotiate the environment it is possible that she or he would not require additional educational services. Orthopedic impairments account for approximately 13 percent of children receiving special educational services (NCES, 2015).

(7) Traumatic Brain Injury

Traumatic brain injury is one of the few disability categories in which a specific etiology is required for diagnosis. According to IDEIA,

> Traumatic brain injury means an acquired injury to the brain caused by an external physical force, resulting in total or partial functional disability or psychosocial impairment, or both, that adversely affects a child's educational performance. Traumatic brain injury applies to open or closed head injuries resulting in impairments

in one or more areas, such as cognition; language; memory; attention; reasoning; abstract thinking; judgment; problem-solving; sensory, perceptual, and motor abilities; psychosocial behavior; physical functions; information processing; and speech. Traumatic brain injury does not apply to brain injuries that are congenital or degenerative, or to brain injuries induced by birth trauma.

(IDEIA, 2004, Sec. 300.8)

Noted in the definition, brain injury can manifest in many ways—including physical-motor, cognitive, emotional, social, and/or speech-language impairments. Less than 1 percent of children receiving special educational services are identified according to this category.

(8) Other Health Impairment

Like traumatic brain injury, the category, "other health impairment," is comprised of health conditions with specific etiologies that may "adversely affect a child's educational performance" (IDEIA, 2004, Sec. 300.8). It means,

having limited strength, vitality, or alertness, including a heightened alertness to environmental stimuli, that results in limited alertness with respect to the educational environment, that—

(i) Is due to chronic or acute health problems such as asthma, attention deficit disorder or attention deficit hyperactivity disorder, diabetes, epilepsy, a heart condition, hemophilia, lead poisoning, leukemia, nephritis, rheumatic fever, sickle cell anemia, and Tourette syndrome.

(IDEIA, 2004, Sec. 300.8)

As with the other categories, the diagnosis of any the mentioned diseases or conditions may not indicate disability. For example, many children have asthma but not all are adversely affected by it in their educational environments. The number of children served through IDEIA under this category has increased steadily since 1990, in which only 1.2 percent of children with disabilities were identified in this group. In 2013, "other health impairment" is responsible for 12.6 percent of children served under IDEIA.

(9) Multiple Disabilities

The category, "multiple disabilities" is imprecise and can refer to any combination of impairments. Like "deaf-blindness," this designation indicates a child whose educational needs arise from a variety of impairing factors. A student categorized with "multiple disabilities" typically has a sensory or orthopedic impairment, a combination of the two, or one of them in addition to another kind of impairment—usually "intellectual disability."

Discussion

Impairments that affect the senses, movement, or health are fairly straightforward to perceive or diagnose in a medical model of disability. The "facts" of such differences or non-typical characteristics are made scientific as we use scales to determine visual and hearing impairments and relate an injuring event to disability. The "facts" of orthopedic and speech and language impairment seem self-evident as cultural norms influence our ideas about "normal" and "abnormal" ways to move and communicate. Approaching impairment from a social model, the degree of disability—if any—that these impairments indicate is related to the context and environment. For example, that a brain trauma occurred is a matter of fact; the meaning of that trauma to indicate disability or handicap is subject to the particular culture and environment in which an individual lives, works, and learns. Similarly, that an individual requires a wheelchair to move from place to place due to an orthopedic impairment is a matter of fact; however, whether they experience *disability* may relate more to the degree to which an environment is barrier-free or to the availability and affordability of the mobility device.

Soft Disability

The final four categories of disability described by IDEIA are (10) mental retardation; (11) specific learning disabilities; (12) emotional disturbance; and (13) autism or Autism Spectrum Disorder (ASD). Distinguishing impairment from disability becomes difficult in what some have called *soft* disabilities. Soft disabilities are those "for which no discernible physical markers are currently known," which makes "the identification process subjective" (Fuchs, Fuchs, & Speece, 2002, p. 33; also, see Reschly, 1996). The disabilities most frequently considered soft are learning disabilities, mild mental retardation, and emotional or behavior disorders. Despite decades of medical research to locate physical and neurological linkages between the body/brain and cognition to what appears to be impaired function, science provides little understanding useful to teachers about the majority of disorders deemed neurological, cognitive/intellectual, and psycho-social in nature. The physiological evidence of cognitive-intellectual and psycho-social impairments is found primarily in comparisons of images of brain activity and brain size and development. Current neurological research can show differences among typical and non-typical activity in individuals already characterized by normal and abnormal function, but researchers have not provided precise understanding of types of impairments based on those differences (Bauman & Kemper, 2004; Fiedorowicz et al., 2001).

It is important to note that some proponents of a social model of disability argue that *all* diagnoses and perceptions of impairment are ultimately subjective, as science itself is informed by cultural beliefs about the "normal" body. In other words, that which a culture perceives as impaired or abnormal is inextricably related to that which is perceived normal and then explained biologically and neurologically. Perceiving learning disabilities, mild mental retardation, and emotional or behavior disorders are particularly subjective processes because they (a) are diagnosed with tools that rely largely on assessment of the individual's relationship to a particular context—often school; (b) are difficult to distinguish from one another and often seem to overlap in school settings; and (c) seem particularly influenced by the belief systems and demands of a given society, as expressed in changes of diagnostic criteria over time and in variations in diagnostic criteria in different places (Kane & Tang-dhanakanond, 2008). Autism/Autism Spectrum Disorder is here discussed as a soft disability because diagnosis relies on assessment of social behavior. Although neurological research is burgeoning, the majority of characteristics associated with autistic individuals are interpreted as soft neurological signs, or abnormalities that are not readily connected to a specific brain region. The final four disability categories in IDEIA are next described, each with extended discussion to elucidate controversies surrounding them.

(10) Intellectual Disability, Cognitive Impairment, Mental Retardation

The terms, "intellectual disability," "cognitive impairment," and "mental retardation," are often used interchangeably in the USA. People diagnosed with "intellectual developmental disorder" are also sometimes referred to as having "developmental disabilities" because one criterion is that it is noticeable before the age of 18—thus emerges during, and has an impact on, development. In the UK and other locales, "learning disability" often refers to what is meant, in the US, to refer to intellectual disability. IDEIA defines mental retardation as,

> significantly subaverage general intellectual functioning, existing concurrently with deficits in adaptive behavior and manifested during the developmental period, that adversely affects a child's educational performance.
>
> (IDEIA, 2004, Sec. 300.8)

The concept of what we presently deem intellectual disability has evolved over many years. As early as the first century A.D. a Roman aristocrat, Aulus Cornelius Celsus, used the term *imbecillus* to denote a general weakness or any form of impairment. The term *idios*, the original Greek form, described a private person—that is, one who did not engage in public life. Both terms became descriptors of forms of intellectual disability much later in the Renaissance (Scheerenberger, 1983).

During the early fourteenth through sixteenth centuries, the term *ideocy* began to be replaced by *dunce*, a term that had its origins with the activities of John Duns Scotus, a Scot who, in 1303, argued against the King of France's proposal to tax the Roman Catholic Church to finance a war with England. In response, the Pope excommunicated the French King, who in return banished Scotus from France. Two hundred years later, Renaissance humanists and Reformation leaders hostile to Duns Scotus's defense of the Papacy began to call any follower of his teachings as a "Duns man" or "dunce"—hence, a dull-witted person (Scheerenberger, 1983).

Terminology changed several more times. In 1846, Samuel Gridley Howe defined persons with "feeble-mindedness" as those who ranged in level of incapacity from those with "reason enough for simple individual guidance plus normal powers of locomotion and animal action" to those who were "mere organisms." In 1914, Henry Herbert Goddard subdivided the classification of feeble-mindedness into the subcategories of "morons," "imbeciles," and "idiots" and linked the levels of function to IQ—a then emerging psychological concept (President's Committee on Mental Retardation,

1975, p. 2). Prior to Goddard's work, the designation of a person as "idiot," "dunce," or "feebleminded" served to describe his or her societal position in relation to their engagement in public life, agreement with the beliefs of those in power, and/or to characterize the perceived intellectual-cognitive abilities of a person. Goddard's linkage of IQ to "feeble-mindedness" provided a scientific perspective on the concept of intellect.

Understanding of how intellectual disability became a scientific concept emerges in the ways that IQ became used in and useful to the culture of the USA. Though he ultimately changed his perspective, Goddard began his research to support eugenics. Eugenics is a philosophy made most popular in the early twentieth century, which sought to shape the human population by controlling the genetic characteristics its members passed down through heredity. Goddard advocated measuring IQ in order to determine those most fit to lead the nation to prosperity, and conversely, those who were a detriment to the society. In addition to providing a "scientific" rationale for forced sterilization of women deemed mentally retarded during the eugenic movement, IQ tests were infamously used to make decisions about military assignments, relegating those with the lowest scores to the infantry and those with higher scores for officer training. In schools, IQ and achievement tests were recommended to "track" high-scoring students into gifted and college-preparation programs in efforts to prepare the "most talented" students to contribute to international supremacy during the Cold War era (Rickover, 1957). Thus, the social practices surrounding the meaning of a "low IQ" conformed to the ways that a designation of idios, dunce, or feeble-minded had been used in the past. The subjectivity and cultural construction of the label, however, became obscured in the science touted by the measurability of IQ.

Rick Heber, in 1959, developed the definition of mental retardation that has received the widest contemporary use. Heber offered: "Mental retardation refers to subaverage general intellectual functioning which originates during the developmental period and is associated with impairment in adaptive behavior." He went on to define subaverage intelligence to mean anyone who tested more than one standard deviation below the "normal" limit (100), or having an IQ of approximately 84 or below. Heber's definition also labeled degrees of impairment as "mild," "moderate," "severe," and "profound" (President's Committee on Mental Retardation, 1975, p. 2).

The *DSM-5* (2013) removed "mental retardation" as a diagnosis, opting instead for "intellectual developmental disorder." Additionally, the guide revised diagnostic criteria to emphasize adaptive function as a primary criterion for assessing severity of disorder, which is a departure from Heber's dependence on IQ. The *DSM-5* recommends both clinical assessment and standardized testing of intelligence. It defines "intellectual developmental disorder," or IDD, as impairment of general mental abilities that impact adaptive functioning in three areas: the conceptual, social, and practical. The conceptual area includes skills in language, literacy, reasoning, knowledge, and memory. The social area involves empathy, social judgment, interpersonal communication, and social relationships. The practical area centers on self-management of personal care, work and responsibilities, money management, and recreation. The new diagnostic criteria emphasize assessment of adaptive function in these three areas but do maintain, from past DSMs, a threshold for IDD to be diagnosed at two standard deviations below an IQ of 100.

Currently, approximately 6.6 percent of children with disabilities in US schools are labeled as intellectually disabled, which is .9 percent of all children (NCES, 2015). Causes of mental retardation are characterized as biomedical, environmental, or psychological. Biomedical causes include over 200 identified central nervous system pathologies including phenylketonuria (PKU), hydrocephalus, microcephalus, and Down syndrome. Between 10–25 percent of persons labeled with mental retardation fall into this category. Environmental causes include poor nutrition, poor physical health, exposure to lead paint or other toxins, and lack of sensory stimulation. Because diagnosis of mental retardation relies on subjective evaluation of adaptive function and IQ, misclassification as IDD is possible when an individual's characteristics affect performance on an IQ battery, or affect an individual's *apparent* adaptive function within particular contexts or conditions. Many professionals and self-advocates challenge the practice of placing individuals into a delimited category based on IQ scores and subjective ideas of what adaptive function might mean. Examining the impact that the designation of intellectual disability has had in societies is especially important as we consider past and future rights and quality of life of those deemed intellectually disabled.

In the past, a diagnosis of retardation could be used to bar entry to school and as evidence to support the forced sterilization of women. In 1979, Sarason and Doris observed that the concept of mental retardation (sic) was not scientific, but embedded in culturally situated values for particular kinds of skills deemed intellectual in nature and a particular idea of the meaning of independence. In other words, that which seems important or valuable to a society is embedded in the kinds of activities expected of its citizens, which change over time. The idea of "mental retardation," however, seems monolithic despite changes among contexts and across time. Furthermore, the diagnostic tools of IQ batteries are infamously biased to privilege the particular competencies demonstrated by the most powerful members of a society (Gould, 1981).

Another issue raised by Blatt (1981) suggests the fallacy of linking the presumption of limited neurological or cognitive function to an experience made meaningful and diagnosed in everyday life. He wrote, "mental retardation is an invented disease [and] mental retardation, itself, can't be appreciated by a study of marbles and holes or neurons and dendrites" (pp. 118–119). In other words, he challenges the utility of a definition that at its heart relies on a *metaphorical* assumption that IQ represents brain function. Theorists in disability studies continue to challenge the concept of IDD as a measurable and knowable "condition" belonging to an individual. Carlson (as cited in Stubblefield, 2007) explains,

> "mental retardation" defies a medical model or essentialist analysis because the diagnosis itself is subjective and unstable. There is no straightforward etiology for mental retardation, and the label has been, and continues to be, applied to a wide variety of people with a wide range of characteristics. Indeed, the so-called normality from which cognitive disability is seen as a departure is itself an unstable

category: there is no absolute quality in contrast to which we can define intellectual abnormality (2003, 158).

(as cited in Stubblefield, 2007, p. 168)

In the absence of an "absolute quality" of intellectual ability, the idea of retardation as a *scientific* concept is revealed to be faulty. Stubblefield (2007) echoes Bogdan and Taylor (1994), who likewise concluded that the concept of intellectual disability is not real but "exists in the minds of those who use it as a term to describe the cognitive states of other people" (p. 7).

It is important to point out that mild intellectual disability is the degree that is most often considered "soft" because of the imprecision of diagnostic tools to distinguish "it" from learning disabilities, for example, in the school setting. Perceiving mild IDD most often relies on the IQ in conjunction with adaptive function measured in relation to the literacy demands of school activities; and not necessarily in terms of other activities in daily life that may rely less on the specific idea of literacy measured in schools. Skeptics—largely comprised of self-advocates (i.e., people with intellectual disabilities) and those involved in disability studies—however, argue that the objectivity underlying assertions of intelligence measures is questionable. Further, the notions of independence and adaptive function professed by a culture also rely on far more subjective and mutable factors than a scientific diagnostic process might infer.

Theorists and persons who challenge the concept of intellectual disability firmly agree that individuals interact, perceive, and communicate differently from one another. They generally agree that individuals perform differently from one another in school and in everyday life; that many of us utilize supports and services to lead the lives that we desire; and that the degree and nature of an individual's needs is important to perceive and respond to. They disagree with the concept of intellectual disability as useful to understand and positively affect the diverse experiences of individuals brought together in the diagnostic category. As Stubblefield (2007) points out, the label is "applied to a wide variety of people with a wide range of characteristics" (p. 168), making the idea of mental retardation (sic) impractical for understanding individuals and their unique bodies and minds and how to best teach them.

(11) Specific Learning Disabilities

The term "learning disabilities" emerged in the 1960s. Earlier terms used to label children exhibiting a wide variety of now-familiar characteristics included "minimal brain dysfunctioned," "brain-injured," "minimal cerebral dysfunctioned," "neurologically impaired," "perceptually impaired," "Strauss syndrome," and "attention deficit disordered," (to name only seven). According to IDEIA,

> Specific learning disability means a disorder in one or more of the basic psychological processes involved in understanding or in using language, spoken or written, that may manifest itself in the imperfect ability to listen, think, speak, read, write, spell, or to do mathematical calculations, including conditions such as perceptual disabilities, brain injury, minimal brain dysfunction, dyslexia, and developmental aphasia.

Specific learning disability does not include learning problems that are primarily the result of visual, hearing, or motor disabilities, of mental retardation, of emotional disturbance, or of environmental, cultural, or economic disadvantage.

(IDEIA, 2004, Sec. 300.8)

Learning disabilities are defined as permanent disorders that affect the manner in which individuals with average or above average intelligence receive, retain, and express information. A scientific-cognitive explanation for learning disability proposes that difficultly in learning occurs when messages traveling between sensory organs and the brain seem to "cross wires" or become scrambled and lead to difficulty processing some kinds of information. The resulting problem involves perception rather than acuity. A child with a visual perceptual disability, for example, may have perfect vision but cannot discriminate between the foreground and background on a photograph. He or she may see it but be unable to perceive or interpret it.

As the concept of learning disability has gained popularity, many sub-types have been named. The following lists six general kinds of learning disabilities and the names that have been given to describe the particular area of difficulty:

(1) reading comprehension and spelling: *dyslexia, alexia*;
(2) written expression: *dysgraphia, dysphasia, agitographia*;
(3) mathematical computation: *dyscalcula, acalcuia*;
(4) coordination: *dyskinesia, apraxia, ataxia*;
(5) memory and recall: *dysnomia, aphasia, anomia*; and
(6) oral language skills: for example, *aphonia, dysarthria*.

Learning disability is, by far, the most common disability diagnosis in American schools. Currently, approximately 35 percent of children with disabilities in US schools are labeled as learning disabled, which is 4.5 percent of all children (NCES, 2015). The 27th Annual Report to Congress (U.S. Department of Education, 2007) reported a 28.5 percent increase in children served under IDEA for learning disabilities from 1991 to 2000, which marked a highpoint in a trend that saw a 300 percent increase in learning disability classifications between 1976 and 2000. Since 2002, Cortiella and Horowitz (2014) report, learning disability classification has declined about 2 percent each year. The steep historical rise in students diagnosed with learning disabilities, alongside reports that point out the disproportionate number of African-American students being diagnosed as having a learning disability, has raised many questions about the scientific validity of the diagnosis process (Losen & Orfield, 2002). In the 2013–14 school year, children labeled learning disabled were 49 percent Black or Hispanic students, yet students with these racial identities only comprise 41 percent of the total school population for the USA. The disproportionate representation of children of color in special education has been both a critical and controversial problem for decades. The history of learning disability, the diagnostic processes to identify learning disabilities, and the meaning of the label itself have been perennially called into question and is, perhaps, the clearest example of how disability labeling is a "soft" process.

The most widespread history of learning disability offers an account of its scientific discovery forwarded by European and American researchers who were intrigued by similarities between the characteristics of some children who were struggling in school and adults with brain injury. Between the 1800s and the early twentieth century, European researchers including Franz Joseph Gall, Adolph Kussmaul, John Hinshelwood, and W. Pringle Morgan endeavored to link brain trauma with mental impairment. American contemporaries including Samuel Orton, Grace Fernald, Samuel Kirk, and William M. Cruickshank extended the work of the Europeans throughout the early to mid century, and ultimately arrived at a convincing argument for linkages between brain function and development of reading and other perceptual-cognitive processes. Kirk is credited with coining the term, "learning disability," in a 1963 address to parents of "perceptually handicapped" children, thus ushering in the modern era of learning disability, which attributes otherwise inexplicable difficulties in learning to neurological cause (Opp, 1994).

Examination of the circumstances surrounding the rise in popularity of the learning disability label has been prevalent in educational literature. While one explanation for its increasing prevalence is scientific and social progress, which have led to greater awareness of and better ability to identify and diagnose learning disability, other historical accounts propose that social and cultural factors are also responsible for the steep rise in diagnosis. Sleeter (1987), for example, describes the correlation between the rise of the learning disability label in the USA with the Cold War era advent of high-stakes testing intended to group students into educational tracks most suited to their aptitude. As privileged children—those in middle and upper social classes and of White, European descent—did not pass muster on increasingly demanding assessments, new ways of preserving their status emerged. Definitions of learning disability characterize those "afflicted" as intelligent despite their school struggle, which afford this group a higher status than children labeled with mental retardation. Thus, "learning disability" became and continues to be a more socially desirable label for mild disability as compared to others available in special education.

Parents seeking a more favorable diagnosis for their struggling children, then, contributed to the rise in popularity of learning disability. Carrier (1986) asserts that parent-initiated groups, including major organizations such as the Division for Children with Learning Disabilities of the Council for Exceptional Children (CEC) and the Association for Children with Learning Disabilities (now the Learning Disabilities Association of America), pushed schools to adopt the idea of learning disability to gain advantages in school for their children through Special Education. Ferri and Connor (2005, 2006) also describe ways in which the new label was attractive to some parents, as it preserved racially segregated spaces in special education. By creating "learning disability classrooms" which housed mostly White, middle-classed students, proportionally higher numbers of Black students in special education were kept separate from them in lower-status classes for children labeled mentally retarded, emotionally disturbed, and culturally deprived. In the mid-century frenzy that surrounded racially integrated public education in the USA, becoming labeled with a learning disability emerged as a way to protect White children struggling in school from being in integrated classrooms with their Black peers.

Each account of the rise of learning disability contributes to understanding its history, which is useful to examining current issues in the field. As Kane and Tang-dhanakanond (2008) point out, the number of children estimated by the APA to have learning disability is much lower than the number of children currently identified in schools. In addition, a troubling pattern reveals that African-American and Hispanic/Latino children are identified as having learning disabilities at higher rates than should be expected (Harry & Klingner, 2005; Losen & Orfield, 2002). Social and historical analyses suggest that these are ongoing effects of both the desirability of the learning disability label, relative to others, and de-facto racial segregation. As Brantlinger (2003) points out, parent advocacy is still a powerful force to secure access to appropriate special education services, which creates contexts in which parents who are not accustomed to the mores and discourses of schools are less able to access appropriate services for their children. The most prominent point of contention in the identification of learning disabilities, however, is the *discrepancy method* of diagnosis.

The way that learning disabilities have been traditionally diagnosed is according to the degree of discrepancy between the IQ and scores on an achievement assessment. If a child is determined to have an average or above-average IQ but scores much lower than the expected range on an achievement assessment, the child may be determined to have a learning disability. Researchers have found many problems with the method. First, in addition to issues discussed previously in the section on mental retardation, the validity of some IQ assessments for students with language difficulties is contested. It is difficult to determine whether a child who struggles with language is able to demonstrate his or her aptitude on a measure that is language-based. If the score on which the discrepancy is based is inaccurate, the overall formula does not measure what it claims. Second, comparing an IQ and achievement measure presumes that the measures statistically correlate to each other, which they do not (Kane & Tang-dhanakanond, 2008). In other words, the scores on an IQ measure and achievement measure are compared to determine a discrepancy, but the scoring methods used on different measures with different purposes may not have equivalent meanings. In the simplest formula for gauging discrepancy, the problem is that a score of 100 on an IQ measure does not mean the same thing as a score of 100 on achievement measures, even when they are properly converted to the respective standard scales.

The most confounding issues in identifying learning disability are noticeable in examining the field of educational practice. The result of vague criteria specified by IDEA, each state was able to develop its own discrepancy formula to determine learning disability. The discrepancy required for a learning disability diagnosis ranged, at one time, from as low as 2.1 percent in Georgia to a high of 8.6 percent in Rhode Island (Clark, 2003). Consequently, a child could be diagnosed with or "cured" of learning disability simply by moving to a different state. Further, while research has led to better understanding of difficulty in phonological processes related to reading and indications that learning disabilities may be hereditary, it has not been able to differentiate between the academic function or improvement in reading, for example, of children whose measurements have a discrepancy between IQ and achievement and those who do not. Ultimately, the precision and usefulness of the learning disability label to better aid individuals' learning are debatable.

It is no doubt that the discrepancy method of diagnosing learning disability is fading from practice. The most current regulations in IDEIA (2004) specify:

> [States] must not require the use of a severe discrepancy between intellectual ability and achievement for determining if a child has a specific learning disability, [and] . . . must permit the use of a process based on the child's response to scientific, research-based intervention and may permit the use of other alternative research-based procedures for determining whether a child has a specific learning disability. . . .
>
> (CFR 300.307(a))

The thrust for the change in using the discrepancy method relates to its statistical problems, but also to the length of time it may take for a child experiencing difficulty to receive appropriate interventions in school instruction. In the discrepancy method a child must fail *before* he or she becomes entitled to special services. Instead, considering the child's responsiveness to intervention, known as "RTI," offers a framework in which diagnosis of disability relates to the outcome of efforts to support the child to learn.

In RTI, children who struggle with school-based learning—typically in reading—are offered interventions to improve. If the child responds positively to the intervention they would ideally continue developing and be able to benefit from the "general" curriculum without additional special services. If the child does not respond positively, they are incrementally offered more intensive services, and may ultimately be identified as having a learning disability if they do not improve from the interventions. RTI circumvents the statistical problems of the discrepancy method, and is likely to lead to lower rates of children identified with learning disabilities—assuming interventions that are provided are effective for many.

RTI, however, does not lead to more precision in refining the *meaning* of learning disability. In the framework, learning disability means, simply, that a child does not learn well from that which is provided in the particular school context. Because school contexts change from year to year, or even class to class, identification as learning disabled is as much a reflection of the school and its practices, as of the individual learner. Varenne and McDermott (1998), for example, observe that the meaning of school struggle is relative, and that whether learning disability is identified as a cause of difficulty depends largely on the teacher and teaching practices in a specific classroom or school (see also, Reid & Valle, 2004). In other words, if children are provided with multiple ways of engaging in learning, there is less likelihood that individuals will demonstrate struggle. Despite sharing similar characteristics with others who may be labeled learning disabled, some children may avoid diagnosis when served in a classroom that is suited to meet a range of educational needs. If we are to believe that learning disability is a matter of an individual's neurological make-up, context should not matter in the way it does.

Other social-cultural analyses of the rise of learning disability focus on the ideology of schools that presumes children do or should develop and respond to instruction in the same ways at the same times. Dudley-Marling and Dippo (1995), for example, propose that the presumption that school *should* be socially efficient and that students *should* be homogeneous and progress in an assembly-line fashion creates a context in which differences become characterized as deficits. Identifying children who struggle within the regimented school curriculum as individually disordered preserves the notion that the structure of teaching in schools is "right" and it is the individual child and his body/mind at blame for his failure. Ultimately, identifying failing students as learning disabled becomes a way to locate the problem of school failure in the child and justify the "rightness" of the school, which protects it from changing despite the number of students failing to thrive (Tomlinson, 2004).

Like intellectual disability, the emergence of learning disability in schools has a complicated history. For those in disability studies, criticism of diagnostic processes and skepticism about the meaning made of learning disability relates to the treatment of children who become so-labeled in schools, and to the maintenance—even justification—of schools and curriculum that do not adjust to meet the needs of those subject to them. All people vary in the ways they perceive and respond to information, and one term is hardly adequate to describe each of the 2.3 million children who are categorized as learning disabled. Given that significant differences are not found between children who have learning disabilities and those with reading difficulties, it is unclear how useful the meaning of learning disability is for teaching practice.

(12) Emotional Disturbance and Behavioral Disorder

Emotional disturbance is a category of disability described as such only in IDEIA (as compared with diagnostic inventories in the psychology field). Children identified with behavioral disorders are included in this category, and children with psychiatric, personality, and conduct disorders with more specific diagnoses may also be able to receive special educational services under it. IDEIA offers the following definition:

> Emotional disturbance means a condition exhibiting one or more of the following characteristics over a long period of time and to a marked degree that adversely affects a child's educational performance:
>
> (A) An inability to learn that cannot be explained by intellectual, sensory, or health factors.
> (B) An inability to build or maintain satisfactory interpersonal relationships with peers and teachers.
> (C) Inappropriate types of behavior or feelings under normal circumstances.
> (D) A general pervasive mood of unhappiness or depression.
> (E) A tendency to develop physical symptoms or fears associated with personal or school problems.
>
> Emotional disturbance includes schizophrenia. . . .
>
> (IDEIA, 2004, Sec. 300.8)

As with learning disability, individual states in the USA are able to define emotional disturbance and specify the criteria to identify children with it. About 5.5 percent of children receive special educational services related to emotional disturbance, which reflects a steady drop since a high of 8.4 percent between 1980–1990. Despite the relatively low numbers of students identified with emotional disturbance, examining the demographic characteristics of those so-identified raises questions to the validity of diagnostic processes and the definition in place. Compared with their peers both with and without disabilities, children identified with emotional disturbance are more likely to be male, African-American, and economically disadvantaged. Thus, being a boy, being Black, and/or poor increases one's likelihood of being identified as emotionally disturbed. While some believe that the overrepresentation relates to challenges that affect a child's school performance intrinsic to each of these life circumstances, as Harry, Klingner, and Hart (2005) point out, the majority of education researchers propose the subjectivity involved in diagnosing emotional disturbance is the problem.

Research conducted by the U.S. Department of Education (2001) suggests that the high identification rates for African-Americans and males may be due both to teacher expectations regarding normative behavior (Horowitz, Bility, Plichta, Leaf, & Haynes, 1998; McLaughlin & Talbert, 1992; Metz, 1994) and to a lack of culturally relevant and linguistically appropriate assessment instruments (Harry, 1994). With regard to the overrepresentation of males, it is possible that teachers are more likely to identify students who present disruptive, or externalized behaviors, which are more common in boys than girls. Ferguson (2001) further argues that the criteria for emotional disturbance medicalize what may be otherwise "normal" feelings experienced by poor, Black youth in the socio-political context of the USA. For those children and young adults in the most disenfranchised communities, suspicion of and anger toward teachers, peers, school curriculum, and the institutions they represent may be a troubling, but not inappropriate response indicating impairment. The failure of our schools to respond to the needs of the nation's most vulnerable groups is well documented (Blanchett, 2006; Kozol, 1991, 2005; Noguera, 2008). As with learning disability, identifying students who struggle as individually pathological allows schools to continue "business as usual" rather than query other reasons that particular groups of students seem to fail in our schools.

Most in education acknowledge and work to reconcile problematic approaches to the identification of children with emotional disturbance that have led to the overrepresentation of boys who are poor and Black in the category. However, the wide variety of approaches and the subjectivity in diagnosing emotional and learning disabilities continue to plague the field. It is possible that stronger federal guidelines could reduce the number of students ostensibly mis-diagnosed with "soft" disability labels. In addition, preparing teachers to work more effectively with culturally, economically, and racially diverse children can mitigate and help teachers better understand and find ways to talk about behavioral challenges that are often the cause to initiate referral to special education (Danforth & Rhodes, 1997). The latter is more promising, as simply revising our practices in diagnosing hardly addresses the underlying questions of validity that our past and fading practices initially raised. If the meaning and diagnosis of these disabilities are so elastic and subjective, it is difficult to have confidence that these labels can ever contribute to meaningful understanding of a child's learning and interactions in school. Their imprecision mitigates their practicality for making educational decisions.

(13) *Autism, Autism Spectrum Disorder (ASD),*
Pervasive Developmental Disorder

In the *DSM-5*, "Autism Spectrum Disorder" integrates former classifications including Asperger's syndrome, pervasive developmental disorder–not otherwise specified (PDD-NOS), autistic disorder, and childhood disintegrative disorder. According to IDEIA,

> Autism means a developmental disability significantly affecting verbal and non-verbal communication and social interaction, generally evident before age three, that adversely affects a child's educational performance. Other characteristics often associated with autism are engagement in repetitive activities and stereotyped movements, resistance to environmental change or change in daily routines, and unusual responses to sensory experiences.
>
> (IDEIA, 2004, Sec. 300.8)

In 2013, 8.3 percent of children receiving special education in USA schools were identified as autistic, which is a huge increase from just 1.5 percent in 2000. In 2013, males were labeled ASD at rates more than five times the number of females. In relation to the total population, these rates demonstrate that children today are five times more likely to be identified with ASD than fifteen years ago.

Over the last decade many have voiced concerns about the increase in children identified as autistic. According to the USA's Centers for Disease Control and Prevention (2008),

> It is clear that more children than ever before are being classified as having autism spectrum disorders (ASDs). But, it is unclear how much of this increase is due to changes in how we identify and classify ASDs in people, and how much is due to a true increase in prevalence.

There have been several theories on the nature of autism over the last eighty years. During the 1940s–1970s, Bruno Bettelheim championed a theory that autism was caused by parents' lack of warmth toward their child, which led to the retrospectively cruel stigma placed on "refrigerator mothers." Contemporary scientists agree that autism is not caused by parental neglect, abuse, or failure to create an emotional bond, and is not a product of psychological factors in the child's environment. In the 1980s–1990s, vaccinations, particularly those that contained the preservative, thimerosal, were suspected of causing autism. In 1999, the pediatric community, public health officials, and vaccine manufactures agreed to reduce or eliminate its use in vaccinations. Research on the links between autism and vaccines is ongoing, though research conducted by the Centers for Disease Control and Prevention in 2007 does not support a connection between thimerosal and neuropsychological function in children (Price, Goodson, & Stewart, 2007). The specific cause of autism remains unknown, although current research suggests that it is neurological in nature and has a genetic basis.

Similar to other soft disabilities, ASD is diagnosed through subjective impressions. Individuals with ASD, or "on the spectrum," are deemed so based on their behavior, affect, and social interaction, which are gauged according to criteria put forth in the *DSM-5*. Autism is often described as occurring on a continuum or spectrum—hence the emergence of "Autism Spectrum Disorder." In a medical model, autism is not usually described as a soft disability, but one that is conspicuous—as "it" is diagnosed by gauging perceptible typologies of social responses, actions, and interactions. We have chosen to group autism with soft disabilities because of the reliance on cultural and social norms to dictate diagnosis, and in relation to the beliefs of many autistic self-advocates who strongly disagree with a medical characterization of autism as disorder and understand being autistic as part of neurodiversity (e.g., Aspies for Freedom; Autistic Self Advocacy Network). Similar to the circumstance presented by severe and profound mental retardation, however, persons diagnosed on the autism spectrum are often perceived as conspicuously "autistic," thus we recognize and acknowledge the unusual, though purposeful, choice to describe autism as a soft disability label.

Another reason that we have chosen to include autism in the description of soft disabilities is because the meaning and experience of autism has increasingly been contested, most notably in relation to breakthroughs in assistive technology and communication methods introduced in the 1970s. Practices such as supported typing or facilitated communication provide an individual with the physical and emotional support to enable them to type or point to symbols in order to communicate using augmentative or alternative communication systems. Learning how to type often begins with a facilitator supporting the arm or hand as the communicator develops precision with typing, pressing, and/or pointing. Some individuals may eventually type independently, and others utilize a range of facilitator support throughout their lives. As with all people, those who use assistive technology to communicate demonstrate a wide variety of social and verbal abilities.

In relation to language use, assessing the cognitive ability of individuals with autism is fraught, especially with children and individuals who experience significant barriers in verbal communication—a skill required by most IQ batteries. This has led to many autistic persons being mislabeled as intellectually disabled, which has also served to reveal the limitations of understanding intelligence as measurable by the most common IQ batteries administered in schools. Studies on the use of measures that are non-verbal in nature, such as *Raven's Standard Progressive Matrices* (Raven, 1958), have shown dramatic increases—altering scores by an average of 30 percentile points—in the measured IQ of autistic persons (Dawson, Soulières, Gernsbacher, & Mottron, 2007). This is not to suggest that using better tools increases the validity of the highly contested concept of IQ, but to point out the problems that emerge in our reliance on them.

The increase in attention to assistive technologies like facilitated communication and our willingness to explore other ways of measuring intellect has led to better understanding of the experiences of a growing number of autistic individuals once deemed "low functioning." Access to communication and increased public interest has enabled many to tell their own stories and contest the descriptors that have been attributed to autism. Social media has exploded with autistic bloggers and contributors and other noted advocates and presenters have emerged from smaller circles to public prominence. Sue Rubin, for example, wrote and was featured in the Academy-Award nominated documentary, *Autism is a World* (Wurzburg & Biklen, 2004); Temple Grandin is a highly accomplished author and professor of animal science (see Grandin & Scariano, 1986; Grandin, 1995, 2007; Grandin & Johnson, 2005). The book, *Autism and the Myth of the Person Alone* (Biklen et al., 2005), features several autistic authors whose stories challenge common assumptions made about autism and autistic lives. The concept of "presuming competence," or initially assuming and treating individuals as though they are intellectually active even when their performance may not suggest typical ways of functioning, is a useful position with which to approach school practices related to those with intellectual disabilities or autism (Biklen & Burke, 2006; Biklen & Cardinal, 1997; Jorgensen, McSheehan & Sonnenmeier, 2007; Kasa-Hendrickson, 2005).

Discussion

The idea of the "soft" disability label is complex and to some extent derived from paradigmatic differences between a medical and social model of disability. Diagnostic criteria for the disabilities and related medical-psychiatric conditions we have described as soft *are* established in the *DSM-5* and many instruments and rating scales for assessing the variety of disabilities *are* proven scientifically reliable and valid. Despite the scientific acceptability of these measures, however, it is widely acknowledged that the human role in rating characteristics like behavior, affect, and emotion is simply subjective and relative, by definition. More importantly, however, the histories of diagnosis and meaning attributed to labels such as intellectual disability, learning disability, behavior disorders, and ASD vary across time and place. Rates of identification that are not changing according to known etiologies, but which are influenced by intersections of race, social class, and locale, demonstrate the particular kinds of disablement that we construe as "soft" categories in education.

CONCLUSION: CONCEPTUALIZING DISABILITY IN SCHOOLS

The perception and diagnosis of disability is inextricably related to the moral, cultural, and geographic context within which a characteristic becomes a barrier, a liability—a marker of abnormality. The influential medical model in education emphasizes a need to determine and diagnose impairment so teachers and professionals can anticipate and address the related educational need and provide special services. An outcome of linking disability categories to educational practice, however, is labeling. Labeling unavoidably promotes stigma and segregation, and therefore reduces the likelihood of achieving equality in educational services. Close examinations of soft disability categories demonstrate, in fact, that such labels can be manipulated and used to invoke de facto racial segregation. Unfortunately, disability is too often used as a rationale to hide racial and economic inequities or preserve excessive standardization. That is, when students do not achieve the explanation is focused on finding the individual to be disordered, rather than on other contextual factors. Understanding that disability is fundamentally conceptualized as a dividing entity in education can help educators seeking inclusive practices to identify and understand deep-seated resistance held in the structures of schools themselves.

6

DISABILITIES AND INITIAL APPROACHES FOR CREATING INCLUSIVE ENVIRONMENTS

Working to create inclusive educational experiences requires purposeful assessment of school practices that impede inclusivity, as well as thoughtful engagement in person-centered planning. For inclusive education to be realized it is useful for all school professionals, especially teachers, to be aware of basic and accurate information regarding the most common impairments or disabilities. The approaches in this chapter offer information and practices that reflect general awareness about disability and inclusive teaching. They are starting points and basics for beginning professional inclusive practice. It is crucial to remember that individuals experience disability uniquely and develop ways to navigate school and society. It is always important to learn about individual students by asking questions about their preferences and needs. Learning from students, families, shared experiences, and other professionals can guide teaching practice beyond the basics.

PRIMARY CONSIDERATIONS
Human Variation is Normal
A basic consideration for working toward inclusive education relates to developing productive dispositions for working with diverse groups of children. Each of us, at all ages, in all life contexts, has different characteristics, preferences, strengths, and needs. The condition of human difference *is* normal (Stiker, 1997; Baglieri & Knopf, 2004). Characterizing children as normal or abnormal, "general" or "special," or dividing the curriculum of a classroom into normal and abnormal practices stigmatizes differences. Even when "normal" and "abnormal" are applied objectively or scientifically, the terms are not neutral descriptions. Rather, they form a hierarchy in which the aspect deemed "abnormal" is nearly always perceived negatively and less desirable. By adopting a perspective that acknowledges variation among students as expected and natural teachers can resist characterizing students and teaching practices in ways that segregate and hierarchize.

Another reason to challenge the use of "normal" is variability in culture and experience. What may seem "abnormal" to one person might be quite "normal" to someone else. For example, if a Deaf student uses American Sign Language as a primary means of communication, it may not be normal for others, but it is normal for her. Similarly, one research participant featured on the website, *Conversations about Graduate School and Learning Disability* (Baglieri & Leber, 2008), points out that other adults recognize her difficulty with writing, but that her process does not feel "abnormal" to her. She notes: "I'm comfortable with [my learning disability] because it's a part of me and I accept it. It feels, you know, normal to me . . ." (http://www.graduateschoolandld.com). Seeking better understanding of how students see themselves and their experiences helps teachers appreciate the many ways that individuals understand themselves and interact with the world around them.

Developing personal attitudes that prepare us to accept and appreciate all of our students as they are is the first and most important step in working toward inclusive education. Making efforts to interrupt our tendencies to perceive and talk about people and classroom instruction as normal and abnormal (or "general" and "special") serve the aims of inclusive education well. Although we cannot possibly anticipate the infinite range of unique characteristics, talents, struggles, and identities that each and every student brings to classrooms, we can adopt beliefs and attitudes that reject the effects of stigma, and make us open to accepting and working with everybody. Inclusive teaching is not a standardized or scripted practice that should be the same across years, or even days. Instead, it is a set of beliefs and practices that enable continual and thoughtful creation of a welcoming and flexible educational environment. Differences among students should be valued in celebration of the diversity of experiences that schools offer through its members.

Everyone Utilizes the Help and Support of Others

Throughout life all humans benefit from the help and support of those around them. All of us—disabled or not—can surely remember a time when we benefited from help or support to learn something new, to reach a goal, or to manage a particular difficulty. Specifying ways for students to ask for help and ways that class members may offer help can facilitate a classroom and school community in which all are cared for and respected. Understanding that all humans are **interdependent** is useful to develop inclusive attitudes.

Persons with disabilities are more vulnerable to having unwelcome "help" imposed on them, to not receiving the particular help that is most beneficial, and/or to being hesitant or ashamed to ask for help because of others' potential perception of incompetence. Help should always be rendered in a way that maintains the recipient's dignity and fosters independence. If a student has not asked for help, but it seems needed, the offer for support may come in two questions: "Can I help you?" If the answer is "yes," the second question should be "*How* can I help?" The student should be treated as the expert on his or her needs and should have the opportunity to specify the kind of help required. It is acceptable to offer and explain a different suggestion that may be helpful, but attending to the desires of the recipient of support should be a priority.

Because some students are afraid that asking for help will signify weakness or invite stigma, they may accept assistance only when absolutely necessary. With the exception of situations in which safety is threatened, class members should not impose help if their offers are declined, and should not feel offended if help is refused. Care should be taken, however, to build understanding that all of us need help sometimes, and that accepting the help of others is simply a part of being human. Additionally, ensuring that students with disabilities are competent contributors to the classroom community can help balance the need for help and the ability to contribute. A student with a disability should be encouraged to take leadership positions and participate in classroom duties just as other children do.

Assess School Practices for Barriers to Inclusivity

Special educational practice emphasizes the need for individualized planning and practice. The need for acknowledging and responding to individuality, however, should not be misinterpreted as focusing on the individual as the sole factor in participation and achievement in school. It is essential to undertake a comprehensive and critical assessment of how school practices and policies may impede inclusivity. Staffing, class scheduling and assignments, resource allocation, physical structures, curriculum, and related service provision may seem like complicated aspects of educational planning that are impervious to change. If we recognize, as disability studies promotes, that many bedrock assumptions about education and disability exclude disabled children by design, then we must be open to analyzing and changing features of schooling, *especially* when they appear to be immovable. The Beyond Access Model (Jorgensen, McSheehan, & Sonnenmeier, 2010) is one process that describes how individualized planning can be construed as a process of critical analysis and assessment of the school, alongside understanding of the individual. In this model, planning includes a comprehensive evaluation of the student and their interactions within myriad school structures and arrangements that may facilitate or impede inclusivity. The posture of this framework is that inclusivity is constructed in interplay of individual and environment. Individualized planning in the Beyond Access Model requires schools to "remediate" its structures to ensure that it is receptive to a child, in contrast to a traditional approach that requires the child to prove their ability to be accepted.

GENERAL INFORMATION ABOUT SPECIFIC DISABILITIES

The thirteen categories of disability described by the Individuals with Disabilities Education Improvement Act (IDEIA) offer explanations of types of disabilities that may necessitate a student's access to special educational services. There are a variety of impairments, syndromes, and medical conditions, however, which may be further specified in consideration of a student's needs. Disability may be experienced in relation to physique and movement, social behavior, communication, or intellect. Some basic information about human variation in these areas can help inform approaches for creating access to physical environments and social interaction.

VARIATIONS APPARENT IN PHYSIQUE OR MOVEMENT

Physical disability is a general term often attributed to those with impairments or conditions that are conspicuous in physique. Disabilities described as physical generally include those related to movement, motor function, and the appearance of the body. Not all people with physical disabilities require special educational services, and there is tremendous variety in the kinds of services required, depending on the whole of an individual's characteristics. Orthopedic disabilities are relatively rare among school-age populations, as are the majority of conditions that may be perceived in physique. In addition, some conditions and diseases that affect physique may also affect other aspects of function, such as social behavior, communication, or intellectual performance. Arthritis, cerebral palsy, craniofacial differences, Down syndrome, dwarfism, multiple sclerosis, muscular dystrophy, seizure disorder (formerly called epilepsy), spina bifida, and Tourette syndrome are disabilities that can present with noticeable affects in appearance. In addition, bodies come in all shapes and sizes, with lots of variation in form and features. Some people have extraordinary bodies due to an acquired injury or disease, including amputation; others have unexpected features that are apparent at birth. Some people may use prosthetics, which are artificial extensions that replace body parts; others may not.

The particular special educational needs required by an individual depend on the nature of the impairment or disability. Amputations, for example, usually occur as a result of accidents or diseases like bone cancer. Because amputations are acquired disabilities, the amount of time and support needed to adjust varies widely among individuals and is based on such factors as age, gender, family support, education, and the extent of the amputation. Those who have had a longer time to learn how to function with their bodies—as with impairments present at birth—may benefit from physical or occupational therapy, or may demonstrate a high level of physical function even at a young age. Some people, though different from most in form or appearance, may not be impaired in the usual sense of the term. But, appearances can be disabling due to stigma and perceptions and responses of others. For example, low self-esteem or constant teasing related to a child's appearance could lead to depression, anger, or difficult social behavior.

Experiencing a Physical Disability

The way a person with physical disabilities experiences the world and school depends on infinite factors, including characteristics related to impairment and the context of an individual's life, in general. We offer a few accounts of adults with physical disabilities to demonstrate some pleasures and frustrations in their experiences. In her 2007 memoir, *My Body Politic*, Simi Linton describes the particular pleasure of visiting a New York City art museum from the vantage point of a wheelchair user.

> While [the Guggenheim Museum] has not always been a totally wheelchair-accessible building (though recent renovations have moved it forward), it is a wheelchair-pleasing building. The wheelchair user, as most visitors do, takes the elevator to the top floor. It is the last stop, but it is not the top of the building. As you leave the elevator, the spiral continues up to the right at a steep angle. . . . When I had visited

the museum in a manual chair, I would ask someone to give me a push up to the top, but that day, with a head full of steam, we [Linton and Rufus, her motorized wheelchair] went up, up, up to that tip of the spiral, then down to the next landing, and, just because I could, up and then down again. What a sensation. . . .

While spiraling down, I am reminded of the most dynamic Impressionist paintings. Impressionists employ color and visible brushwork to show the dissolution of form in light and atmosphere. It is said that with the advent of train travel, painters in increasing numbers were leaving Paris to go to the South of France to paint. As the trains moved (more quickly than horse-drawn carriages) and light caught images and fractured those images, painters began to visualize form in more component parts than the more static view of earlier painters.

A painter on a train going to the South of France, and me spinning down the ramp at the Guggenheim, are different creatures, and we each have used our velocity for different ends. Yet in our new vehicles, we both have been catapulted into a new way to see art.

(pp. 187–189)

In contrast, Long (1985/1990) offers a list of frustrating aspects of being physically disabled:

(1) The frustration you feel when you're the guest of honor at the "Handicapped Person of the Year" award luncheon but the rest room doors are too narrow for the wheelchair and you have to urinate in a broom closet.
(2) The rage you feel when someone says to you, "Oh, you have muscular dystrophy? If that happened to me, I'd kill myself."
(3) The annoyance that comes from not being able to turn the radio on or the television off.
(4) The indignity of having to see everything from about four feet off the ground. (How'd you like to go to a cocktail party where all you can see are rear ends at eye level?)
(5) The indignity of having to ask, all the time.
(6) The restlessness of having to sit in one place for 9 hours and then to come home and sit in a different chair for 7 hours.
(7) The frustration of feeling violence and anger and having absolutely no strong physical way of expressing it.

(p. 81)

Several frustrations that may affect children with physical disabilities are clear in Long's list, while Linton describes a distinctive pleasure of using a wheelchair. Experiencing pleasures and frustrations are universal aspects of human life, however we can glean some common-sense approaches that can reduce frustrations. Having equal access to rooms and facilities, providing furniture for others to sit on to facilitate eye-level interaction, plus ensuring control over objects (e.g., televisions, radios) can reduce frustration with the environment. Other frustrations may relate to coping with one's body and function, which necessitates the empathy and non-judgment of others.

Common-Sense Approaches

Creating barrier-free environments that facilitate freedom of movement and access to materials and activities is essential for students with physical disabilities. In addition, a direct approach to addressing questions and curiosity about variations in behavior and appearance is most useful to reducing fear and nurturing belonging and understanding. Classroom adults and peers should be attentive to talk and interactions about disability, impairment, and difference. Children may demonstrate curiosity about a classmate's variation in physique or behaviors like tics, and it is not helpful for questions to be avoided, discussed secretively, made "taboo," or overly emphasized. Encouraging adults and children who have questions to ask respectful, direct questions of the person of subject is recommended. Simultaneously, all should learn to respect a person's option to decline to answer. Explicitly teaching responses such as, "Why do you want to know?"; "I don't know you well enough to answer that"; "I'm not comfortable telling you"; or even, "That's not your business," can facilitate respectful ways to deal with curiosity. Other precepts useful for addressing needs of students with physical disabilities follow.

(1) In the classroom, desks and other furniture should be arranged so that students with physical disabilities can move around the room comfortably, with full access to peers and class materials. Consistency in the layout of furniture and locations of materials is recommended to support the independence of students with visual impairments.

(2) When planning off-campus events like class trips make sure that the transportation and buildings at the destination are barrier free. An in-person "walk-through" of the site by someone who knows the needs of the members of class is best, but a detailed conversation with a site employee may also suffice. Pay careful attention (or be sure to ask about) access to parking lots, walks, ramps, entrances and exits, steps and stairs, floor surfaces, restrooms, water fountains, telephones, elevators, switches, and controls.

(3) When planning a recreational or social event, care should be taken to choose an activity with a facility that is generally accessible to all, and which can be enjoyed by all in some facet. In planning a ski trip or trip to an amusement park, for example, a facility that offers accessible, alternative, and/or adaptive activities should be chosen. For students with significant healthcare or mobility needs, advance notice to the family can facilitate careful thought about preparation to travel to an unfamiliar place.

(4) Students who use manual wheelchairs may appreciate some help on difficult terrain—for example, steep uphill or downhill grades, dirt or stone paths, high pile carpeting, pot holes, or curbs. However, peers, teachers, and other school staff should never push a classmate's wheelchair without the occupant's permission, and should always discuss the wheelchair occupant's preference for "cruising speed" and destination.

In general, though, school and classroom members should be provided with an opportunity to learn how to operate the chair safely, which can allow for natural, spontaneous, and safe invitations or offers to give a push. "Persons accustomed to pushing shopping carts tend not to realize that wheelchairs are less steady and that hitting even a small bump in the ground can send the occupant face down on the pavement" (Maloff & Wood, 1988, p. 11). Wheelchairs are heavy and can gain quick momentum on a hill. In addition, people should become familiar with the dimensions of the chair—for example, with how far the foot plates protrude out the sides. Maloff and Wood (1988) cited the thoughts of one wheelchair user:

> I hate being pushed in malls. The person pushing me always underestimates how far my feed stick out and my foot plates mash people in the ankles. I spend the whole time getting looks and saying, "I'm sorry, I'm sorry, excuse me, I'm sorry." It's embarrassing.

> (pp. 11–12)

To avoid embarrassment and injury, people pushing an occupied wheelchair for the first time need to become familiar with the experience slowly and cautiously.

(5) In the school cafeteria, in a restaurant, or at a party, it may be difficult for a classmate with motor or craniofacial impairments to eat or manage certain foods because of difficulty moving his or her arms or hands or mouth. Once help is accepted, the meal becomes more manageable if the meat is pre-cut and put back and re-shaped, corn is sliced from the cob, or fruit is separated from its rind (Maloff & Wood, 1988).

(6) Remember and teach that wheelchairs, crutches, and other orthotics are personal items and should not be touched without their user's consent. Putting an item like food or a book on the arm of wheelchair is an invasion of the user's privacy.

(7) Welcome and become familiar with assistive devices. These include standing tables, wheelchairs, head sticks, prostheses (devices designed to replace, partially or completely, parts of the body), and orthoses (devices designed to restore, partially or completely, a lost function of the body, such as crutches or braces).

ABOUT LOW VISION

The idea of blindness can be both frightening and fascinating for youngsters, who often draw upon images of dark glasses, a white cane, a tin cup, a guide dog, and perhaps a sad life of hopelessness and eternal darkness to form attitudes. The thought of becoming blind may frighten youngsters particularly because of their familiar experiences of stumbling and groping for articles in the dark or perhaps wearing a blindfold—experiences leading to the assumption that blind persons live in a dreary, black world. But, in reality, only about ten percent of all persons labeled as blind are totally without sight (Scholl, 1986). Most are able to respond to some visual stimulation like light and dark, or shadows or moving objects, providing them with some functional vision.

Blindness occurs rarely in children—in fact, in less than .10 percent of the population between the ages of 6 through 17. Thus, the chances are high that a student with blindness will be the only one in his or her school or even community with that disability. The low incidence of blindness in the young can isolate that student, and encourage stereotyped misconceptions on the part of others. As one student with blindness urged, "I want you to know you shouldn't overreact when you see people who are blind, but just treat them like anyone else" (Westridge Young Writers, 1994, p. 88).

Depending on the degree of sight, students may benefit from materials with enlarged print, strong contrast, Braille, or audio information. Such students are usually able to distinguish the presence or absence of light, and any partial vision may be used effectively for learning mobility and orientation as well as other tasks. Students considered to be partially sighted or with low vision may be able to see objects near at hand with magnification and proper lighting.

Dispelling common myths about blindness and low vision can facilitate a young person's positive experience in school. Common myths include the notions that persons with blindness can not see at all, are all alike; have exceptional musical ability and hearing, live a sad and melancholy life, are dependent and helpless, are led around by their guide dogs, need to be taught Braille, and have become blind as punishment for past sins. Although blind persons may rely on hearing to gather information about their surroundings more readily that those with sight, and therefore might be more attuned to aural information, blind persons do not have super hearing, nor does the degree of hearing increase as a result of visual impairment. As for all, some persons with blindness do have natural musical talent, and some develop a musical talent, but a lot do not. In addition, those persons with blindness who use service animals, like guide dogs, are not taken where they want to go by their dogs. The individual determines the destination, using the dog as a prosthesis and protection against unsafe areas or obstacles.

As with most disabilities, the effect of blindness on an individual's activities and interactions with others relies on several factors like whether the disability is congenital, adventitious, stable, progressive, hidden, or visible. Because one's motor development depends highly on one's sight, youngsters born with blindness or a visual impairment may have difficulty with both gross and fine motor performance. Their physical skill and coordination deficiencies are generally attributable to environmental factors—for example, seldom being encouraged to participate in physical activities or being unable to see small objects and thereby lacking practice in picking them up. Children should be encouraged to explore their environments and be provided with ways to learn how to orient themselves.

Experiencing Blindness or Visual Impairment
Attending to experiences of low vision or blindness invites opportunities to consider varied perceptions of the world around us. Hull (1990), for example, made the following entry in his diary:

For me, the wind has taken the place of the sun, and a nice day is a day when there is a mild breeze. This brings into life all the sounds of my environment. The leaves are rustling, bits of paper are blowing along the pavement, the walls and corners of the large buildings stand out under the impact of the wind, which I feel in my hair and on my face, in my clothes. . . . The sound of the wind creates trees; one is surrounded by trees whereas before there was nothing. . . . The misunderstanding between me and the sighted arises when it is a mild day, even warm, with a light breeze but overcast. To the sighted, this would not be a nice day, because the sky is not blue.

(p. 16)

In a later work, he notes a difficulty related to the mystery of non-verbal communications, in which not being able to see and respond to a smile or a wink affects interactions. Hull (1990) explains,

Nearly every time I smile. I am conscious of it. I am aware of the muscular effort; not that my smiles have become forced, as if I were pretending, but it has become a more or less conscious effort. Why is this? It must be because there is no reinforcement, there is no returning smile, I am no longer dazzled by a brilliant smile. I no longer find that the face of a stranger break into sudden beauty— and friendliness. I never seem to get anything for my efforts. Most smiling is responsive. You smile spontaneously when you receive a smile. For me, it is like sending off dead letters. Have they been received or acknowledged? Was I even smiling in the right direction? In any case, how could my sighted friend make acknowledgment?

(p. 34)

The ability of any individual with low vision to deal with the physical and social environment is affected in various ways. Because low vision affects one's ability to read print, maneuver in unfamiliar places, and perceive one's surroundings and such social cues as a wave, a wink, a smile, or other type of body language, some particular considerations in developing inclusive school environments are recommended.

Common-Sense Responses

In order to interact with persons with low vision in positive and meaningful ways students should consider the following ten common-sense approaches:

(1) When greeting and communicating with students with blindness, remember to communicate verbally. It is important to identify oneself and anyone else present—for example, "Hi there, this is Susan and on my left is Joe Smith."
(2) Class members should know that it is considered extremely rude to gesture about a classmate with low vision to someone else who may be present. In addition, it is possible that the gesture would not be as covert as some might think: persons with low vision are often able to perceive movement and can become aware of other cues that signify such gestures.
(3) Using common words like "look" and "see" to refer to experiences will generally not be received offensively. These words are part of everyone's vocabulary,

and it is fine to ask a student with low vision if they watched a television show or saw so-and-so at the mall. Expressions like, "I'll see you later" are also perfectly acceptable.

(4) Class members should practice being relaxed and smooth in supporting a classmate with low vision to move from one place to another if asked. The proper "sighted guide" method involves the student with low vision taking the other's elbow. This enables guidance, rather than propelling or leading, as the person being guided responds to the motion of the guide's body to tell when curbs, steps or turns are encountered. To avoid surprises, the student being guided may walk a half step behind the guide. It is useful for the guide to verbalize specific directions and numbers like "on the right two yards" or "seven steps including the landing." Providing precise directions are much more useful than indications such as, "over there" or "go straight up and to the left." When facing someone using directions like right or left, one should specify whose right or left. Pointing is not likely to help.

(5) Guiding others' hands to objects can be useful, but a person who may need help to locate an item should be asked if help is needed and whether it is alright to guide his or her hand—do recall that some objects may be more visible than others based on color or the degree of light available, so help may not always be needed. It is not acceptable to grab someone else's hand without asking permission. However, the more familiar class members become with one another, the more they will know about the kind of help that is desired and hence, received favorably as a friendly gesture even without a request. Teaching and using clock directions can help describe more detailed directions or where things are placed in close relation to the person (i.e., in reaching distance). For example, "the pencil is at 3 o'clock." When offering seating to a student with low vision, it can be useful to ask to place his or her hand on the back of the seat and state which way it is facing.

(6) Students with low vision should be oriented into classrooms and other settings in the school environment, such as restrooms, the cafeteria, and other common areas. This may be done by either walking around and pointing out places of interest with the student as they explore, or guiding the student to varying places. It is best to ask the student how they would like to get to know the environment, as it is likely that they have a method to remember where things are. These include counting paces from a landmark like the doorway or a desk or learning the setup of a room by which areas are proximal to others.

In classrooms, students should be made aware of the shape of the classroom setting and where landmarks like student desks, the teacher's desk, bookshelves, permanent cabinets, lockers, wastebaskets, windows, pencil sharpener, doorways, windows, bathrooms, chalkboards, and bulletin boards are situated. Wastebaskets and other movable items should be made stationary or kept in the same place. The student should be told of any changes in a familiar furniture arrangement. In the restroom, the student with a visual disability should be guided to the location of the toilets, urinals, sinks, towel dispenser or hand dryer, especially if they are in a public facility like a restaurant.

(7) Be familiar with adaptive aids and assistive technologies. These include book-stands, Braille writers, large print books, canes, raised line paper, writing guides, audio books, and talking calculators. There is an ever increasing array and range of software and technologies that convert text-to-speech and vice versa.

(8) A visually impaired student may sometimes be unaware of events in the classroom, and a sighted student seated nearby might inform him or her of helpful, non-verbal cues like a smile, a facial expression, a nod or a beck-oning arm movement. Persons with visual impairments enjoy a wide variety of recreational activities including bowling, movies, and the theater. Just like describing non-verbal gestures, a friend can quietly describe some of the purely visual aspects of movies and theater performances like opening scenes, costumes, and special effects. Visual description service is increasingly available at public performances and events.

(9) People with visual impairments may exhibit particular mannerisms, which include, head rolling, eye poking, rocking, or adaptive behaviors such as click-ing or stamping feet to orient to the environment with sound. Class members should be encouraged to practice acceptance and care may be taken to deter-mine the nature of the behaviors to determine whether a course of reduction or development, in the case of potentially useful behaviors, is needed.

(10) Students should be reminded that a service animal is working and responsible for the safety of its master. Such a dog is not just any pet and should not be distracted or petted without the consent of its master, especially while it is working.

COMMUNICATION AND SOCIAL BEHAVIOR

There are several kinds of human variations and impairments that become dis-abling primarily in social contexts, meaning those that require communication and interaction with others. Students who are d/Deaf or hard of hearing and those with communication disorders may require accommodations to provide or enhance their access to classroom talk and to facilitate their ways of communicating with others. Students identified as on the autism spectrum, or with emotional or behavioral dis-orders may also have ways of communicating, acting, and interacting that become disabling in the school setting. Descriptions and common-sense approaches for students who require considerations and accommodations to participate in social contexts follow.

ABOUT STUDENTS WITH DISABILITIES IN COMMUNICATION AND SPEECH

Addressing the social disablement of students with variations or impairments in speech, language, and communication is especially important because of the size of this group. Statistics indicate that as many as 20 million Americans have a speech, lan-guage, or hearing impairment that affects communication. Because verbal skills are so highly valued, language judged deviant is quickly targeted for therapy and intervention, and oral methods (practices that focus on speaking and understanding speech) for d/Deaf children and adults often become the priority in school instruction. It is important to remember, however, that there are many ways to communicate, and members in a community should be recognized, valued, and enabled to participate in social contexts.

Speech impairments refer to difficulties or variations in the production of speech or articulation. Verbal non-fluency (stuttering), lisps, and other impediments to speech production, notably in those with cerebral palsy, are types of speech impairments. Communication disorders affect the way a person understands or expresses language relative to meaning. Aphasia refers to the loss of ability to comprehend or express language, and can affect language received aurally or expressed in speech; and/or in understanding or producing writing. Those with aphasia may have difficulty with "finding" or choosing words to express oneself; with making speech cooperate with one's thoughts; and/or with comprehending the meaning of received language. Aphasia can be an expression of learning disability or learning disability can be an expression of aphasia.

Children with speech or communication impairments often work with an SLP (speech language pathologist) to learn how to form different sounds and/or to develop strategies that can aid in getting through a "block" or finding a word. Care should be taken to follow professional practices in diagnosing speech and communication disorders. Because speech and language are intrinsically related to culture and access to oral language, many variations in speech are not indications of impairment or disorder. Accents and pronunciations related to speaking languages and dialects other than Standard English (in the US), for example, should not be confused with impairments. Similarly, the need for more time than expected to understand, select, and say words can also relate to a student's prior learning or simultaneous use of another language, and is not an indication of disorder or impairment. In addition, children of Deaf adults, or CODAs, may have learned to say sounds and words without substantive access to speakers on whom to model their talk or who might guide children to "correct" pronunciation.

Experiencing Speech and Communication Disabilities

The problem with having speech impairment is often less that one has difficulty communicating than society's stigmatizing attitudes toward what it considers to be unacceptable speech. When a person with a stutter, for example, says "h-h-h-hello," the listener usually understands. A disabling context arises because the interaction is uncomfortable for the speaker, the listener, or both. Similarly, a person with a communication disorder can usually participate in communicating, but allowing more time than usual for interacting or the use of supplemental methods to communicate may be required.

Ruch (1967) listed three types of frustration that can arise from disability, and relate strongly to communication: environmental, personal, and conflict. Among the frustrations found in the environment are those related to one's social surroundings.

During interaction, the attitudes and reactions of others have an enormous influence on an individual with so-called "deviant" speech. Carlisle (1985) observed:

> very few people know what to do when faced by a stutterer. Do you help the guy begin his word? Do you look at him or look away as he struggles to speak? Do you smile encouragingly or sit there like a stuffed dummy? Most people look away, fidget, and think of ways to escape; or if they happen to be holding a cup of coffee, stir it as though their lives depended upon it. Many just flee in alarm as the stutterer battles his way to the next word. Few know what to do, and uncertainty breeds fear with its attendant tension, rudeness, hostility, and anger. To make matters worse, stutterers' own attitudes vary; some welcome help and others do not. All stutterers welcome a little patience.
>
> (p. xi)

Although this example relates to stuttering (verbal non-fluency), others who require more time to communicate or are difficult to understand experience similar environmental barriers.

To avoid or counteract frustrations related to communication, teachers and class members can slow down the speed of talk, demonstrate willingness to repeat talk, and take the time to listen. These changes in talking and listening behavior, along with other common-sense approaches listed later, can significantly reduce the frustrations experienced by a child with a speech or communication disability.

ABOUT STUDENTS WHO ARE D/DEAF OR HARD OF HEARING

Being d/Deaf or hard of hearing (HOH) becomes apparent in social interaction, and may affect a student's understanding of language, mode of communication, and development of identity and culture to varying degrees. The nature of a related disability depends on many factors including the degree of hearing possessed, the age or period of development during which hearing loss occurred, and the response to deafness chosen by the student and family. Teachers and other school professionals need to be aware of the wide range of options in language, hearing, and interventions available to children who are d/Deaf/HOH, and to be respectful of student and family preferences. Two general areas of consideration are whether to enhance a child's access to auditory information with technology and which communication mode or modes to use and teach.

There is a wide range of technologies that can enhance a child's access to auditory information, which include hearing aids, amplification devices, and cochlear implants. The type of technology chosen, if any, depends on the kind of hearing loss and the choice of the family. Conductive hearing loss relates to an interference in the middle or outer ear and can usually be addressed by medical treatments to remove or relieve whatever is interfering with the conduction of sound—possibly fluid, wax, a tumor, or another foreign body. Sensorineural hearing loss relates to problems in the cochlea or auditory nerve and is not medically treatable. However, hearing aids and amplification devices can be useful. Hearing aids are worn by the child on one or both ears and amplify sounds and improve auditory discrimination (the ability to differentiate sounds). Many styles and models of hearing aids are available, and include those placed almost entirely inside the ear, which can be nearly invisible, as well as those that are visible on the outside of the ear, usually as a cuff that forms to the curve behind the outer ear. There are also a variety of amplification devices, such as FM systems, that allow a speaker to wear a microphone in order to broadcast her or his voice to a receiver worn by another person. In the classroom, this can improve a HOH student's access to teacher's directions amidst background noise made by moving chairs and classroom chatter, for example.

Among the more controversial issues for d/Deaf/HOH persons is the cochlear implant, which is a technology developed to provide access to auditory information for those with severe or profound sensorineural hearing loss, but whose auditory nerves function in whole or part. Cochlear implants do not amplify sound, but electrically stimulate working auditory nerves inside the cochlea to produce auditory information. A cochlear implant has both internal and external parts. A stimulator is surgically inserted into the cochlea, which connects to a magnetic receiver that is implanted in the skin of the skull, just above the outer ear. The external microphone, speech processor, and transmitter—contained in a single, connected apparatus—is then magnetically attached to the implanted receiver. Cochlear implants destroy any natural hearing, and as with any surgery, implantation carries risks. These include infection, nerve damage, and paralysis of the face. Those with implants experience a very wide range of outcomes. Some recipients, especially those who developed language before hearing loss and very young children who initially develop language with an implant, regain or gain significant access to auditory information and speech. Others gain minimal access and the surgery can fail entirely, for others. Among the considerations in gauging the success of an individual's cochlear implant are the availability and quality of the speech-language therapy that follows surgery and the preference of the individual to be part of the "hearing world" and adhere to the therapeutic routine (Kelsay & Tyler, 1996; Schramm, Fitzpatrick, & Seguin, 2002).

The central controversy surrounding cochlear implants relates to a second broad consideration for d/Deaf/HOH children regarding the mode of communication chosen and taught. Members of Deaf culture identify themselves primarily by the use of signed languages—American Sign Language (ASL) in the USA. As with other cultural groups, aspects of shared history, relations to the "hearing world," and the lineage of ASL connect Deaf people to one another, and many see the use and proliferation of ASL as an affirmation of a positive linguistic and cultural identity (Padden & Humphries, 1988; Rosen, 2006). Because cochlear implants are recommended for persons with profound or severe hearing loss—the same group who might otherwise communicate with ASL—some members of Deaf culture see the implant as a threat to their community and culture (Aronson, 2000). It is more likely that a deaf child with Deaf parents will be encouraged to use ASL, but the majority of profoundly deaf children are born to hearing parents, and fewer than 30 percent of their families use signed languages regularly (Gallaudet Research Institute, 2003).

The National Association of the Deaf (NAD) (2000) opposes the characterization of cochlear implants as a cure to deafness, and due to the variability of success rates, cautions professionals and parents against the automatic implantation of young children and the setting of therapeutic goals that relate only to hearing and speaking. Children who receive implants are encouraged to develop and practice ways of communicating using hearing and speech, and discouraged to use or continue to use other methods, including ASL. In the longer term, an implanted child may not develop hearing useful to understanding speech and language, and being denied the opportunity to learn ASL or other methods of communication during critical periods for language development can have serious impact on a child's development of literacy.

This brief overview of considerations surrounding d/Deaf/HOH children demonstrates the multiple and complicated possibilities and decisions families face with regard to communication mode. It is essential for teachers and school professionals to work with families to understand their ways of communicating, their desires and expectations for their child, and to respect and observe the choices they make. The following list provides descriptions of possible modes of communication.

(1) **American Sign Language (ASL)** is a signed *language*, which means it has an established shared vocabulary and follows standardized rules of grammar and syntax. ASL is performed by using one or both hands and fingers to make distinctive shapes and movements in specific locations relative to the body. Its rules of syntax are reflected in spatial position, orientation, direction, facial expression, and body position. The syntax of ASL is different than spoken and written English, so interpretation of ASL involves much more than "translating" word-by-word. Other nations and cultures also have signed languages, which include the French language, Langue des Signes Française (LSF); Spanish sign languages, with local dialects present in Spain, Mexico, and Columbia, among others; Australasian, in use in Australia and some parts of Asia; British Sign Language (BSL); and Israel, China, Japan, Pakistan, Belgium, Germany, Ireland, and Quebec, among many others, also have signed languages.

(2) **Signing Exact English (SEE), Signed English, or Manually Coded English (MCE)** is performed using many ASL signs, but follows the syntax of spoken English.

(3) **Finger spelling** is performed by utilizing manual hand signs for the English alphabet. Finger spelling is literally writing in the air; individuals spell out the entire conversation.

(4) **Manual communication** refers to a combination of signed language and finger spelling; it may also refer to communication methods that rely on gesturing and pointing to symbols, typing, or writing.

(5) **Oral communication or oral method** refers to the use of speech and speech reading as the primary modes of communication. The receptive component

of the oral method is often called "lip reading." Kisor (1990) explains that the biggest problem with lip reading is that many sounds look identical:

> *M*, *p*, and *b* are made by bringing the lips together. *T*, *d*, and *l* all take shape with the tongue on the roof of the mouth just behind the teeth. As a result, the words *bat*, *bad*, *ban*, *mat*, *mad*, *man*, *pat*, *pad*, and *pan* all look exactly alike. To the eye there is no difference between *s* and *z*. Sounds formed in the back of the throat are impossible to distinguish from one another. *Cat* and *hat* cannot be told apart, let alone *mamma* and *papa*.
>
> (p. xii)

In fact, only between 6–30 percent of speech can be read on the lips (National Child Traumatic Stress Network, 2004), therefore being able to understand and respond to the context of talk is an essential part of making meaning from lip reading. Developing speech in the oral method requires intensive therapy, as children must learn how to form their mouth structures and control air flow to make sounds, but may have limited ability to hear the sounds they make and self-correct.

(6) **Cued speech** is a system of communication in which a selection of eight hand gestures made next to the speaker's mouth cue "listeners" to the initial sound or syllable being spoken. It is a method used to supplement and enhance the information that can be gathered from lip reading. In ASL the signs represent words, whereas in cued speech, the signs represent sounds.

(7) **Simultaneous communication** means the combined use of speech and Signed English.

(8) **Total communication** refers to a philosophy that implies the acceptance, understanding, and use of all and any methods that may aid communication. Those utilizing total communication may use any of the above approaches in whole or part.

It is likely that a d/Deaf/HOH individual will use many methods to communicate throughout their lives, and that those methods will vary by context. It may seem like a total or simultaneous communication approach is the obvious philosophy for working with children in schools because they seem to offer the most flexibility. School professionals should consider, though, that children may be working toward specific language development goals, and that the use of one method (or many) can interfere with development in another. It is very important to work with families and other professionals—usually audiologists or SLPs—to ensure that everyone is aware of how to best support the child to participate in school *and* develop language and literacy.

Teachers who plan to work specifically with d/Deaf/HOH students generally engage in specialized preparation, and specialized schools and classrooms are often recommended for students who are users of ASL. One reason for the recommendation and preference of a separate setting relates to language. Because deafness is relatively rare among children and the majority of teachers do not know ASL, students who use ASL may have better opportunities to fully develop their language when surrounded by children and adults who do. A specialized school or class may be comprised of children from a broader geographic area, therefore creating a Deaf community. From another angle, the inclusion of Deaf children in integrated school settings offers the opportunity for others to become interested in ASL and Deaf culture (Rosen, 2006), which reflects a value of pluralism generally espoused as a benefit and rationale for inclusive education.

ABOUT AUTISM

Those "on the spectrum" are recognizable mainly through their social behavior. Although there is tremendous variation in degree and effect on the individual, children identified with ASD experience difficulty with verbal communication and/or understanding and responding "appropriately" to social cues, which can make verbal communication, social interaction, or group participation difficult or awkward. For example, autistic children and adults may not seek out or respond to others, make eye contact, or respond to emotion or other non-verbal cues (i.e., body language) and subtleties of conversational conventions. Needing to raise one's hand to speak in class or knowing when a pause in speech indicates a time to talk may be small mysteries to autistic individuals.

Those on the spectrum often experience sensitivity to sensory stimuli like touch, sound, or light, which makes some environments or interactions unbearable and a cause for reaction even when others are not affected. Other sensations may be sought through self-stimulating behaviors, which include repetitive body movements like rocking or flapping one's hands. These are usually not harmful, but do attract the attention of others. Self-injurious behaviors, such as banging one's head or biting oneself, may be forms of self-stimulation, a response or reaction to a specific event, and/or efforts to communicate, but are harmful and require intervention.

Some autistic persons' preferences for following strict routines can make participation in variable situations difficult. Some autistic students may need the same, detailed regimen to be followed for specific activities; or may demand perfect adherence to the schedule for a day or week. Others tolerate change, but may require plenty of warning and preparation when changes in schedule or people in an environment are imminent. Aversions to being touched or hugged and to interacting with others in play or talk are also associated with autistic individuals. Thus, "anti-social" behavior can also raise the concerns of others and can be especially difficult for families.

A final characteristic that is stereotypically associated with autistic persons is the presence of splinter or savant skills. Splinter skills are discrete abilities that stand out as remarkable for the individual. Somewhat similar, those who demonstrate marked exceptionality or talent in an entire area of function may be referred to as having Savant Syndrome (Young, 2005). An enduring public impression of Savant Syndrome is found in the 1988 movie, *Rainman* (Johnson & Levinson, 1988), which featured actor Dustin Hoffman as a fictional autistic character who possessed exceptional memory and ability to manipulate numbers. The terms "autistic savant" and "idiot savant" have been used to refer to the syndrome, but the prior is inaccurate, as savant skills have been noted in persons who are not autistic, and the latter is pejorative. Research into the meaning of savant skills in relation to general intellectual performance is ongoing. A critical view may challenge the underlying premise that intellectual performance is or should be inherently uniform. A variety of interventions for speech, communication, unusual social behaviors, and harmful behaviors are proffered to children on the autism spectrum.

Speech and Communication

Individuals on the spectrum perform speech and language to various levels of proficiency. Common speech peculiarities associated with autism include echolalia, the immediate or delayed repeating of sounds, words, or phrases; unconventional word use; and the production of unusual tones, pitches, and inflections. Although some autistic children do not develop functional, or reliable, speech, many can learn to communicate through a variety of methods, including sign language. Other options include the use of augmentative or alternative communication systems, sometimes abbreviated by the acronyms AAC, AC, and AACS. Communication boards are boards with symbols, pictures, words, or letters to which an individual can point. Software that offers extensive databases of printable pictures and words are commercially available, as are digital devices that can display pictures digitally. There is a wide range of communication applications available for tablets and smartphones. Other augmentative/ alternative systems utilize technologies that enable a person to communicate by typing or using a head pointer to select letters on a keyboard or screen. Communication may then be expressed in writing or "spoken" with a digitized voice. The use of alternative and augmentative communication technology is not exclusive to people on the spectrum, and is widely used among those with physical disabilities that affect speech articulation.

Learning to communicate with alternative systems takes time and requires skills such as controlling intentional movement, which may be difficult for people with autism (Broderick & Kasa-Hendrickson, 2006). Supported typing and facilitated communication (FC) are promising practices in this regard, though have been a topic of controversy. FC refers to a process by which a communicator is physically supported by a facilitator to enable typing, pressing, or pointing. The facilitator usually supports the arm and creates tension by gently holding it back, which allows the communicator to intentionally point or press. The relationship between a communicator and facilitator is also important, as the partnership can serve as an emotional support, which may help motivate an autistic person to communicate and increase her or his confidence in communicating. Ideally, a goal of FC is for the facilitator to decrease the support over time as the communicator moves toward independence. Some individuals gain complete independence and others continue to rely on some degree of support beyond the training period.

According to Douglas Biklen, who is credited with popularizing FC in the USA, and co-author, Jamie Burke, a user of an alternative communication system who learned through FC, "controversy about the method of [FC] centers on the question of authorship" (2006, p. 173). Noted by Biklen and Burke (2006), there are studies that have shown that "a facilitator's physical touch of the typist's hand or arm may influence the person's pointing" (p. 173); an equal number of studies, however, *have* demonstrated authorship. In addition to studies cited by Biklen and Burke (see p. 173), the Academy-Award nominated documentary, *Autism is a World* (Wurzburg, 2004) and the book, *Autism and the Myth of the Person Alone* (Biklen et al., 2005; see also: Crossley, 1997), offer powerful, FC-user accounts of the benefit of providing the option of FC to autistic children and young adults. Although picture exchange systems (e.g., communication boards) offer an extensive selection of symbols that depict things, actions, and feelings, they do not offer communication as flexible as access to language does, and do not support the development of a sophisticated level of literacy. Therefore, offering a variety of approaches to communication can help to ensure that a child has the opportunity to develop language. Assessing each individual, rather than denying access to an approach because it has not been proven for others, should determine whether the approach should be introduced or continued. *Any* given educational approach—related to autism or not—may work for some children and not others, and waiting for a resolution to a debate over a non-harmful practice is not a justification for denying a child access to a possibility.

On Autistic Behavior

It is important to differentiate unusual behaviors from harmful behaviors when considering interventions for autistic children. Some behaviors, such as having an attachment to an object or flapping one's hands occasionally, may be unusual, but not harmful. Trying to change these behaviors may take a lot of time and effort, but actually benefits others who are disturbed by the behaviors rather than substantively improve the life of the autistic person (the effect of stigma aside). Learning or improving behavior related to social interaction can support an autistic person to better participate in school and beyond, but it is important that the behavioral goals consider the desires of the child. A teacher or parent may want a child to initiate conversations or play with others more frequently, for example, but the child may be very satisfied playing alone. Indeed, school should provide opportunities for new experiences and meeting other children, but while introducing and encouraging an autistic child to try new things, she or he should not be wholly denied access to the activities—however unusual or "anti-social"—that are otherwise enjoyed. There are a variety of approaches used to teach desirable behaviors or change harmful ones.

Applied Behavior Analysis (ABA) refers to a child-specific type of intervention designed to identify undesirable and desirable behaviors, determine the environmental stimuli to which the behaviors relate, and then use rewards or positive natural consequences to increase desirable behaviors and eliminate undesirable behaviors or replace them with more desirable ones. Methods in ABA include discrete trial training and naturalistic intervention. Discrete trial training is when a child works one-to-one with a "trainer" on a particular skill in a controlled environment in which the training is the main event. The person is presented with a stimulus, prompted to respond, then rewarded for the desirable response—usually with a favorite food, object, or activity. Naturalistic interventions, including Pivotal Response Intervention (Koegel, Koegel, Harrower, & Carter, 1999; Koegel, Koegel, Shoshan, & McNerney, 1999), takes place in the context of a classroom or other daily activities. Trainers or teachers identify desirable behaviors—such as communicating, making choices, or playing with others—and prompt and reward the child as the opportunity to engage in a desired behavior presents itself.

Worthwhile to note, Lovaas ABA, named for developer, O. Ivar Lovaas, is a frequently recommended intensive program that utilizes the principles of ABA to improve speech and response to language, and reduce "autistic" behaviors. Francis (2005) describes:

> Skills in receptive/expressive language, attending to social stimuli, imitation, preacademics (e.g. rote counting, knowledge of spatial relationships, etc.), and self-help that are deficient, are broken into discrete components. They are then taught on a one-to-one basis, in school and/or at home, using rewards for the successful completion of each step. Behavioural techniques of reinforcement (mainly positive), backward chaining (i.e. the process of teaching each component of a behaviour starting with the last step needed to complete the sequence), shaping, and prompt and prompt fading are used. Physical aversives are no longer employed. Initially, food and favourite objects are used as reinforcers, and are later replaced by more social ones, such as praise. Learned responses are repeated until firmly embedded. . . . After the initial assessment, the children follow a comprehensive curriculum, tailored to their individual needs for approximately 40 hours per week with their trainers. Parents are also encouraged to contribute to the programme in order to achieve generalization of the skills learned.
>
> (p. 495)

Generalization—the transfer of discrete skills to real-world situations—is one of the more important and controversial elements to consider in choosing an ABA approach, alongside the cost and intensity of Lovaas ABA, in particular. The long-term effects of both discrete trial training and naturalistic intervention to increase independence are debatable, though ABA is generally recognized to have positive effects (Francis, 2005; McConnell, 2002).

Despite the dominance of ABA and other child-specific approaches used in a medical model, several inclusive approaches to addressing the social behavior of children on the spectrum are available. Collateral skills interventions emphasize training in skills that seem unrelated, yet lead to improved social behavior (McConnell, 2002). Practices in this category favor an inclusive setting (one in which autistic and non-autistic children learn and play together), in which all children learn and participate in more structured play activities. The opportunity to play with others in activities designed to facilitate interaction offers a welcoming, predictable environment, which can lead to increased interest in engaging with others in various situations. Somewhat similar, peer-mediated interventions involve the direct teaching of social skills to all children in an inclusive setting. Here, class members learn how to actively invite and involve each other in activities.

Sensory Integration Therapy

Attentiveness to the sensory experiences of autistic people is sometimes necessary, and a variety of therapies are being investigated to respond to this need. OTs or other therapists may provide sensory integration therapy, which was first proposed by A. Jean Ayres and aims to improve motor and academic skills by stimulating senses in ways that effect and improve neurological processing of sensory information (Ayres & Tickle, 1980). Sensory Integration therapies range from offering deep-pressure brushing or massaging to exercise or movement protocols to special diets to immersion in environments that are flooded with sound and light (Baranek, 2002). Work on theories underlying the linkages made between sensory integration therapy and neurological effect is ongoing; as are investigations into therapeutic outcomes. As with any therapy, careful attention to the needs and characteristics of each individual is necessary to determine which approaches to introduce or continue. For the most inclusive approach to related services, efforts to implement therapies alongside and within general education curriculum and settings are highly desired.

ABOUT EMOTIONAL DISTURBANCE AND BEHAVIOR DISORDERS

Students identified with emotional disturbances or behavior disorders receive special services due to difficulty interacting within the social environment to an extent that interferes with learning. We often find emotional disturbance described through two subgroups consisting of externalized and internalized behaviors. Externalized or "acting out" behaviors are characterized by impulsive, anti-social, hostile, or aggressive actions directed toward others. Boys exhibit this type of behavior much more than girls and, therefore, have a higher identification, referral, and classification rate. Internalized behaviors, more prevalent in girls, are often characterized by social withdrawal, fear, immaturity, shyness, depression, an excessive craving for control and the development of self-directed symptoms like cutting oneself, bulimia, and anorexia. Internalized behaviors are often hidden or masked (Gearheart, Mullen, & Gearheart, 1993; Hunt & Marshall, 1994; Smith & Luckasson, 1995). Although relatively rare among school-age children, there are a variety of psychiatric and psychological conditions that may underlie behavior and emotional responses that seem "disturbed." Some include anxiety, post traumatic stress disorder (PTSD), obsessive compulsive disorder (OCD), depression, bipolar disorder, and schizophrenia.

Behavioral Disorders

Who becomes categorized as "emotionally disturbed" due to a behavior disorder generally depends on many ambiguous factors. Society, schools, and teachers set standards for acceptable behavior and expectations for children and adults, and such conditions as the individual's age, the characteristics of the surrounding society, and the conditions under which behaviors occur each influence how people in authority judge the appropriateness of behavior (Smith & Luckasson, 1995). What is disturbing to one person may be viewed as independent, humorous, appropriate, or creative by another. Relevant to the problem of such a subjective category of disability classification, it is important to differentiate between children who demonstrate rational, purposeful, and communicative challenging behavior and those whose behaviors seem aggressive or reactive without an age-appropriate or contextually/culturally germane rationale

(Ferguson, 2001). Oppositional Defiant Disorder (ODD) and Conduct Disorder are two diagnoses related to behavior disorders.

Students who are identified as having behavior disorders may need assistance and guidance designed to help them learn how to cope with their environments by establishing positive interpersonal relationships or engaging in prosocial behavior. The goal of inclusive education is to provide an environment that will support the student's development of healthy behavior, enhance the student's feeling of self-worth, and enable the student to reach academic goals.

Common-Sense Approaches

It should be apparent that disabilities affecting communication and social interaction relate to a wide range and variety of access needs, impairments, or psychological conditions. Our grouping of common-sense approaches, however, relates to the similar attitudinal and environmental considerations and accommodations that are useful to facilitate the inclusive school experiences of those whose ways of communicating and interacting necessitate particular attention.

(1) Practice and teach to others acceptance, tolerance, and empathy

Stated earlier, variation among humans is normal. In addition to acknowledging differences in appearance, senses, and communication methods, students and teachers need to be aware that people relate to people, objects, and events differently from one another, and some respond unusually or dramatically to sensory stimuli, group environments, or authoritative instruction. When necessary, these ways of responding should be addressed candidly in order to cultivate understanding and acceptance of difference. Class members should be made aware of noises or kinds of activities or interactions that may be uncomfortable for classmates, and helped to avoid them as a show of respect and empathy toward others. Conversely, class members should also be taught and encouraged to practice ways of interacting that are supportive and welcoming to each other. These are essentials for building a sense of community among class members, in which working together leads to the betterment of the whole.

Students with disabilities may more frequently seem to be at the center of class interruptions or adult support, and class members should learn to be tolerant during disruptive events. For example, teachers should have a plan in mind for how to deal with dramatic disruptions in the case of a student engaging in self-injurious or aggressive behaviors. Typically, two or more school professionals are available in a classroom that includes students at risk for these kinds of behaviors, and a plan that addresses which adults will manage the safety and security of all students should be agreed upon before an incident might occur. Following an incident, students should be provided an opportunity to respond to and discuss what happened. Keeping communication open and straightforward can reduce fear and stigma, as well as provide opportunities to help all students learn to cope with interruptions and unexpected phenomena, gain understanding about other people, and even develop ways that they can help, when appropriate. Academic learning is integral to school, but so is learning how to coexist respectfully in a diversified world. Adopting an open process for discussing unpleasant occurrences is not limited to disability-related interruptions and can be a useful method for addressing issues of teasing, name-calling, bullying, and other conflicts common in schools, as well. In an inclusive class, the occasion to address aspects of shared experiences toward nurturing acceptance, tolerance, and empathy for others should not be viewed as interruptions in curriculum, but a central part of it.

(2) Accept, teach, and encourage many ways of communicating

Be sure to explain to all class members the many ways individuals communicate, and help students and professionals to learn how to interact with communication boards, assistive or augmentative technologies, or signed languages. In addition, make sure that class members have access to and are comfortable asking a specialist, such as an ASL interpreter or communication facilitator, to help them communicate with users of these methods. To cultivate acceptance, provide plenty of opportunities for communication in a variety of arrangements. For example, ensure that there are times for one-to-one conversations, large-group, and small-group communication built into class instruction, and encourage social conversation during recess, lunchtime, and other non-instructional times. Some students' instructional goals may relate to engaging in social relationships and are, in fact, quite common for students labeled with emotional and behavioral disabilities and autism.

In teaching acceptance and promoting many ways to communicate, it is important to encourage students who use assistive technologies, like hearing aids, FM receivers, and augmentative systems, to use them. However, it is also fairly common for children to reject technologies as they are getting used to them or in response to teasing, the curiosity of others, and stigma. Adults should be sensitive to the reasons children may reject their technologies in figuring out how to respond. Asking the family about their preferred response is essential, and might even help to reveal a problem with the technology itself. At minimum, teachers should gain basic familiarity with how technologies are powered and operate in case the need to help a student change a battery or troubleshoot arises.

(3) Slow down the pace of talk, pause between topics, and take turns

Slowing down the pace of talk can improve understanding for students who need time to process the meaning of language or who lip read, who may need a minute to respond to instructions, and is necessary to support accurate ASL interpretation. In addition, willingness to slow down the pace of conversation and listen more carefully offers a welcoming context for classmates with communication difficulties to join in. A student with a speech impediment, for example, may speak slower than usual, and it will put the speaker more at ease if class members simply accept the fact that the conversation will proceed slower and that there is no need to rush it. Students and teachers should remain calm and relaxed, listen attentively, and become the kind of people with whom others like to converse.

Pausing after a classmate with speech impairment speaks or a communicator uses a board or other method can ensure that s/he has finished the thought. Similarly, pausing between ideas offers a natural moment for someone else to interject or offer a new topic. It is important, in other words, to take turns during talking, and making an effort to give another person a turn may be needed for those who need more time to "jump in." Pausing and turn-taking are relevant to children who need time to process the meaning of language, who have difficulty pronouncing and articulating speech, those who use augmentative communication or interpreters, those who need help interpreting social cues, those with anxiety, and even those who have trouble keeping quiet for long periods. Making sure that appropriate times to talk are made available can welcome all to communicate and reduce behavioral conflicts.

(4) Model and teach respectful communication practices

Direct teaching, or explicit instruction, on respectful communicative and interactive practices may help support the positive participation of students with behavioral difficulties or autistic students, and enhance the classroom community overall. Topics may include turn-taking and pausing, described above, and may also address other conventions like initiating conversation, ending one, changing subjects, reading body language, or declining an invitation. Expectations about talking and listening within groups may also be a part of direct instruction on respectful social interactions. Other practices specific to providing access to speech and supporting those with communication disabilities follow.

Talk and questions should be directed to the conversation partner, even if an interpreter or other facilitator meditates the communication method. The interpreter or facilitator will not be offended if the conversers do not look at her or him. Respectful communication also includes attending to the needs of a listener. Even though a speaker's respect is communicated by looking at the person to whom one is talking, it is important to understand and accept that a communication partner may need to look at an interpreter or facilitator, and not at a speaker. Attention should be given to ways that show respect for people who read lips as a primary or supplemental way to understand speech. Body, face, and mouth position can make the difference between being understood or not. Speakers should avoid standing directly in front of a light source because it darkens and obscures a face in front of bright light. It is best to face persons who are lip reading squarely, and stand or sit at their level. Be mindful of turning to the side or backwards, and placing books, papers, or hands in front of the mouth. It is also advisable to avoid eating and chewing gum; and a teacher with a moustache or beard needs to know that facial hair often obscures the mouth, making lip reading difficult. That is not to suggest that a teacher must be clean-shaven, but that he pays closer attention to making himself understood. Finally, it is important to speak clearly and a slightly higher volume than usual may help; but avoid yelling or over-exaggerating speech, as these cause contortions of the lips that make understanding more difficult.

Do not stop, correct, or interrupt a student with verbal non-fluency (i.e., stutter); and encourage him or her to talk as he or she naturally does, as trying to avoid or move too quickly through a stutter or block during talking increases frustration and anxiety and is likely to make communication more difficult. Unless the preference of the speaker/communicator is explicitly known, others should not finish a sentence or assume the meaning of a communication, even if the expresser has difficulty and even if the listener is pretty sure what the end of the thought will be. The "receiver" may be wrong, for one, and denying someone the right to his or her voice is simply disrespectful. Additionally, the way others respond to a person with a stutter will affect his or her speech. It is important to use good manners, hear the person out, avoid finding excuses to leave or end the conversation, and avoid offering unsolicited advice about the speech impairment (Johnson, 1956; Carlisle, 1985; Maloff & Wood, 1988; Lessen, 1994).

It is perfectly permissible to ask a speaker to repeat himself or herself, and requests to repeat or clarify should be respectfully obliged. Clarifying means to re-phrase, shorten, or expand; repeating means to re-state. Although repeating or listening to a repetition can take time, care should be taken to attend to the entirety of the initial exchange. Although a sentence or idea may be able to be clarified in fewer words, few of us want to participate in a "watered down" conversation (especially in a mixed group in which others *did* receive the full communication). It is easier, in fact, for students who read lips to grasp a word's content or meaning in context rather than in isolation. Finally, learners deserve to understand the fullness of instructional talk, so differentiating between a need to clarify and repeat is essential for instruction.

(5) Be aware of and reduce environmental barriers
to positive social interaction

Try to reduce unnecessary sounds and noise pollution. It is easier for most to listen when noises and sounds in the atmosphere are reduced, and students who are hard of hearing can hear better away from telephones, radios, and other noise sources, including traffic sounds from outdoors and noise from a school corridor. When listening is not essential (i.e., during independent work or reading), some students may prefer wearing headphones that muffle sounds, turning off hearing aids, or moving to a quieter location. Sound-muffling headphones, or ones with music, can also support students with sensitivities to sound to feel comfortable in noisy classrooms and schools. Raising everyone's awareness to sources of disturbing noises and sounds is recommended, and can offer an opportunity to find creative solutions. Students might need to be reminded if they are unknowingly or repetitively making noise, most pertinent to students who are autistic or d/Deaf. A solution to reducing the excruciating classroom noise of chairs scraping the floor when they move, for example, is to apply felt feet to furniture, or even use "gutted" tennis balls to cover them.

The seating arrangement should be suitable for the students and conducive to the attainment of the program goals. Students who sometimes exhibit disturbing behaviors should be positioned for optimum interaction with their teachers and those peers who are appropriate role models, and may be sources of peer help. In addition, students should be provided enough space to feel comfortable. Creating space between children may help to eliminate pushing, shoving, or other contact that may lead to aggression or retaliatory behavior; however, it is also useful to teach how to interact respectfully when proximal to others. After all, it is not possible to avoid being near to others in life. School is a great context to learn how to behave, respect others' personal space, and deal with conflicts. An opportunity may be lost if separation is our only response.

Disabilities related to social interaction relate not only to methods of interacting, but also to access to interactions. Ensuring that school arrangements and environments are friendly to a wide variety of children makes interactions possible. Environmental barriers that can impede a child's access to other children relate to lighting, temperature, and even the taken-for-granted presence of many students and teachers talking and moving. Especially fluorescent lights can cause headaches and discomfort for many people; and the large buildings and rooms of schools, many older, may not have good climate control. It is not possible to eliminate all barriers, but being aware of them, reducing them when possible, and having integrated alternatives can facilitate the inclusion, hence social interaction, of many individuals. Being near a bright window or having an incandescent desk light can reduce the effects of fluorescent lights; dimming lights or turning them off when possible can also be helpful. Moving a whole class to an air-conditioned room or allowing the use of a small fan when it is very warm would be welcomed by many, and may be a necessary accommodation for students with low thresholds for discomfort, as may be students with autism or emotional/behavioral disabilities. Finally, making sure to provide breaks, allowing individuals to take breaks, and offering an alternative, less noisy or less hectic setting in which a heterogeneous smaller group can socialize, work, or eat lunch, for example, can be helpful to facilitating inclusive school environments.

(6) Structure class activities and routines for positive group interaction

The pace of activity, talk, and the many explicit and implicit demands that are made of children in classrooms means there is a lot of information and even more rules to negotiate in order to interact as expected in the social environments of schools. Children and adults generally learn the variable expectations and rules of behavior in many different contexts through experience. As we encounter new situations in which we want to participate, we observe and adopt the behaviors of those around us. More experienced members of a group, such as adults and other children, serve as models or may explicitly guide novices to enact appropriate and expected ways of behaving and interacting. The age, family mores related to social behavior and authority, and prior experience of school or other group activities affect the kind of social rules and expectations that children will know and be ready to abide by when they join a new class.

To facilitate positive group interaction, all class members should have ample opportunity to learn the routines and expectations of a class, which may include: procedures for taking a turn to talk, asking questions, requesting help, going to the bathroom, taking a break, and accessing learning materials; rules that relate to behavioral norms, which often include keeping one's hands to oneself, using "nice" language, and being quiet when others are speaking; and instructions for engaging in particular kinds of repeated activities such as a morning meeting, homework review, putting materials away, entering and leaving class, being called to attention, and changing from one activity to another. To deter rule-breaking, teachers may specify types of rule infractions and the consequences, usually punishments, students can expect from a violation. In the same family as ABA, behaviorist approaches that rely on positive reinforcement may be used as a strategy to shape desirable behavior. Examples are: systematically praising by name all students who are sitting down as expected (and not those who aren't); or noting the good behavior of students who raise their hand to speak. Ideally, students who are not sitting or raising their hand will begin to in order to earn the praise of an adult, though this approach is highly dependent on whether the indirect instruction is comprehended. Teachers cannot assume that others understand the "hidden" agenda. Systems including token economies and behavior charts provide a structure through which individual students or a whole class can earn tokens (like gold stars, play money, or checkmarks) for pre-determined desired behaviors and then exchange them for prizes, privileges, or parties—to name a few common rewards.

Before a systematic reinforcement method is considered, however, it is important to remember that in order for anyone to learn and abide by routines and expectations, individuals need to understand them, be able to perform them, and desire to be a participant in the setting to which they relate. In order to cultivate group understanding, adults and students should cooperatively develop classroom procedures, rules, and instructions. This can ensure that aspects of group participation are reasonable to all and that the language used is understandable to all in the class. It is important for class members, especially adults, to remember that learning and learning from mistakes is part of school and life. It is unreasonable to expect that individuals of any age or ability/disability status will immediately learn and be able conform to all of the routines and expectations of a class based on a list of rules or single day of procedure-development.

Commencing punishment or the denial of a "gold star" in the first days and weeks in a new environment can exacerbate undesirable social behavior if individuals feel as though they have already failed or disappointed, and is a sure way to squash a student's desire to participate. Students should be afforded time and positive guidance to learn and be able to participate in routines and expectations.

The type and topics of class activities have a tremendous effect on students' social behavior. It is important that instructions for each activity are provided, and that teachers or class members ensure everyone's hearing, understanding, and ability to abide by them. Offering instructions in talking and in writing, making sure to clarify understanding, and breaking down complicated tasks can be helpful. Adults should *expect* students to need direction and clarification as they engage in work, as some clarifying questions will not arise until the activities are attempted. Considering students' engagement and motivation with regard to class topics is also essential to reduce problematic social behavior. A teacher should provide challenging and interesting curriculum that is appropriate to the age and skills of students. Students who are engaged in activities that are interesting and that provide success are much less likely to present challenging behaviors. Activities and schedules should provide variety and diversity, be both active and passive, and take place individually, in small groups, and with the whole class. Varied teaching techniques, sports and other extra curricular activities, and interesting materials and resources, like computers, help arouse and retain student interest. In addition, the instructional program should be appropriate to the student's need, skill level, and learning style. Offering subject matter that is relevant to students' lives and connects to familiar ideas or experiences is always recommended to cultivate engagement.

A final note on structuring a class for positive social interaction relates to schedules and social procedures. Having a consistent flow of class activities and implementing particular procedures for working with others can support students who require predictable activities, need to be alerted to changes from one activity to another, benefit from knowing the time parameter of activities to manage frustration, and help with interacting with others. Autistic individuals often resist changes in their routines, and those who experience anxiety or paranoia may be discomforted by novel situations. Knowing exactly how long they have to attend to a particular subject matter or kind of activity may support students who have low tolerance for frustration. Tolerating something displeasing can be easier when an endpoint is known and having warning about the end of an activity can help students who hate to leave work unfinished. Finally, some class members may need to leave class at scheduled times for health-related needs, supplemental therapies, or academic support. Having a consistent and predictable schedule can make the environment comfortable for many and reduce the amount or kinds of experiences students miss if they must leave the class. For students who need time to adjust to or get ready for an impending change, providing advance knowledge or alerts can be helpful. For example, a student or class may have a class schedule that they set up each day; be alerted to the imminent end or start of an activity and count down to its close or beginning; or check off or manipulate a pictorial schedule to signify a change. From another angle, individuals may be enabled to work at their own paces if moving on too quickly causes distress.

Incorporating cooperative learning or collaborative work and teaching specific social procedures that support cooperation is highly recommended for cultivating desirable and productive group interactions. Cooperative learning is usually performed in small-group activities in which students are to learn from working together. It is often recommended that specific roles and tasks that relate to a whole product or process be specified in order to ensure that all members participate and benefit. The benefit of well-designed cooperative learning experiences is touted frequently as offering a most engaging form of school activity, since students must be active, as well as implementing a democratic vision of classrooms as supportive communities (Johnson & Johnson, 1999; Slavin, 1999). Because the nature of cooperative learning incorporates role-defining and purposeful social interaction, its structures are supportive to students who need help to interact, are better enabled to participate in working with smaller numbers of others, and who benefit from clear rules of interaction.

(7) Practice respectful and meaningful individual interventions for undesirable interactions

There are many, many reasons why students may not initially (or ever) adhere to the rules of the social environment of classrooms and schools. The developmental period of adolescence is virtually defined by the needs of its members to "test" rules and societal norms in order to define one's own place and identity in the world—often accomplished by dressing and talking in ways different from adults, challenging adults, or defying the rules of adult-life in or outside of school. Most adolescents ultimately gain from participating in school, and therefore generally adhere to the rules that allow them to access school and avoid conflict with authority figures. Other children and adolescents, however, either do not or do not feel that they gain from participating in school and may engage in behaviors—purposefully and not—to avoid school, classes, or authority.

The vast majority of undesirable behaviors that arise in the course of a school day are minor and may be annoying to others, but do not indicate a need for planned intervention. Positive guidance or reminding of "the rules" will usually do; as will extending time to talk or time to cool down in the case of a conflict. It is a human virtue to offer acceptance and understanding for children and adolescents who may have acted or reacted unfavorably, but are simply having a bad day or are involved in the throes of a peer conflict, which can be dramatic, but are usually not serious. Conflicts and undesirable behaviors are sure to occur in any school setting, and some immediate responses helpful to resolve them follow.

(A) Reminders of class rules that many students may occasionally neglect to observe may be noted aloud, and the class permitted to continue.

(B) In the case of non-compliance with a direction, make sure students have had enough time to respond to it and allow them the chance to get it right before prompting them or repeating it. Additionally, make sure that the direction was clear. For example, saying, "Why don't we all put away our notebooks?" or, "I think it's time to put away our notebooks," are not the same as saying, "Everyone please put away your notebooks." The first is actually a question, the second a comment, and only the third is truly an instruction.

(C) Some negative behaviors are best ignored. By purposely avoiding eye contact and overlooking the student's behavior, the teacher may discourage the behavior rather than fuel it. The misbehaving student may be testing the teacher. By ignoring the behavior, the teacher gives the student time and a chance to reduce anxiety or anger. Of course, the application of the strategy of "planful ignoring" always depends on the situation. Never ignore behavior if the student is liable to harm to self or others.

(D) Initiate a "signal system." Many teachers use a prearranged signal to alert a student or the entire class to unwanted or unacceptable behavior. Such signals may include turning the classroom lights off and on, raising a hand, sitting down in one's chair, putting a finger to the lips, or using other gestures to indicate a need to control undesirable behavior. But, remember that signals are usually most effective during the early stages of misconduct to keep small incidents from growing.

(E) Individual oppositional or refusing behavior should be handled privately and quietly. An adult may go over to a child and address him or her quietly, or ask the child to meet in a private other area. In these cases,

• The undesirable behavior should be described clearly to ensure that the adult's perception is accurate and that the student understands the problem. Because disruptions happen quickly and in the midst of other activities, it is not uncommon for students to be unsure of the precise problem noted by the teacher, or a teacher to be mistaken (Vavrus & Cole, 2002).

• The student should be asked directly what the class and teacher might do to make the situation better. In just a brief conversation the teacher can help a student arrive reasonable changes that can be done on the spot.

- Adults should ensure that the student understands and is able to participate in the activity underway. Students may be overwhelmed by an activity and embarrassed or too upset to ask for help.
- The student should be offered the opportunity to start over or take a break to calm down and try again. The object may be to ask for help or clarification, to share an object of conflict, to raise a hand, or exchange a respectful comment or question for a disrespectful one. The meaning of the repeat performance is essential, and offering the opportunity to try again is not the same as demanding a student repeat a routine over and over as punishment.
- Offering a change in the nature of the activity or redirecting the interest of the student can be helpful.
- Individual students should never be made "responsible" for a whole class being punished. Avoid threats or punishments that require a whole class to "pay" for the undesired behavior of one or many. These kinds of practices are more likely to increase antagonism between an individual and adults, and can create conflicts and anger among students.

In the case of recurring undesirable behavior, intense, or harmful ones, an assessment and intervention plan may be necessary. Behavior is a form of communication, and students may "act out" to express feelings or exercise control. Common communicative purposes of behavior include expressing frustration, anger, discomfort, or difficulty, seeking attention, avoiding a person or activity, and needing help. The most easily and quickly performed assessment can be done through open communication, which consists of talking with the student to try to figure out the reason for the behavior. Once the reason is established, alternative ways to express needs may be posed or strategies for coping with anger or frustration may be taught. Some coping strategies include:

- Asking for help;
- Taking a break from the work;
- Counting or breathing exercises to regain composure;
- Alternating engaging in the frustrating task with an enjoyable one;
- Temporarily leaving the environment to regain composure.

In the course of a school day, students are posed with different subjects, kinds of activities, environments and people. Any number of possibilities may make a situation uncomfortable for a student, leading to behaviors that permit him or her to avoid them. To reduce behaviors performed to avoid a situation:

- The student should be asked how to improve the situation.
- Effort should be made to emphasize the abilities and belonging of the student in relation to the setting or topic.
- Teachers should ensure that tasks are understood and manageable.
- Help should be offered and sustained until the student gains confidence in the activity.

- Consider providing a temporary alternative setting or format of assignment in which the student can gain confidence or tolerance for the activity or setting and return to the group.
- Consider that dealing with disciplinary consequences may feel more desirable than engaging in the activity or setting. Teachers should deal with the conflict in the situation and setting in which it occurred, as students will quickly learn how to repeat or escalate behaviors to escape to the principal's office, for example.

Although the desire for attention is often described as problematic within the context of schools and classrooms, needing affirmation from others and asserting one's presence and belonging in a group are hardly pathological. Children and adolescents who do not feel belonging are more likely to "announce" their presence in undesirable ways. Some helpful ways to instantiate belonging and respectfully reduce negative attention-seeking behaviors are:

- Make sure to emphasize all individuals' strengths in private acknowledgements and public praise. It is essential, however, for praise to be authentic and meaningful. If offered too frequently for the same thing, for every kind of thing, or without enthusiasm, individuals will not feel acknowledged.
- Offer ways for individuals to contribute to the class and recognize those contributions.
- Proactively call on, move near, or attend to students who may need help.
- Offer positive attention when appropriate, and create situations in which a student can be caught "doing good."
- Handle disruptions privately and quickly, which communicates that negative behaviors will not result in the public attention a student may seek.

(F) Provide a program that allows students to "let off steam" in acceptable ways. Learning activities should provide relief from tension and exhaustion, which may provoke unwanted behaviors. A student who exhibits disturbing behaviors needs opportunities to drain off anger and frustrations in order to regain self-control. The youngster should have an opportunity to express his or her personal feelings openly to classmates or teachers.

(G) Provide direct teaching and support. Sometimes problems arise in the classroom because a youngster cannot cope with some aspects of the program. If this occurs, specific help—for example working on the assignment directly with the student—may make what he or she thinks difficult easy. The teacher's focus should be on teaching the child to overcome the learning problem at hand, rather than on the student's misconduct.

(H) Provide "teacher proximity." Teachers tend to sense potential problems, and a teacher's physical nearness at such times may help a student control his or her behavior. A teacher may avert an outburst in a stressful situation if the student draws reassurance from the teacher's nearness and support. The teacher can provide the student with a model of self control, self concept reinforcement, and on-the-spot encouragement.

(I) A teacher can usefully anticipate and allow for changes in the environment. If the youngster is exhibiting a problem in his or her environment, it may be helpful to change that environment until self-control returns. The emphasis should be on ameliorating the unruly behavior and helping the child "get over it."

(J) Reinforce and reward positive behavior. Rewards can communicate others' recognition and appreciation for desired behavior, which can encourage a child to "keep up the good work."

(K) Avoid threats and blame. Some youngsters who exhibit disturbing behaviors interpret blame as rejection. Always keep the behavior and the individual separate: "I don't like what you are doing but I still like you." But a teacher who states firmly the consequences of an action may help the child retain self-control. "Positive affirmation" of desirable student behavior builds positive self-concepts. Teachers who call attention to positive peer behaviors promote appropriate role modeling.

DISABILITIES AFFECTING ACADEMIC PERFORMANCE

Schools are dynamic, social places and it is often difficult to precisely determine whether barriers to participation and learning in school relate to the social behaviors and interactions of class members or are attributable to differences among the ways learners perceive and respond to class instruction. A learner's ability to perform well on academic tasks expected in school has as much to do with one's particular abilities and prior experiences as the social environments and manner in which instruction is provided. Common sense approaches for students with identified learning and intellectual/cognitive disabilities presented here relate primarily to accommodations that are often specific to provisions listed on IEPs.

Learning Disabilities

Learning disabilities, according to IDEIA, are permanent disorders that affect the manner in which individuals with average or above average intelligence receive, retain, and express information. Students deemed learning disabled constitute the greatest number of children receiving special education services. Biological bases of learning disabilities unknown, many critiques have been raised regarding the diagnostic process and the disproportionate numbers of students of color placed into special education under the category (Blanchett, 2006; Ferri & Connor, 2005; Losen & Orfield, 2002). An argument can be made that variations in learning are natural and the steep number of disability diagnoses indicates the inflexibility of school practices, more than the prevalence of learning disorders in children (Harry & Klingner, 2005; Reid & Valle, 2004). The nature of learning disability notwithstanding, students presumed to have learning disabilities may benefit from support in any or all of the following general areas: reading comprehension and spelling; written expression; mathematical computation; coordination; memory and recall; and oral language skills. No one person would experience all of these difficulties.

Public awareness about learning disabilities has increased over the past decade and teachers are generally much more informed on the subject. Students with learning disabilities, however, had long been misjudged as lazy, stubborn, or "dumb" by teachers and classmates (Shapiro & Margolis, 1988). Because the category is embracive of many kinds of otherwise inexplicable learning difficulties, it is problematic to compile a list of "classic" characteristics. Further, learning always takes place in context, and how well a person can perform a particular skill strongly relates to their interest and prior experience with the content and the type of performance demanded. For example, a student's performance will depend on whether the task is to read fiction or expository text; to answer a question, write a response, or discuss an opinion. Ways to support children who seem to have difficulty learning include attending to how well instructional practices and materials enable access for those who may struggle with visual discrimination, memory, sequencing, figure–ground perception, visual motor coordination, auditory discrimination, spatial sense, or abstract reasoning.

Common-Sense Responses
The best way to support students with learning disabilities is to be flexible. Learning disability varies from one student to another and, often, affects the same person differently according to the situation and task at hand. Flexibility in teaching practices is helpful, as is flexibility in day-to-day activities. The following suggestions can help teachers begin to create classroom environments that are supportive of students with learning disabilities.

(1) Instruct in Varied Formats. Ensure that class instruction and directions are delivered in multiple formats. For example, provide directions aloud and in writing and offer many ways to present and respond to information and assignments.

(2) Provide Flexible Work Environments. Students may benefit from working on independent activities in an area designed to reduce distractions. For example, cubicles or desks with a carrel may be helpful, if desired by the student. In contrast, students may learn better with a partner or in a group, where ideas can be presented and thought through by a variety of people.

(3) Get to Know the Individual. Create a positive climate in their classrooms by communicating on a personal level with all students and attending to specific needs. Knowing students well enables teachers to develop personalized supports and creates a relationship wherein the student is comfortable asking for help and suggesting new ideas.

(4) Assign Meaningful Work. All students should be provided with meaningful work. Even when offering alternate assignments, work should be on topic and appropriately challenging.

(5) Address Student Questions. A teacher should address questions like these from curious peers openly and honestly:

- How come he's lazy and doesn't pay attention?
- How come he's so clumsy?
- How come she is allowed to use a calculator in math and we can't?
- How come we get more homework than she does?
- How come he gets good grades with such sloppy writing?

Refusing to answer these kinds of questions can create suspicion among students and too-brief answers that simply indicate special education or special needs as a reason can lead to stigma. Rather than avoid them, these kinds of questions give the class a chance to discuss disability and diversity, or the broader idea of fairness. One approach is to conceptualize the concepts of equality and equity. "Equality" means everyone gets treated alike; "equity" means everyone gets what he or she needs (Welch, 2000).

(6) Provide Supplemental Information and Organizers. Students with learning disabilities (and many others) may learn better if provided supplemental instructional guides, outlines, and graphic organizers. For example, a list of the three or four major points to be covered that day with room for developing those points can help to focus attention to the main ideas. A written outline of each unit can also be helpful. Providing frameworks for organizing information, such as outlines with space for fill-in or grids for note-taking, can also be helpful.

(7) Provide Clear and Organized Materials. Assignment sheets and reading materials should have a clear font with a streamlined, straightforward format. Directions should be positioned prominently.

(8) Set Students up for Success. Invite students' participation on aspects of the lesson in which they are likely to succeed. Providing discussion questions or challenging problems ahead of time so that a student can prepare a response may help build confidence and participation.

(9) Use Technology. Learn how to use of different kinds of technologies for reading, writing, studying, taking notes, responding to assignments or examinations. Welcome and permit students to use them in and out of class.

(10) Be Generous with Time. One of the greatest supports a student with a learning disability can have is time—for example, extra time to read, complete an assignment or test, or simply think about the task at hand. Make arrangements for providing extra time in advance so that the student's work is disrupted as little as possible.

(11) Consider Self Concept. School can be very unpleasant and demoralizing for students who have difficulty with academic demands. A critical element in helping the child with a learning disability is building a strong, positive self-image. Providing an understanding environment, honest praise, and tasks that invite success and progress, can help build confidence in learning.

About Intellectual Disabilities

Students deemed to have intellectual disabilities are diagnosed based on their adaptive behavior and IQ. Previously discussed at length, both areas are highly subjective and relative to the social context and environment. Some general areas that are assessed in terms of adaptive behavior, however, are:

(1) **Social behavior**, which includes: interpersonal skills, interaction and play, dealing with conflict and interpreting social cues or body language;

(2) **Intellectual and Academic Performance**, which includes: memory, rate of learning, abstract concepts, and applying learned information to new situations;

(3) **Speech and language development**, which includes: articulation of speech, vocabulary, and understanding of the nuances of meaning.

Common-Sense Responses

Intellectual disability is diagnosed on a spectrum, from mild to profound. Accordingly, experiences of intellectual disability are tremendously varied. As with working with students with learning disabilities, flexibility in teaching and instruction and getting to know the individual are important guidelines. The following recommendations can also guide educators:

(1) Presume Competence. For example, engage in dialogue, offer choices, and age-appropriate materials and activities.

(2) Teach, Re-Teach, and Reinforce. Offer opportunities and support for repetition, practice, and reinforcement when teaching a new concept or skill.

(3) Provide Supplemental Materials. Offer encouragement and provide supplemental materials to aid attention, memory, and avoid frustration. For example, a multiplication table, vocabulary word list, quick fact sheet, and so on.

(4) Be Precise and Detailed. Students with cognitive disabilities may have difficulty reasoning abstractly, which can make it hard to make connections in concepts and instructions. Providing specific details on content and on instructions to complete assignments can be very helpful. Offering practical experiences to support the transfer of learning from one activity to another can also aid understanding and retention of knowledge and skill.

(5) Provide Orientation to School and Schedule. Students may benefit from help finding the school office, school nurse, lockers, cafeteria, art room, music room and lavatories, and so on. Reminders of school schedules and routines can also be helpful. Facilitating relationships and partnerships among peers with the same schedule can be a good way to ensure all students get where they need to go.

(6) Appropriate Expectations. Students with intellectual disabilities are at risk for having poor self-images and low tolerances for frustration. The development of poor self-image can relate to repeated failure on tasks that are inappropriately demanding. On the other end of the spectrum, when students are frequently posed with tasks that are too easy they may resist challenges and develop a low tolerance for frustration. Either situation can lead to learned helplessness, which is when a person acts incapable or waits for others to do for them, based on past patterns, usually of others helping too much. It is important that students are provided reasonably challenging and meaningful work and that they are provided enough support to learn, but not so much that they fail to develop a sense of self-efficacy.

(7) Facilitate Relationships. Another source of poor self-image among students with intellectual disabilities can relate to social isolation. Especially

for adolescents, it can be difficult to establish peer relationships when social behavior and language may seem child-like. Teachers can encourage positive social relationships by making interaction a part of class instruction. Cooperative learning and other kinds of group work can help students get to know each other and provide opportunities for relationships and friendships to form.

CONCLUSION

There is tremendous variation among individuals with disabilities and the practices that can best support students with disabilities in schools are equally varied. The information this chapter offers is merely a starting point for professional practice. Teachers are encouraged to see the information as useful to demystifying impairment and conditions that may otherwise seem foreign, frightening, or off-putting. The beginning practices should pose initial ways of thinking inclusively about educational practices. It is essential to remember that children are individuals, not labels. The best way to learn how to effectively welcome and educate students is by gaining specific knowledge through building relationships with them.

Part III

CURRICULUM AND INCLUSIVE EDUCATION

7

APPROACHES TO STUDENT DIVERSITY
An Overview

A perusal of mass media or educational research readily yields scores of news items, articles, and studies that describe challenges facing American schools and the related targets of reform. Diversities among students are frequently highlighted as a challenge for educators. The monikers, "urban school reform" and "special education reform" are two popular topics that encapsulate either the difficulties faced by children in urban or special education or the difficulties schools have meeting needs presented by children in these contexts. We can add to the list of targets of reform the needs of recent immigrants and English learners, concerns about gender equity and the many other varieties of learning needs presented by children in the present day. When we sort the diversities that characterize students in classrooms by a presumed "type" or point of origin of struggle, the recommendations for reform and improvement of schools and teaching to meet each need seem quite daunting. It seems that reaching equity in education is an additive process, with each newly proposed concern stacking upon another. The purpose of this chapter is to illustrate that the approaches schools have taken toward diversities of all kinds have actually been markedly similar over time. Although specific knowledge and practice have developed for varied groups and needs, the arrangements between "general" education and education for Others emerge in strikingly similar patterns. In perceiving these patterns, inclusive education may be seen not as an additive process of stacking up different ways to attend to student diversities, but in the possibility of deconstructing the barriers common to all.

The development of American public schooling, Carl Kaestle (1976) proposes, responded to the needs and values of the society in relation to the dominance of Protestant culture, the development of capitalism, and the hope for representative democracy. Public education was construed as a force that would advance a morality built on value for hard work, moderation, rugged individualism, personal advancement, and participating in governance toward the common good. These values are recognizable in the contemporary practices of schools and in its curriculum traditions. For example, achievement is linked to personal effort with the promise of advancement in the economic meritocracy. Curriculum content aims to demonstrate societal progress made through the achievements of Western thought and Christian values. American schooling, we may argue, is an enterprise designed to shape the habits and values of children in ways that carry on the dreams of its founders—a vision of a common good built with democracy, rather than directed by sovereignty.

Growing around the 1830s, common schools were developed to prepare children for adult lives newly defined in changes to the agrarian society. Urban schools sought to assimilate immigrants and other children of color who were characterized as culturally deprived into dominant culture. Within the pro-education milieu, institutions founded to contain blind, deaf, and feeble-minded children adopted an educative mission, characterized by vocational training and self-help in activities of daily living. Southern Black communities in the Reconstruction era labored to build educational systems, as public funds were diverted from Black schools to White schools amidst the sentiment of landowners who believed that "school actually spoiled a good field hand," and "preferred their laborers illiterate or at best semiliterate" (Anderson, 1988, p. 149). Education, overall, was performed as an act of transmission—with teachers delivering the skills, content, and values of the dominant culture.

As attendance increased throughout the American periods marked by industrialization and urbanization in the early twentieth century, schools came to resemble the current structures that, historians and philosophers observe, have remained largely unchanged. The introduction of child labor laws and an emphasis on the role that education could play in shaping or reforming immigrant youth through an image of American values expanded the numbers and diversity of children entering schools. The influence of industrialization, capitalism, and their emphasis on efficiency was also felt in schools. Frederick W. Taylor developed ideas and practices for industry that focused on simplifying tasks, creating systems of accountability for workers that emphasized speed and productivity, and organizing work spaces and what we might now call workflow. Scientific efficiency, or "Taylorism," characterized teachers as technicians who should aim to deliver instruction in efficient ways. Students would be the "products." Children were organized by age or levels and movement between classrooms became ruled by bell systems. Teachers documented their work to ensure their accountability of time and children's learning was assessed using measures of accuracy and speed (Rees, 2001). The development of pedagogy was focused on discerning systematic steps and processes to make teaching technically efficient. The work performed in schools became modeled on the image of a well-oiled machine in industry. The technical rationalism and scientific efficiency developed in the early twentieth century continue to shape many perspectives and practices in education.

The mission of schooling to shape values and knowledge in alignment with capitalism, Protestantism, and a values-laden view of cognitive rationality as a framework for democracy coupled with scientific efficiency created a structure that would readily accommodate social exclusions already woven into the fabric of American society. Those deemed deficient within the cultural mission would be separated and tracked according to their lesser potential for economic or societal contribution. Students who underperformed would be separated so as not to disrupt the efficiency of the school. A present view on schooling emerges, then, at the interstices of the cultural supremacy of values associated with Whiteness and the assertion of technical rationality as a neutral philosophy of pedagogy. The presumption that the school curriculum, structure, and practices were moral, efficient, and configured through the fact of scientific development propelled understandings that the occurrence of struggle for children in schools was a burden for individuals, their families, and cultural communities to bear. Herein, the construction of diversity among students as a problem and challenge of education takes form.

TOWARD INTEGRATION OF PUBLIC EDUCATION

As attending school became more commonplace toward the late nineteenth century, public schools were mostly attended by White children and separate schools were developed for Black children and for children with disabilities. Early disability-specific schools typically catered to teaching the orientation and communication skills useful, and often empowering, to students who were blind or visually impaired, deaf or hard-of-hearing, and both (Wright, 1999). They offered vocational training for boys, "home-keeping" training for girls, and the teaching of basic academic skills. Through the Reconstruction era and Jim Crow south, Black children attended schools developed by Black communities. Varied traditions of thought emerged about the education of Black children, which vacillated between preparation to create trade and vocational futures to improve Black-centered economies and education to enter into the intellectual and economic structures dominated by White culture (Anderson, 1988).

While some children with sensory and intellectual disabilities attended private schools, special classes within public schools had also emerged for so-called "backward children" in the early twentieth century (Franklin, 1994). Separate classes for students who were unable to keep up with the students in the "general" class were created as places in which struggling learners could develop at their own rates, with the goal of "catching up" and re-joining the general class. Others followed a different curriculum that focused on vocational training or life skills. The school experience offered to children with disabilities was dependent on many factors: the kind and degree of impairment or disability, the availability and kind of education placement, and the prediction made about a child's future. At the same time, Black-established, as well as racially segregated public schools developed. Schools attended by African-American children were infamously under-resourced in the Jim Crow south, leading to the ruling in *Plessy v. Ferguson* (1896) that schools should be made equal, even while racially segregated. Gaps in resources and funding for racially segregated schools persisted. The 1954 decision in *Brown v. Board of Education*, recognizing that segregated schools reflected and exacerbated economic inequity and racism, forced schools to end policies and practices that resulted in racial segregation and take proactive measures to achieve integration.

The view of school as an enterprise characterized by efficient work toward the cultivation of children to contribute to civic and economic progress in society was sharpened in the 1950s. Mid-twentieth century thinkers advanced the idea of schools as competitive places that should strive to identify those "most talented" in order to provide advanced education for potential leaders who would win the Cold War for Americans (Rickover, 1957). Struggling students who could not keep up with increased academic expectations were increasingly labeled in a new category—learning disability—and placed in segregated environments. Labels like "culturally deprived" were given to African-American students, and achievement tests were used to separate children into different classes that focused on a curriculum appropriate to their presumed potential. Students were divided into programs that prepared them for differing post-school opportunities such as college preparation, vocational or technical studies, or basic skills preparation. The parallel system of special education, alongside the development of educational tracks, became a way to maintain racial segregation in spite of the movement to integrate schools. Black students who had been in sub-par racially segregated schools found themselves again segregated, but this time for what were deemed psychological, social, cultural, and cognitive deficiencies.

In the mid-century, the practice of special education became marked by contradiction. Efforts fueled by White parents to understand and address the needs of a new category of learning disabled children coincided with negative effects for Black children, who now had a new arbiter of separation to reckon with. Classes for students categorized as "mentally retarded," "culturally deprived," and "emotionally disturbed"—majority Black—became places for racial containment (Ferri & Connor, 2005). Like the "backward children" before them, new categories of disability and the resulting segregated placements trapped a new group of students in a parallel system. Both already made, by history, into objects of fear and dread, the intertwined assertion of intellectual and cultural inferiority enacted upon Black children and other children of color and the presumption of the incompetence of disabled children guided practices that rationalized their exclusion from "general" education. The making of school struggle and race into medical, intellectual, and cultural deficiencies allowed education to be thought of as a democratic and equalizing enterprise amidst sorting and tracking practices that actually limited access to education for many (Skrtic, 1991).

The current enterprise of public education characterizes schools in their responsibility to enable children to attain college and career-readiness. Education is proposed as a means to cultivate adults who will seek and secure America's status within the global knowledge economy and who will serve domestic interests as a skilled labor force, while reaping individual benefits through attaining personal wealth. Acknowledging the emphasis on a common curriculum and demonstration of achievement on statewide and national measures is unavoidable. The assertion that teachers and their preparation are the blame and hope for the condition of education proliferates in educational research and popular media (Kumashiro, 2012). Each of these components echoes the character of public education forwarded since the early twentieth century. Contemporary public education is contested terrain on which the battles for economic, cultural, and racial equity are fought. Proponents of Critical Race Theory (Harris, 1993; Ladson-Billings, 2009) observe that attainment of education, as it is marked by diplomas and degrees, make schooling a form of property. Achievement in schooling may be deployed to access privileges, which is a common view forwarded in the current aim of ensuring students' readiness for college and career. Hierarchies that are created through merit that may be gained in school ultimately seem to justify the unequal distribution of goods and status within a capitalist society. Ladson-Billings and Tate (1995) argue, however, that de-facto segregation and funding inequities for schools that serve students of color result in poorer access to high-status and high-quality curriculum and instruction and are exacerbated by the impact of penalties linked to assessment-focused accountability measures. Scholars in Dis/ability Critical Race Studies (Annamma, Connor, & Ferri, 2013) observe that racism and ableism are so ingrained in culture that it seems natural and rational for students with disabilities and students of color to fail in school. Poorer progress compared to able-bodied and White peers is made into a fact of disability, culture, poverty, and/or color. Work toward inclusivity in education strives, in theory and practice, to subvert the assumptions about schooling and children that make inequality appear inevitable.

TEACHING OTHERS

The structure and curriculum of American public schools were formed, designed, and developed in values-laden contexts that designated technical rationalism and White culture, white bodies, and the Western ideal of cognitive rationality as paramount. Children of color, those with conspicuous impairments, and those using languages other than English did not fit the mold. Disability was ascribed to children who fit the mold but struggled nonetheless. The proliferation of classes and curriculum that we would now associate with remedial education, special education, teaching English to speakers of other languages, and multicultural education was the School's response to the categories of Others it created. Sleeter and Grant first provided a taxonomy of research in multicultural education in 1987, which is described in the book, *Making Choices for Multicultural Education*, now in its sixth edition (Sleeter & Grant, 2007). They describe five categories of research and practice in education that focus on students of color and Others. The categories are: Teaching the Culturally Different, Human Relations Approach, Single Group Studies, Multicultural Education, and Multicultural Social Justice Education. The schema laid out in these categories provides a useful organization to consider the broad relationship between the "general" course of education and the circle of surrounding practices generated to serve students Othered within education. What emerges is a history of practice that illustrates the maintenance of a circle of privilege, encoded as "general" education, and the pushes and pulls that seek to enter Others into the circle and increasingly, to widen or dissolve its boundaries.

We draw from the histories and practices of multicultural education and special education to describe approaches to the education of Others in four themes: (a) An Individual Approach to Difference, (b) Pluralism as a Social Practice, (c) Diversity as a Curricular Practice, and (d) Pedagogies for Liberation, some of which are also described in Baglieri (2016). At the outset, it is important to point out that each of these approaches have been and can be configured as empowering or oppressive constructs. In other words, there is not one framework that is inherently inclusive because all educational practices are influenced by context-specific enactments of power and privilege. We highlight how each of these conceptualizations is configured within ideas of inclusive education.

An Individual Approach to Difference

A prevalent approach to responding to differences among students is to address the aspects of particular individuals that appear to place them "at risk" of failure within the curriculum. Descriptions of meeting "diverse" and "culturally diverse" students' needs and ways to meet the "challenge" of diversity are abundant. Additionally, educational literature highlights needs associated with varied "learning styles" and special educational needs related to disability. The aims of education that seek to address diversity often emerge in recommendations of instructional approaches that respond to individual needs. The individual approach to difference, then, is not conceived as change to the general curriculum, but rather inserts supplemental and remedial practices in response to the needs of particular individuals and groups.

The primary philosophy of individual approaches revolves around the aim to assimilate "diverse" students and those with unruly bodies into the culture of power that presumably defines School and characterizes the expectations of college and career beyond. Emphases are on speaking and writing in Standard English and normalizing behavior and appearance to make students acceptable within the dominant culture. Courses of study may emphasize basic skills, remedial instruction or curriculum designed to address specific skills. In inclusive contexts, an individual approach is characterized by practices that highlight the need to individualize instruction or craft materials and instructional approaches that cater to the presumed needs of student groups. The influence of technical rationalism is evident in the individual approach and most notable in traditional special educational practices and in some threads of culturally responsive teaching.

Traditional special education practice is premised on documenting the ways in which an educational program may be individualized for a student with a disability, which is written in the Individualized Education Program. A student may have a prescribed list of remediative or basic skills instruction designed to support their eventual participation in a content-based curriculum. Pugach and Warger (1996) describe these approaches as essentially "acurricular." The focus is solely on the individualized course of instruction with the hope it would lead to the ability to participate in the general curriculum. An acurricular practice of special education largely relies on a reductive view of learning that purports that a student should master and be able to express or perform each component of a skill before moving onto a sequential step (Heshusius, 1989). In this orientation, access to general or inclusive education is often predicated on the concept of readiness. In other words, we focus on whether students are academically, emotionally, or behaviorally "ready" to enter into the circle of general education.

In multicultural education, the framework of "Treating the Culturally Different" (Sleeter & Grant, 2007) focuses on educational approaches that target students in non-dominant linguistic or cultural groups. Providing targeted English language instruction and/or moving students to remedial and lower-tracked classes—often populated by students of color and poor or working class children—are similar to the aims of special education and the striving toward "readiness" to enter general education. Culturally responsive teaching is a widely forwarded concept, which refers to the body of practices that positions student linguistic and cultural experiences and racial identities as relevant and essential to their learning the discourse of schooling that will enable their academic achievement. The argument for culturally responsive teaching is drawn from the culmination of sociological, psychological, and curricular research that reveals curricular and instructional discourses as privileging ways of knowing, speaking, and acting more likely accumulated through White and middle-classed experiences. School achievement for Others, then, may be sought by honoring students' experiences and knowledge as educative and centering them in school activities. Explicitly teaching Standard English and other academic mores that reflect the culture of power are engaged as practices that acknowledge the "reality" of the domination of Whiteness in ways of knowing, communicating, and behaving. That individuals and Othered groups are targeted as the beneficiaries of culturally relevant teaching is what situates culturally relevant teaching within the individual approaches category. The concept that drawing from students' experiences and identities as resources for attaining capital in relation to the culture of power is decidedly assimilationist in philosophy.

With regard to inclusive education, individual approaches have dominated the practice of special education and are forwarded for all in the presently popular discourse that sees individualization and differentiated instruction as beneficial for all students. The ideas that cultural diversities and individual diversities of "learning styles," interests, and preferences may be discerned and leveraged toward promoting individuals' success in the general curriculum are flourishing. A practice of inclusive education in the individual approach depicts classroom efforts as a technical-rational pursuit of matching instructional strategies to the specific needs assessed for each learner.

Pluralism as a Social Practice

Another approach present in literature on multicultural and inclusive education conceives of inclusion and pluralism toward the development of positive intergroup social human relations (Sleeter & Grant, 2007). This family of practices positions knowing about the Other as beneficial to peace, recognition, and appreciation of diversity. Desegregation, in terms of race and disability, is argued to assert togetherness as a mechanism to enable young people to resist stereotypes. In educational orientations that forward pluralism as a social practice, Othered students are presumed to benefit from integrated education as they are provided access to standard curriculum while surrounded by peer models who exemplify normative standards. Children already presumed to be entitled to general education gain the opportunity to practice tolerance and acceptance of the Other. It is through this framework that racial integration and disability inclusion became palatable within a narrative of education and society that presumed general education as a privilege reserved for White and abled children.

Early efforts toward inclusion for students with disabilities provided part-time integration that offered children a mixture of social benefits of participating in the "mainstream" and developmentally appropriate academic instruction in a separate setting. In 1986 the Regular Education Initiative (REI), developed by Madeline Will and issued by the U.S. Department of Education Office of Special Education and Rehabilitative Services, challenged the assumption that the self-contained special education classroom was the most effective setting in which to teach students with disabilities (Stainback & Stainback, 1996). A lively debate between those in support of inclusion and major reforms to special education and those wishing to be more cautious emerged in the research field (Andrews et al., 2000; Paul & Ward, 1996). Among the top points of debate were (1) whether to conceptualize inclusion as a moral imperative, aligned with civil rights and a humanistic perspective on the role of schools in society (Gallagher, 2001); and (2) whether to wait for an empirical body of research demonstrating positive outcomes for students with disabilities before moving toward "full inclusion" (Kavale, 2002).

The public had previously engaged in debate over the IDEA, with many concerned about a perceived drain on fiscal and human resources presented by special education. On public perceptions gathered in newspaper editorials, Rice (2006) describes the creation of an "us vs. them" dialogue:

> Early presentations of special education set students with disabilities up against other children. The early view and regular repetition of this perspective . . . sets "special education" up for suspicion and resentment. In this narrative, education is a zero-sum game, with "winners" and "losers": the "contest" being between special and general education students.
>
> (p. 38)

The idea of inclusion and the REI exacerbated the division made between "us vs. them." With schools positioned as places for competition among children, concerns about the amount of time a teacher would dedicate to students with disabilities at cost to non-identified children were raised, as were questions about a general education teacher's responsibility to craft a separate curriculum for an "included" child (Yell & Drasgow, 1999).

The right to due process granted under IDEA led to further interpretation of the LRE and inclusion in the courts. As Yell and Drasgow (1999) and Kavale (2002) point out, the language in IDEA regarding the LRE was (and is) purposefully vague, leading to a fuzzy notion of inclusion that placed the impetus on IEP Teams to determine the practices that best fulfilled the needs of an individual and the intention of the law. Initial arguments for inclusion posed social skill development as a rationale for the importance of severely disabled students' inclusion in general education. A principle of the REI also put forth the belief that all students, regardless of the nature of their differences, are more alike than different. The prevailing public acquiesced, perhaps, to disability inclusion within a climate of liberal progressivism that endeavored toward a post-race, post-ability worldview. In views that forward inclusivity as pluralistic social practice, differences among people are presented as objective and neutral. The person-first language movement emerged in the late 1980s, along with "color-blind" orientations toward race. Together, these conceptions of difference emphasize the practices of looking past or through difference to surmise the core of a person who might "happen to be Black" or "happen to have a disability." Popular television shows like *The Cosby Show* (Cosby, 1984–1992), featuring a thriving African-American family, and *Life Goes On* (Braverman, 1989–1993), which starred Chris Burke as a high school student with Down syndrome, exemplified the public's interest in imagining the promise of the equal opportunities made possible in a socially progressive society.

In schools, the practices of inclusion and integration were seen as efforts and examples of harmonious intergroup relations. Downplayed in social pluralism, however, are the losses that children with disabilities and Black children experience in integration. As Black children were bussed and integrated into White schools, for example, they lost connection to Black communities and teachers and, noted earlier, found themselves tracked into low-ability curriculum through remedial and special education. "Included" students gained proximity to non-disabled peers, but too often found themselves excluded within the general curriculum, leading to decreased access to learning and in environments that sharpened the stigma of disability (Miller, 2001). Characterizing pluralism as a *social* practice emphasizes togetherness, but fails to reckon with or ignores systemic conditions of oppression that mitigate the promise of equity to eventually emerge through the march of time or the actuality of what is able to be accomplished through individual grit.

In school curriculum, adding information about diversity was seen to enrich and enhance the curriculum and school experience for all. In multicultural education, social pluralism emerges in what Banks (1993) describes as Contributions and Additive approaches, and which Steinberg and Kincheloe (2009) regard as liberal and pluralist practices. Adding materials that depict notable accomplishments and contributions of people of color, those with disabilities, women, people with lesbian and gay identities, and other underrepresented social groups, are seen to allow all students to broaden their knowledge toward empathy for and appreciation of diversity. Awareness activities, and cultural/identity pride events or special history "months" (e.g., Black history, Women's history) characterize curriculum in social pluralism.

Of contemporary practice, Steinberg and Kincheloe (2009) argue that liberal pluralism, rather than contributing to inclusive experiences for children of color, actually "exoticizes difference and positions it as necessary knowledge for those who would compete in the globalized economy" (p. 4). When diversity is primarily celebrated in special events, in other words, the boundaries between the sanctioned knowledge associated with White, Western traditions and the histories and experiences targeted for awareness or special celebration are sharpened. Steinberg and Kincheloe's (2009) second point reflects the observation that the celebrations and awareness of diversity that circulate within social pluralism seem designed to primarily contribute to the acquisition of empathy and additive knowledge to benefit White and abled children. Multicultural additions to curriculum and bilingual education are characterized as benefiting everyone, toward increased understanding and skill in a globalized economy. Practices such as co-teaching, individualized instruction, specific types of strategy instruction, and accommodations traditionally associated with disability are touted as being beneficial to everyone. That utilizing varied approaches to instruction is "just good teaching" is a widely used phrase, for example. Palpable in these arguments is what Bell (1980) calls interest convergence. Efforts to improve conditions for

Othered groups are taken up by the mainstream only when they are seen to contribute to the benefit and privilege of dominant interests. The outcome is reduced advancement toward the specific goals and interests of Othered groups in favor of directing practices and policies toward serving the maintenance of power relationships embedded in the dominant culture.

Inclusive educational efforts that conceptualize pluralism as a social practice are characterized by contradictions. They simultaneously erase and mark diversities, with thorny outcomes. Efforts to include children construed as "diverse" in general education and to develop curriculum that acknowledges the diversity of culture and bodies reflects values of acceptance and tolerance, which seem like worthy efforts. When inclusion is construed as a social or additive practice, however, difference is equated with the exotic and disabled students are positioned outside curriculum and instruction leading to a state of exclusion within general education. Educational practices associated with social pluralism strive to emphasize the differences that characterize all people, therefore neutralizing conceptions of disability, race, gender, and culture. At the same time that social plurality forwards the benefit of finding common ground and seeking togetherness within the normalcy of difference, there is a risk of downplaying the effects of racism and ableism. Neutralizing color or disability, in other words, can also make systems of discrimination seem invisible or obsolete and erase the impact of impairment on an individual. Even as multicultural education was initially characterized as knowledge practices designed to empower Black and brown learners, analysts argue that it has been taken up in the mainstream and practiced in ways that further White and abled privilege.

Overall, orientations toward pluralism as a social practice in education undoubtedly offer actionable philosophies toward increasing and asserting value for multicultural education and disability inclusion. Social pluralism is arguably the most easily discernible philosophy of inclusion and multicultural education in school practice. Even as marred by practices that critical educators find disingenuous, social pluralism is an argument and strategy that has enabled integrating classrooms and putting diversity on the curricular map within otherwise unreceptive contexts.

Diversity as Curricular Practice

Conceptualizations of pluralism as social practice rely on assimilationist orientations and advance multiculturalism and inclusion as examples of how Others may contribute to or be embraced by the dominant culture. Approaches that conceptualize diversity as curricular practice center diversity as a productive force in societal knowledge and advancement. These perspectives depict the creation of knowledge as a constructive process in which varying worldviews and experiences coexist, merge, and contrast as we seek to understand the past and present human condition. A view of diversity as curricular practice relates to Sleeter and Grant's (2007) framework entitled "Multicultural Education," which they describe as an integrative practice that strives to articulate knowledge production as a diversity-rich endeavor. Banks (1993) describes the complementary idea of Knowledge Construction, which attends to the power relationships expressed in curriculum. Changing the knowledge construction of school curriculum compels us to examine the way in which school curriculum depicts diverse people in, for example, historical events—to what extent are African-American experiences characterized primarily by enslavement and the Civil Rights Act? Attention to knowledge construction also demands thoughtfulness about varying perspectives on events imbued with conflicting accounts, such as European exploration and colonization. The basis of an analogous approach in disability is found in disability studies. Mitchell, Snyder, and Ware (2014) describe a method of "curricular cripistemologies" that seeks to perceive of knowledge construction through the lens of disabled and cripped perspectives. Applying these viewpoints as enabling productive insight into humanity, rather than incidental or failed expressions of the body, situates disability as a valued position at the crux of identity and experience. Proponents of diversity as curricular practice strive to generate an anti-colonial pedagogy that embraces Othered experiences, knowledges, and ways of knowing in schools.

A consideration of curriculum content is the role that curriculum plays in students' development of identities and understanding of their positions in society. Means of changing cultural narratives in curriculum are notably articulated in the oeuvre of Banks (1993) and Asante (1991). Connor and Baglieri (2009) cite disability-critical approaches to history and literature, as guided by works including Longmore and Umansky's (2001) *The New Disability History* and Mitchell and Snyder's (2000) *Narrative Prosthesis*. The collective arguments of multicultural and disability studies draw from the desire to write difference into the knowledge tapestry taught in schools in ways that (a) render difference visible, and (b) pose "Othered" experiences as empowered or resistant, rather than incidental or perpetually subjugated, as in colonial discourses. In other words, curriculum content can enable learners to understand history and literature, especially, as characterized and nurtured through diversities in culture, experiences, geographies, and consciousness. Perceiving multiple and varied perspectives is necessary to understand and interpret aspects of the human condition in this view.

The emphasis in a view of diversity as curricular practice is foremost on how students experience their identities and positionalities in relation to the culture of power, characterized by White, Eurocentrist, and ableist histories and norms. Changing the content of traditional curriculum is believed to shift how learners become included in the school canon and thus, in schools themselves. Curriculum reform might aim for a version of multicultural education described as Critical Diversity and Multiculturalism (Steinberg & Kincheloe, 2009), which relates to Banks's (1993) Transformation and Social Action approaches to curriculum reform. Pedagogical approaches to inclusivity in this orientation aim to expand the ways of knowing that are valued and made valuable in school practice. Examples of such pedagogies include critical multiculturalism, culturally sustaining pedagogy, and universal design in education.

Critical multiculturalism relates to what Sleeter and Grant (2007) describe as Multicultural Social Justice Education in an approach that conceives of diversifying curriculum and pedagogy as an eternal project-in-progress characterized by vigilance and critical reflexivity. Critical multiculturalism and what some deem "critical" disability studies examine the nature of power relations that assert the domination of particular perspectives and subvert others. These perspectives depict knowledge construction as agentive processes, which actively affirm or produce ideologies that reflect the culture of power. Education that is disability-critical and critically multicultural works toward social justice by direct engagement in cycles of reflection to perceive injustice and take action to increase equity.

Culturally sustaining pedagogy and universal design in education are conceptualizations of educational practice that emerged to differentiate anti-colonial practices from assimilationist constructions of inclusive teaching. While the philosophical nuances between anti-colonialism and assimilation are critically different and defined, in fact, by their opposition, educational vocabulary and the process to articulate these differences in research and practice yields many overlaps in the terms to describe essentially opposing pedagogies. For example, practitioners of culturally relevant teaching may nod toward the decidedly anti-colonial works of Gloria Ladson-Billings (1995), Luis Moll, Sonia Nieto, and Carol Lee, for example, but interpret the ideas as assimilationist by emphasizing the acquisition of the culture or language of power without significant attention to the critique and construction of such powered relationships (Ladson-Billings, 2014). They utilize cultural responsiveness as strategy, but fail to enable development and maintenance of non-dominant heritages (Paris, 2012). Universal design in education is widely emphasized as an inclusive instructional strategy intended to reform general education as an endeavor of community and embrace of difference in schools (McGuire, 2014; Glass, Meyer, & Rose, 2013). More often, however, universal design is touted as an efficient solution to the problem or challenge of student diversity, with emphasis on how teachers may individualize, perhaps segregate, instruction within a shared space. Far from attributing value in the embrace of student diversities, many practitioners espouse a pedagogy of universal design as a strategy to manage and organize students' needs relevant to the traditional course of instruction. In this construction, universal design does little to work against ableism and toward, for example, curricular cripistemologies (Mitchell, Snyder, & Ware, 2014). In acknowledgement of the vacillating vocabulary surrounding the works-in-progress of the anti-colonial efforts described in culturally sustaining pedagogy and universal design in education, we recognize that similar conceptual framings are described using other terms and that practices using the same terms are not always articulated through the same ideals and commitments.

Both culturally sustaining pedagogies and universal design emphasize the value and development of learners' ways of knowing and doing that are associated with cultural and ability diversity and traditionally Othered in schools. These pedagogies seek to situate students and their experiences at the center of educative practices that promote the study of materials and development of skills that inform the development of the self and support positive affiliation and group identities. Supporting and developing multiple literacies and valuing many ways to express literacy enable learners to participate in learning with rigor and toward engagement and mastery of the varied ways of knowing essential for navigating and using the mélange of text, images, multimedia, languages, and vernacular that comprise and enrich contemporary life. As school practices move toward broadening curriculum and practice, both ease of achievement and experiences of struggle are, perhaps, likely to shift. As a class engages, for example, in learning American Sign Language or Spanish; practicing visual literacies instead of text-based; posing varied perspectives on disabled or raced experiences and their understandings as important learning, different knowledges, experiences, and ways of knowing and doing emerge as alternatingly comfortable and foreign. All learners are challenged by the rigor developed through seeking and developing academic traditions held within and outside the self. Changing the knowledge construction and engaging in anti-colonial practices toward sustaining culture, nurturing positive identities, and seeking school achievement for Others characterizes what most mean by multicultural and inclusive curriculum. Different from additive or compensatory approaches, diversity as curricular practice centers the aims, goals, and needs of people of color, disabled people, and other groups who are oppressed within schools. Different from individual approaches, we argue that change is systemic and not limited only to contexts that contain Others. In a view of diversity as curriculum practice, inclusivity is sought not through catering to the presumed needs of Others relative to the culture of power, but in shaping pedagogy to change what is powerful to know, understand, and be able to do in a culture that desires to embrace and cultivate everyone's participation.

Pedagogies for Liberation

Recall the metaphor of school as circles in which the privilege and promise of general education is inscribed as a center with boundaries defined by the accomplishment of White and abled normativity. Within the metaphor, an individual approach to difference strives to enable learners with the competencies allowing them entry in the circle; pluralism as social practice creates interlocking circles, like a Venn diagram, in which intersections are enabled, but the center is preserved; and diversity as a curriculum project aims to widen the circle to embrace all. Each of these frameworks, varyingly cognizant and critical of the relationships among race, ability, racism, ableism, and school privilege, advance education to be a desired commodity. Efforts are to expand access to the privileges attained through school. A fourth metaphor for conceiving inclusivity in education is one that depicts a dissolving circle. Proponents of deschooling, unschooling, and critical pedagogy seek to remake the relationship of learning to schooling. Though different in approach, each philosophy and theory of practice discerns schooling as an enterprise primarily in service to capitalism and the industrial machine that require people to become docile contributors to the material advancement of the dominant class. Advocates of deschooling and/or critical pedagogy desire to construct a view of education in which learning enables the liberation of people to pursue hope, desire, and possibility in the human experience, which are occluded by capitalism and alienation.

Liberatory pedagogies reflect the critical theories of the Frankfurt School, which employ Marxist philosophy to articulate the machineries of capitalist ideology. Critical Race Theory (Ladson-Billings & Tate, 1995) and Materialist theories of disability (Oliver, 1999), for example, discern exploitative relationships between social classes that are driven by economic power and justified by hierarchies naturalized within, for example, racism and ableism. Using Dis/Ability Critical Race Studies or DisCrit, Annamma, Connor, and Ferri (2013) argue that racism and ableism intersect in ways that make it impossible to address one aspect of marginality without engaging the other in perceiving inequity in schools. As people of color were once deemed incompetent to participate in democracy and consigned to labor and enslavement on the basis of biological determinism, racism and ableism collude in contemporary education to explain persistent patterns of poverty and disenfranchisement in the notion that Black students are poorly educated. The concept of disability in a medical model within capitalism continues to rely on biologically determinist narratives about the unsuitability of some bodies for participation in work and democracy (Erevelles, 2000). Russell (1998) complicates a view of disability and society to point out that capitalism creates an "ethic that equates human value with work." Many disabled people, with others who are dispossessed within the economy, become trapped in a system that, first, requires poverty, then attributes poverty to individual failure in education, and then assigns lesser value to impoverished persons. School, in these views, then, functions as an ideological state apparatus (Althusser, 1971), which serves to rationalize injustices and the disenfranchisement in the class system that is necessary in capitalism.

It would seem that those invested in a thriving economy may desire to improve education conditions to enable more people access to the circle of privilege constructed in schools, thereby increasing the workforce and the number of people able to spend or invest in capitalism. Russell (1998) points out that advances in disability rights have largely benefited disabled people who are also affluent, which enables such investment. The subjugated positions of most people with disabilities are maintained, however, which she describes as a "straightjacket" of dwindling public aid maintained by the concomitant lack of voice experienced by those reputed as recipients of charity. In a materialist critique, Oliver (1999) further establishes that disablement in school and society gives rise to economies that are exploited for profit. Special education, rehabilitation and nursing facilities, medicine, and innumerable other goods and services related to the management of impairment and disability offer opportunities to capitalize on the educational and economic marginality of disabled people.

A neoliberal view of school reform is similarly present in current education literature and in mass media. Proponents of neoliberal school reform point to the achievement gap and the poor state of education, especially in urban areas that serve high proportions of students of color. To remedy histories of sub-par education, they argue that private-sector entities may develop, fund, and/or manage schools in addition to the public provision of such services. Families may then choose among semi-privatized or public schools. The market-driven notion of "school choice" is proposed to yield faster and better improvements in schooling overall. Like the economy that has risen up around disability, Saltman (2007) and Collins (2015) employ the concept of disaster capitalism to point out the logic of neoliberal educational reforms. Saltman (2007) points out the discourse of failure made of public education at large—in news headlines that vilify public schools for achievement gaps between children in the US and in comparison to other nations—but especially of urban education. Collins (2015) describes the impact of neoliberalism in New Orleans in the wake of the massive flooding triggered by Hurricane Katrina and caused by the failure of city levees in 2005. The production of the achievement gap, presented as apparent by standardized testing, contributes to the ongoing designation of schools that primarily serve children of color as disaster zones. In turn, the need for "development" provides opportunities for profit. In material analyses critical theorists argue, then, that capitalism is sustained by disablement and school failure. Ableism and racism are convenient products of history that are relied upon and deployed anew to rationalize social and economic stratification.

Deschooling

Critical theories discern the relationships among School, capitalism, and economic and political disenfranchisement. Critical Race Theory, materialist critiques of disability, and DisCrit further describe how racism and ableism are inscribed in these relationships. While many perceive these relationships as able to be transformed within and through education as we endeavor toward curriculum reform, as in those who approach diversity as a curricular practice, other critical theorists find the institution of education to be inescapably fraught within the condition of capitalism. Schools cannot escape their fundamental function to sort and rank children at the core of the mission. There are those, like Ivan Illich (1971), who argue that all societal institutions, including education, corrupt and make the mind and body dependent. His argument for deschooling emphasizes the difference between schooling and learning. Schooling is a corrupting force that prevents humanity from pursuing hope and being generative except in relation to roles and expectation inscribed by institutional life. He writes:

> School has become the planned process which tools man for a planned world, the principal tool to trap man in man's trap. It is supposed to shape each man to an adequate level for playing a part in this world game. Inexorably we cultivate, treat, produce, and school the world out of existence.
>
> (p. 47)

Through Schooling, learning is presumed to be the acquisition of a laid out, standardized curriculum that we have come to believe is best carried out and controlled by the institution of School. An emancipated view of learning, in contrast, is a pursuit of curiosity related to the search for belonging, purpose, and function in communities and in service to others. Illich's hope is for people to discover the unpredictable possibility in the world. He characterizes learning as engagement in the world wherein all objects and people are regarded in their potential to constitute curriculum and act as teachers.

Illich (1971) proposes that learning occur not according to a construct of what children should know and be able to do, but what they grow into desiring to do and know. As deschooling refers to the realization that schooling is not the same as learning, unschooling, coined by John Holt (1964, 2004), describes a related practice that emphasizes children's pursuit of learning as emergent from and in their natural life contexts, variability presumed. In both frameworks, the family and community may enable learning by providing resources or networks to enable individual and group pursuit of knowledge and experience. These require, in Illich's (1971) terms:

1. To liberate access to things by abolishing the control which persons and institutions now exercise over their educational values.
2. To liberate the sharing of skills by guaranteeing freedom to teach or exercise them on request.

3. To liberate the critical and creative resources of people by returning to individual persons the ability to call and hold meetings—an ability now increasingly monopolized by institutions which claim to speak for the people.
4. To liberate the individual from the obligation to shape his expectations to the services offered by any established profession—by providing him with the opportunity to draw on the experience of his peers and to entrust himself to the teacher, guide, adviser, or healer of his choice. Inevitably the deschooling of society will blur the distinctions between economics, education, and politics on which the stability of the present world order and the stability of nations now rest.

(p. 44)

A main idea is that what is useful to learn is best learned through engagement with what is or may be made available in the world and through reliance on the community at large, rather than contained and narrowed by the institution of school. Important to both deschooling and unschooling is recognizing and building upon the curiosity and acts of learning in which children engage through play and the activities they choose to pursue. Self-directed learning undertaken in the home and "real world" is understood to be more meaningful when sought out by the child and engaged in community contexts. Proponents of deschooling, in sum, favor a local and community-centered way of life built on knowing and caring for other people, seeking belonging, and becoming generative, all made authentic through self-direction, rather than as configured by institutions.

Critical Pedagogy

More widely described in relation to diversity and inclusivity in education, critical pedagogy is a family of practice that seeks to liberate people from the corrupting power of institutions by working toward transforming oppressive ideologies. Described in his work, *Pedagogy of the Oppressed*, Paulo Freire (1970) established the concept of critical pedagogy as education that transforms self and others through engagement in cycles of reflection and action, referred to as praxis. Critical praxis resists a "banking model" of education in which learning is perceived as the acquisition and accruement knowledge—akin to depositing information and ideas into learners as if they are vessels waiting to be filled. Banking models are characterized by the static and oppressive power enacted by the knower onto the learner. In this arrangement education forwards the culture of power that is woven into the canon to be learned. To be "wide awake" in learning, to use the words of Maxine Greene (1971, 1977), is to avail oneself of the richness and complexity of interpretation of the human experience, rather than merely acquire lessons delivered in an oppressive didactic. Essential in critical pedagogy, then, is recognition that both oppressor and oppressed are damaged within injustice. All are prevented from realizing the expansive promise and humanizing effect that learning can offer. Practitioners of critical praxis seek to construct relationships in which all participants in a learning community are knowers and learners. The knowledge and experiences of all participants are posed as contexts through which the nature of injustices can be understood and anti-oppressive actions may be enacted. A cycle by design, critical pedagogy does not end with a solution, but comprises what is meant by the course of education. In these frameworks imbalances of power are seen to be inescapable, but individuals and groups can work toward social justice by creating contexts in which power can circulate. In other words, there is not an endpoint where a utopian state of equality or equity are reached. The premise is that the pursuit of democracy is defined by struggle, wherein equity is configured as a constant striving.

Critical pedagogy is proposed to be dialectical in which individuals create society as they are also created within its social, political, historical, and economic contexts. Peter McLaren (2003) offers:

> A dialectical understanding of schooling permits us to see schools as sites of both domination and liberation; this runs counter to the overdeterministic orthodox Marxist view of schooling, which claims that schools simply reproduce class relations and passively indoctrinate students into becoming greedy young capitalists.
>
> (p. 70)

Unlike in deschooling, proponents of critical pedagogy find hope in education. They see the potential of constructing "school not simply as an arena of indoctrination or socialization or a site of instruction, but also as a cultural terrain that promotes student empowerment and self-transformation" (McLaren, 2003, p. 70). Learning is the process through which people gain understanding of the interplay of self and society to enable empowerment and action toward seeking justice and inclusivity.

Practitioners of critical pedagogy in schools may seek inclusivity by examining practices and curriculum that serve to exclude Others and changing them. What differentiates critical pedagogy from other efforts, however, are the people involved in examination and action. In this orientation, all school and community members, especially students, are positioned as generative sources of knowledge and experience, and charged with participating in reflexive learning. Students and teachers work together to share their lives and desires, experiences of school and the world outside, to pose problems, seek understanding of them, and endeavor toward change. The curriculum is generated from those brought together in the immediate context and reflects the expressed desires of the people and places engaged. The collaborative generation of curriculum and insistence on teacher and student action set critical pedagogies apart from other critical practices in inclusive education. Many critical educators engage in reflexive practice as they consider their own role in curriculum and teaching with regard to equity and inequity and enact change toward inclusivity. The orientation that describes diversity as a curriculum practice, in fact, insists upon the teacher's criticality and reflexivity. The problems identified as critical study for students, however, emerge as the teacher's curriculum that can just as readily be delivered in a banking model of education, even as the content of study seems intended to spark students' criticality. Critical pedagogies begin with problems that the community of learners—together—raise and discern, struggle through, seek understanding of, and most importantly, take action on. This view of pedagogy is what makes the unscripted nature of critical pedagogy a radical possibility for schools.

DIVERSITY AND INCLUSIVITY: TOWARD
A THEORY OF PRACTICE

The four orientations we have articulated provide an organizational framework of approaches to diversity and embedded assumptions about the history and project of seeking inclusivity in education. Essential to developing a theory of practice for inclusive education is to consider how the role of the teacher shifts across the various frameworks for addressing student diversities in education. In the individual approach and pluralism as a social practice, teachers must master specialized approaches to work with individuals' diversities. A view of inclusive education in these frameworks means that a single teacher is responsible for learning and doing the work once accomplished by several people with specific preparation and training. More common, recommendations related to individual and plural approaches suggest that teachers with specialized knowledge work in collaboration with each other to provide specific support based on student need. In diversity as a curricular practice, teachers are responsible for preparing and planning in ways that are likely to be accessible and meaningful to all. Classroom practice here is less characterized by implementing specific strategies meted out by learner category and more reflective of providing an array of opportunities likely to engage all. While the range of teaching knowledge and practice expands, it is related to student needs as they are presented in context, rather than in strict prior mastery of fields of specialization. In pedagogies for liberation, the teacher's role shifts dramatically. Instead of being solely responsible for generating curriculum and instruction, the assumption is that adults and children learn and grow together. The pressure of knowing "everything" is lessened, as the course of learning and teaching is meant to be shared and developed. There is space and expectation to reflect, make mistakes, and try again. Engagement in disability studies and multicultural education, the primary fields informing this work, is premised on paying close attention to individuals and sustaining their identities within collective histories. Recognizing and responding to racism and ableism is core to both fields. Most simpatico with diversity as curriculum practice and envisioning education in its liberatory potential, then, a disability studies perspective on inclusive education emphasizes three areas of study for educators. First, the teacher's role is to be a student of diversity and equity, who studies widely and critically while understanding that all knowledge is partial. Second, the inclusive educator pays close attention to students and families and their desires for school, emphasizing collaboration and equal voice in educational planning, teaching, and assessment. Finally, they see instructional design and curriculum content not as means to an end, but as an active practice of inclusivity. In the next chapters, we offer an overview of directions in collaboration, instructional design, and curriculum practice that relate to these efforts.

8

COLLABORATIVE PLANNING AND PRACTICE

There are many parties involved in the education of a child. Students, families, teachers, and other school professionals can work together to ensure that learners have positive and productive experiences in school. The IDEIA guarantees a free and appropriate public education to children with disabilities, access to the least restrictive environment, as well as specifying the need to engage in collaborative planning and practice. The history of collaboration related to disability and education is peppered with accounts of positive and negative, productive and ineffectual experiences for families and school personnel. Consideration of barriers to collaboration and enactment of efforts to reduce difficulties can move educational planning and practice for children and adolescents with disabilities forward.

A SEAT AT THE TABLE: INTERRUPTING THE EXPERT DISCOURSE

Interest in the nature and outcomes of family involvement in schools has been a consistent theme in educational research (Booth & Dunn, 1996; Epstein, 2001; Fan, Williams, & Wolters, 2012; Grolnick & Slowiaczek, 1994). For families of children with disabilities, involvement in educational planning is specified as a protection and entitlement offered in the IDEIA. Parents must be part of the decision to evaluate a child for eligibility for special education and are members of the team that develops the Individualized Education Plan (IEP) each year. The expectation of school involvement for parents of children with disabilities is welcome by some and uncomfortable for others (Lareau, 1996; Valle, 2009). One reason to support and nurture family participation, from a disability rights perspective, is that the need to advocate alongside and on behalf of a child or family member with a disability may persist into adulthood. Schools can provide a supportive context in which families are initiated into the structures and discourses that may come to characterize a lifetime of effort to secure disability entitlements and protect against discrimination. Families also can provide insight and knowledge built from deep experience with their children that can contribute to educational planning.

A basic consideration for inclusive practice, then, is to invite, welcome, and take seriously the information, ideas, and desires of students and their families in relation to school planning. School professionals contribute a wealth of knowledge to help understand and support students who experience struggle in schools. Teachers and other school professionals have studied curriculum and instruction and spend most of their workday with children, which add to their expertise. While the contributions of professionals are essential, students and their families should also be considered and treated as experts. Consider, for example, Pam Steeves's (2006) reflection on life with her son, Matthew: "It is by living up close with Matthew that I have come to know stories of Matthew as knowledgeable, as using playful and improvisatory ways to participate, communicate, and contribute to the world" (p. 107). She further describes the way her experience of Matthew enabled her to help school professionals arrive at better understanding of her son's attachment to a stuffed toy cat named Tony—a topic of discussion when he changed schools at age 11. She recollects the phone call:

> After a few pleasantries, the "issue" of Tony, the stuffed toy cat, came up. I must admit that viewed from the outside, it seemed pretty crazy to defend this cat, but I was looking from a different vantage point. I was attending to what Tony meant to Matthew from the inside. Tony helped Matthew be strong; Tony was always there; Tony was funny and could do things that would make other people laugh, and then Matthew could join in, too. Matthew wanted more than anything to belong, to have a place. Tony helped him to do that.
>
> (p. 109)

Matthew was able to keep Tony with him in school. Steeves notes,

> Matthew shifted the landscape from one where he held a fixed position as a child with disabilities to a child who was trying to figure out how to fit into a situation. For Matthew, Tony was the way in. Matthew was able to participate because Tony created a common ground.
>
> (p. 109)

Listening to the stories of parents and attending to their understandings of their children is essential to developing a whole portrait of a student, their desires, and needs in school.

Although most would agree on the importance of family participation in planning and educational decisions, many studies into parents' perceptions of interactions, especially in special education evaluation and planning meetings, demonstrate their negative experiences (Reiman, Beck, Coppola, & Engiles, 2010). Common sources of parents' negative feelings are: the density of professional talk and confusion about the goals and purpose of the meeting; the failure of school professionals to include them in the planning process; and the undesirability of attending meetings in which negative talk about their child prevails, especially when they feel blamed for their child's difficulty in school (Reiman et al., 2010; Valle & Aponte, 2002; Hale, 2008). These problems are exacerbated for families who speak languages other than English (Kalyanpur & Harry, 1999; Lo, 2008; Salas, 2004). Other barriers to participation include meetings scheduled in conflict with working or caring for other children; securing transportation to the school; and poor translation or interpretation for families who speak languages other than English (Kalyanpur & Harry, 1999; Rogers, 2002). The two frameworks of cultural reciprocity and person-centered planning provide promising guidelines to create more affirmative and productive collaborative planning.

Cultural Reciprocity

Disability advocates and researchers have long observed that the medical model of disability positions professionals as experts on disability and the treatment of disabled persons. One of the ways this presumption of expertise is practiced and upheld is in what Kalyanpur and Harry (2012) identify as the often unspoken mores performed in a culture of special education. The culture of special education, which also reflects a broader culture of schools, presumes that teaching is a practice of technical rationalism in which there is an objective and scientific approach for any given need. With regard to disability, the prevalence of the medical model compels educators to perceive the impairment as the primary need according to which educational approaches are recommended. Traditional planning practices for students with disabilities, then, have primarily emphasized a child's problems with reliance on professionals to direct a course of remediation. The type of remediation and accommodation have often related to assumptions about the disability category, rather than with specific attention to the particularities of the individual or understandings of the family. The culture of special education, Kalyanpur and Harry (2012) describe, forwards disability as an objective, therefore neutral, position. For families, however, as Reiman et al. (2010), Valle and Aponte (2002), Danforth and Smith (2005), and Lalvani (2012) describe, the discourse of disability in schools shapes negative and impersonal characterizations of the child, and can also devalue family experiences and understandings. First, parenting is an experience characterized by emotion and depth of relationship, which is positioned in opposition to the veil of objectivity often advanced in school discourse. Second, the understandings about disability forwarded in the medical model may be inconsistent with families' understandings about disability as informed by their cultural or religious traditions.

In addition to conflicts between school talk and family perceptions about children, another barrier to productive and equitable relationships may be found in special education language. One way that the expertise of trained professionals is expressed and asserted is through the use of clinical language. Special education discourse is rife with acronyms (e.g., IEP, LRE, LD, ABA, etc.), euphemisms (e.g., "special needs"), and jargon (e.g., self-contained, one-to-one, transition, resource room, etc.). More specific locales are likely to have idiosyncratic ways to refer to special education practices. "12 to 1," for example, as in, "She can go into a 12 to 1," is a way that a district might refer to a special education class that has a ratio of 12 students to 1 teacher. A layperson attending a special education evaluation or planning meeting can understandably become confused in the "alphabet soup" of talk. It is also possible that a parent may not realize the implications of what is being discussed when euphemisms veil direct language about disability or the nature of the class or accommodations that are being recommended. The use of special education language not only interferes with clarity, but also serves to position families as outsiders to the discussion. Many parents, when entered into the special education process either at the birth of a child with a disability or at entry to school, quickly adopt a posture of advocate and strive to learn the discourse of special education in order to attain a more powerful position in educational discussions (Lalvani, 2012). Families who are already privileged within the culture of power, which associates authority with Whiteness and credibility with high social class and the use of standard English, learn to affirm their privilege through accruing the benefits of additional resources through special education (Brantlinger, 2003; Hale, 2008). Families with less privilege and whose parenting, cultural, and language practices are either unsupported or systematically devalued within the culture of power, are more likely to experience special education as an oppressive force imposed on their children (Blanchett, 2006; Collins, 2003; Rogers, 2002). Ample studies demonstrate, however, that many families—privileged and not—experience special education and entry into clinical disability discourses as combative, rather than supportive, engagements with professionals (Rogers, 2011).

Creating a seat at the table for families of children with disabilities may be conceived of through the relational process of cultural reciprocity (Kalyanpur & Harry, 2012). Because professionals in special education are in the presumed position of power with regard to school practices, much of the work in building cultural reciprocity may begin with the course of professional preparation and proceed in ongoing reflective practice during work with children and families. Professionals may:

- Seek awareness of varied ways that individuals, cultures, and religions may conceptualize disability and the treatment of disabled people, with a posture of openness, not evaluation.
- Engage in outreach and ongoing conversations with the individual families with whom they work to learn about shared and conflicting ideas and goals, with a posture toward mutual understanding and respect.
- Seek self-awareness of assumptions and stereotypes—related to race, culture, social class, sexuality, language, and gender—that may influence interactions, and work toward reducing bias and prejudice in work with families.
- Adopt a position as partner, rather than expert; advocate and facilitator, rather than director.
- Seek knowledge and understanding about varied approaches to parenting and views of schooling, in consideration of differences between home and school contexts.
- Be aware of professional jargon and make purposeful efforts to, (1) limit euphemisms and unnecessarily complicated language, and (2) ensure that all parties have opportunities to learn language and concepts that are essential to informed participation. In other words, eliminate language that is needlessly confusing, and explain important terms.

A key idea in practicing cultural reciprocity is understanding that professional discourses in special education are not neutral, or objective—they relate to a medical tradition that is fraught with subjectivities and values just as any other system of meaning. There are many truths and perspectives about disability and education and all may be considered and treated respectfully in work with disabled children and their families. Working toward mutual understanding is one way to construct relationships in which all those who participate in the care and education of a child may be valued for their role and contribution.

Person-Centered Planning

Person-centered planning refers to practices that seek to de-center medical narratives of disability and disablement and work toward holistic and situated understandings of individuals and educational planning. Rather than generate goals and plans in relation to an assumption of what disability may mean for an individual, person-centered planning takes fuller account of unique aspects of identity, desire, and the relationships and life contexts that inform the development of a meaningful education. Consistent with disability rights, person-centered planning may be coupled with the aims of nurturing positive disability identity and self-advocacy. A positive disability identity is not one that ignores or seeks to erase impairment or disablement, but one that embraces and strives to value the self in a culture that more often characterizes disability as relative dysfunction and failed potential (Johnson, 2005; Linton, 2007; Muragami, 2009; Valente, 2011). Self-determination is active and meaningful participation in directing the course of one's life, while self-advocacy additionally emphasizes that being and becoming self-determined often requires people with disabilities—especially those deemed intellectually disabled or autistic—to simultaneously engage in work to expose discrimination that prevents self-determination. In disability communities, self-advocacy may be perceived functionally, as the development of a skill-set for communication and expression, but is also forwarded as a political activity in response to the widespread characterization of disabled persons as incompetent. There are many frameworks, guidelines, and protocols available that illustrate person-centered planning, with varying degrees of attention to disability identity and self-advocacy.

Making Action Plans, typically referred to as MAPS, was first developed in 1989 by O'Brien, Forest, Snow, Pearpoint, and Hasbury. MAPS provides a protocol for gathering a group of family members, friends, and professionals to create a holistic portrait of a person's identity, dreams, and needs in preparation for developing an educational plan. In MAPS, a facilitator guides the person of focus to describe their history, dreams and hopes, and fears, while they or another group member records what is communicated on corresponding sheets of chart paper that all can see. Other participants also contribute to the discussion and add to the charted ideas. Two other charts are: "Who is . . .?," that should capture a ranging account of aspects of identity, and "needs," which is developed by the group as they review and synthesize the ideas represented on the other charts. The "needs" chart, in other words, should directly reflect the bridges required to realize the dreams of the person of focus and reduce factors contributing to fears, in concert with identity and history. Ideally, the person of focus and family members select participants and the facilitator of the process, which may enable them to feel more in control of the planning process than has historically been the case. The MAPS process is designed to precede the development of a formal education plan, such as an IEP or transition plan. This type of gathering has the potential to de-mystify the process of educational planning and create contexts through which shared understanding can be built.

Building Relationships between Schools and Families

Cultural reciprocity may be used as a framework to inform the purpose and process of shared planning protocols, like MAPS. When brought together, the MAPS process can help students, families, and school professionals to articulate and make visible similarities and differences in thinking. To move forward, a posture of cultural reciprocity can ensure that all perspectives are discerned and contemplated. There are many other ways teachers can strive to build affirmative and productive interactions with families.

Before a formal process like MAPS may be planned, contact families at the beginning of the school year as an introduction and also to gain insight into their experiences, thoughts, and desires for their child. This can be a great opportunity to listen to ideas about how the child was successful in the past, as well as finding out about her or his interests and/or life outside of school. Initiating early and open communication is a great way to start positively, and will make it easier to reach out to the family if conflicts or challenges arise.

Provide families with contact information and the best times to be reached—for example, during preparation periods or before and after the school day. Consider that email or phone may not be comfortable or accessible to everyone. Providing multiple ways to communicate demonstrates interest in two-way communication.

Although most schools offer special events for families to meet teachers and visit the school, it is also beneficial to extend a personal invitation for family members to visit the class. This may be especially welcome for those who are unable to attend events offered only once.

Sending out periodic newsletters or social media posts describing what the class is studying can be interesting to families. Students may also enjoy suggesting what to include and participate in creating them. Family members who have related knowledge, experiences, or ideas may be guest presenters or help facilitate a field trip. It is important, however, to ensure that the format is accessible to families—do consider the languages families may be most comfortable with and communicating in multiple formats. For example, using a text-based blog (web log) with translation and screen reading or read aloud tools can ensure wide accessibility, as well making sure to also send paper copies for families with limited access to technology.

Avoid using a "call home" as a threat to students. Communication between families and teachers is better construed as an ongoing relationship, rather than an occasional means of punishment. Interactions surrounding students' negative behavior or performance are, in fact, linked with reduced family involvement in school (McNeal, 2012). In other words, while teachers may aim to gain or increase family support by reporting student difficulties, such reports may produce the opposite effect. From another angle, regularly communicating successes and accomplishments is more likely to nurture a satisfying partnership among teachers and families.

There are many ways that teachers and schools can promote positive and productive relationships with students and their families. It is important, however, to take cues from the community to understand the kind of partnerships and understand that multiple efforts may be required. Not all families (or communities) have had pleasant interactions with schools. Extending oneself is certainly in the best interest of the student, and the benefits of school–family collaboration can be immense.

DEVELOPING THE INDIVIDUALIZED EDUCATION PROGRAM

Building relationships and working toward developing shared understandings among students, families, and professionals are useful goals for educational practice and planning. Being aware of barriers to participation and taking actions to reduce them over a long term can make the formal process of developing the annual IEP for a child with a disability a constructive and satisfying experience for all. The requirement of an IEP is often described as the cornerstone of the IDEIA, as it is a binding document that defines how the school will provide a child with an appropriate education in the LRE. It is a contract between a child, family, and the school, which describes aims and criteria for success, as well as the special educational services that will be provided to enable progress and achievement. An IEP must include:

(1) a description of the child's current levels of academic performance, which addresses how the disability affects her or his participation in learning and school;
(2) measurable educational and functional goals and objectives that should enable the child to make progress in the general curriculum;
(3) a description of how progress toward the goals will be measured;
(4) a description of the classroom setting(s), special education services, and supplementary aids that will be provided to the child, which must adhere to the LRE requirement;
(5) a description of accommodations required or alternate measures to enable the child to participate in State or school-wide assessments;
(6) the dates for beginning the educational program and intermittent assessment of progress;
(7) for students 16 and older, a description of goals and instruction to support the student to make the *transition* from school to post-school life.

The descriptions of the child and her or his educational program written for the IEP are developed by an IEP Team. The IEP Team includes: (a) the parent(s)/guardian(s); (b) at least one special education teacher or service provider; (c) a general education teacher, if the child is or might participate in general education; (d) a representative of the school district, usually a school administrator; (e) an individual who can interpret the results of educational assessments, usually a psychologist or other licensed educational evaluator; (f) any other parties with supporting knowledge or experience with the child, at the parent(s)' or school's discretion; and—most important—(g) the child, "whenever appropriate," to quote IDEIA.

An IEP should be developed according to the expertise and contributions of all members of the IEP Team. At minimum, the school must hold at least one meeting per year to review the child's progress and plan or review the IEP for the subsequent annual period. The IEP should be agreed upon by all parties, and the parent/guardian consents to its implementation by signing. It is the responsibility of all teachers and personnel who work with a child who receives special educational services to read his or her IEP, and to comply with the goals, objectives, services, assessment methods and schedule, and accommodations described within. To ensure the implementation of an IEP, cultivating collaborative practices among all members of the team is essential. As earlier described, work to build such relationships precedes the IEP meeting. The IEP, then, may be seen as a culmination of shared planning, rather than the place to start.

COLLABORATIVE IEP MEETINGS

There are many practices professionals can implement to make the IEP meeting more affirmative and productive for everyone, including the MAPS process. Creating a constructive climate concerns the arrangements made before the meeting, as well as interactions during it. In scheduling the meeting it is useful to offer various options for the meeting time and place, which demonstrate consideration of the family member's work and other responsibilities. Making sure teachers' and other professionals' schedules are clear is also essential so that they are not pressured during the meeting. Providing travel arrangements to family participants is part of IDEIA, so ensuring parents know it is a right and not a "favor" communicates the school's interest in working together. Ensuring translating or interpreter services are arranged and are of high quality is essential for families who speak languages other than English. Parents in one study suggested that IEP forms be provided in advance of the meeting so they could review and be prepared to discuss them (Simon, 2006). An advance phone discussion about any changes or developments may also be warranted, so that parents do not feel ambushed at the meeting. Beginning the collaborative process begins with facilitating parents' ability to attend the meeting and enabling them to be prepared to participate.

When it is time for the meeting it is useful to have a planned format that aims for collaboration and equal participation among the members of the IEP Team. Kroeger, Leibold, and Ryan (1999), for example, offer a vision of IEP meetings as collaborative processes of educational planning and suggest ways to make them more accessible to students and families. A facilitator, not a "leader," may begin with having members, including the student, set a format for participation and a time frame. Visual cues can help keep everyone on track: A chalkboard, whiteboard, or chart can be used to record participants' knowledge about the learner's strengths, talents, difficulties, and educational needs. A shared vision for the student's goals and desires should be developed through attending to the recorded knowledge, prioritizing areas of need, and arriving at consensus about the best ways school and related services can enable the learner to meet his or her goals. The facilitator's role should aim to cultivate active participation by all, ensure that members understand each other, and keep track of time—to be respectful of participants' schedules and avoid a need to rush to decisions.

Having a protocol that maximizes everyone's understanding of the meeting content and that provides a process for all to participate nurtures collaboration and mutual respect. A format like this may also be used to resolve disagreements about an IEP (Mueller, 2009). Adding a neutral facilitator and setting ground rules for respectful communication and turn-taking can help turn contentious situations into productive ones. Being able to solve IEP disputes collaboratively is surely preferred to taking them to formal mediation, as IDEIA allows.

Schools are busy places and school professionals are usually working with many students in what never seems like enough time. Additionally, far too many schools are understaffed and poorly resourced. These constraints often lead to IEP meetings feeling rushed and as though they are formalities, rather than collaborations. This is especially the case when the planning seems already completed and documents are merely presented for parents to sign; when parents and students attend a meeting only to listen and nod (Fish, 2008). This type of meeting creates a situation in which families must ask to make changes instead of having been part of the process to begin with. To practice IEP meetings as spaces of genuine collaboration requires them to be envisioned as such. School professionals can be open to parents' and students' ideas and suggestions about the educational program. School administrators, especially, need to provide time and support so that teachers and other school professionals can devote the necessary time to cultivating relationships and working with students and families.

Student-Led IEP Meetings

If collaboration with families is important, then including the student in the IEP process is essential. MAPS provides one protocol for centering the student in educational planning. It is also strongly recommend that students attend their IEP meetings and desirable that they be placed in leadership roles to guide their annual review meetings (IDEIA, 2004; Mason, McGahee-Kovac, & Johnson, 2004; Martin et al., 1996). Students can learn about the purpose and structure of the IEP meeting, and should be encouraged to express their thoughts about their educational progress, their immediate goals, and long-term desires. Students of all ages can participate. Mason, McGahee-Kovac, and Johnson (2004) note:

> Although it is perhaps easiest for teachers to envision students in high school preparing to leave school as IEP team leaders, we have experience implementing student-led IEPs with students as young as 6 years of age. The vocabulary is different, and the degree of responsibility is different; however, the concept of leadership is maintained through the emphasis that is placed on asking the child about what is important to him or her and using that information in planning goals.
>
> (p. 22)

Some professionals and families may be hesitant to include children and adolescents in IEP planning because of the presumed need to talk about difficulties, which may be upsetting to a child and uncomfortable to professionals; or to protect the child from knowing the disability with which they have been labeled. Perhaps the rationale for including students is evident in reasons offered to exclude them: Professionals can learn how to talk about students in candid, but respectful ways; and children and adolescents have a right and need to know the disabilities attributed to them and should not be made to feel ashamed. Providing opportunities for students to learn how to self-advocate and play a role in educational planning places the individual at the center of his experiences, and honors the values of independence and self-determination, most dear to disability rights.

School professionals and families can support students to engage in their IEP meetings by encouraging their early attendance and explaining the process. There are also a number of programs and guides for assistance available. The Self-Directed IEP, developed by Martin, Marshall, Maxson, and Jerman (1996) is a program that includes lessons, video, and other materials that can be used to teach students about the IEP meeting and develop skills that can enable them to lead their meetings. Participating in the meetings empowers students to direct their education, as well as provides a forum for others to perceive their competence.

The IEP meeting has long been a source of negative feelings for families of students with disabilities. There are, however, many practices that school professionals can implement in order to use this meeting time as the collaborative space for which it is intended. Recognizing the positive contribution families and students can have in the process is the first step; planning for attendance and participation is the second; and developing respectful, inviting procedures for collaboration during the meeting is the third. Working proactively and amenably benefits all stakeholders. Students especially benefit, as they participate in their educational planning and self-advocate for their needs and desires, a major aim of disability rights and disability studies.

PROFESSIONAL COLLABORATION IS ESSENTIAL

In addition to collaborating with students and families in educational planning and problem solving, the inclusive educator should expect to work with a variety of other school professionals. Inviting and welcoming consultation and engaging in collaborative planning and teaching is a necessity in ensuring that the needs of students with disabilities are addressed comprehensively, consistently, and holistically. In addition to sharing specific kinds of expertise to best meet the needs of students, a benefit of collaboration is in building and maintaining relationships that can facilitate a friendly and satisfying work environment. For all collaborations, standards of professional interactions should be followed. In other words, all should be given respect and treated as welcome classroom members or consultants. When working together, members of a professional team should be introduced to all students and adults. Whenever possible, classroom routines and the instructional plans for a given day should be developed together; at minimum, a description of instruction or service provision should be shared with all who may attend a class. Establishing roles and discussing the kinds of instruction or support that are being performed or may be needed can help with negotiating the changing environment of a classroom and ensure that all adults are able to contribute in appropriate and supportive ways. Descriptions of the most common kinds of professional collaboration follow.

Consulting and Supportive Roles

Special educators provide a variety of instructional services that can be performed in many structures and settings, which reflect the continuum of settings and services specified in the IDEIA. Supplemental support, sometimes described as resource rooms, refers to a service in which a special educator works with an individual or small group of students with disabilities to provide support on curriculum offered in another setting or to provide a specialized curriculum. Supplemental support may be provided within a large-class setting or in a small-group or individual setting. In either arrangement, the special educator should work with students' other teachers to understand their needs and performance in other settings, the design and requirements of grade-level curriculum, and to offer her or his own experience to help other teachers work with shared students.

Collaborative Teaching, or Co-Teaching

Collaborative teaching generally refers to a teaching arrangement in which a general education teacher and special education teacher work together to provide instruction to a class of students with and without disabilities. Collaborative teaching is the arrangement that best relates to inclusive education. Students in co-taught classrooms have the benefit of two teachers with whom to learn and gain support. Just as teachers support students, they can also support each other. To best implement co-teaching, teachers can:

(1) Get to know and work with all children in the class, regardless of disability status;
(2) Plan curriculum and instruction together, and in a way that allows both teachers to contribute their experience and expertise—ideas for planning inclusive curriculum are addressed in Chapter 9;
(3) Share responsibilities and classroom roles;
(4) Participate in the assessment and evaluation of all children, regardless of disability status.

In brief, co-teachers work as a team—with equal status and responsibilities. Collaborative teaching is high on the list of initiatives in inclusive education, and resources with ideas for how to structure classes, determine roles and responsibilities, and establish effective planning and teaching practices are widely available.

Specialists and Related Services

Schools employ a variety of specialists who may work with teachers and students to address needs related to learning, health, and/or access to schools and instruction. A related service is broadly defined in IDEIA, and can include anything from school health services to speech therapy to psychological, and even family, counseling. Specialists of all kinds may work with an individual or group of students outside of the usual instructional environment in a "pull-out" arrangement or they may "push-in" to a class and address needs of an individual or group in conjunction with class instruction. Some of the more common specialists and related services are described in terms of typical services performed in schools.

Paraprofessionals or School Aides

It is possible that a class may have a paraprofessional or teacher's assistant assigned to support class instruction. An individual student may have a paraprofessional or aide assigned specifically to him or her to help with health and personal needs or with instruction.

Speech-Language Pathologists

Speech-Language Pathologists (SLP) or therapists are specialized professionals who work with children who need help with articulating speech or language development. An SLP is not the same as a teacher who specializes in teaching English to speakers of other languages.

Audiologist

An audiologist is a specialist in hearing, who may diagnose, treat, and monitor auditory disorders. She or he may provide training for teachers or students related to using hearing aids, amplification devices, or cochlear implants.

Interpreters

Students' right to assessment in their native language is described in the IDEIA. Interpreters for languages other than English may be a part of the assessment process, or may assist at meetings with families who require them to participate in school planning. Interpreters for American Sign Language (ASL) may be permanent members of the classroom if there are students who communicate with ASL.

Counselors and Psychologists

Schools may provide any variety of mental heath or therapeutic services. Students may receive individual or group counseling or therapy as part of their school program and related services. A mental health counselor, counseling psychologist, or school psychologist is a licensed mental health professional and is different from a guidance counselor, who is a licensed school professional. The school psychologist is part of the IEP Team and may perform assessments and/or provide therapy or counseling. Except in crisis situations in which harm to others or self is imminent, counselors and psychologists must respect the confidentiality of students and families. However, collaboration and professional communication among parties can lead to joint efforts to support a student's psychosocial development and goals.

Social Workers

Social workers are part of the IEP Team, and may also provide services to students and their families. The social worker connects children and families with social resources and networks to improve quality of life, which may include anything from connecting families with support groups to helping them seek better housing; from connecting a student with a potential employer to dealing with issues of abuse or neglect.

Occupational Therapists

Occupational therapists (OT) generally provide consultation and instruction to support the fullest participation and independence in life activities for students with physical, motor, or sensory impairments. They may help assess and adapt the physical environment, provide adaptive equipment, or provide exercises or training to enable independence in school tasks and life activities. For example, OTs may provide a pencil grip to enable independence in writing, offer training or exercises to help a student build dexterity in order to better grip a pencil, or work on helping a student use a different method for written expression—like typing. OTs or orientation specialists may also support students with orthopedic or visual impairments to learn how to negotiate the physical environment using a cane or crutches, for example, as well as how to perform life activities, such as eating, dressing, or cooking. A final role that an OT may fill is in working with students to develop skills and strategies that support social interaction, play, and responding to sensory stimuli in the environment.

Physical Therapists

The work of physical therapists may overlap with occupational therapists, though the focus of "PTs" is on improving, developing, or teaching ways of moving the body that aim to strengthen the body and/or manage or reduce pain toward maximizing physical function. In schools, PT may be provided for students who are working on increasing strength and technique to adapt to physical impairment, for example, or as a way to maintain strength or range of motion.

Health Professionals

Health professionals typically include nurses or specialized aides who attend to physiological needs, although mental health professionals, or a psychiatrist, may also be a part of this category. Nurses may administer medication or help monitor a student who has had a seizure, for example; aides may assist with health needs such as eating or going to the bathroom.

Related services have traditionally been offered outside of classrooms. That is, the therapist would take a student or small group of students to an office and provide instruction or therapy there. The students would then return to class. The "pull-out" model has long been thought to provide students specialized instruction in a highly focused environment in which to practice a much needed skill. There are also criticisms of the model, however. First, the pulled out students presumably miss the activity that is occurring in the classroom. The students, at worst, miss instruction and have to make-up work. At best, they miss social experience and have to catch up with their peers at a later time. Either way, there is a gap in the students' experience with regard to class activities. A second criticism is that skills learned in isolation are more difficult for students to transfer, or generalize, to the classroom contexts in which they will be most useful. For example, using specific reading strategies to decode challenging words is most needed when reading a text in social studies. The ability to grip a pencil is key in mathematics, and using methods to manage frustration or anger are best utilized in the setting where the emotions are likely to occur. Because of these criticisms, it is increasingly recommended that related services be provided within the classroom instruction—in other words, inclusively. When related services are provided in a classroom, collaboration among professionals, similar to co-teaching guidelines, may be appropriate. All professionals should be aware of each other's goals and efforts should be made to integrate aims as much as possible.

CONCLUSION

The African proverb, "it takes a village to raise a child," is a wise comment applicable to the development of collaborative educational practices. Children benefit from families and professionals who work together on their behalf. Whether co-teaching, consulting with professionals, or reaching out to families, working closely with others is a necessity for inclusive education. While there are barriers that can prevent effective communication and partnerships, there are also many ways that teachers can initiate and nurture positive relationships.

9

INSTRUCTIONAL DESIGN FOR INCLUSIVE EDUCATION

Instructional design refers to the way educators organize activities of teaching and learning. It involves consideration of learning goals, materials, and experiences that are offered to students in connection with understandings about the way people learn. The decisions we make about instructional design are rooted in learning theory, as well as relate to particular values of public education. In other words, we desire to teach in ways that are likely to support students to learn academic content and how to work with others in a democratic society. We begin this chapter with an overview of values and theories of learning that relate to inclusive practice. We then offer an introduction to the application of universal design in learning as an organizing framework for inclusive instructional design.

RESISTING NORMATIVE PRACTICES

The concept of the norm is a statistical assumption, much more than is a reality in the complexity of human lives and experiences. Differences enable our distinctive appearances, talents, and interests, therefore variety in academic performance should also be anticipated. The central ideals of inclusive education are to query the problem of narrow conceptualizations of normality. It is only when we determine a norm, expect it, and favor those who seem to comply with our expectations that we label and marginalize. A tenet of inclusive teaching practice is to resist beliefs and practices that promote one "normal" way to live and learn. Instead inclusive education seeks to broaden the range of experiences that can be valued and embraced in schools.

The tradition of parallel systems of general and special education ingrained in most educators' experiences inhibits our ability to think creatively and broadly about all kinds of learning that happens in the "general" environment. Similarly, the idea of a single curriculum in which all children are supposed to do and learn in the same ways is a powerful, long-lasting image of classroom instruction that is simply not viable for inclusive education. Similar to reflecting on what we think about "normal" and "abnormal," thinking inclusively about teaching starts with developing beliefs and images of schooling that emphasize the growth of the whole child and all children.

To resist normative practices educators may critique existing curriculum and teaching practices to discern embedded assumptions about the nature of knowledge and understandings about diversity of culture and experience. Engaging in criticality requires applying a consciousness of cultural privilege and marginality to examine the ways that curriculum likely centers, for example, Whiteness, ability, heteronormativity, masculinity, or Anglo-European language and culture. Preparing to offer multicultural curriculum can begin with ensuring that materials for study offer a diversity of perspectives and that the course of study enables learners to develop their own criticality about the culture of power and collective work to learn, embrace, and sustain traditions and identities of self and others. To further engage in critical practice, however, educators must attend to the immediate context of teaching and learning. A philosophy and organization of classroom practice that makes visible the contributions and desires of learners, teachers, and the broader ideas about curriculum that influence both, is necessary.

Democratic schooling is an educational concept and philosophy that relates to the creation of curriculum that engages learners in shared dialog and work with others to enable them to be active participants in a democratic society. In the foundational work, *Democracy and Education*, philosopher and education theorist, John Dewey (1916), described:

A democracy is more than a form of government; it is primarily a mode of associated living, of conjoint communicated experience. The extension in space of the number of individuals who participate in an interest so that each has to refer his own action to that of others, and to consider the action of others to give point and direction to his own, is equivalent to the breaking down of those barriers of class, race, and national territory which kept men from perceiving the full import of their activity.

(p. 87)

In other words, democracy is a way of life in which communities of people shape their worlds and actions in concert with each other. Engagement in dialog and shared action with many individuals allows many perspectives and experiences to be considered for action toward mutually beneficial goals.

The relationship of democratic schooling to inclusive curriculum and critical multiculturalism is strong. Oyler (2001) offers four considerations for teaching that can enable students to learn how to engage in democracy through school curriculum. They are:

1) Searching for strengths in all learners
2) Expanding beyond the whole-class, uniform-lesson format
3) Utilizing flexible grouping strategies
4) Fostering collaborative problem solving

(p. 29)

The first three recommendations change the traditional teaching and learning arrangements. Instead of looking only for problems, educators search for strengths; instead of assuming students must all learn in a teacher-centered format or only with same-ability peers, varied grouping and formats may be used. The fourth recommendation to foster collaborative problem solving provides the opportunity for students to play a central role in proposing areas of study. The opportunity in using problem-posing and problem-solving as the basis for learning offers deep and meaningful contexts to draw from students' lived experiences, build on their knowledge of self and community, and extend understanding of inequity and relationships of power.

Students of all ages can find problems to investigate in the real world. Incorporating their ideas and making learners' interests central to curriculum increases their engagement and provides experiences in the democratic process itself. Oyler (2001), for example, described the shift in a course of study on ancient nomadic life when a student, named Rachel, wondered about similarities between nomads and people without permanent homes in contemporary society. The course of study bloomed into an investigation that provided students the opportunity to explore current news media and community resources toward understanding a contemporary problem. Schultz (2008) similarly describes fourth-grade students' yearlong investigation into the failure of their city's government to repair or replace their dilapidated school. What began as a group brainstorm of problems that affected students in the class exploded into a vigorous campaign to petition for a new school. Students studied political process and media analysis by studying documents and literature related to their cause and actively engaging in these forums as concerned and informed citizens.

Both Oyler (2001) and Schultz (2008), among many others, have demonstrated the impact that engagement in democratic processes of education has on students. When student-identified interests and problems are taken up as courses of study, we engage them in real and important work—as students in Schultz's class noted; and we allow them to live the benefits of engaging with others in shared study and dialog—as Rachel, in Oyler's (2001) essay, pointed out. Hardly detracting from students' development of academic skills in literacy, for example, Schultz notes the "spectacular" growth of students enabled by this kind of personally meaningful curriculum. To end with Dewey's (1916) words, a democratic society,

> must have a type of education which gives individuals a personal interest in social relationships and control, and the habits of mind which secure social changes without introducing disorder.
>
> (p. 99)

Inclusive education is best developed as practices that engage students in authentic problem solving that emanates from their experiences. Rather than needing to retrofit curriculum to be culturally or ability responsive, beginning with context-specific problems provide a compelling and inclusive context for study. The nature of group problem solving offers a natural distribution of tasks that allows varied ways of participating, opportunities to learn from others, and the development of interdisciplinary content-area knowledge and academic skills.

LEARNING THEORIES

The basis for democratic schooling primarily relates to ideals in active political engagement, though is also supported by psychological-cognitive, and social theories of learning and development. Constructivism refers to a family of theories of learning and development, initially posed by Swiss psychologist, Jean Piaget, during the early twentieth century. Piaget was interested in describing and understanding the importance of children's play to their cognitive development (Fosnot, 2005). The essential tenet of constructivism is that children generate knowledge (i.e., learn) from their own experiences. Through experiencing the world by engaging with natural phenomena and information gathered through the senses, children build "theories" about how things work and what things mean, then "test" those theories in order to arrive at knowledge. The theories and knowledge that children generate and understand as truth change, however, as varying cognitive abilities develop, as they accrue more experiences, and as they gain access to the knowledge of others, including formal knowledge.

The implications of constructivism for curriculum and teaching center on children's need to learn through experience, or learn by doing. As children actively engage with phenomena to be studied, they are able to build ideas about what is happening from their own perspectives and then test those theories against subsequent experiences, which may include an introduction to a formalized concept. For example, children can learn that *to add* means to increase quantity through manipulating building blocks to create lesser and greater quantities, then matching those quantities to numbers. As the child is able to see and feel the increase of quantity, he or she can understand that adding means to increase quantity. In constructivist approaches to learning, children are provided with authentic (i.e., manipulating blocks), rather than abstract (i.e., only working with numbers and symbols), experiences through which to develop understandings about phenomena.

Constructivist approaches to curriculum and teaching correspond well to inclusive education because they place the learner at the center of his or her knowledge-making. It is expected that children will develop knowledge and understanding through different means and at different rates because we all have varied experiences and prior knowledge that will inform the ways we encounter and learn new ideas. Common educational approaches that relate to constructivism include: "hands-on" learning, discovery learning, the Montessori method, named for developer Maria Montessori, and Reggio-Emilia methods, which are named for a region in Italy (Fosnot, 2005).

Social constructivist theories of learning, initially described by the Russian psychologist, Lev Vygotsky (Vygotsky, 1986), are similar to constructivist theories. Both theories posit knowledge to be actively constructed by learners, though social constructivism offers a more extensive focus on the social and cultural contexts in which learners form motivation and intent to learn and acquire the tools to generate knowledge—primarily, language. Although Vygotsky was developing ideas at the same time as Piaget, Vygotsky's work was relatively unknown to the Western world until the English translation of his works during the 1960s. The contribution of social constructivism to educational approaches is most evident in the concept of learning as *apprenticeship*. In this view, children learn through their active engagement with members who are more experienced in the activity. In the classroom, those more experienced may be teachers or other students. Three basic relational stages of growth toward mastering an activity can be characterized as: *novice*, in which the apprentice observes and/or copies actions that seem important to an activity; *dependence*, in which the apprentice can accomplish some facets of an activity with support; and *independence*, in which the learner is able to fully engage in an activity and direct his or efforts appropriately to a novel task of the same kind.

Three related concepts intrinsic to social constructivism have, perhaps, the greatest influence on contemporary approaches to teaching and efforts to refine instructional methods.

- *Zone of Proximal Development* (ZPD). The ZPD refers to the range of skills or tasks that a child cannot do independently, but can with support. It is this "zone" from which goals and objectives for a child's curriculum should be drawn. Nearly all kinds of classroom-based assessment aim to determine the ZPD in order to meet the needs of children.
- *Scaffolding.* As a child acts as a novice-apprentice, the more experienced "expert" acts to *scaffold* the tasks or activity by providing the necessary support to enable to novice-apprentice to learn the essential skills. Scaffolding learning is analogous to a scaffold in construction—external supports that enable work to be done on a structure before it is internally sound. Modeling, or demonstrating how to engage in a task or activity, is an initial kind of scaffold. Offering guided practice, or leading learners through the steps of an activity, is also a way of scaffolding.
- *Mediation.* Finally, *mediation* describes the context and means by which novices learn from experts. For example, the social context in which a skill is learned, the materials presented to a learner, and the language and style of language in which instruction is offered are each intervening, middle forces, that substantively affect the course of learning. *Cultural mediation* refers to the tremendous impact of culture on the ways in which people learn to use language, think, and behave. Members of varying cultures value and perform ways of interacting and thinking and kinds of knowledge differently from one another. *Sociocultural perspectives* on teaching and learning put forth the implications of cultural mediation to education. Collins (2003) succinctly describes, "a sociocultural perspective suggests examining the intersection of environment and individual to understand how they mutually construct each other" (p. 3). Social models of disability are derived from this family of thought.

The centrality of understanding students' and teachers' prior experiences toward establishing effective ways to construct learning activities cannot be overstated. Construed generally, it is essential to attend to how learners interact with materials and others and how they are enabled to interact with these mediating forces in the classroom. The concept that students performing varied ranges of competence and with varied backgrounds and experiences learn from each other while engaging in shared activity relates strongly to ideals of democratic schooling. Aside from the innumerable methods for teaching that recommend differentiating instruction according to students' ZPD and practices that act as scaffolds, methods of teaching that strongly relate to sociocultural theories of learning include: Guided Inquiry (Burns, 2005; Palincsar, 1998) and Cooperative Learning (Gutierrez, Baquedano-Lopez, Alvarez, & Chiu, 1999; Johnson & Johnson, 1999).

UNIVERSAL DESIGN IN EDUCATION

Both constructivism and social constructivism offer theories that characterize learning as dynamic processes influenced by the culture and prior knowledge of the individual, in conjunction with the social context in which instruction is provided. Support for these approaches to instruction for students with disabilities is growing (Morocco, 2001). The ideal of the democratic classroom aims to offer school experiences that value and respond to diversity and provide students with knowledge, skills and dispositions to interact within and be able to influence a democratic society. Universal design in education provides a broad framework to conceptualize the kinds of teaching practices that can meet our aims.

Universal design frameworks for curriculum development and teaching practice were developed on the ideas of architect and wheelchair-user, Ronald Mace (Mace, Hardie, & Place, 1990), who first proposed *universal design* (UD) as the creation of physical spaces that are both functional and elegant for the broadest possible constituency (McGuire, Scott, & Shaw, 2006). Mace and his colleagues conceptualized UD as a philosophy not only of access, but of community. The seven principles that define UD are: (a) equitable use, (b) flexibility in use, (c) simple and intuitive, (d) perceptible information, (e) tolerance for error, (f) low physical effort, and (g) size and space for approach and use (Connell et al., 1997). For example, a building designed universally might feature a gently sloping incline as an entrance, rather than having both a set of stairs and a designated wheelchair ramp. Designing this way provides entry to many, and might also maximize the use of space and be more aesthetically pleasing than building two entryways. In education, UD seeks the same elegance and functionality in a conceptualization of planning, teaching, and learning that presumes all students possess unique sets of strengths and needs.

Early developers drew from the ideas of universal design to apply them to education. Silver, Bourke, and Strehorn (1998) and Bowe (2000) developed the concept of Universal Instructional Design (UID). McGuire, Scott, and Shaw (2006) also draw from the UD principles established by Mace and colleagues to develop the Universal Design of Instruction (UDI) framework. UDI interprets how the seven principles can be interpreted for instruction and adds two additional principles: community of learners and instructional climate. Burgstahler's (2009) description of UDI provides eight categories to consider: (a) class climate, (b) interaction, (c) physical environments and products, (d) delivery methods, (e) information resources and technology, (f) feedback, (g) assessment, and (h) accommodation. The UDI frameworks include attention to class climates that "adopt practices that reflect high values with respect to both diversity and inclusiveness" (Burgstahler, 2009) and that strive for a community of learners that "promotes interaction and communication among students and between students and faculty" . . . and in which "instruction is designed to be welcoming and inclusive" (McGuire, Scott, & Shaw, 2006, p. 170). Especially clear is that UDI is grown from values of inclusivity and community and embraces a social justice mission.

The Center for Applied Special Technology (CAST) is a not-for-profit organization that has been exploring ways of increasing access through technology since 1984. Orkwis and McLane introduced the concept of Universal Design for Learning (UDL) in 1998 (McGuire, Scott, & Shaw, 2006). They described initiatives that could open up access in education by capitalizing on advances in technology, which could make general curriculum more accessible to a variety of learners. Why couldn't schools offer text, digital, and audio versions of a book, for example? Why couldn't a learner type an answer to a question or dictate a response to someone else, instead of performing only in handwriting? Why wouldn't schools presume that many ways of engaging with instruction were possible? Since then CAST researchers have developed the concept of UDL to be a widely recognized framework for instruction. UDL is an orientation to instructional design that aims to anticipate learner diversity and presumes the school's responsibility to take learner variation into account from the start (Rose & Meyer, 2002). In the *Higher Education Opportunity Act* (HEOA), UDL is recommended as means to provide appropriate accommodations toward high achievement expectations for "all students, including students with disabilities and students who are limited English proficient" (HEOA, 2008). Most recently, the *Every Student Succeeds Act* (ESSA, 2015) includes UDL in the definition of comprehensive literacy instruction.

There are two central components of CAST's framework for UDL. First, CAST proposes that UDL is a scientifically valid framework. Founders point to analyses of "experimentation and brain-imaging technologies" (Glass, Meyer, & Rose, 2013, p. 100) that demonstrate diverse patterns of neurological activity across people and within the same person, depending on different affective and disciplinary contexts (Rose & Meyer, 2000; 2002; Meyer, Rose, & Gordon, 2014). They recommend, accordingly, that schools provide flexibility in instructional approaches. The second component of this "brain-based" idea of pedagogy is that flexibility is created to activate specific brain networks associated with learning. Rose and Meyer (2000) discern three main barriers, which correlate to areas of the brain activated during learning, that prohibited the access of students with disabilities to school curriculum:

(1) The mode of *representation* of materials and instruction;
(2) The mode of *expression*, or how students were enabled to perform their learning;
(3) The mode of *engagement*, or method by which students were engaged in learning.

Each of these elements of pedagogy, CAST purports, can be construed to meet the needs of broader, more diverse groups of learners. Pertinent to learning theories described previously, readers will note that each element relates to a mediating force in the social context of classrooms.

Finding ways to modify or adapt materials and practices to include students with disabilities in the general curriculum is commonplace work in special education. Offering larger print materials, using digital texts, and adapting or modifying text were ways to open access to classroom materials. The possibility for students to use technology like computers, word processors, or augmentative communication devices broadened the methods by which students could express learning. Students with disabilities did not need a separate curriculum as much as ways to gain better access to the general curriculum. The shift to imagining inclusion as practices of accessing curriculum signified a shift in the ways inclusion had been thought about, especially for students deemed severely disabled. Wehmeyer (2006), for example, notes the first aim of inclusion was to provide entry to schools and to "the mainstream"; and the second, to improve teaching practices aimed at supporting students with disabilities in inclusive environments, such as co-teaching. The third wave—current practices—aims to improve access to the general education curriculum, and also seeks to ensure students' benefit and progress through instruction. If not evident already, moving away from the one-size-fits-most model of planning and teaching is essential, as captured in Oyler's (2001) advice to expand "beyond the whole-class, uniform-lesson format" (p. 29).

Offering accommodations and modifications to extend access for students with disabilities to the general education environment is necessary, and highly recommended in the IDEIA and education literature. However, there is one caveat in this way of conceptualizing curriculum planning. The notion that some students require "extra" accommodations or modifications to engage with a course of study can categorize and stigmatize students. In other words, constructing provisions for access as supplemental to an otherwise "normal" course of study partitions children into "general education" students and those with needs deemed "special." Unfortunately, children may become characterized by the modifications and accommodations that are needed, which stigmatizes the individual. In addition, work to support children requiring accommodations and modifications may be seen as "extra" work by teachers. Rather than imagine curriculum as a stock set of practices that can become accessible by making "special" accommodations and modifications, it is useful to envision curriculum as flexible and able to be crafted for diverse needs from the beginning. This way of thinking presumes and anticipates learner diversity, rather than aims to retrofit curriculum when a student struggles.

Instruction derived through UDL is equivalent to conceptualizing teaching as a way to offer a spectrum of possibility. Planning with the assumption that learners are individuals who will benefit from a variety of materials, interactions, experiences, and opportunities better attends to the tenets of the most noted learning theories. In addition, presuming diversity and planning for an anticipated range of student ability and competencies reduces the problems caused when students must first fail before getting help. Spooner, Baker, Harris, Ahlgrim-Delzell, and Browder (2007) conducted workshops to introduce UDL to undergraduate and graduate students studying to be general or special educators. They propose:

> universally designed concepts might save teachers an extensive amount of time by creating modified lesson plans rather than changing them after the fact. By

designing lessons before the fact, considering all students using the components of UDL, teachers have a better opportunity to teach a curriculum that actively involves all students. Participants in this study were given approximately 20 min to complete lesson plans during the posttest, and they were able to create a lesson plan with modified instruction for all students, including those with disabilities, within that 20-min time period.

(p. 114)

In UDL, curriculum and instruction can already be designed for the many ways that learners can engage in learning, thus allowing opportunity to emerge in each new moment, in each new day. UDL promises classroom design that is, in Pisha and Coyne's (2001) words, "smart from the start" (p. 197).

UDL IN PRACTICE

Developing teaching practices through a framework of UDL requires attention to three main elements that affect students' access to learning opportunities: (1) planning curriculum; (2) developing materials and instructional methods; and (3) assessing instruction and reflecting on teaching to inform future work.

PLANNING CURRICULUM

There are many factors to consider when figuring out which topics and skills to present for students' study and learning. Some schools use a scope and sequence or curriculum map of topics for study and accompanying skills that teachers are expected to follow. Others use programs and material sets, including textbooks, which lay out the topics of study. In the USA, individual states also describe standards for learning and most provide core curriculum for subject areas, which describe the knowledge and skills students are expected to master. In standardized curriculum, benchmarks for progress are provided and assessed at the ends of the primary, middle, and secondary grades—for example, fourth, eighth, and twelfth. Despite the interest in ensuring all students of the same age are able to meet standards, natural human variation and differences in the kinds of school and out-of-school experiences students have make aiming for a singular goal for all impractical. A more useful concept for inclusive teaching is to ensure all students have ample opportunity to make progress toward individualized goals, while having access to and gaining experience toward meeting State-developed guidelines.

Planning curriculum for a whole class, then, has the dual aims of being both cohesive and individualized. *Differentiated Instruction* is a named approach to this kind of curriculum planning, quite popular in contemporary schools. The term had been used, however, as early as 1959 by Donald Durrell and others. John Dewey had also posed the necessity of developing constructivist curriculum to match individual students' needs, lives, and interests in 1938. Although differentiating instruction is a hot topic in current teaching practice, the ideas that instruction is best developed to meet a range of students' needs and competencies is not one new to the field. To describe recommended practices for planning curriculum in a UDL framework, however, we draw from a selection of contemporary literature to best reflect current educational language.

Developing Coherence in Curriculum

Coherence in curriculum is achieved by developing a broad set of related concepts for a class to study over an extended period of time. These are typically organized as *units of study* that can range anywhere from a few weeks to several months, or even a whole year (described in Schultz's 2008 work, noted previously). Organizing curriculum into units supports the natural ways that people learn new information. We organize new knowledge by building on what we already know. If students are presented with many ideas surrounding a central base of concepts over a period of time, they are better able to organize the information for long-term understanding. In addition, sustained study on a set of central concepts offers more time and the possibility of providing many experiences through which students may develop understanding.

Onosko and Jorgensen (1998), among many others, suggest that inclusive curriculum planning begin with identifying a central unit issue or problem to investigate. The issue or problem should relate to students' lives and enable them to refer to their prior knowledge and experiences. Posing instruction as sets of problems to solve or issues to investigate provides a learning context in which children are able to brainstorm what they already know in order to set directions for new learning, then explore and generate ideas to inform their shared goal of problem-solving, and culminate in deeper understanding of an issue. Because there are many ways to solve problems and investigate issues, everyone can participate in the investigation to her or his own levels of comfort. *Big ideas* and *essential questions* are two concepts to help teachers figure out how to pose problems and issues for study.

Big ideas are conceptual organizers that students will revisit multiple times during the course of their education (McTighe & Brown, 2005). In order to determine big ideas, McTighe and Brown (2005) recommend "unpacking" curriculum standards provided by the state to identify conceptual organizers. An example of a "big idea" related to social studies and a unit on immigration, perhaps, is: People move for a variety of reasons, including economic opportunity, greater freedoms, or to escape something (McTighe & Wiggins, 2004). A big idea may also be broadened to apply to a variety of subject and study. For example, instead of focusing only on the immigration of people, a theme of "movement" might also encompass study on animal migrations. Seeking food, shelter, and more favorable climates could be other reasons posed for movements of these kinds. Even broader, a study of movement could include examination of the various ways that individuals move. Opportunities to explore movement technology and access could easily incorporate disability-related study, and certainly encompass movement goals that a child with physical or multiple disabilities may be working toward in replacement of or in addition to content-area learning.

Essential questions capture problems or issues posed for students to investigate, toward conceptual understanding. They may be big ideas written in question form;

for example, *How have people come to live all over the world?* Or, *How does moving shape the human experience?* Characteristics of essential questions are:

(1) They help students become investigators
(2) They involve thinking, not just answering
(3) They offer a sense of adventure and are fun to explore and to answer
(4) All students can answer them
(5) They require students to connect different disciplines and areas of knowledge.

(Jorgensen, 1996, p. 224)

In the two examples above, opportunities for students to connect study to their varied, individual lives and experiences are abundant. Students may explore their own ways of moving or places they move, or family histories of movement. They may investigate transportation, any number of mass movements of people over history, or any kind of movement of other organisms. Beginning with a shared big idea and set of organizing concepts offers many possibilities for individuating curriculum.

Key concepts, big ideas, and essential questions may be developed according to students' interests in problems they define; in terms of state standards; and/or in terms of other topics and areas of study provided by the school. It is most likely that teachers will consider each of these sources of curriculum. For example, the teacher may present a broad theme recommended by the state and/or school, and then refine it based on student contributions and questions that emerge along the way.

Individuating Curriculum at the Planning Stage

While developing problems, issues, big ideas, and essential questions to characterize the coherence of a unit and shared work around a theme, it is recommended that teachers also consider ways that individual students will demonstrate their understanding of the big ideas. In the *Understanding by Design* framework, Wiggins and McTighe (1998) describe a process of backward planning. Backward planning begins at the end—that is, thinking about the desired end goals in order to support students' learning toward them. Backward planning with inclusive design requires teachers to consider the many ways students may learn toward a theme and ultimately demonstrate their learning. End products or performances that help teachers assess student learning are called *culminating projects* or products, and should directly relate to the big ideas and essential questions initially posed.

Assessments should require students' demonstrations of understanding, not just recall of information or formulaic modeling. Understanding is best revealed through multiple forms of understanding, including real-world applications, explanations involving the construction of claims and arguments supported with evidence; analysis of perspectives associated with significant debates and controversial issues; expressions of empathy, with students encouraged to walk in the shoes of others; and self-reflection, involving students' growing ability to reflect, revise, rethink, and refine.

(McTighe & Brown, 2005, p. 236)

Continuing with the examples related to "movement" above, varied ideas for culminating projects can suit a range of learners' needs. Some may aim to construct a map, noting the many places people live; others may increase the sophistication of a map by including movement patterns with dates, reasons, and details about cultural or geographic groups that have immigrated over time. Other students may focus on family histories or personal patterns and ways of moving. As we consider the class as a whole unit of problem-solvers and investigators, the great variety of culminating products imagined from the start of curriculum planning can result in a robust and substantive study of movement in which all participate and contribute.

DEVELOPING MATERIALS AND INSTRUCTIONAL METHODS

Once a unit theme, big ideas, and some possibilities for a range of culminating projects are proposed, attending to instructional methods for daily instruction is in order. A general guideline is that lessons are linked to the central issue or problem and daily instruction should engage students in work that will be useful to the development of culminating products (Onosko & Jorgensen, 1998; Tomlinson & McTighe, 2006; Wiggins & McTighe, 1998). This requires teachers (and students) to consider what is needed to investigate the theme. General areas to consider are:

(1) *Increasing knowledge about an area of study*, which may include activities such as: accessing literature and other informational media on the theme; learning vocabulary and symbols pertinent to a new area of study; performing experiments to work with models or observe an area under investigation; working with "expert" guests in or out of school; or finding real-world examples and areas for study in the community.

(2) *Developing skills to access information*, which may include instruction in: reading, or particularly useful reading strategies for different kinds of text; searching for and locating resources; interviewing; observing; listening; reading maps, graphs and charts; or any other forms of data.

(3) *Developing modes of inquiry to engage with ideas*; which may include instruction in: collaborative work and discussion; ways of conducting investigations and experiments; analytical and critical thinking in general, or specific to disciplines (e.g., working with mathematical/computational systems); or reflection.

(4) *Developing ways of performing the knowledge and skills learned*, which often include writing, speaking, word-processing, displaying mathematical algorithms, charting, and graphing (and test-taking). Other forms of expression may also be areas for instruction, including: the visual arts, theatrical and musical performances, and the wide variety of media arts and computer-related forums for expression (e.g., presentation software and web-pages).

Sourcebooks containing ideas for lesson planning, materials, and teaching methods are abundant. For the purposes of considering inclusive, differentiated instruction we offer an overview of methods and material ideas consonant with these aims.

Materials

A main tenet of UDL is the provision of varied materials to reduce barriers in the mode of representation. Having multiple formats of a material is one way to diversify. For example, when offering reading material it is useful to have the text version, a larger-print text version, a digital format that can be viewed or read aloud on a computer, an audio version, and perhaps a Braille version. Ideally, these materials would be obtained at the same time to be ready-to-go for anyone who could benefit from them. Preparing for students with diverse needs before a need arises reduces frustration and barriers that can occur when available materials are inadequate to support the class. If varied formats are not available or able to be acquired, teachers may plan to engage the whole class in read-aloud, shared, or partnered reading so that all have access to the text. Similar methods may also be used to include students who cannot read. Of shared reading and reading aloud, Browder et al. (2008) point out that "the two primary outcomes for literacy are enhanced," including, "quality of life through shared literature and increased independence as a reader" (p. 3).

In addition to having varied formats of texts, providing modified texts may also be appropriate and helpful. One example of modified texts that are available for purchase is abridged versions of books. They are shortened versions of materials that include main plot elements, characters, and essential story lines. Many "classics" in literature and mythology are available in many versions written or re-told in differing levels of sophistication. Educators can certainly create modified text materials, as well. Students may be offered a photocopy of a page with only the main headings or central ideas visible; or a text that is highlighted to alert them to the main ideas, as correlated, perhaps, to individuated instructional goals. Providing modified texts can enable a student to participate in conversation and class activities without becoming frustrated with an overwhelming task. Or, a modified text may be useful for homework or independent work, when sources of classroom support may not be available.

Beyond offering multiple or abridged versions of a shared material, it is recommended that educators collect or locate many kinds of materials that offer similar information in a variety of formats and that relate to and incorporate various cultures and people. Resources of these kinds are necessary for robust thematic and unit planning. Having rich, detailed, and diverse source materials increases the potential to engage and be interesting to the widest range of class members (Onosko & Jorgensen, 1998). Efforts in inclusive education are best designed to create contexts for learning in which every student can identify with and connect to the school's culture and organizational life (see Dei et al., 2000, as cited in Wotherspoon & Schissel, 2001). Inclusive schooling, according to Wotherspoon and Schissel,

> Incorporate[s] social and cultural resources such as the accumulation of significant pools of informal learning, or the presence of individuals with special skills or life histories, that are often ignored in schooling or not considered as legitimate learning resources (Livingstone, 1999).
>
> (2001, p. 332)

In other words, when seeking materials, it is useful to consider human resources, community organizations, and all kinds of available experiences that may be related to a theme of study. In general, teachers may consider having books and readings on similar topics on many levels and in many text types (i.e., novels, magazine articles, picture books, text books); a selection of videos; websites; and hands-on materials all related to a theme provide many ways for students to obtain information for study. Students can all have a chance to choose materials most interesting to them, gain experience working with varied forms of information, and can expand, enrich, or review learning throughout the duration of study. Van Garderen and Whittaker (2006) offer an important further note to keep in mind: "regardless of the degree of heterogeneity of a district or classroom, all students should learn about the history and experiences of diverse groups so that they can function in a global society" (p. 13).

Finally, just as material sources of information can be varied and modified, so can assignment handouts, class notes, and any other material provided in class. Supplemental materials and aids, such as reading or vocabulary guides, calculators, or graphic organizers—such as charts, Venn diagrams, concept maps—are also ways of opening access to understanding and participation. The possibilities for providing a variety of materials and supplemental tools for organization or ease of completion of assignments are innumerable and are best derived from considering the needs of individual students as teachers get to know them. Resources containing ideas to modify and develop supplemental materials are abundant. Although IDEIA guarantees the modifications and accommodations listed on a student's IEP, there is no reason that supplemental and varied versions of materials can be offered *only* to students with IEPs. Offering everyone the opportunity to benefit from the range of resources and practices available in a UDL curriculum can maximize learning for many.

Methods in UDL

The methods chosen for teaching and learning are greatly determined by the skills, modes of inquiry, and performances of learning that are desired. The educational philosophy of a democratic ideal for inclusive teaching also has significant impact on the kinds of skills and modes of inquiry addressed. For example, engaging in and gaining from shared dialog requires class members to learn how to present their ideas clearly, acknowledge and listen to others, and be able to clarify and incorporate others' ideas and contributions (Palincsar, Magnusson, Collins, & Cutter, 2001). Sociocultural theories of learning offer a framework that supports engagement in shared work, in which students learn by modeling their thought and actions on more experienced class members. Constructivist theories also support the necessity of learners' interaction in authentic experiences that allow them to construct ideas toward the development of conceptual understanding. McTighe and Brown (2005), offer:

> Students learn best when they are engaged in purposeful, active, and inquiry-driven teaching and learning activities, rather than passive variations of didactic instruction. The more learners are situated at the center of their own learning process, the greater the extent of their understanding and mastery of desired outcomes.
>
> (p. 236)

The family of methods related to guided inquiry and cooperative learning seem well suited for inclusive teaching (Morocco, 2001; Palincsar, Magnusson, Collins, & Cutter, 2001).

Guided inquiry provides students with problems to investigate and an interactive, social forum to share ideas and gain guidance toward developing disciplinary understanding. In other words, students are enabled to develop their own ideas, which are posed to the group (including teachers), and then refined as content-area knowledge through further questioning, clarifying, and investigating. The teacher's roles are to develop, or help students develop, activities to illustrate and animate the concepts of study; to guide students' thinking and doing toward productive directions by modeling and questioning; and to provide direct teaching of skills, instructions, and information likely to support students' ability to engage in inquiry. Cooperative learning generally refers to work in which students learn by working together (Johnson & Johnson, 1999), and is an integral component of guided inquiry.

Morocco (2001) offers four broad considerations for planning in a guided inquiry method: (1) Authentic Tasks; (2) Cognitive Strategies; (3) Social Mediation; (4) Constructive Conversation.

(1) Authentic Tasks. Authentic tasks pose students with real-world scenarios and/or actual materials to manipulate in order to investigate concepts or phenomena. A few real-world scenarios are:

- Preparing for a trip by investigating a place to go, mapping a route, and calculating mileage and costs. The most authentic work might feature actual planning to go on a field trip, though planning for an imagined trip can also be quite engaging.
- Investigating a current social problem, posing ideas for action, and getting involved in anything from volunteer work to communicating with government official—the closer to students' lived experiences, the more authentic the work.
- Mathematical problems involving calculating area, volume, perimeter, and other geometric skills are frequently posed through scenarios in which students will plan to paint a room, plant a garden, or build a building. Science experiments and lab work are frequently designed to provide materials to manipulate and phenomena to observe.

(2) Cognitive Strategies. Addressing cognitive strategies relates to the teaching of steps or thinking processes in which people engage to complete tasks. In guided inquiry, teachers may listen for and reinforce desired ways of thinking and talking as they emerge naturally in student talk and work. For example, a student may be asked to share a particular idea or way of interacting that highlighted an instructional aim. Teachers may also directly teach cognitive strategies to deepen and better enable student understanding. In mathematics, a common example of teaching cognitive strategy is found in supporting students to differentiate important and unimportant information given in word problems. When learners first encounter word problems, teachers or other students may lead them through a step-by-step process to identify the question the problem is asking, the information that seems useful to answering the question, and the information that is not useful to the question. Oftentimes, key-words for operations are highlighted to enable students to figure out how to manipu-late the numbers to answer the question (e.g., "altogether" usually refers to addition).

Another well-documented cognitive strategy is Reciprocal Teaching, which relates to reading comprehension of nearly any kind of text for any kind of content (Lederer, 2000; Palincsar & Brown, 1984; Slater & Horstman, 2002). Reciprocal Teaching pro-vides a series of strategies in which readers actively engage in discussion to arrive at shared meaning during reading. First, a group reads a common selection of text. Next, they generate questions prompted by the selection and try to answer them. After that, readers raise issues that need to be clarified for best understanding of the selection. Summarizing the passage is next, and finally, readers predict what might happen in the subsequent text. The next section of text is read, and the process is repeated. Each of the four steps may be taught in isolation from one another, with the goal to be able to practice them altogether. Ultimately, Reciprocal Teaching breaks down and makes explicit the skills of questioning, clarifying, summarizing, and predicting text in order to gain accurate understandings, while also highlighting the importance of dialog and shared meaning.

(3) Social Mediation and **(4) Constructive Conversation.** Learning is an interac-tive process and can be characterized as exchanges of ideas through which individuals and groups develop shared understandings. In guided inquiry, the sharing of ideas and propositions followed by group discussion to clarify and question supports learn-ers to develop and refine understandings. In the examples above, the teacher usually provides directions and demonstrations of each step, and then supports students as they practice the steps with the whole class, and then in smaller groups of students, which increases everyone's opportunity to engage with and practice the strategies. As students practice, they act as models for each other and all refine their understanding of material and gaining competence with the strategies. In this method, it is essential that students have the opportunity to practice and learn how to engage in construc-tive conversations or communication. Just as cognitive strategy instruction may be provided, strategies for sharing and listening to ideas may also be directly taught and practiced within the context of authentic experiences.

There are many ways that daily lessons can be structured, and the kind of activity in which students will engage is likely to dictate the flow of a lesson. Madeline Hunter (1982), for example, offered a seven-step model of lesson planning for direct teach-ing that incorporates the teacher's scaffolding, which may be useful when introduc-ing cognitive strategies. Workshop models for teaching reading and writing add the concept of the "mini-lesson" (Calkins, 1986). The characterization of lesson delivery, or direct instruction, as "mini" emphasizes the need for students' active engagement and time for exploration and dialog. We offer five lesson components that are useful to structure daily planning for a balance of direct and inquiry-based instruction:

1) Activate prior knowledge or anticipatory set. Students are invited to consider and share knowledge and experiences related to the objective for the day; review prior learning from the unit of study; or are offered an "attention-grabbing" activity or idea to increase their anticipation of the activity for the day.

2) Mini-lesson. Students are provided instruction on a particular cognitive or social strategy of focus that will guide them to be successful in the day's activity, or that will further their development in an ongoing investigation. Introducing new information pertinent to the area of study may also be offered.

3) Check for understanding and offer opportunities for guided practice. Students are guided through a model application of the new concept or strategy. Students may role-play, observe, and comment on others' practice; and/or follow along as teachers or peers demonstrate. Care should be taken to provide clear directions and explanations to enable students to understand the purpose and process of the lesson.

4) Interdependent practice. Students are provided with authentic tasks or problems through which to practice their new learning, initiate, or continue an investigation. Ideally this is a time that students work together. Teachers can circulate among groups to ensure understanding of directions and to pose questions or model language to deepen conversations. When groups are enabled to work interdependently, this can also be a time for teachers to have individual conversations with students or provide additional support or enrichment for small groups.

5) Sharing and reflection. The class community, in guided inquiry, is thought of as a learning community in which all members learn from each other and contribute to the whole of class accomplishment. Small groups or individuals may present on their learning and activity for the day and/or participate in a larger group discussion or work. This is often a time in which broader conceptual understandings emerge and can be highlighted. Teachers may also take note of understandings, strategies, and concepts that can be emphasized in subsequent lessons.

In planning for a unit and guided inquiry model of teaching, the overall framework is guided by big ideas, concepts, and instruction needed to work toward culminating projects. Topics for the mini-lessons can emerge from students' learning along the way, as areas of need and interests are noted; or relate to more specific skills students are expected to learn.

There are several reasons that guided inquiry and workshop models are recommended for inclusive teaching. First, students work in learning communities on a shared problem or issue. Any given big idea, concept, essential question, and investigation poses the need for many different kinds of information and ways of engaging in joint, culminating efforts. Everyone can contribute to class learning toward a theme while working on individual goals. In UDL terms, guided inquiry and workshop models provide ways of differentiating the mode of engagement in learning. Similarly, as Tomlinson (1999) describes of differentiated instruction, the process by which students practice and perform learning can be varied. For example, a group can work together to search for information on a shared topic, with some doing Internet searches, others watching a documentary, others reading texts, and so on. All members can contribute information from different sources of information. One group or class member may create a visual display of information by making a collage of related words or pictures, while another writes a report of the information, another develops a website, and another presents an oral presentation. Each member can work individually, but in concert toward a shared aim.

Second, because students are working on similar concepts and topics, they are enabled to support and deepen each other's learning. "Students are thought of as having and using distributed expertise" (cited in Mariage, Paxton-Buursma, & Bouck, 2004, p. 541), which means that it is expected that students will develop understanding and competencies at different rates and through varied means. Engagement in dialogic work provides any individual with several "models" who may act as learning scaffolds. The openness of instruction similarly poses infinite opportunities to arrive at novel ideas and understanding and allows students to interact in ways most familiar to them while gaining experience and instruction. This allows for a valuing of students' ways of knowing alongside the development of culturally dominant styles of interacting (van Garderen & Whittaker, 2006; Gutierrez, Baquedano-Lopez, Alvarez, & Chiu, 1999; Mariage, Paxton-Buursma, & Bouck, 2004; Reid & Valle, 2004).

Third, planning in units provides a context for sustained study that deepens over the course of the unit. Spending a greater duration dedicated to related areas of study allows more time for learners to develop understanding or to complete assignments without feeling left behind. Finally, supporting students to work interdependently provides a structure in which teachers are able to plan for small-group or intensive instruction when necessary. Rotating combinations of heterogeneous groups for themed work with homogeneous groups for specific skill instruction can provide flexible teacher and peer support. Some ideas for grouping include:

- Student groupings can be created by interest in a common type of product. For example, all students who wish to create a visual product may work together to share ideas, draft work, share materials, create products, and offer constructive criticism. Assuming a variety in skill level and experience in art-making, peers can support each other to develop better products than they would without each other. A teaching artist or more advanced student of the arts would be an excellent classroom visitor to advance this group's skills.
- Student groupings can be created to gather students with a range of abilities and competencies with the express purpose of their supporting each other. Roles can be assigned by ability, process, or product to appropriately structure students' participation and increase the likelihood of success.
- Student groupings can be created according to affinity or interest groups. These groupings can increase student engagement or support the building of relationships and friendships.
- Students can be grouped according to specific needs of instruction, which allows teachers to provide scaffolded instruction that they are best equipped to facilitate. These groupings and intense instruction benefit students who may need support to engage in an enriching task and those who need support revisiting a concept or skill.
- Teachers can make the most of small-group, intensive instruction by changing groupings regularly and varying the complexity of assignments. For example,

when intensive instruction for a small group of students is required, other groups may be assigned to continue work-in-progress or a task that is likely to be comfortable. These help ensure a balance of attending to students' needs with an organized and productive class.

- Most cognitive strategy instruction will be useful to all. To ensure that students are able to make progress, materials and ways of applying strategies in independent work can be differentiated to provide appropriate levels of challenge.

Developing ways of teaching that support students toward interdependence can make time for combinations of whole-group, small-group, and individual instruction, as well as position students as teachers and leaders in areas of strength. There is no formula or ideal balance that can apply to all classes of students; and the process of thinking about differentiated instruction can be messy, even chaotic. However, the following ways of thinking about grouping, student strengths, and cognitive and social strategies instruction are a place to start. In addition to considering the general guidelines for guided inquiry, there are many guidelines and tools available to support the work of cooperative learning. Johnson and Johnson (1999), for example, provide the following elements of cooperative learning activity design:

- *Positive Interdependence*: The task requires all members to contribute in order to complete the assignment. To support positive interdependence students may choose or be assigned specific roles to fill. These may relate to aspects of a product or process. For example, there may be a time keeper, material manager, note-taker, and facilitator to support the social process of a shared task; or students may be differently assigned to create a visual display, outline, a writing piece, or a speaking component based on shared understanding of an experiment, piece of text, or problem.
- *Individual Accountability*: Individuals' contribution to the group must be acknowledged and assessed. Assigning roles or asking students to describe their contributions supports the participation of all members.
- *Face-to-Face Promotive Interaction*: Group work should require students to interact with each other in ways that will advance their pursuit. A jigsaw, for example, is when individual members of a group are responsible for learning different aspects of a task, then come together to share, explain, and ensure that all group members understand all of the varied aspects. Another possibility is that all members need to use their learning toward solving a shared problem. In either case, students must interact to complete the assignment.
- *Social Skills*: It is essential that students be provided guidelines and instruction toward respectful and productive interaction. Offering direct instruction in social skills and providing ongoing reinforcement and acknowledgement of good communication is a necessity of cooperative learning, as well as a primary value in democratic schooling. Even if it takes time for students to develop respectful and productive ways of interacting, taking the time to teach students to work with each other is well aligned with the goals of an inclusive classroom. Beyond establishing general norms of mutual respect, instruction in strategies

to cultivate conceptually meaningful dialogue is a central principle of guided inquiry communities. Students can learn how to acknowledge others' contributions, re-phrase ideas, form questions, and clarify, and build on each other's ideas.
- *Group Processing*: Cooperative learning can be built upon and furthered as students (and teachers) develop values for shared work and evaluate successful elements of group work. Group work should include a time and forum for the group to identify successes in the group process and areas that can be improved. In fact, these kinds of reflections and learning can be great ideas for follow-up mini-lessons or ways of identifying goals for the next time the group works together.

Cooperative learning experiences can promote greater acceptance of differences and interpersonal attraction between students with disabilities and students without disabilities. Direct contact and interaction through cooperative experiences can move students beyond one-dimensional prejudices to multidimensional views of one another. Teachers can help students reduce their prejudices by allowing them to learn cooperatively and encouraging them to value each other (Conrad, 1988). Practiced cooperation leads to spontaneous cooperation, the polar opposite of prejudice. Assigning students with disabilities to work cooperatively with their non-disabled peers creates a pattern of positive interaction. Guidelines to facilitate a productive experience include (Yuker & Block, 1979):

(1) The interaction of non-disabled students and their peers with disabilities should rely on collaborating rather than helping. This orientation must be taught. Many students both with and without disabilities simply lack the necessary skills to interact with each other. Thus, a teacher needs to teach collaboration.

(2) The interactions of non-disabled students with their disabled peers should be cooperative rather than competitive. Techniques like cooperative learning that emphasize group accomplishment and de-emphasize competition nurture self-esteem by building confidence and inviting students to achieve their potential.

(3) The interactions of non-disabled students with their disabled classmates should be intimate rather than casual in order to lead to positive attitudes toward one another.

(4) The interactions of non-disabled students with their disabled classmates should be frequent rather than occasional.

(5) The interactions of non-disabled students and their classmates with disabilities should take place on settings that make them equals. Students with disabilities should not be treated as "guests" who earned their way into the mainstream, but as students who belong in that classroom as much as any other student.

Cooperative learning increases contact between students, gives them a shared basis of similarity (group membership), engages them in pleasant activities together, and encourages them to work toward common goals. The outcome of these kinds of experience can be friendships and long-lasting impressions that counteract stereotypes about disability. An important psychological outcome of cooperative learning is the positive effect it can have on self-esteem and self-confidence. The students' realization enables them to withstand life's disappointments, to be confident decision makers, and ultimately to be happy and productive individuals.

ASSESSMENT AND REFLECTIVE PRACTICE

Assessment

Assessment involves examining students and their work to support planning and instructional design to best meet their needs. IEP development includes assessment processes, and is one tool that describes goals and areas of study for individuals useful to daily practice. In addition to attending to IEP goals, it is essential for teachers to assess students in the particular instructional environment and in relation to the specific unit of study. For example, a question to guide assessment might be, *How will Juan best benefit from and engage in study about movement?* Or, *How will Shannon's IEP goal of increasing reading comprehension be met in a study of movement?* The overall purpose of assessment is to gauge the competency of students with regard to the four areas above. In other words, (1) What do students know about the area of study, and from what sources? (2) What skills do students possess that will enable them to access information? (3) In what modes of inquiry are students able to engage? and (4) In which kinds of formats are students comfortable performing or demonstrating their learning? Based on general answers to these questions, teachers can develop ideas that will emphasize students' strengths as areas on which to build and help identify areas to pose for growth.

Assessment for planning can take many forms. Inviting student input is, perhaps, the most straightforward way to begin assessment for planning. A number of surveys, tools, and methods for discerning students' interests, learning strengths, and prior knowledge are available. Student interest surveys and simply having group or individual discussions about interests may be used to inform areas of study likely to be engaging. Asking students about the kinds of school activities that they found enjoyable in years past may also help teachers figure out practices that are familiar and likely to be successful. Some questions to guide a conversation include:

- What was your favorite subject last year?

  - What kinds of work did you do in that class or on that subject?
  - Do you have any examples of that work from last year?

- What was something you feel you learned very well last year?

  - What kinds of things did you do to learn that?

If possible, talking to students' past teachers about what was successful and engaging to students can give a new teacher great ideas for where to begin planning.

Having an idea of what students already know is also very helpful to planning for daily instruction. The KWL Chart was originally developed as a tool for helping students to more deeply engage with and comprehend reading materials (Ogle, 1986). It has subsequently become a frequently used strategy for assessing students' prior knowledge, discerning students' interests, and charting progress throughout a unit of study. KWL stands for What I Know, What I Want to Know, and What I Learned. To create a KWL Chart, simply create a three-column chart with one heading for each column. The class then fills in the chart with what they Know about a given area of study, as well as what they Want to know. Teachers and students then have a shared way of determining areas for study. As the class learns the areas proposed (and others), they can fill in the "Learned" column for a dynamic display of class accomplishment.

In addition to asking students directly, observation and reviewing student work are other straightforward ways to get a sense of students' comfort zones and areas of need. A suggestion for beginning practice is to watch students as they work on a variety of open-ended tasks on familiar topics. Perhaps the most familiar topic is oneself, and beginning a school year with activities that allow teachers and classmates to get to know each other is highly recommended. For example, asking students to create a product to express what they did over the summer, the previous night, or over the weekend is a way to give a familiar task that can be completed in many ways. Students may choose to write, draw, select pictures from magazines, or any other creative way to present a recent experience. Taking note of which students gravitate to which form can provide insight into the kinds of work students are most comfortable doing. The work samples can provide valuable information about students and their experiences, as well as suggest students' areas of strengths and needs. In addition, many diagnostic tools are available to help teachers determine the ZPD. Being sensitive to what students are able to do and able to do with help in the context of their actual work is most helpful to planning.

While assessment is useful to get a broad idea of the kinds of activities most likely to result in success, sociocultural theories emphasize the importance of context to learners' achievement. It is likely and desirable that students will be able to perform more sophisticated knowledge and skills in the context of authentic problem scenarios and when they have many models on which to "apprentice." Rather than imagine assessment as occurring once at the beginning of a year or unit, it is useful to attend to individual students' progress each day and in different kinds of activities that emerge as a unit develops. This kind of attention enables teachers to note and repeat (or further develop) topics or kinds of activities in which students perform best.

A final consideration for methods in UDL and differentiated instruction is providing variety in the ways students can perform their learning—that is, varying the mode of expression. Already noted in earlier sections, planning instruction and learning activities around themes provides varied goals that individuals in a class can be working toward, while engaging in shared aims. Earlier described, students may be working on a range of goals. Reisberg (1998), for example, points out:

> The infusion of goals, objectives, and activities from the areas of self-help, independent living, and social and learning skills is limited only by a teacher's imagination and subsequent planning. Some skills and knowledge fit better and are more effectively related to particular themes than others; however, through careful planning

and development, teachers can address, in the general education classroom, many of the learning goals needed by students with disabilities.

(pp. 276–277)

Performance-based assessment refers to a way of gauging student growth based on what they are able to perform in an authentic context of application. The most common way of assessing learners on complex projects and application of skills is with evaluation rubrics and task checklists. A rubric is usually formatted as a grid that lists key competencies with a range of criteria that describe performance levels or qualities. Task checklists are lists of components or processes that should be included or performed as part of the assignment.

Ideally, students may use the same rubric to gauge progress over a course of similar study. For example, a rubric for writing an essay may be used for a variety of kinds of essays, but specify general components such as thesis, supporting details, organization, style, and editing. To gauge content-area knowledge and conceptual understanding, a rubric may be developed according to big ideas, key concepts, or essential questions. A range of product types can be assessed according to the range and depth of content and concepts displayed in them. Rubrics can be developed for any goal—academic, social, or other skills—by identifying and describing the range of competence most appropriate for the student. Because the rubric offers descriptive details of different performance levels or qualities, students are provided specific feedback on how to improve. Rather than simply provide a grade or level, assessment can guide instruction and provide a goal for further work, useful to both teacher and student. Using rubrics and descriptive, performance-based assessment practices focus attention to individual progress, rather than emphasize comparisons to others or performance relative to a norm.

Reflective Practice

Teaching is dynamic because of the many variable factors that influence joint engagement in shared work. All class members are affected by events, moods, and the ups and downs of life. In addition, many factors influence how an individual or group will respond to class activities on any given day—the topic, prior knowledge and experience of class members, nature of activity, materials provided, members of a group, and so on. Although planning universally and differentiating instruction can maximize the potential of daily lessons to provide students with success and growth, no degree of planning can account for all of the variations that affect classroom life. Teachers, however, can engage in practices that help increase the effectiveness in planning for teaching.

Students grow through opportunities to re-visit and practice ways of thinking and talking over time. Conceptual understanding develops and deepens as students engage in similar processes and encounter similar, related phenomena over time. Deep learning does not "happen" in one day or in a single experience. Therefore, teachers should not be discouraged by students' needs to re-visit concepts. In fact, planning a unit emphasizes and builds on learners' needs to engage in sustained study that deepens—through scaffolding—over time and experience. That said, teachers do need to be attentive and responsive to factors in class design that can be improved. Assessment applies not only to gauging students' growth and progress, but also to teachers' growth in the design and implementation of instruction.

It is recommended that teachers take time to consider and reflect on teaching practices in order to inform subsequent planning. Certainly, thinking about the events of a day and making mental notes about what is going well and not, and responding to student work are ways that teachers gain insight into students' learning in order to adjust instruction. However, after a long day of work, details that could inform knowledge about students and effective or ineffective teaching processes are likely to fade in memory. A first step toward being enabled to reflect on teaching practice, then, is to develop a means for noting and recording details of teaching. Taking notes while teaching or right after a lesson, keeping a written or audio journal, or even periodically recording video or audio of a class are possible ways to create detailed accounts of practice.

Korthagen (1999) defines reflection as "the mental process of structuring or restructuring an experience, a problem or existing knowledge or insights" (p. 193), and offers the ALACT process of ongoing reflection and action suggested for teachers. Described as a spiral, the ALACT model is an acronym for stages of reflective practice. Guiding questions follow the stages listed below.

1) *Acting*: The act of teaching. Key questions to consider are:

  • What did I want to achieve?
  • What did I want to pay particular attention to?
  • What did I want to try out?

2) *Looking back on the action*: Recording descriptive details of the actions

  • What were the concrete events?
  • What did I want?
  • What did I think?
  • How did I feel?
  • What did I do?

3) *Awareness of essential aspects*: Discerning, from the description, key areas of interest or a problem

  • What is the connection between answers to the previous questions?
  • What is the influence of the context/the school as a whole?
  • What does that mean for me?
  • What is the problem or the positive discovery?

4) *Creating alternative methods of action*: Posing ideas to solve a problem or repeat and further effective practices

  • What alternatives do I see? What are ways to make use of my positive discovery?
  • What are advantages and disadvantages of each?
  • What do I resolve to do next time?

5) *Trial*: Trying out the new ideas. The process then spirals back to the acting stage.
(p. 197)

In this open design, teachers can aim to describe a particular event or challenge, or write a narrative description of a longer period of time. The more that is recorded, the more enriching and comprehensive the process can be. It is important to remember that events and interactions preceding a challenging situation may influence it; so, developing descriptions that precede a particular event can give further insight and awareness.

The ALACT model is quite flexible. The process can be used for open inquiry— describing actions in order to gain insight into teaching practices; and it can be used to examine specific areas of interest. McTighe and Brown (2005), for example, describe responsive teaching as practice that,

> demands diagnostic and ongoing assessments of student progress in relationship to required content and performance standards. Through this process, teachers decrease skills and knowledge gaps, as well as accommodate individual students' demonstrated strengths, interests, and personal learning goals.
>
> (p. 237)

The ALACT model can be used to describe and reflect upon individual students' progress in terms of the content and performance standards planned for in a lesson. Teachers may choose to specifically "Look back" at how students were enabled (or not) to develop the big ideas of a lesson.

ALACT can also be used individually or for collaborative reflection and action. Especially useful in collaborative teaching, teachers can each describe aspects of a lesson or day, then work together to gain awareness of essential aspects (some of which may not be apparent to only one person), create alternative methods for action, and trial teach together. The benefit of having multiple insights and sources for generating ideas is tremendous.

RESEARCH SUPPORTING UDL AND DIFFERENTIATED INSTRUCTION

There is a growing research base to support the impact of UDL and differentiated instruction on student learning. In addition to sociocultural and constructivist frameworks, other contemporary theories of learning support differentiation as an approach to teaching, including brain-based learning and multiple intelligences. For example, proponents of "brain-based instruction" propose that a comfortable learning environment, an appropriate level of challenge, and activities that allow students to attach meaning to concepts through significant associations enable students' cognitive process (Tomlinson & Kalbfleisch, 1998). Lynch and Warner (2008) offer the following review of research that demonstrates support for differentiated instruction:

> Patricia Hodge (as cited in Subban 2006) found that students who had received differentiated instruction had increased gains in mathematics scores. McAdamis (2001) reported that differentiated instruction resulted in significant improvement in test scores for low-achieving students across grade levels. In addition to

improvements in test scores, another result of differentiated instruction, according to other studies, is increased student engagement. Johnsen (2003) found that differentiated techniques were engaging and stimulated student interest. In a study by Linda Affholder (as cited in Subban 2006), teachers who used differentiated techniques experienced a greater sense of effectiveness and were more willing to try new instructional approaches.

(p. 11)

In addition to support for differentiated instruction, the benefit for planning curriculum to develop conceptual understanding and engage students in active dialog is well established. The REACH project—a multi-year study examining the conceptual learning of students with disabilities—has yielded successful demonstrations of the role and impact of dialog. In a brief summary, Morocco (2001) describes:

> Some studies in special education have focused on the effect of constructive conversation on the learning of students with disabilities. For example, Woodward and Baxter (1996) identify questioning strategies in teachers' conversations with young adolescent students with disabilities as a way to build students' conceptual understanding in mathematics. Echevarria (1995) successfully embedded dialogue within strategy instruction within a curriculum focused on conceptual understanding of concepts for Hispanic students with disabilities. Palincsar, Magnusson, Marano, Ford, and Brown (1998) described the role that conversation can play in enabling students to synthesize evidence from science experiments.

(p. 9)

In a classroom-based study, Morocco and Hindin (2002) explain the learning accomplished through students' active engagement in discussions. In working with a teacher who modeled and scaffolded language practices that supported engagement with others' ideas, students were able to deepen their understanding. The researchers observed:

> The students demonstrate their developing ability to negotiate interpretations of literature through specific discourse practices that include stating claims, elaborating upon one another's claims, countering one another's claims with alternative views, and using arguments to support their claims. By requiring precise wording . . . these four students reveal their understanding of the value of close attention to their language.

(p. 156)

Additionally, because students are able to incorporate knowledge of their own lives in the open format of discussion, they were able "to better interpret and hypothesize about the choices that [the character] makes in the text," which enabled them to "deepen their understanding" (p. 156). The promising work done by teachers, students, and researchers in the REACH project offers support for guided inquiry and the concept of the learning community as an inclusive space. That is, one that provides many open opportunities to engage with instruction, deepen learning, gain support for developing cognitive and social strategies, and activities that capitalize on students' contributions and experiences.

In addition to examining how UDL practices relate to students' opportunities to learn, researchers continue to clarify the types of teaching practices that reflect UDL. A pluralistic practice of UDL describes learner-centered approaches, that aim to complement learning characteristics of individuals, and include "brain-based" (Katz & Sugden, 2013; Kurtts et al., 2009) approaches that may wish to activate and shape neural networks associated with learning. Pluralistic approaches to UDL emphasize differentiated instruction, student choice, and individualization of instruction (Edyburn & Edyburn, 2012; Jimenez, Graf, & Rose, 2007; Kurtts, Matthews, & Smallwood, 2009; Lieberman, Lytle, & Clarcq, 2008; Meo, 2008). A social justice approach to UDL emphasizes collaborative learning experiences that engage learners in problem-posing, dialogue, and taking action to solve problems. Ideally, learners strive toward learning from and with others in situations that encourage diversity of perspective and ways of learning toward a shared goal. Practices associated with UDL as social justice include critical curriculum approaches, including curricular cripistemologies (Mitchell, Snyder, & Ware, 2014), critical multiculturalism, and critical pedagogies (Kozleski & Thorius, 2014; Waitoller & Artiles, 2013). Attention to the development of multiple literacies, rather than a narrow focus on Standard English text and talk, is also featured as social justice work in UDL (Flores, 2008; Glass, Meyer, & Rose, 2013). A third approach examines UDL as specific intervention. The emphasis in this framework is often on providing learners with explicit or direct strategies with which to approach learning activities and typically provide step-by-step procedures derived from a task or content analysis of the instructional goal or cognitive process presumed to be related to the learning goal. UDL practices in an intervention framework include the use of scaffolded digital readers and tools (Dalton et al., 2011; Hall, Meyer, & Rose, 2012; Proctor et al., 2011; Rappolt-Schlichtmann et al., 2013)); scaffolded digital games (Marino, 2009; Marino, Black, Hayes, & Beecher, 2010; Marino et al., 2014); and the use of multi-modal and multimedia instruction (Kennedy, Thomas, Meyer, Alves, & Lloyd, 2014; King-Sears et al., 2015).

Research on the impact of UDL practices in instructional environments is still in an early phase. There is growing evidence for the positive impact of UDL on student engagement and for the promise of UDL to increase support for inclusive education. Katz and Sugden (2013), for example, conducted a case study of implementing UDL practices, in which a teacher's comment highlights the possibility for the model to create experiences through which children at risk of being marginalized may find belonging:

> This program changed the trajectory of a child in my class with severe behavior, he would have been moved to a special program the next term, now he is engaged and wants to be with his "learning family."
>
> (Katz & Sugden, 2013, p. 17)

Dymond et al. (2006) similarly report that teachers who implemented UDL with positive impact for students with cognitive disabilities hoped that inclusive experiences could be provided to more students. They "expressed concern that students in the section of the course that was not receiving the redesign were not meaningfully engaged." The teachers "had difficulty accepting the discrepancy between the two course sections when they had observed what could happen as a result of [UDL] redesign" (p. 305).

Examining student engagement is a common interest of researchers who are studying UDL. King-Sears et al. (2015), Marino et al. (2014), Kortering, McClannon, and Braziel (2008), Hall et al. (2015), Dymond et al. (2006), and Katz (2013) all report higher levels of student engagement during UDL-informed instruction. Marino et al. (2014) report, for example:

> Students described talking with their peers, yelling and cheering each other on in class, and sharing their game experience with family. . . . In addition, they reported gaining an in-depth understanding as they interacted with scientific content in novel ways.
>
> (p. 97)

Despite the reports of engagement and students' self-reports of depth of understanding, however, results on measures of learning do not always demonstrate efficacy of the UDL design for most students across many of the studies. Marino et al.'s (2014) question, "Why would students and teachers react so positively to the UDL units if their test scores were not improving?" (Marino et al., 2014, p. 97), points to an important query to be raised within future UDL research. Rappolt-Schlichtmann et al. (2013), however, propose that "high and persistent levels of interest and excitement reported among students using the UDSN" may reflect "the generation of feelings of competence and autonomy in their work" (p. 1221), which may have longer-term benefits for students' persistence in school study.

A final area of study in support of learning communities and cooperative learning relates to improving the school experiences specifically for students with disabilities. Though work on strategies useful to realizing inclusion has been underway for some time, positive social interaction among labeled and non-labeled students has not been a natural outcome. In 1980, Guinagh noted that most "mainstreamed" children begin their regular classes with slight and unplanned social contact with their peers, and found that "[helping] children become better friends is not central to instruction" (p. 2). Johnson and Johnson (1980), in fact, had found that placing students with disabilities into the mainstream without the proper support and preparation can be extremely harmful:

> Placing handicapped students in the regular classroom is the beginning of an opportunity. But, like all opportunities, it carries the risk of making things worse as well as the possibility of making things better. If things go badly, handicapped students will be stigmatized, stereotyped, and rejected. Even worse, they may be ignored or treated with the paternalistic care one reserves for pets. If things go well, however, true friendships and positive relationships may develop between the non-handicapped and handicapped students. . . . What is needed is an understanding of

how the process of acceptance works in a classroom setting and an understanding of the specified teaching strategies that help to build positive relationships between handicapped and nonhandicapped students as they attend the regular classroom together.

(p. 10)

Notable, further attention has been given to aspects of learning communities in terms of opportunities for collaboration and friendship.

Techniques like cooperative learning—where children engage in small group activities in which they are the primary talkers and doers—that emphasize group accomplishment and de-emphasize competition nurture self-esteem by building confidence and inviting students to achieve their potential. As Slavin (1990) stated,

> Because cooperative learning methods are social interventions, they should provide social effects. The criteria for positive intergroup relations are similar to the widely accepted antecedents of friendship formation or cohesion.... These include contact; perceived similarity; engaging in pleasant activities; and, once again, cooperation where individuals who work toward the same goal come to see one another as providers of rewards. Cooperative learning increases contact between students, gives them a shared basis of similarity (group membership), engages them in pleasant activities together, and has them work toward common goals. As such, it can clearly be hypothesized that they would increase positive affect among students.
>
> (p. 49)

Van der Klift and Kunc (1994) also remind us, however, that friendships develop from mutual respect and reciprocity. "Friendship is not the same thing as help" (p. 393).

Though children can and should learn to help each other through collaboration, it is important that all children have occasions to help and to accept help from others. In using practices that emphasize collaboration among children, we teach in consideration of academics . . . and more. Noddings (1994) also focuses her work on the importance of human relationships in learning. Through providing instructional arrangements where students support and interact with each other in continual, meaningful ways, teachers promote relationships that lead to mutual caring. When teachers model positive language and attitudes toward difference, students also are affirmed in the development of their peer relationships. A classroom discourse that dialogically and pedagogically explores and embraces differences nurtures relationships within the classroom community and leads students toward a broader appreciation of difference.

CONCLUSION

Designing instruction that caters to individual students seems a daunting process when considering a classroom of 25, and often more, students. Practice born in UDL begins with a holistic conception of the potential for many possible learning experiences, in which the emphasis shifts from a focus on the benefits to an individual to the benefit of the whole community; from determined outcomes to those interpreted through open inquiry in assessment. When many possibilities are presented, learners are poised to interact with the multitude of variations in context that inform whether a task is achievable one day, but not another. Teachers are positioned to assess and plan based on learner strengths that show themselves in context, occasionally in surprising ways.

Research demonstrates that a sociocultural framework effectively guides and supports all students' learning. By using instructional arrangements that provide opportunities to form cooperative relationships in which students support each other and serve as learning models, students have multiple models and guides to practice and encourage the development of new and emerging abilities (Gindis, 1999). By providing multiple opportunities to participate in the learning community, student learning is both social and individualized and is reinforced through interaction with knowledge in several ways, a favored method in current learning theory (Gardner & Hatch, 1989). The use of this model allows and encourages multiple ways to participate and also reinforces the value of difference in the classroom and society. In this way, difference is reconstructed as normal in the classroom community. As Sapon-Shevin (2000/2001) explains, educators can "move beyond discussions of diversity as a problem in the classroom to a conceptualization of differences as natural, inevitable, and desirable, enriching teaching and learning experiences for teachers and students alike" (p. 35).

10

DESIGNING CURRICULUM TO ACCOUNT FOR DISABILITY

To develop and maintain inclusive schools and communities, children and teachers can see themselves as change agents, willing and able to confront and challenge stereotypes and oppressive, discriminatory behavior. Ableism is systemic discrimination toward persons with disabilities and is akin to racism, sexism, and heterosexism. More than twenty years ago, the United States Commission on Civil Rights reported, "Many perceive handicapped people's disadvantaged social and economic status as resulting from innate limitations caused by handicaps. Authorities from every branch of government have concluded, however, that prejudice and discrimination are major causes of the disadvantages confronting handicapped people" (Bell & Burgdorf, 1983, p. 17). Ableism, like other "-isms," is carried out in relationships between privilege and disadvantage. People with disabilities are disadvantaged by assumptions that they cannot, should not, or do not desire to participate in education, employment, and other life activities. People who do not identify or appear as disabled benefit from a presumption of competence that is not always afforded to people with disabilities. Although the provision of reasonable accommodations to enable people with disabilities to participate in work, education, and other life activities is required by the ADAAA, some employers and businesses focus on assumed burdens, rather than contributions, that disabled workers or consumers might pose. In working toward the realization of civil rights for disabled people, one action that educators may take is purposeful work toward enabling learners to replace stereotypes about disability with knowledge and understanding about the wide range of disability experiences. We can also develop critical understanding of ableism to promote awareness of the impact of prejudice and discrimination on disabled people.

Expanding diversity-focused curriculum to include disability can follow the pathways that multicultural education has forged. Featuring works of people of color, women, and others with underrepresented identities and experiences is important to recognize the variety of perspectives and voices that contribute to human experience.

Directly discussing and analyzing prejudice, discrimination, varying perspectives, or development of particular social group identities is also useful to highlight in all topic areas. Examples of questions that can spark such explorations include: How is work on the human genome perceived differently depending on the perspective of disability? What are varied ways that disability rights have been enacted and resisted? How might authors' experiences and identities influence their creative works?

Although the need to educate students about disability is important and perhaps even self-evident as part of diversity curriculum, critical perspectives on discrimination and ableism are less common than "awareness" activities focused on increasing sympathy or empathy. Designing curriculum to challenge ableism enables consideration of disability as more than a one-time event, as some awareness activities or special sporting days might be. Attention to anti-ableist action must go on continually in the school to help students become aware of stereotypes, prejudice, and discrimination and gain exposure to a variety of ways of being and living. Learning about disability can occur alongside key competencies in most all disciplines and subject areas. All age groups can be taught about disability and ableism in meaningful ways.

DIVERSIFYING CURRICULUM CONTENT

The study of disability can enhance many subject areas commonly addressed in school curriculum. When infusing information about disabilities, it is best to offer instruction at appropriate content points rather than offering "special" lessons or units. Earlier chapters of this book provide a wealth of information and ways of thinking about disability and disabled persons that can inform efforts to deepen content-area curriculum especially in social studies, literature, and media studies.

Although people with disabilities have always existed, they are often absent in histories we write. When disability is noted, it is described as personal tragedy or insult, rather than as an aspect of culture to be explored (Baynton, 2001). Historians in disability studies instead propose that disability "sit squarely at the center of historical inquiry, both as a subject worth studying in its own right and as one that will provide scholars with a new analytic tool" for understanding human relations (Kudlick, 2003, pp. 2–3). In social studies, historical study may include knowledge about disabled persons in different eras and cultures. Incorporating the roles and experiences of people with disabilities into studies on daily life and governance in past civilizations contributes to a fuller body of knowledge and exemplifies that disability has always been a part of human experience. When studying contemporary history, especially other movements for civil and human rights, it is useful to include disabilities rights movements and laws like The Education for All Handicapped Children's Act, Section 504 of the Rehabilitation Act and The Americans With Disabilities Act. Disability Rights and ableism can be a topic of investigation in the same way that some schools explore the issues of sexism and racism. Background information may include the meanings of the terms "disability," "stereotype," "prejudice," "discrimination," and "stigma." Ableism can certainly be posed for study.

The study of science, technology, and engineering can provide varied opportunities to think about disability. The documentaries, *Freedom Machines* (Stobie & Cole,

2004), and *FIXED: The Science/Fiction of Human Enhancement* (Brashear, 2013), each focus on the impact of technology on the meaning of disability and on the lives and possibilities for people with disabilities. Engineering projects can incorporate ideas about universal design in the development of products and buildings. Students may construct disability-related products as a design challenge. Research related to disability and examination of bioethics are current, relevant, and enriching areas of study for biology and philosophy classes alike. Physical Education and kinesiology curriculum can highlight the ways that people with varied bodies illustrate and experience physicality. The athleticism and skill of Paralympians can be posed alongside the accomplishment of able-bodied athletes. The incorporation of disability into the frame of school curriculum can be accomplished by adding it as a perspective or facet of themes already in place. Critical analysis of disability and ableism, however, may require more sophisticated approaches to narrative analysis.

Analyzing Literature (Fiction)

Studying literature offers innumerable opportunities to consider plot development, characterization, symbolism, and imagery related to disability. According to Fiedler (1996), for example, Shakespeare's characterization of the king in *Richard III* provided "the prototype for the innumerable maimed villains who follow" (p. 41). "Richard's deformity is inextricably tied to his malevolent lust" (Thurer, 1980, p. 13). Useful to literary analysis, however, Dearing (1981) points out,

> Richard III was an able soldier, a skillful politician and a capable monarch, who in the two short troubled years of his reign still managed to enact a number of excellent laws still on the books in modern England. Only a man of unusual physical strength and intellectual power could have achieved the career objective history concedes him. The myth, of course, is that Richard was evil incarnate, that he was a cruel, unfeeling villain, a disastrous and destructive leader and a grotesque hunchback born with a full set of sharp teeth. He was vilified as a hunchback toad, a venomous spider, and a savage wild boar. . . . The truth seems to be that he had one shoulder a little higher than the other, largely because of an overdeveloped sword arm; he personally wielded the heavy weapons of the period in his many military campaigns as the principal field general of his brother King Edward IV. His contemporary portraits reveal a handsome, somewhat ascetic countenance.
>
> (pp. 32–33)

Thus, it becomes apparent that Shakespeare used physical deformity as a literary device—the twisted mind in the twisted body—to symbolize mental and spiritual ugliness. Shakespeare exploited his audience's negative perceptions of physical disability by distorting the appearance of the king, who in life was not disabled (Rogers, 1978), to accentuate the evil side of his personality.

Melville, too, used disability to symbolize a warped personality. In *Moby Dick*, Ahab loses his mind over the white whale's destruction of his leg and sacrifices himself and his crew in a mad, obsessive pursuit of revenge. As Kriegel (1982) observed,

Melville's Captain Ahab is not merely crippled—his leg torn from his body by the white whale—he is "crippled" in the deepest metaphysical sense. His injury became his self-hood.

(p.18)

The reader's fear of Ahab is further heightened by the description of Ahab's scar, which begins under the hair of his head and extends to the length of his body (Margolis & Shapiro, 1987), and when Ishmael describes hearing Ahab's wooden leg tapping back and forth across the deck in the middle of the night (Biklen & Bogdan, 1977).

Similarly, Biklen and Bogdan (1977) describe the disability images found in Stevenson's classic, *Treasure Island*. In evoking the terror and suspense that mark this book's opening pages, the key elements are the disabled characters Black Dog and Blind Pew. The former is introduced as a "tallow-faced man, wanting two fingers." This minor disability sets a tone that is built up when the second man is described as that "hunched and eyeless creature," and it is the latter who hands Billy Bones the dread black spot. In addition, when Long John Silver is introduced as a good guy, there is only a casual mention of the fact that he has a wooden leg. Later, when his treachery is revealed, the references to his "timber" leg become ominous and foreboding (p. 7).

Disability, Mitchell and Snyder (2001) point out, is both a "stock feature of characterization and [employed as] an opportunistic metaphorical device" (p. 47). Garland Thomson (1997) demonstrates how literary plots benefit from stereotyped representations of characters with disabilities, as she asks:

How could Ahab operate effectively if the reader were allowed to see him as an ordinary fellow instead of as an icon of monomaniacal revenge—if his disability lost its transcendent meaning? What would happen to the pure pity generated for Tiny Tim if he were portrayed as sometimes naughty, like a "normal" child? Thus the rhetorical function of the highly charged trait fixes relations between disabled figures and their readers. If disabled characters act as real people with disabilities often do, to counter their stigmatized status, the rhetorical potency of the stigma would be mitigated or lost.

(pp. 11–12)

Literary analysts such as Rosemarie Garland Thomson and David Mitchell and Sharon Snyder, among many others, have demonstrated the importance of examining the powerful role disability plays in canonical works of literature, often studied in school.

Literature and Attitude Development

In addition to engaging students in critical, contemporary forms of literary analysis by attending to disability, teachers can also consider the messages transmitted in the works students read. Classical literature, in particular, transmits values, provides interpretation, teaches in the form of allegory, and provides models for identification and behavior (Baskin, 1975). A message in a classic receives respectability and even prestige, making it doubly difficult for those with disabilities to overcome deeply entrenched, complex prejudices (Margolis & Shapiro, 1987). As Margolis and Shapiro (1987) emphasize, however,

> The issue is never that of banning or censoring but of discussing and explaining symbolism so that damaging messages are negated. When literature is taught without an explanation of the moralistic meaning assigned to disabilities, those with impairments may find it difficult to overcome deeply entrenched prejudices.
>
> (p. 21)

Thus, instead of censoring the material that contains prejudiced ideas, teachers can use it as object lessons to offset stereotypes. This can be accomplished by teaching students to discern stereotypes and stereotypical representations related to disability, including those noted earlier: the object of pity—the diseased or sick patient; the sub-human organism; sinister or evil: the menace or the monster; the unspeakable object of dread; the holy innocent or the eternal child; the object of comedy, ridicule, and curiosity; the burden; the victim of violence; and the "supercrip" or the extraordinary disabled person.

Interdisciplinary explorations of literature and related historical contexts can enhance understanding of history, literature, and their embeddedness in social and cultural frames of understanding. For example, John Steinbeck's 1937 classic, *Of Mice and Men*, offers the opportunity for research on disability and its history to understand the characters' actions in the context of time and place. The character, Lennie, exemplifies a view of intellectually disabled persons as social menaces contributing to genetic decline and social disorganization that proliferated during the era of eugenics. Kanner (1964) captured the essence of this image. He noted that

> [In the early 1900s] mental defectives were viewed as a menace to civilization, incorrigible at home, burdens to the school, sexually promiscuous, breeders of feebleminded offspring, victims and spreaders of poverty, degeneracy, crime and disease.
>
> (p. 88)

Further, the President's Committee on Mental Retardation (1977) provided three interesting "articles of belief" from 1912 during the eugenics movement, which guided practice in the treatment of "feebleminded" individuals during the early part of this century:

> First, there is always danger of uncontrollable and impulsive brutality and dangerous aggressiveness, even in the most mild appearing mental defectives, especially as they reach adult age. They are of essentially violent nature.

> Second, the feebleminded are prone to crime and delinquency, contributing to a large proportion of the criminal population. Since they do not distinguish right from wrong, their behavior tends to be dominated by primitive anti-social drives.

Third, feebleminded persons, especially females, have abnormally strong sex drives which they are unable to control. They tend, therefore, to be degenerate and prolific.
(pp. 138–139)

The moral quandary over whether George was justified in killing Lennie, which is often posed as a topic for study in relation to *Of Mice and Men*, can be animated and enlivened by featuring the views of disability in Steinbeck's time. Additionally, the opportunities posed to discuss changes in views of disability over time, modern "mercy killings" of disabled persons, and/or disabled persons' position in the contemporary criminal justice system can enhance interdisciplinary study in schools.

Works of literature that feature disabled characters are abundant in the traditional canon offered in many schools, as well as increasingly present in contemporary works. Mark Haddon's (2003), *The Curious Incident of the Dog in the Night-time*, R. J. Palacio's (2012), *Wonder*, and Susan Nussbaum's (2013), *Good Kings Bad Kings: A Novel*, are just three acclaimed works of fiction that are increasingly featured in school curriculum. Interpretations of each of these works yield possibility for exploring lenses and perspectives of characters with disabled identities and experiences. In all three, the portrayal of disability moves beyond its presence as only symbolic by offering multifaceted treatments of plot and perspective.

Margolis and Shapiro (1987) offer some general recommendations to examine disability as part of literary study, as have others. Some guidelines may include:

(1) "carefully examine excerpts that introduce and describe persons with disabilities;

   a. "explain how each adjective, phrase, or expression influences their responses;
   b. "enumerate the number of positive and negative qualities the author attributes to the person with the disability;"
   (Margolis & Shapiro, 1987, p. 20)

(2) read works of fiction, drama, poetry, and non-fiction to include works that portray the experiences of persons or intentionally challenge stereotypes and tropes with disabilities alongside typical reading assigned in school;
(3) ask students to rewrite the book or a book excerpt with the disabled character no longer disabled, and have them discuss, "How does it affect the story?" (Students may also rewrite the story from the disabled character's point of view)

The following questions, adapted from Margolis and Shapiro (1987, p. 20) offer a starting point to guide discussion:

(1) How would you describe the character's disability? Does the author specifically state it or is it implied?
(2) What specific words does the author use to describe the character with the disability? How realistic is the description of the impairment and what are other ways that people may experience the type of impairment?

(3) When was this book written? How are the attitudes toward disability related to the time in which it was written? How do the attitudes and language used in the book compare with current society?

(4) What stereotype(s) of disability are portrayed (for example is the character pitiable, evil, amusing, weak, burdensome)?

(5) Are the characters with disabilities portrayed as people or as literary devices (for example, "the twisted mind in the twisted body" or "the foreteller of ominous events")? And/or, Does the overall theme of the book rely on disability?

(6) How are the relationships among characters portrayed? (e.g., disabled individuals are often depicted in literature as pitiable "receivers" in their relationships with able-bodied characters.)

(7) In what settings and contexts are disabled characters featured? (e.g., in segregated or inclusive contexts?)

(8) Why do you think the author chose to make this character disabled?

(9) How do you think such depictions and descriptive passages influence the way readers feel about disability?

There are many ways to find literature for children and young adults that offer the opportunity to explore disability and disability experience. The American Library Association, for example, offers a bibliography of "Children's Books about the Disability Experience," which is promoted through the Schneider Family Book Award. Many other lists can be found on disability-specific websites and as categories in other literature lists. As with selecting any books for educational use, it is important to consider how well the book complements the purpose for learning. In striving to enable learners to appreciate disabled perspectives and experience through literature, we recommend that teachers select works that offer narratives and stories that include disability and disability experiences instead of works that are primarily informational. In other words, we propose approaching disability through works that contribute to broader literary aims and feature opportunities, for example, to study plot, setting, characterization, and so on. Selecting fiction that demonstrates literary craft is favored to using fictional works that are contrived to be didactic presentations of disability. Here is a short list of recommended fiction:

Themed for Children

Bell, C., Lasky, D., & Amulet Books. (2014). *El Deafo*. New York, NY: Abrams.

Cottin, M., Faría, R., & Amado, E. (2008). *The black book of colors*. Toronto, Canada: Groundwood Books.

Elliott, R. (2010). *Just because*. Oxford: Lion Hudson.

Ely, L., & Dunbar, P. (2004). *Looking after Louis*. Morton Grove, IL: Albert Whitman.

Herrera, J. F., & Cuevas, E. (2004). *Featherless*. New York, NY: Children's Book Press, an imprint of Lee & Low Books Inc.

Polacco, P. (1998). *Thank you, Mr. Falker*. New York, NY: Philomel Books.

Stryer, A. S., & Dodson, B. (2007). *Kami and the yaks*. Palo Alto, CA: Bay Otter Press.

Tingle, T., & Clarkson, K. (2010). *Saltypie: A Choctaw journey from darkness into light*. El Paso, TX: Cinco Puntos Press.

Willems, M. (2010). *Can I play, too?* New York, NY: Hyperion Books for Children.

Themed for Young Adults

Chambers, A. (2012). *Dying to know you*. London: Bodley Head.
Draper, S.M. (2010). *Out of my mind*. New York, NY: Atheneum Books for Young Readers.
Haddon, M., & Rogers D. Spotswood Collection. (2003). *The curious incident of the dog in the night-time*. New York, NY: Doubleday.
Nussbaum, S. (2013). *Good kings bad kings: A novel*. Chapel Hill, NC: Algonquin Books.
Palacio, R.J. (2012). *Wonder*. New York, NY: Random House.

Analyzing Non-fiction

Reading autobiographies and memoirs and engaging students in writing about their own lives and experiences is a typical part of school curriculum for all levels of study. Students may create picture books, illustrated works of their lives and experiences, memoirs, narratives, photo essays, and multimedia works. Planning units on memoir or life writing offers excellent opportunities to include picture books and autobiographical narratives by persons with disabilities. Literature consistently proves itself a powerful means for providing information and influencing the attitudes and development of individuals, and according to Friedberg, Mullins, and Sukiennik (1985),

> Nonfiction carries the unique power of verifiable authenticity, giving special effect to biography, autobiography, concept, and information books about people who are disabled. Children are born without prejudice toward disabilities, but as they meet those who differ from themselves in significant ways, they are affected by societal attitudes as well as by their own individual reactions. Books that sensitively and honestly depict persons with disabilities expand limited experience and can mitigate the uneasiness that stems from material that helps them deal with anxieties and suggests ways that problems can be solved and the good life lived, even in the face of imperfection and adversity.
>
> (p. ix)

Thus, a useful method to studying issues of disability is to read and evaluate a variety of memoirs, essays, and weblogs authored by a people with disabilities. Ensuring students read a variety of works demonstrates that there are many experiences of disability, which, in turn, deflects stereotypes.

For children with disabilities, reading accounts of others can support their efforts to develop a positive self-concept. Kokaska and Brolin (1985) offer the concept of bibliotherapy:

> [O]ne means of helping individuals with disabilities to understand their difficulties is by exposing them to works of literature in which characters with limitations confront and, in most instances, succeed in life's challenges. The key element to the process, aside from the physical act of reading the book, occurs when the individual identifies with the character or circumstance, transfers insights from the literature, and applies them to his own situation. . . . Bibliotherapy has received expanded interest among teachers, counselors, and therapists who are attempting to broaden

the individual's perspective of his situation and potential problem-solving behaviors that increase the student's self-confidence. This interest has been aided by the fact that a greater number of literary works by individuals with a disability have found their way into print.

(p. 136)

Grindler, Stratton, and McKenna (1997) listed five research conclusions regarding the effects of bibliotherapy on children:

(1) bibliotherapy can produce positive attitude change related to the reduction of children's fear,
(2) listening and reading used in conjunction with discussion may change attitudes more than listening or reading alone,
(3) positive changes in self-concept can be attributed to bibliotherapy,
(4) bibliotherapy provides children with knowledge of strategies they might employ in particular situations, and
(5) books can be useful in helping children solve problems and in helping children realize the usefulness of books for this purpose

(p. 7).

When assigning a non-fiction book for its bibliotherapeutic value, teachers may want to consider the following 11 questions in selecting a book:

(1) Who wrote the book and for what purpose was the book written? (e.g., memoir/autobiography; informational or instructive; support or inspiration for others with similar experience; for adults, young adults, or children).
(2) What is the nature of the disability and how did it occur?
(3) How did the disability affect the author's education, home life, friends, and job?
(4) What problems were encountered by the author as a result of the disability?
(5) What were the author's accomplishments, contributions, goals, and hopes?
(6) What is the message of the book—and to what extent does it reinforce or challenge stereotypes or tropes related to disability?
(7) Is the language and terminology used respectful and current?
(8) Does the book offer multifaceted ways of understanding experiences related to disability?
(9) Did you find the book meaningful, relevant and realistic? Why or why not?
(10) Do you believe that an individual in a context like the author's would find this book bibliotherapeutically relevant? Why or why not?
(11) What did you learn about the disability experience you were unaware of before?

When choosing to assign readings for bibliotherapeutic value, students might read two to three books by different authors to compare and contrast experiences and themes.

Six questions to compare and contrast the authors' approaches, feelings, points of view, and attitudes include:

(1) On what issues do they agree?
(2) On what issues do they differ?
(3) What views and what important issues do they share?
(4) What experiences do they have in common? What experiences are unique?
(5) What are their individual feelings toward the medical model?
(6) What do they have to say about labeling and language?

Media Studies

Studying news, political cartoons, media, film, and television programs are excellent ways to incorporate multi-media materials in teaching and support students to develop critical thinking skills. Being able to understand and interpret varied sources of information is a necessity for navigating the "information society" that characterizes the contemporary USA. Individuals and organizations involved with disability rights have become increasingly critical about the biased way the media cover disability issues and stories. Prominent among these complaints are demeaning language, inaccuracy, bias, stereotypical representation, and ethical lapses. Mass media has a long legacy of using disability to deliver messages of tragedy, pity, charity, or brave and inspiring struggles. Less often have people with disabilities been spotlighted for their take on serious issues (Haller, 2010). The proliferation of social media and the accessibility of works of disabled self-advocates who author and produce disability-related media diversifies the media available for public consumption. To find varied perspectives on a news item, in other words, is made easier in the growth of access to internet content.

Teachers can challenge negative, inaccurate, and stereotypical images of persons with disabilities perpetuated by newspapers, magazines, television programs, films, political cartoons, and other mass and social media by:

(1) identifying and discussing current examples of distortion, inaccuracy, or misdirected attention and using instructional techniques that encourage students to examine their own thoughts, thought processes, and attributions so as to help them discover in a safe way the personal biases and beliefs they were unaware of;
(2) inviting persons from disability rights and news organizations to discuss the issues of media coverage;
(3) organizing instructional units that analyze and evaluate news coverage and compare findings to explicit criteria (for example, Does this story ignore major issues facing persons with disabilities?), and reviewing magazines concerned with disabled persons can add a unique perspective to the unit.

Analyzing the News Media

A lively project that lends itself to cooperative learning is analyzing the news media. Teachers at the junior or senior high school levels consistently confront prejudices already embedded in their students' minds, and examining the beliefs students already hold is the first step in unmasking stereotypes. Next comes organizing instructional units that analyze and evaluate newspaper, magazine, and television coverage of disabled persons that requires students to compare their findings with explicit criteria. Combating stereotypes of the disabled in newspapers and magazines can be different at each schooling level, but in every case combating stereotypes means examining assumptions, discussing issues, and critically responding to societal injustices. For example, a teacher can use the following nine questions as beginning criteria for analyzing news stories:

(1) Does this story ignore major issues facing persons with disabilities?
(2) Does the story accurately reflect persons' abilities as well as disabilities?
(3) Does it use the proper terminology?
(4) Does it use person first language? (Are people described as "voters with disabilities" rather than "disabled voters?")
(5) Is disability being portrayed in a positive sense rather than as a fate worse than death? (Do words like "tragedy," "sufferer," and "afflicted" appear?)
(6) Does disability appear in the story unnecessarily? (Is the person's disability referred to even though it has no relevance to the story?)
(7) Is the disabled individual described in sentimental or pop terms? (Are words like "courageous," "heroic," "inspiring," "special," or "brave" used?)
(8) Is disability portrayed as overcoming barriers and a challenge? (Are terms like "in spite of his handicap," "overcame her disability" used?)
(9) Is the terminology accurate? (Are terms like "Down's syndrome," "handicapped parking," and "disabled seating" used rather than "Down syndrome," "parking for disabled persons" and "accessible seating?")

Analyzing Editorial (Political) Cartoons

Another important area in the mass media for teachers to address when striving for an anti-ableist curriculum is the very common use of negative disability images in political or editorial cartoons. These images depict idioms and metaphors drawn from disability stereotypes like:

Turning a deaf ear
Lame duck
Crippled by fear
Blind to the situation.

Editorial cartoonists do in pictures what writers do in words. They work in the language of symbols involving visual metaphors. The value of the cartoon is based on its instantaneous exposition of an idea. It's actually a direct attack on someone or something and says one thing at a glance reducing complex issues to a single image. It has the ability to convey meaning in an extraordinarily concentrated manner.

Editorial cartoons are *political* (and often referred to as political cartoons) because they focus on the relationship of *power* between dominant and marginalized groups. They use satire and metaphor to hold up to contempt what they believe are vices, follies, and stupidity. A political cartoon's most important elements—exaggeration, humor, and ridicule—often use disability as a metaphor of *powerlessness* and *incompetence*. Depicting the target in a wheelchair, or wearing dark glasses with a cane, or on crutches often portrays this. In order to interpret a political cartoon, the following five issues should be addressed:

(1) What is the issue or point the cartoonist is trying to get across?
(2) What is the viewpoint or motivation of the cartoonist?
(3) Does the use of exaggeration and visual symbolism depict disability as a negative trait?
(4) If so, what does the cartoonist intend the symbol to stand for?
(5) What other techniques could the cartoonist use to make the point of the cartoon?

In order to fashion an anti-ableist environment teachers and students need to become aware of the ubiquitous subtle images that stereotype persons with disabilities in editorial cartoons and be able to discuss them. It develops critical thinking and is necessary to expose biased images.

Organizing a Media Watch

Few cooperative learning instructional techniques engage students at any level quicker than a media watch campaign. These campaigns can help students cooperatively correct misconceptions about persons with disabilities inadvertently perpetuated by newspapers and magazines and thus increase understanding. The concomitant benefits of these campaigns include the development of critical reading and thinking skills and improved attitudes toward persons with disabilities. Because media images of persons with disabilities are often superficial or biased, they provide teachers with continual examples of negative language, prejudice, and stereotypes.

A media watch campaign is a planned method of monitoring the media and then providing reporters, newscasters, editors, and producers with responses, often in the form of personal letters that commend appropriate disability terminology and portrayals or suggest positive, constructive alternatives when problems appear. In addition, a media watch campaign teaches about prejudice by encouraging students to challenge biased coverage of disabilities, especially in news reports and human-interest stories. As a cooperative educational technique, such a campaign can help students learn how to analyze critically what they read and view about persons with disabilities. It also provides, of course, an excellent opportunity for implementing cooperative learning experiences. A media watch campaign can easily include various cooperative learning groups, each assigned to a different newspaper, television or radio station, with follow-up responsibilities for the whole class.

A media watch campaign allows students cooperatively to exert a direct impact on improving public attitudes toward persons with disabilities and exposing ableism in the media. Students personally and directly become involved in the media's ability to communicate, influence, and shape social values in our society. The class gains the experience of becoming involved through direct interaction with media professionals who have often been criticized for creating and perpetuating stereotypes through inaccurate or sensationalized portrayals of persons with disabilities. Such interaction challenges those image-makers who consider themselves responsible and responsive to their audience. Media watch campaigns also provide a way for students to encourage positive media portrayals by communicating constructively with the media when their story or article is well written.

Establishing a media watch campaign takes a lot of work and commitment on the part of both the teacher and the class. The class must understand the purposes and structure of the cooperative campaign assignment. The first step is to decide what particular goals the class hopes to accomplish so it can focus on exactly what it wants to do. Letters and phone calls to the media must reflect clear goals to be attained. The class may have several possible purposes or goals. It may want to focus, for example, on any or all of these six purposes:

(1) diversifying images in the media of persons with disability;
(2) offering alternative terminology and language to discuss disability;
(3) increasing the frequency of features about disability or issues concerning people with disabilities;
(4) encouraging the media to include features or present information for the benefit of disabled persons in the community (for example, encouraging restaurant critics to provide accessibility information in their restaurant reviews, or encouraging chambers of commerce to promote accessible community activities in their promotional brochures);
(5) promoting coverage of policy decisions that affect persons with disabilities, (for example, broad coverage of how recent mass transit decisions affects disabled persons);
(6) increasing inclusion of persons with disabilities in reaction or public comment segments.

The next step in establishing a media watch campaign is to set the scope of activities. Once the goals of the project are established, the class must then cooperatively decide on the scope of its activities. Possible activities include monitoring, taking action, and evaluating what it does. Many questions need to be answered. For example, monitoring procedures need to be clearly established. Some guiding questions for monitors can include reports on the following:

(1) What is the origin of the feature? Is it local or from a newsgathering service like the Associated Press?
(2) What type of disability does the article cover? Over time, an analysis of the prominence of some disability categories can yield interesting findings.
(3) What is the effect of the terminology used to describe disability?
(4) What is the purpose of the media item in relation to disability/disability perspective?

(5) How important and persistent is the issue? The principal criterion for determining its importance is the daily impact it has on the lives of persons with disabilities. The class must also decide if it will treat a "repeat offender" differently from one with a past record for covering disability issues fairly.

The class will need to decide which media sources will be monitored, whether to monitor several newspapers or one, and whether to monitor local or national magazines, and television and radio stations. When setting goals, the class should consider monitoring comparatively few media sources regularly. It will need to discuss other important issues relating to its goals as well. For example, if the class decides to monitor newspapers, on what items will it focus? The possibilities include, local, national and international news stories; regional features; sports and entertainment; editorials; business items and advertisements; and even comics and political cartoons.

The class must also decide how long to conduct its campaign. Will it monitor news features for a day, a week, or a month? Elkins, Jones, and Ulicny (1987) found that daily monitoring is best. But, once the class sets the schedule, it must be followed. Only a regular monitoring schedule can measure the project's effects accurately; success depends on the consistency of the class's monitoring and response letters. The class needs to agree on how long the campaign will last and at what intervals will it decide whether to continue—say a whole school year, a half-year, or less?

The next step in the process is deciding on appropriate action. Having decided what and when to monitor, the class must then decide what specific kinds of action it intends to take. If a student monitor brings in an article with an obvious ableist bias how will the class follow up? It is critical that the entire class discuss the ableist aspects of the article and then agree on an appropriate action. Elkins, Jones, and Ulicny (1987) mentioned the following four options for action:

(1) *Educating the media professionals.* Such education may include sending a brochure to the media. In addition, the class could invite a media professional to speak to the class or it could appoint a representative to meet personally with media professionals, or with an editorial board of a targeted paper or station. The more personal contacts the class makes, the better its chance of establishing a positive relationship with the media. Personal meetings increase the class's credibility and its opportunity to bring about change.

(2) *Rewarding positive articles.* The class may send a personal letter to a reporter or editor complimenting a story.

(3) *Providing corrective responses to negative or undesirable articles.* The class may send letters to a reporter or editor mentioning problems with a particular story or feature, identifying negative aspects (for example, unacceptable portrayals and language) and then suggesting suitable alternatives. In addition, the class may want to quantify the problems and let the editor or reporter know how often such problems have occurred in the past.

(4) *Providing corrective activities for uncooperative media professionals.* The class must also decide how it will deal with media professionals who remain

uncooperative and insensitive to disability issues. The class, for example, may opt to contact an agency, organization, or individual with the influence or power to make change—like an editor, a publisher, a sponsor who buys lots of advertising or even the Federal Communications Commission.

Expanding the watch to monitor other groups who are subject to media bias offers a way to expand or diversify a media watch. Students might work in small groups to consider representations of race, sexuality, gender, nationality, religion, economic status, or geographical region.

The last step in establishing a media watch campaign is assessment. To determine whether or not the campaign has reached its goals, the class can develop a method of evaluating outcomes. A flow chart that tracks group reports can be helpful; it can, perhaps measure whether negative portrayals, language, and terminology have decreased, increased, or remained unchanged. The class can judge whether the media are changing their portrayals and terminology over time. Thus, both the teacher and students must monitor the monitors for accuracy and consistency.

DISABILITY AWARENESS PROGRAMS

Infusing the study of disability into school curriculum aims to incorporate a facet of study that has been omitted in the past. A focus on diversifying curriculum is akin to the long-term societal benefits of educating students with disabilities in public schools and in inclusive settings to reduce of fear, bias, and discrimination. Although incorporating the study of disability into content-area instruction is most desirable, schools may also choose to address disability during particular days, weeks, or months designated for "disability awareness." Disability awareness is observed in states including Indiana and Missouri and in cities across the USA in March. The US Congress designates October as National Disability Employment Awareness Month, and Idaho, North Carolina, and New York also name October as a time to focus on disability history.

Disability awareness events tend to offer activities like charity drives to benefit cure research and guest presenters who share experiences related to disability. Schools may also utilize a disability awareness curriculum to spread knowledge about disability in classes or workshops, or may engage students in activities to alert them to disability discrimination, reduce fear about disability and disabled persons, and/or develop empathy for people with disabilities. Because attitude change often comes in the aftermath of targeting an abundance of messages upon an individual or audience, it is possible to use disability awareness events to promote positive attitudes toward persons with disability.

From the literature on disability awareness, one can adduce the following 20 goals for a comprehensive disability awareness program:

(1) One's value as a human being is not earned, it is a given.
(2) People are more alike than different.

(3) Differences can be seen as both positive and negative. Different does not imply one is better or worse than another person. Differences need not to be stigmatized.

(4) All persons benefit from a diverse population.

(5) Although people are different, an overall transcending humanness unites us all.

(6) All persons can learn.

(7) Disabilities are normal.

(8) People are unique individuals, not labels. Everyone has a right to be judged on individual merit, not prejudged by group membership.

(9) It is hurtful to judge others.

(10) Feelings are important. A caring person avoids hurting others.

(11) Self-esteem helps an individual grow.

(12) Language is a critical ingredient in framing our thoughts and attitudes.

(13) Disabling environments, as opposed to impairments, per se, are situational and environmental and therefore can be eliminated.

(14) Disabled persons have basic rights that must be safeguarded for everyone's benefit.

(15) Positive attitudes and understanding help us all develop empathy.

(16) Developing empathy, understanding, compassion, and concern for others enhances our own growth. Cruelty to others hinders personal growth. Persons with disabilities deserve empathy rather than sympathy or pity, and exercise of empathy is a valuable and compassionate skill.

(17) We can most fully experience life by concentrating on our abilities and doing what we can do.

(18) Each disability group is unique, special, and significant, as is each individual member of that group. We can learn valuable lessons from each disability group and each disabled individual.

(19) Negative attitudes toward persons with disabilities are deeply ingrained in our culture, language, media, and history.

(20) Integration is preferable to segregation.

A comprehensive disability awareness program should stress goals that facilitate integration by establishing a classroom climate in which students with disabilities can find acceptance and respect as their peers learn about the benefits, advantages, and opportunities of living in a diverse and pluralistic society. To support and promote integration and inclusion, one can usefully consider the following guiding principles.

Emphasize Sameness while Appreciating Individual Differences

When teaching about disability awareness, it is useful to emphasize sameness, while taking care not to erase or overly downplay the impact of impairment. For example, when teaching about persons with mobility impairments emphasize the commonalities in people. We may do some things differently, but we do the same things. Although some people get around with the use of a wheelchair, we all need transportation. Some people communicate with sign language or assistive technology, but we all communicate. In fact, although we are all different, we are also all the same and more alike than unlike. Educators may emphasize the idea that people are individuals who represent themselves, not a group, and each has a right to be different. Lessons and activities should reflect an appreciation for differences and diversity and avoid stereotypes and stigmatizing. Information included should stress how every individual contributes to the culture and classroom, and every student is equally worthy. Students, in turn, need to become equipped with a positive way to express their curiosity, concern, and acceptance of those who appear different. Whatever the disability, the classroom discussion should encompass and emphasize individual differences and an appreciation of uniqueness. Similarly, when a guest with a disability comes to class, remind the students that her or she speaks only for himself or herself, not for all disabled people.

Get Involved

Students may become aware of the enormous impact public attitudes have on the potential for acceptance and inclusion of persons with disabilities into community life and how negative impressions lead to prejudice, discrimination, and segregation persons with disabilities encounter every day. When students begin to understand the issues that affect their classmates and others with disabilities, they will be more likely to support social policies and programs that promote inclusion and independence. Further, people typically have to do something in order to change attitudes. Attending lectures or reading ideas, without engagement with them, seldom changes attitudes. Work toward attitude change must include active participation, including thinking, communicating, and taking positive action. This is precisely why longer-term curriculum is likely to be most productive and enriching.

INFLUENCING ATTITUDES TOWARD DISABILITY

Some effective ways to influence attitudes toward disability are experiential (active participation) techniques (Schroedel, 1979; Donaldson, 1980; Watts, 1984). These include social gaming (for example, role-playing, behavior rehearsing, and simulation activities, always followed by discussion); value confrontation and learning about inference; interaction with persons with disabilities (including cooperative learning with disabled peers and exposure to guest presenters with disabilities); the provision of basic information on disabilities by exposure to books, articles, and a wide variety of audio-visual media, including resources available on the Internet; and exposure to assistive technology.

Assessing Existing Attitudes

Teachers can assess class members' general knowledge of and attitudes toward persons with disabilities. Specifically, they may assess their students' current attitudes, common assumptions, and misconceptions in order to plan experiential techniques effectively. Engaging students in self-examination is a good starting point. What myths do students believe to be truth? What paradigms regarding disability do they recognize?

For example, does the student or teacher regard stuttering as amusing? Does he or she believe that persons with mental retardation are dangerous or that persons with disabilities can never be happy? Does he or she consider it foolish to take an individual with blindness to an art museum? What are beliefs regarding integration and segregation. For example, should children with disabilities go to separate schools and if so, why? Do they regard persons with disabilities as a homogeneous group of persons who lead lives quite different from those of the rest of society? Do they associate physical disability with evilness or retribution? Such self-examination should be as intense as possible and should always include discussion. Those who actively participate are far likelier to change attitudes while no change is likely to occur in those who remain passive.

Four effective basic techniques used for assessing attitudes toward disabilities are direct observation, student "opinionnaires," sentence completion techniques, and drawings. All four encourage learners to reflect on their attitudes and thoughts toward persons with disabilities, which the teacher may use to inform planning. Any method used to assess attitudes and beliefs may also prompt discussions of issues related to disabilities.

Direct observation. Observing students as they interact with each other, respond to representations of disability in literature, photos, or media sources, or with adults with disabilities is a way to assess their perceptions and comfort.

Student opinionnaires. The Measurement of Attitudes Toward People With Disabilities, by Antonak and Livneh (1988), includes opinionnaires on all levels for assessing pertinent information. Most of these opinionnaires use a Likert rating scale that includes the familiar range of answers: strongly agree, agree, undecided, disagree, and strongly disagree. They should be used only for "instructional" purposes, not "comparative" or "normative" ones. Teachers may want to develop opinionnaires that include items appropriate for the level of the students they teach and based on the curricular material they teach. In addition, they may want to adapt an existing opinionnaire for younger students who require explanations of language and terms. Teachers may want to rephrase, explain, or simplify questions, or even change them to a true and false format (Antonak & Livneh, 1988).

Student sentence completion techniques. Sentence completion provides another method for adducing feelings and attitudes of students. A student reads a series of open-ended statements to complete. Again, the teacher may want to develop additional or different to match the level of the class and or a specific curriculum.

Student drawings. Yet another valuable attitude assessment strategy is to ask younger students to draw a picture of a scene depicting persons with disabilities. For example, if the student draws a picture of a character with blindness, is the individual wearing dark glasses, holding a cane or tin cup, or using a guide dog? What is the expression on the character's face? If the child draws a picture of a parent of a child with a disability, is the parent sad? If both a parent and a disabled child appear, where are they spaced in relation to each other? If possible, the teacher may want to sit with the child as they draw. As DiLeo (1983) stated, "Articulate children are likely to talk as they draw. These comments should be noted as they may clarify what may or may not be visibly evident" (p. 4). In addition, to assess a youngster's feelings accurately, a teacher should ask them to write a story explaining the picture (Salend, 1994).

EXPERIENTIAL METHODS

Demystifying Aids, Appliances, and Adaptive Technology

Many students with disabilities benefit from using supportive devices, aids, materials, and appliances. These materials include audio books, hearing aids, speech synthesizers, wheelchairs, Braille, and adaptive technology devices. Children with little or no exposure to people with disabilities are often fascinated by all the "gear." Because their fascination focuses on the equipment, they sometimes seem unaware of the person using it. In other words, people often concentrate more on the wheelchair than its user.

One aspect of the stigma of disability lies in the mystification of its accompanying equipment—like wheelchairs, crutches, braces, and walkers—to the extent that people may be afraid to touch these objects, as if they might "catch" the disability. Unfortunately, charity drives reinforce these attitudes. In their quest to make their disability the most debilitating so the public will donate, they often use aids and appliances in a shocking way in their advertising. For example, to dissuade teenagers from drinking and driving, a Blue Cross and Blue Shield of Pennsylvania ad featured an empty wheelchair with the caption, "Is this the set of wheels you've been saving for?" Another ad shows a wheelchair with the caption, "Thousands of youngsters are sentenced to the chair each year." The message is plain: living your life in a wheelchair is the worst thing in the world. An ad for the Muscular Dystrophy Association shows a glass-box like terrarium with a child's leg brace in it. The top has a slit like a bank to collect money. A sign on the box reads, "Help Jerry's kids bury the brace." If such campaigns must convey their points in a negative way, they should focus on what causes the handicap and disability, not what helps the individual overcome it. Such ads make it imperative that teachers, introducing a unit on physical disabilities or sensory impairments, show prostheses and wheelchairs as positive objects that help people deal with environmental barriers.

Recently, various juvenile books have been written that familiarize children with different kinds of equipment. In addition, various magazines, targeted for persons with disabilities, carry ads and information on adaptive equipment. Teachers may have their students read them to learn about adaptive equipment. Such equipment may be shown in a light-hearted context (for example, electric wheelchairs go quite fast, much faster than a person on foot, and can be pictured in races or tag games) to counteract the link between this equipment and injury, death, disease, and vulnerability. Having "practiced" with the equipment, children are less likely to find it strange or frightening. When something is overwhelming, children sometimes react with fear or aggression—in order to make themselves feel more secure. Relieved of their resistance or fear, they can learn to take the paraphernalia for granted and recognize the persons using it. Teachers can introduce these devices in interesting ways that help youngsters develop an appreciation for their purpose, to liberate persons with disabilities.

Inventors, engineers, designers, therapists, and imaginative lay people have devised a wide range of ingenious aids to help disabled people in all phases of their lives—for example, at home, traveling, at work, at recreation. From a simple homemade reacher that retrieves dropped articles, to a sophisticated breath-controlled switch that operates a typewriter, these devices help persons with disabilities live more independently. Aids can simplify eating, grooming, dressing—in fact, almost all the basic tasks of daily living. A few specialized gadgets can make household chores like cleaning, cooking, and laundering easier. Among the more sophisticated adaptive apparatuses are electronic systems, telephones, reading and writing contrivances, and alternative and augmentative communication devices. Automobile adaptations, special controls, and transfer aids make driving possible. Wheelchairs, walkers, hoists, lifts, and ramps increase outdoor and indoor mobility.

The thousands of devices and aids range from expensive equipment obtainable only from specialists to simple gadgets catering to the need of persons with physical disabilities. The large number and wide variety of these products make it impossible to mention every one. For example, just in the area of automobile transportation, automated controls help a physically disabled person drive his or her own car. These include parking brake extensions, left-foot accelerators, built-up brake and gas pedals, left-hand shift levers, and light-weight folding van ramps.

Similarly, a wide assortment of kitchen and cooking aids include a safety-cutting fork designed with the cutting edge along one side designed specifically for either the right or left hand. For those with limited arm range, an angle-handled utensil of stainless steel with a plastic handle is available. Also obtainable are slip-on or large handled utensils. An inner-lip or suction cup dinner plate keeps food from sliding. Microwave ovens come with tactile touchpads, tactile dials, and Braille kits for the controls. A talking bread and dough maker comes with an optional voice feature that can be activated to guide users through all phases of the baking process. A variety of aids for dressing and other daily living needs include an elongated no-stoop shoehorn, elastic shoe laces that permit shoes to be slipped on or off without tying or untying, zipper pull rings or long reach zipper pulls with 18-inch plastic cords and metal hooks and rings, and a one-handed dental flosser which features floss storage and tension control in one handle. There are innumerable tools and adaptive equipment that can be demonstrated to show how people with disabilities navigate daily living.

Thus, students may be introduced to aids, appliances, and assistive technology, and can be provided time to examine and try out the devices that persons with disabilities might use. In their own classrooms they can learn to write in Braille and to use finger spelling and some sign language. They can learn to operate and take care of hearing aids. They can use wheelchairs, walkers, and crutches. They can examine braces, artificial legs, and other prostheses. Schools may borrow the aids and appliances from local agencies, or other schools in the area. Students may even design adaptive equipment as science, technology, or engineering projects.

Leaders of the Disability Rights Movement believe that technology will be the equalizer of the twenty-first century. Technology already enhances our independence and productivity, whether or not we have disabilities. When a person with a disability uses a technology application, it is commonly referred to as "assistive technology."

Assistive technology may be high or low tech; it may be an item available at a local department store, like a large-key telephone, or a specially designed product, like an electric wheelchair equipped with a sip-and-puff control. In the next decade, this technological "liberation" is likely to free more and more of our citizens with disabilities. Combined with civil rights, improved access, and education, assistive technology can help us transcend the myths and prejudices that have limited persons with disabilities for so many years and usher in a new age of inclusion for those so labeled.

Wherever possible, it would be best for students with the disabilities using adaptive equipment to introduce and explain the aids and devices they use themselves. They can show their classmates the devices and allow them to touch and experiment with the equipment. For example, a student with a hearing impairment could explain the parts and maintenance of the hearing aid, and then invite other students to use a hearing aid briefly. If the student with the disability feels uncomfortable explaining the aids he or she uses, a physical therapist, teacher, guidance counselor, or parent might do so. Adaptive devices may be obtained from a variety of sources and placed in a central location within the room. Students could then examine and then experiment with the devices at different times during the school day.

Alternative communication systems, such as Braille, sign language, and finger spelling, can be introduced to students in a variety of ways that simultaneously promote academic skills. Teachers can teach students the manual alphabet, then have them practice their spelling words by spelling them manually. Teachers can include hand signs for numbers as part of a math assignment. For example, rather than writing the numbers of a division computation on the board, the teacher could present the problem with numerical hand signs. Teachers could introduce the students to basic signs and then use them to give directions and assignments. Students who have learned Braille might be assigned the task of reading Braille books, and writing their names or compositions in Braille.

Simulations

Experiencing simulations is much like role-playing. Both are forms of social gaming. Learning through simulations takes place by creating circumstances and working out solutions to problems that might arise in a particular situation. The difference between role-playing and simulations is in the role that participants occupy. Role-plays assume that the participants respond as themselves; simulations ask participants to "try-on" the experience of another. Burgstahler and Doe (2004) explained, "A simulation creates a representation of elements of reality to develop a learning activity so participants develop skills, gain knowledge or change attitudes about that reality" (p. 8). They further stressed, "Simulations have been found to stimulate interest in a topic and the desire to learn more. They are reputed to change perspectives, increase empathy, increase self-awareness, and increase tolerance for ambiguity" (p. 9). Thus, a simulation allows the learner to experience essential aspects of a situation during active participation, which, ideally, generates insight into the real world.

Popular simulation activities include engaging students in blind-folding, ear-plugging, wheelchair-riding, and/or tying back limbs or fingers, then sending them to complete either planned tasks, like an obstacle course, or to try to follow a usual routine as an impaired person. The widely used Frustration Anxiety and Tension workshop, known as F.A.T. City (Lavoie, 1989), is a video that invites participants to make meaning of nonsense words and complete impossible activities to simulate the experience of students with learning disabilities. Although the most favorable outcomes of simulations can result in empathy and appreciation for the challenges disabled persons face from environmental barriers, this learning comes at a steep price. Simulations can also result in heightened fear and negative perceptions of disability.

Burgstahaler and Doe (2004) warn,

> In actuality, most disability-related simulations are designed to result in negative feelings. By disabling participants and simulating problematic experiences, given their new limitations participants learn how difficult it is to maneuver a wheelchair, how frustrating it is to be unable to hear or read, how frightening it is to be visually impaired, or how impossible it is to participate without the use of their hands. They focus on what people with disabilities cannot do with appropriate access, technology, or skills.
>
> (p. 11)

Brew-Parrish (1997, 2004), a disabled activist, recalls her daughter's experience of a disability simulation from which students emerged "terrified of their newly created disabilities," and with ideas that "persons with disabilities had horrible lives. A few thought they might be better off dead."

On the problems with disability simulations, Wright (1987) quoted Laura Raucher, a disability rights advocate with a physical impairment:

> I don't encourage simulations because I think they're based on a false assumption that fifteen minutes, or two hours, or two weeks in a wheelchair or walking around blindfolded could give someone any idea what it's like to be disabled. . . . What a simulation approximates is not the reality of being disabled, but the trauma of becoming disabled—the awkwardness, humiliation, and fear of confronting a world that isn't set up for you and frankly looks down on you, with tools you haven't yet mastered. . . . The point we are missing, in the terrifying blackness behind the blindfold or the sweaty confusion of our first bout with double doors, is that people learn to manage, and manage well with disabilities.
>
> (p. 4)

French (1996) similarly found,

> Simulation exercises have the aim of informing non-disabled people of the situation of disabled people, but they clearly provide false information. At best these exercises only simulate the onset of disability, but even that is not achieved because the people concerned know very well that at the end of the day, or any time they choose, they can stop being "disabled" and return to their non-disabled status. It is

quite obvious that if a person is suddenly deprived of his or her hearing, sight, or ability to walk or use his or her hands, difficulties will be experienced and fear and frustration may be felt, but this is not the situation disabled people are in because they have had to develop coping strategies or unusual dexterity or strength in other areas of their bodies, and are therefore likely to be far more calm and able than the non-disabled person's experience would suggest, which is not to minimize the difficulties they do experience.

(p. 117)

Alternatives to Simulations

The most common goals for a disability simulation include providing students with experiential activities through which to develop awareness of environmental barriers; and to increase knowledge about how persons with disabilities experience daily life—including joys and struggles. Both of these goals can be achieved through experiential activities that do not require simulation. Art Blaser offers "Some Alternatives to Simulation Exercises" in *Ragged Edge Magazine*, some of which are included in the list below.

(1) Talk about doing simulations—without doing them.

(2) Survey your school or neighborhood to assess everyday barriers. Students may note places inaccessible except by stairs, cars parked over driveways, unleashed dogs, color contrast on stairs, branches that can hit a blind person, or note audible cues, such as horns honking.

(3) Survey your school or neighborhood to assess accessibility features. Students can count the number of businesses that have ramps or elevators; explore how to gain access to an elevator in a subway or train station; hunt for accessibility measures found in the environment, including curb cuts, "bumpy tiles" that indicate street intersections or train platforms, Braille plates or signs, the options for auditory instructions. They may evaluate restaurants for table heights and clarity of menus, and so on.

(4) Listen to a person with a disability—one in your neighborhood, your class, around school. Develop a list of questions to ask them about their life—not focused only on medical aspects of the disability.

(5) Take a tour of a familiar place with a person with a disability to gain insight into how she or he negotiates various places.

(6) Find out what confronts a family traveling and living in motels or hotels. Visit a local hotel. Find out where TDD/TTY phones are and how you would find one if you were deaf.

(7) Search for a personal assistant in the classified ads. Find out what the job entails.

(8) Evaluate your home for accessibility according to one or many kinds of impairment. Get an estimate on what it would cost to install accessibility features in your home.

(9) Create or visit an arts exhibit that can be experienced by many senses: touch, hearing, sight, and maybe even smell. For example, consider the texture of oil painting, sculpture, and relief; incorporate sound or narration into an exhibit; or use essential oils to offer ambient scents to an exhibit.

(10) Attend or watch a sporting event that features professional disabled athletes. The Paralympics, for example, features well-known sports like basketball, rugby and tennis, as well as lesser-known competitive team sports like goal ball.

INVITING GUESTS WITH DISABILITIES

Another way to increase students' awareness and understanding on disability is to invite guests with disabilities to interact with or give a presentation to the class. Introducing persons with disabilities into the daily classroom routine provides an ideal first-hand learning opportunity. In general, students benefit from working with community and family volunteers who may work with students on everyday work (e.g., reading buddies) or assist with a special project related to a visitor's professional expertise (e.g., planning a business to learn about economics; planting a garden to study botany). Teachers may specifically invite volunteers, family members, or professionals with disabilities to provide opportunities for direct contact and interaction that does not relate only to disability.

Presenters can also be invited to specific disability awareness events. Class guests with different disabilities can provide experiential knowledge and offer students a chance to have personal contact and to interact with an individual who at first may seem to be different, but in actuality is much like them. The experience gives the youngsters an opportunity to learn how persons with impairments accommodate their disabilities and accomplish what non-disabled persons do only differently. They get the chance to see persons with disabilities as individuals, each with their particular personalities, lifestyles, interests, jobs, problems, and ideas. It is best to seek out a visitor who is accustomed to working with children and offering presentations related to disability, especially for the first visit, or if only one guest is planned. Classroom encounters with guests with disabilities should be well planned and the next pages present preparatory considerations.

Selecting a guest presenter. For the encounter to be meaningful, teachers should be cautious in the identification, selection, and preparation of guest speakers. A teacher can rely on a number of ways to identify potential speakers. Guests with special needs can be located through local branches of national agencies like the Association for Retarded Citizens (ARC) and the United Cerebral Palsy Association (UCP). In addition, every state has a Developmental Disabilities Council, and most publish directories of agencies and services within that state. Local agencies are also listed in the Yellow Pages under Human Service Organizations or Social Service Organizations.

Selecting the number of guests. Teachers sometimes conclude that the experience will be more valuable if they invite several guests with similar disabilities at the same time. They feel one visitor may be more comfortable with others. But, this decision should be considered carefully. Guests expounding conflicting perspectives or personalities may not appreciate being on the same panel without warning; and unplanned tension can result in confusion and discomfort for everyone involved. If a debate is desired or a presentation of divergent perspectives is intended, it is essential that guests are informed and comfortable and that students know the purpose of the presentation.

Screening potential guests. Having identified potential guest presenters, a teacher should interview them informally. Contact the person, introducing yourself, and explain the interest of your class. Briefly describe the purposes and related activities so that the presenter knows the context into which he or she is entering. It is important to explain what preparation the students will have before the visit. Explain, as well, what you expect in a guest presenter, to help the potential guest speaker decide whether he or she would be comfortable participating in the program, and the kinds of things he or she would like to talk about. From this initial conversation, you might determine that the guest's perspective and experience is not well aligned with the curriculum or students' interests. If the guest does seem like a good candidate, you could gain some principles to include in the curriculum, as well as consider how your class might best interact with the visitor. An introductory conversation should help you get an idea of the person's personality and comfort with children, which can support the planning of a positive experience for all.

Important characteristics to look for in a presenter. If the guest comes from an organization he or she will probably be accustomed to working with groups, though it is useful to consider the age groups with which the presenter has worked before. Potential presenters who are not accustomed to working with children or being "in the spotlight" need to know ahead of time the kinds of questions students may ask. The introductory conversation can be a time to alert presenters to the likely need to be able to respond candidly, respectfully, and age-appropriately to questions that may seem inappropriate, naive, or intrusive by adult norms. Declining to answer some kinds of questions is, of course, acceptable, but ground rules should be made explicit to students and are best established by the presenter.

Making arrangements. In addition to establishing a date and time, compensation, and other arrangements, it may be particularly important to discuss transportation and access requirements. Teachers should be aware of whether public transportation is accessible and convenient to the school, in terms of the guest's needs. It is also essential to evaluate the accessibility of the school itself: consider entrances and exits, the classroom space, and restrooms. Also important is to consider and ask about interaction with students. Will students need an interpreter or other assistive technology to interact with the guest, for example? If so, how will those arrangements be made? If a service animal (e.g., a guide dog) will attend class, it is important to consider allergies and/or students' fears.

Preparing the presenter. Teachers should keep foremost in their minds the importance of planning and preparation. When inviting a guest who will be compensated for his or her work and time, she or he should know ahead of time what the class expects. Teachers should explain the class's purpose for the invitation and what students should experience or learn, and guests need to know how long a presentation should be (an hour is usually about right for young students; more time may be useful for older); how much of the time to allow for questions; and what kinds of questions will be asked. For example, consider whether the class will have been learning about environmental accessibility, adapting to daily life, vocations, discrimination, personal experiences, being a child, and so on. When inviting a guest who is volunteering his or her time, providing information about length of time and structure is also necessary, but it is essential to ask and respond to the *guest's* preferences for the type of presentation that will be made and the kind of discussion that will be invited. A volunteer should not be asked to prepare something outside of his or her areas of comfort, unless she or he offers.

Preparing the students. Inviting guests with disabilities should be part of an inclusive, multidimensional classroom experience. Therefore, the students should have already engaged in some learning to prepare for the visit. If students know something about the visitor's life and characteristics, their interest will be heightened and they will tend to ask more meaningful questions. It is useful to describe the guest to students—age, where she or he lives or grew up, profession or job, interests, hobbies, and disability. Students may then generate topics of interest or questions they may like to ask. Generating ideas for questions provides an opportunity to help students evaluate appropriate or inappropriate kinds of questions, as based on the teacher's knowledge about the guest.

Addressing feelings. Be sure to allow opportunities for both the guest and children to express their feelings about being with each other. Such a visit may be the first experience youngsters have had to interact with a person with a disability. If the experience is positive, open, and natural, it will influence the way the youngsters may approach others with disabilities when they meet them. It is better to talk openly in front of most guests than talk about them after they have left. Persons with disabilities live with a need to express their feelings, and teachers should understand that individuals with disabilities are more comfortable with questions than non-disabled adults realize. In fact, the conclusion that persons with disabilities avoid talking about their impairments or are ashamed of them is, itself, a form of prejudiced thinking. Moreover, discussing people now out of sight encourages shyness in children.

Expressing appreciation. Among the best ideas to follow-up a visit is to invite students to write thank-you letters, emails, or record messages to your presenter. This experience provides the class an opportunity to express gratitude, comment on what they learned, and maybe ask more questions and build a relationship.

Questions for Classroom Discussion

All classroom activities—including role-playing and hosting guests with disabilities—should include thorough de-briefings and discussions. When presenting any information on disability as diversity awareness, teachers may find any or all of the following questions helpful for promoting classroom discussions. These questions also lend themselves nicely to writing assignments.

1. Human Variation is Normal

   - Why are all children normal and all children special?
   - What is meant by the statement, "People are different in degree rather than kind?"
   - What is your definition of normal?

- How are all people more alike than different?
- How can differences be seen as both positive and negative?
- Why is it important to see people as individuals, not labels?

2. Attitudes and Actions

- How do our feelings influence our attitudes and behavior?
- How does our language reflect our attitudes?
- How are negative attitudes toward persons with disabilities deeply ingrained in our culture, language, and history?
- How is your perception of yourself shaped by the way others perceive you?
- In what ways might experiences at school affect the self-image of persons with disabilities?
- Why is it wrong to judge someone by something he or she cannot change?
- What is the difference between "laughing at" people and "laughing with" them?
- How can a disability obstruct people's views of each other?
- What causes peer cruelty? Why do we tend to laugh at something or someone who is different?
- Why is it important to treat all persons as individuals?
- What are the implications of calling someone a "vegetable"?
- What do the concepts of "monster" and "freak" imply?
- What are the implications for persons with disabilities of beliefs like "social Darwinism," "eugenics," and "racial hygiene"?

3. Stereotypes and Self-Image

- Why do you think many people with disabilities describe themselves as "ordinary" and wonder why others do not see them in the same way?
- How do labels become stereotypes? What other negative effects do labels have?
- How do labels affect self-image?
- What are the different effects of being born with a disability and acquiring one later in life?
- Why is it wrong to base judgments of others on appearances?
- What is a "stigma"? How does it affect how we think about someone?
- Describe the concept of "stigma spread." How does a disability become an "all-defining" characteristic?

4. Disability Rights and Awareness

- Why must the basic rights of persons with disabilities be safeguarded for everyone's benefit?
- Why do many people with physical disabilities view telethons and similar fund-raising methods as demeaning?

- Why do most persons with disabilities want us to "empathize" with them rather than "sympathize" with them?
- What is meant by the statement, "An impairment is a characteristic of a person; a disability is a characteristic of the environment"?
- What is meant by the statement, "disabilities are situational?"
- What are the differences and similarities between the concepts of ableism and racism, sexism, or heterosexism?
- What are the differences between "equity" and "equality"?
- Describe what a socially inclusive society would be like.

CONCLUSION

The expansion of curriculum to include disability and disability perspectives is essential to promoting inclusivity through education. Providing opportunities for students with and without disabilities to live and learn together in inclusive classrooms is an important element in developing values for all ways of being. There are also many ways that the study of disability and the experiences of disabled people can become part of school curriculum. Ongoing attention to disability contributes to broader movements to diversify curriculum and provides learners opportunities to explore and sharpen critical perspectives on ableism. Experiential techniques are direct approaches to teaching about disability and may be useful to address specific needs and questions within the inclusive classroom.

FINAL THOUGHTS

This is a book for all teachers. The development of inclusive education affects everyone and involves everyone. As stated in Chapter 1, schools have a responsibility for encouraging diversity and tolerance, eliminating discrimination, increasing among learners an understanding of those perceived to be different, and respecting and protecting the rights of all diverse populations within our pluralistic society. Each individual child is the responsibility of the school and has a right to attend and feel as though they belong. Considering the "three R's"—recognition, respect, and responsibility—as tenets to guide educational practice can inform productive dialogue and the building of collaborative relationships with students, families, and other professionals.

The emergence of disability studies challenges and resists the medical model and segregation, as well as examines the perpetuation of these paradigms in the media, our culture, and schools. Directions toward inclusive education, such as universal design for learning and developing and practicing curriculum to be multicultural and ability diverse offer promising practices to provide rigorous learning and the development of community to the benefit of all children. In turn, developing practices that are responsive to the anticipated diversity of learners mitigates the need to separate children from one another. Scholars in the fields of disability studies and disability studies in education firmly acknowledge that schools and teachers do not, alone, shoulder all of the responsibility in working toward societal and school integration. The historical legacy of marginalization; the paradigms of disability that inform societal institutions, bureaucratic structures, and policy; and slow, sometimes contradictory forces of school reform movements—including standardization—all complicate efforts toward the realization of inclusive schools. In addition, negative attitudes among educators (and the public) toward the inclusion of students with disabilities persist. In the face of seemingly insurmountable challenges, however, there is much possibility. The emergence of disability rights and progress made toward inclusive education over the past decades is testament to the ability of schools and societies to become places in which everybody belongs.

Inclusive education is a project and a way of approaching teaching, learning, and development of schools. It is not a destination, but a struggle to be wide-awake in our thought and action. As we are able and willing to recognize assumptions and practices that reflect and enact ableism, we are more able to take action as self-advocates, allies, and accomplices working toward disability rights and education for all. In every moment teachers, students, families, and communities have the opportunity to create community and express a value for diversity. What will your moment be?

REFERENCES

ADAPT v. Skinner, 881 F.2d 1184, 3rd Cir. (1989).

Adler, S., Richard, Y., & Horowitz, J. (2008). *Tropic Thunder* director/star Ben Stiller says disability advocates' planned boycott is unwarranted. *MTV.com*. Retrieved August 11, 2008, from http://www.mtv.com/movies/news/articles/1592544/story.jhtml

Advisory Committee on Human Radiation Experiments [ACHRE]. (1994). *Interim report*. Washington, DC: U.S. Government Printing Office.

Advisory Committee on Human Radiation Experiments [ACHRE]. (1996). *Executive summary and guide to final report*. Washington, DC: U.S. Government Printing Office.

Albrecht, G., Seelman, K., & Bury, M. (2001). *Handbook of disability studies*. Thousand Oaks, CA: Sage Publications.

Althusser, L. (1971). Ideology and the ideological state apparatus. In F. Jameson (ed.), *Lenin and philosophy and other essays* (pp. 1–29). New York, NY: Monthly Review Press.

American Library Association. (2016). Select bibliography of children's books about the disability experience. Retrieved from http://www.ala.org/awardsgrants/schneider-family-book-award

American Psychiatric Association. (1973). *Diagnostic and statistical manual of mental disorders* (6th change; 2nd ed.). Arlington, VA: American Psychiatric Association.

American Psychiatric Association. (2013). *Diagnostic and statistical manual of mental disorders* (5th ed.). Arlington, VA: American Psychiatric Association.

Americans with Disabilities Act Amendments Act of 2008. PL. 110–325. Stat. 3406. (2008).

Americans with Disabilities Act of 1990. PL. 101–336. 104 Stat. 327. (1990).

Anderson, J.D. (1988). *The education of Blacks in the South, 1860–1935*. Chapel Hill, NC: University of North Carolina Press.

Andrews, J.E., Carnine, D.W., Coutinho, M.J., Edgar, E.B., Forness, S.R., Fuchs, L.S., . . . Wong, J. (2000). Bridging the special education divide. *Remedial and Special Education*, *21*(5), 258–260, 267.

Annamma, S.A., Connor, D., & Ferri, B. (2013). Dis/ability critical race (DisCrit): Theorizing at the intersections of race and dis/ability. *Journal of Race, Ethnicity, and Education*, *16*(1), 1–31.

Antonak, R., & Livneh, H. (1988). *The measurement of attitudes toward people with disabilities: Methods, psychometrics and scales*. Springfield, IL: Charles C. Thomas.

Arad, A., Foster, G., Milchan, A. (Producers), & Johnson, M.S. (Director). (2003). *Daredevil* [motion picture]. United States: 20th Century Fox.

Arieno, M. (1989). *Victorian lunatics: A social epidemiology of mental illness in mid-nineteenth century England*. Cranbury, NJ: Associated University Presses.

Asante, M.K. (1991). Afrocentric curriculum. *Educational Leadership*, *49*(4), 28–31.

Asch, A. (2000). Why I haven't changed my mind about prenatal diagnosis: Reflections and refinements. In E. Parens & A. Asch (eds.), *Prenatal testing and disability rights* (pp. 234–258). Washington DC: Georgetown University Press.

Aspies for Freedom [website]. Accessed May 1, 2009, at http://www.aspiesforfreedom.com/

Astor, C. (1985). *Who makes people different: Jewish perspectives on the disabled.* New York, NY: United Synagogue of America, Department of Youth Activities.

Autistic Self Advocacy Network [website]. Accessed May 1, 2009, at http://www.autisticadvocacy.org/

Ayres, A. J., & Tickle, L. S. (1980). Hyper-responsivity to touch and vestibular stimuli as a predictor of positive response to sensory integration procedures by autistic children. *American Journal of Occupational Therapy, 34,* 375–381.

Baglieri, S. (2016). Toward unity in school reform: What DisCrit contributes to multicultural and inclusive education. In D. J. Connor, B. A. Ferri, & S. A. Annamma (eds.), *DisCrit: Disability studies and critical race theory in education* (pp. 167–181). New York, NY: Teachers College Press.

Baglieri, S., & Knopf, J. H. (2004). Normalizing difference in inclusive teaching. *Journal of Learning Disabilities, 37*(6), 525–529.

Baglieri, S., & Leber, J. (2008). *Conversations about graduate school and learning disability* [website]. Accessed June 3, 2008, at http://www.graduateschoolandld.com

Ballard, K. (ed.). (1999). *Inclusive education: International voices on disability and justice.* London: Falmer Press.

Banks, J. A. (1993). The canon debate, knowledge, construction, and multicultural education. *Educational Researcher, 22*(5), 4–14.

Banks, J. A. (2005). Approaches to multicultural curriculum reform. In J. A. Banks & C. A. McGee Banks (eds.), *Multicultural education issues and perspectives* (Vol. 5, pp. 242–264). Hoboken, NJ: John Wiley & Sons.

Baranek, G. T. (2002). Efficacy of sensory and motor interventions for children with autism. *Journal of Autism and Developmental Disorders, 32*(5), 397–422.

Barnes, C., Mercer, G., & Shakespeare, T. (1999). *Exploring disability: A sociological introduction.* Malden, MA: Blackwell Publishers.

Barrie, J. M. (1904). *Peter Pan: The boy who wouldn't grow up* [performance]. London: Duke of York's Theatre.

Barrie, J. M. (1911). *Peter and Wendy* (AKA Peter Pan). London: Hodder & Stoughton.

Barton, L. (ed.). (1996). *Disability and society: Emerging issues and insights.* New York, NY: Addison Wesley Longman.

Barton, L., & Armstrong, F. (2001). Disability, education and inclusion: Cross-cultural issues dilemmas. In G. Albrecht, K. Seelman, & M. Bury (eds.), *Handbook of disability studies* (pp. 693–710). Thousand Oaks, CA: Sage Publications.

Baskin, B. (1975). The handicapped in children's literature. In *Proceedings of the Special Study Institute: Fostering positive attitudes toward the handicapped in school settings* (pp. 132–164). Rensselaerville, NY: New York State Education Department.

Bauman, M. L., & Kemper, T. L. (eds.). (2004). *The neurobiology of autism* (2nd ed.). Baltimore, MD: Johns Hopkins University Press.

Baumeister, A., & Butterfield, E. (eds.). (1970). *Residential facilities for the mentally retarded.* Chicago, IL: Aldine Publishing Co.

Baynton, D. (2001). *Disability and the justification of inequality in American history.* In P. Longmore & L. Umansky (eds.), *The new disability history: American perspectives* (pp. 33–57). New York, NY: New York University Press.

Befort, S. F. (2013). Empirical examination of case outcomes under the ADA Amendments Act. *Washington and Lee Law Review, 70*(4), 2027–2071.

Bell, C., & Burgdorf, R. (1983). *Accommodating the spectrum of individual abilities* (Clearinghouse Publication #81). Washington, DC: United States Commission on Civil Rights.

Bell, D. (1980). *Brown v. Board of the Education* and the interest convergence dilemma. *Harvard Law Review, 93,* 518–533.

Benioff, D., & Weiss, D. B. (Producers). (2011). *Game of thrones* [television series]. New York City, NY: Home Box Office.

Berenbaum, M. (1993). *The world must know: The history of the Holocaust as told in the United States Holocaust Memorial Museum.* Boston, MA: Little Brown & Co.

Berman, P. (Producer), & Dieterle, W. (Director). (1939). *The hunchback of Notre Dame* [motion picture]. United States: RKO Radio Pictures.

Biklen, D. (1981). The Supreme Court v. retarded children. *Journal of the Association for Persons with Severe Handicaps, 6*(2), 3–5.

Biklen, D. (1989). Redefining schools. In D. Biklen, D. Ferguson, & A. Ford (eds.), *Schooling and disability* (pp. 1–24). Chicago, IL: National Society for the Study of Education.

Biklen, D., with Attfield, R., Bissonnette, L., Blackman, L., Burke, J., Frugone, A., . . . Rubin, S. (ed.). (2005). *Autism and the myth of the person alone.* New York, NY: New York University Press.

Biklen, D., & Bogdan, R. (1977). Media portrayals of disabled people: A study in stereotypes. *Interracial Books of Children Bulletin, 8*(6 & 7), 4–9.

Biklen, D., & Burke, J. (2006). Presuming competence. *Equity & Excellence in Education, 39*(2), 166–175.

Biklen, D., & Cardinal, D. N. (eds.). (1997). *Contested words, contested science: Unraveling the facilitated communication controversy.* New York, NY: Teachers College Press.

Biklen, D., Ferguson, D., & Ford, A. (eds.). (1989). *Schooling and disability.* Chicago, IL: National Society for the Study of Education, University of Chicago Press.

Binding, K., & Hoche, A. (1975). *The release of the destruction of life devoid of value.* R. Sassone (ed.). Santa Ana, CA: Life Quality Paperbacks (original work published 1920).

Blanchett, W. J. (2006). Disproportionate representation of African-American students in special education: Acknowledging the role of White privilege and racism. *Educational Researcher, 35*(6), 24–28.

Blaser, A. (2003). Awareness days: Some alternatives to simulation exercises. *Ragged Edge Magazine,* September/October. Retrieved from http://www.raggededgemagazine.com/0903/0903ft1.html

Blatt, B. (1970). *Exodus from pandemonium: Human abuse and a reformation of public policy.* Boston, MA: Allyn & Bacon.

Blatt, B. (1981). *In and out of mental retardation: Essays on educability, disability, and human policy.* Baltimore, MD: University Park Press.

Bleul, H. (1973). *Sex and society in Nazi Germany.* Philadelphia, PA: J.B. Lippincott.

Board of Education v. Rowley, 458 U.S. 176 (2nd Circuit Court 1982).

Bogdan, R. (1986). Exhibiting mentally retarded people for amusement and profit, 1850–1940. *American Journal of Mental Deficiency, 91*(2), 120–126.

Bogdan, R. (1988). *Freak show: Presenting human oddities for amusement and profit.* Chicago, IL: University of Chicago Press.

Bogdan, R., & Taylor, S. (1994). *The social meaning of mental retardation: Two life stories.* New York, NY: Teachers College Press, Columbia University.

Booth, A., & Dunn, J. (eds.). (1996). *Family–school links.* Mahwah, NJ: Lawrence Erlbaum.

Bowe, F. (1978). *Handicapping America: Barriers to disabled people.* New York, NY: Harper & Row.

Bowe, F. G. (2000). *Universal design in education.* Westport, CT: Bergin and Garvey.

Brantlinger, E. A. (2003). *Dividing classes: How the middle class negotiates and rationalizes school advantage.* New York, NY: Routledge.

Brashear, R. (Producer/Director). (2013). *FIXED: The science/fiction of human enhancement* [motion picture]. United States: New Day Films.

Braverman, M. (Creator). (1989). *Life goes on* [television series]. Burbank, CA: Toots Company/Warner Brothers.

Brew-Parrish, V. (1997). The wrong message [electronic version]. *Ragged Edge Online,* March/April. Retrieved April 10, 2008 from http://www.raggededgemagazine.com /archive/aware.htm

Brew-Parrish, V. (2004). The wrong message—still [electronic version]. *Ragged Edge Online.* Retrieved April 10, 2008 from http://www.raggededgemagazine.com /focus/wrongmessage04.html

Broderick, A. A., & Kasa-Hendrickson, C. (2006). "I am thinking that speech is asinine": Narrating complexities and rethinking the notion of "independence" in communication. *Equity & Excellence in Education, 39*(2), 176–186.

Browder, D. M., Mims, P. J., Spooner, F., Ahlgrim-Delzell, L., & Lee, A. (2008). Teaching elementary students with multiple disabilities to participate in shared stories. *Research and Practice for Persons with Severe Disabilities, 33*(1–2), 3–12.

Brown v. Board of Education of Topeka, 347 U.S. 483 (1954).

Buck v. Bell, 143 Va. 313, 130 S.E. 516, 517 (1925).

Bullock, C., & Mahon, M. (1997). *Introduction to recreation services for people with disabilities: A person-centered approach.* Champaign, IL: Sagamore Publishing.

Burgdorf, R. (1980). *The legal rights of handicapped persons: Cases, materials and text.* Baltimore, MD: Brookes Publishers.

Burgdorf, M., & Burgdorf, R. (1975). A history of unequal treatment: The qualifications of handicapped persons as a *Suspect Class* under the Equal Protection Clause. *Santa Clara Lawyer*, *215*(4), 855–910.

Burgdorf, R., & Burgdorf, M. (1977). The wicked witch is almost dead: "Buck v. Bell" and the sterilization of handicapped persons. *Temple Law Quarterly*, *50*(4), 995–1034.

Burgstahler, S. (2009). Universal Design of Instruction (UDI): Definition, principles, guidelines, and examples [website]. Seattle: DO-IT, University of Washington. Retrieved from http://www.washington.edu/doit/Brochures/Academics/instruction.html

Burgstahler, S., & Doe, T. (2004) Disability-related simulations: If, and how to use them in professional development. *Review of Disability Studies: An International Journal*, *2*(2), 8–18.

Burleigh, M. (1994). *Death and deliverance: "Euthanasia" in Germany 1900–1945*. New York, NY: Cambridge University Press.

Burns, M. (2005). Looking at how students reason. *Educational Leadership*, *53*(3), 26–31.

Burns, R. (1995, August 18). 16,000 used in radiation experiments. *The Times* (Trenton, NJ), p. 3B.

Calkins, L. (1986). *The art of teaching writing*. Portsmouth, NH: Heinemann.

Cammarota, J., & Fine, M. (2008). *Revolutionizing education: Youth participatory action research in motion*. New York, NY: Routledge.

Campbell, F.K. (2009). *Contours of ableism*. Basingstoke, UK: Palgrave Macmillan.

Carlisle, J. (1985). *Tangled tongue: Living with a stutter*. Reading, MA: Addison-Wesley.

Carrier, J.G. (1986). *Learning disability: Social class and the construction of inequality in American education*. New York, NY: Greenwood Press.

Centers for Disease Control and Prevention. (2008, June 30). *Autism Spectrum Disorder: Data and statistics, prevalence*. Retrieved from https://www.cdc.gov/ncbddd/autism/data.html

Charkins, H. (1996). *Children with facial difference*. Bethesda, MD: Woodbine House.

Cherry v. Mathews, 419 F.Supp. 922 (United States District Court, District of Columbia. 1976).

Civil Rights Act of 1964. Pub.L. 88–352, 78 Stat. 241 (1964).

Clandinin, D.J., & Raymond, H. (2006). Note on narrating disability. *Equity & Excellence in Education*, *39*(2), 101–104.

Clark, C.T. (2003). Examining the role of authoritative discourse in the labeling and unlabeling of a "learning disabled" college learner. *Journal of Adolescent and Adult Literacy*, *47*(2), 128–135.

Cohen, S. (1977). *Special people*. Englewood Cliffs, NJ: Prentice-Hall.

Collins, K.M. (2003). *Ability profiling and school failure: One child's struggle to be seen as competent*. Mahwah, NJ: Lawrence Erlbaum Associates.

Collins, K.M. (2015). A disability studies in education analysis of corporate-based educational reform: Lessons from New Orleans. In D.J. Connor, J.W. Valle, & C. Hale (eds.), *Practicing disability studies in education: Acting toward social change* (pp. 217–233). New York, NY: Peter Lang.

Collins, L. (Producer), Stanton, A., & MacLane, A. (Directors). (2016). *Finding dory* [motion picture]. USA: Disney Pixar.

Connell, B.R., Jones, M., Mace, R., Mueller, J., Mullick, A., Ostroff, E., . . . & Vanderheiden, G. (1997). *The principles of universal design*. NC State University, The Center for Universal Design. Retrieved from https://www.ncsu.edu/ncsu/design/cud/about_ud/udprinciplestext.htm

Connor, D.J. (2008). *Urban narratives: Portraits in progress. Life at the intersections of learning disability, race, and social class*. New York, NY: Peter Lang.

Connor, D.J. (2012). Does dis/ability now sit at the table (s) of social justice and multicultural education? A descriptive survey of three recent anthologies. *Disability Studies Quarterly*, *32*(3). Retrieved from http://dsq-sds.org/article/view/1770/3095

Connor, D.J., & Baglieri, S. (2009). Tipping the scales: Disability studies asks "How much diversity can you take?". In S. Steinberg (ed.), *Diversity and multiculturalism: A reader* (pp. 341–362). New York, NY: Peter Lang.

Conot, R. (1983). *Justice at Nuremberg*. New York, NY: Carroll & Graf Publishers.

Conrad, B. (1988). Cooperative learning and prejudice reduction. *Social Education*, April/May, 283–286.

Corbett, J. (1996) *Bad-Mouthing: The language of special needs*. Bristol, PA: Falmer Press.

Cornfeld, S., McLeod, E. (Producers), & Stiller, B. (Producer/Director). (2008). *Tropic thunder* [motion picture]. United States: DreamWorks/Paramount Pictures.

Cortiella, C., & Horowitz, S.H. (2014). *The state of learning disabilities: Facts, trends, and emerging issues* (3rd ed.). New York, NY: National Center for Learning Disabilities.

Cosby, B. (Producer). (1984). *The Cosby show* [television series]. New York: Carsey-Werner Company.

Crissey, M., & Rosen, M. (1986). *Institutions for the mentally retarded: A changing role in changing times.* Austin, TX: Pro-Ed.

Crossley, R. (1997). *Speechless: Facilitating communication for people without voices.* New York, NY: Dutton/Penguin Books USA.

Crutchfield, S., & Epstein, M. (2000). *Points of contact: Disability, art, and culture.* Ann Arbor, MI: University of Michigan Press.

Dalton, B., Proctor, C.P., Uccelli, P., Mo, E., & Snow, C.E. (2011). Designing for diversity: The role of reading strategies and interactive vocabulary in a digital reading environment for fifth-grade monolingual English and bilingual students. *Journal of Literacy Research, 43*(1), 68–100. doi:10.1177/1086296X10397872

Danforth, S., & Rhodes, W.C. (1997). Deconstructing disability: A philosophy for inclusion. *Remedial and Special Education, 18*(6), 357–366.

Danforth, S., & Smith, T.J. (2005). *Engaging troubling students: A constructivist approach.* Thousand Oaks, CA: Corwin Press.

Daniel R.R. v State Board of Education, 874 F.2d 1036 (5th Circuit Court 1989).

Darder, A., Baltodano, M.P., & Torres, R.D. (2009). *The critical pedagogy reader* (2nd ed.). New York, NY: Routledge.

Darke, P. (1998). Understanding cinematic representations of disability. In T. Shakespeare (ed.), *The disability reader: Social science perspectives* (pp. 181–197). London: Cassell.

Davis, L. (1995). *Enforcing normalcy: Disability, deafness and the body.* London: Verso.

Davis, L. (ed.). (1997). *The disability studies reader.* New York, NY: Routledge.

Dawson, M., Soulières, I., Gernsbacher, M.A., & Mottron, L. (2007). The level and nature of autistic intelligence. *Psychological Science, 18*, 657–662.

Dearing, B. (1981). Literary images as stereotypes. In D. Biklen & L. Bailey (eds.), *Rudely stamp'd: Imaginal disability and prejudice* (pp. 33–47). Washington, DC: University Press of America.

Dei, G.J.S., James, I.M., Karumanchery, L.L., James-Wilson, S., & Zine, J. (2000). *Removing the margins: The challenges and possibilities of inclusive schooling.* Toronto: Canadian Scholars' Press.

Dewey, J. (1916). *Democracy and education.* New York, NY: MacMillan.

Dewey, J. (1938). *Experience and education.* West Lafayette, IN: Kappa Delta Pi.

Dickens, C. (1843). *A Christmas carol.* London: Chapman & Hall.

DiLeo, J. (1983). *Interpreting children's drawings.* New York, NY: Brunner/Mazel Publishers.

Disabled in Action of Pennsylvania v. Coleman (E.D., Pa. 1976).

Doll, W. (2004). The four R's—An alternative to the Tyler rationale. In D.J. Flinders & S.J. Thornton (eds.), *The curriculum studies reader* (pp. 253–260). New York, NY: Routledge.

Dolmage, J., & DeGenaro, W. (eds.). (2005). Responding to *Million Dollar Baby*: A forum. *Disability Studies Quarterly, 25*(3). Retrieved June 21, 2009, from http://www.dsq-sds.org/article/view/590/767

Donaldson, J. (1980). Changing attitudes toward handicapped persons: A review and analysis of research. *Exceptional Children, 46*(7), 504–514.

Du Bois, W.E.B. (1903). *The souls of black folk: Essays and sketches.* Chicago, IL: A.C. McClurg & Co.

Dudley-Marling, C., & Dippo, D. (1995). What learning disability does: Sustaining the ideology of schooling. *Journal of Learning Disabilities, 28*, 406–414.

Durant, W. (1944). *Caesar and Christ.* New York, NY: Simon & Schuster.

Durrell, D.D., Scribner, H.B., McHugh, W.J., Manning, J.C., & Rochfort, G.B. (1959). Adapting instruction to the learning needs of children in the intermediate grades. *The Journal of Education, 142*(2), 1–78.

Dymond, S.K., Renzaglia, A., Rosenstein, A., Eul Jung, C., Banks, R.A., Niswander, V., & Gibson, C.L. (2006). Using a Participatory Action Research approach to create a universally designed inclusive high school science course: A case study. *Research and Practice for Persons with Severe Disabilities, 31*(4), 293–308.

Edwards, M. (1996). Ability and disability in the Ancient Greek military community. In E. Makas & L. Schlesinger (eds.), *End results and starting points: Expanding the field of disability studies* (pp. 29–33). Portland, ME: The Society for Disability Studies and The Muskie Institute.

Edyburn, D.L., & Edyburn, K.D. (2012). Tools for creating accessible, tiered, and multilingual web-based curricula. *Intervention in School & Clinic, 47*(4), 199–205. doi:10.1177/1053451211424603

Eiseland, N. (1994). *The disabled god: Toward a liberatory theology of disability.* Nashville, TN: Abington Press.

Elkins, S., Jones, M., & Ulicny, R. (1987). *The media watch campaign manual.* Lawrence, KA: The Research & Training Center on Independent Living, The University of Kansas.

Epstein, J.L. (2001). *School and family partnerships: Preparing educators and improving schools.* Boulder, CO: Westview Press.

Erevelles, N. (2000). Educating unruly bodies: Critical pedagogy, disability studies, and the politics of schooling. *Educational Theory, 50*(1), 25–47.

Evans, D. (1983). *The lives of mentally retarded persons.* Boulder, CO: Westview Press.

Every Student Succeeds Act (ESSA). (2015). Pub. L. No. 114–95. In 114th Congress.

Fan, W., Williams, C. M., & Wolters, C. A. (2012). Parental involvement in predicting school motivation: Similar and differential effects across ethnic groups. *The Journal of Educational Research, 105*(1), 21–35.

Ferguson, A. A. (2001). *Bad boys: Public schools in the making of black masculinity.* Ann Arbor, MI: University of Michigan Press.

Ferguson, P. (1994). *Abandoned to their fate: Social policy and practice toward severely retarded people in America, 1820–1920.* Philadelphia, PA: Temple University Press.

Ferri, B. A., & Connor, D. J. (2005). Tools of exclusion: Race, disability, and (re)segregated education. *Teachers College Record, 107*(3), 453–474.

Ferri, B. A., & Connor, D. J. (2006). *Reading resistance: Discourses of exclusion in desegregation and inclusion debates.* New York, NY: Peter Lang.

Fiedler, L. (1978). *Freaks: Myths and images of the secret self.* New York, NY: Simon & Schuster.

Fiedler, L. (1996). *Tyranny of the normal: Essays on bioethics, theology, and myth.* New Brunswick, NJ: Rutgers University Press.

Fiedorowicz, I. C., Benezra, E., MacDonald, W., McElgunn, B., Wilson, A., & Kaplan, B. (2001). Neurobiological basis of learning disabilities: An update. *Learning Disabilities: A Multidisciplinary Journal, 11*(2), 61–74.

Finerman, W., Starkey, S., Tisch, S. (Producers), & Zemeckis, R. (Director). (1994). *Forrest Gump* [motion picture]. United States: Paramount Pictures.

Finger, A. (1992). The idiot, the cretin and the cripple. *Disability Rag, 13*(6), 23–25.

Fish, W. W. (2008). The IEP meeting. Perceptions of parents of students who receive special education services. *Preventing School Failure, 53*(1), 8–14.

Fleischer, D. Z., & Zames, F. (2001). *The disability rights movement: From charity to confrontation.* Philadelphia, PA: Temple University Press.

Fleming, P. M. (2000). Three decades of educational progress (and continuing barriers) for women and girls. *Equity & Excellence in Education, 33*(1), 74–79.

Flores, M. M. (2008). Universal Design in elementary and middle school: Designing classrooms and instructional practices to ensure access to learning for all students. *Childhood Education, 84*(4), 224–229.

Fosnot, C. T. (ed.). (2005). *Constructivism: Theory, perspectives, and practice* (2nd ed.). New York, NY: Teachers College Press.

Foucault, M. (1965). *Madness and civilization: A history of insanity in the age of reason* (R. Howard, Trans.). New York, NY: Vintage Books.

Francis, K. (2005). Autism interventions: A critical update. *Developmental Medicine & Child Neurology, 47*(7), 493–499.

Franklin, B. M. (1994). *From "backwardness" to "at-risk": Childhood learning difficulties and the contradictions of school reform.* Albany, NY: State University of New York Press.

Freire, P. (1970). *Pedagogy of the oppressed.* New York, NY: Continuum.

French, R. (1932). *From Homer to Helen Keller: A social and educational study of the blind.* New York, NY: American Foundation of the Blind.

French, S. (1996). Simulation exercises in disability awareness training: A critique. In G. Hales (ed.), *Beyond disability: Towards an enabling society* (pp. 114–123). Thousand Oaks, CA: SAGE Publications.

Friedberg, J., Mullins, J., & Sukiennik, A. (1985). *Accept me as I am: Best books of juvenile nonfiction on impairments and disabilities.* New Providence, NJ: R. R. Bowker.

Friedberg, J., Mullins, J., & Sukiennik, A. (1992). *Portraying persons with disabilities (nonfiction): An annotated bibliography of nonfiction for children and teenagers.* New Providence, NJ: R. R. Bowker.

Friedlander, H. (1995). *The origins of Nazi genocide: From euthanasia to the final solution.* Chapel Hill, NC: The University of North Carolina Press.

Fries, K. (ed.). (1997). *Staring back: The disability experience from the inside out.* New York, NY: Penguin Books.

Fuchs, L. S., Fuchs, D., & Speece, D. L. (2002). Treatment validity as a unifying construct for identifying learning disabilities. *Learning Disability Quarterly, 25*, 33–46.

Funk, R. (1987). Disability rights: From caste to class in the context of civil rights. In A. Gartner & T. Joe (eds.), *Images of the disabled, disabling images* (pp. 7–30). New York, NY: Praeger Publishers.

Gabel, S. (2005). *Disability studies in education: Readings in theory and method.* New York, NY: Peter Lang.

Gabel, S.L., & Danforth, S. (2008). *Disability and the politics of education: An international reader*. New York, NY: Peter Lang.

Galinsky, A.D., Hugenberg, K., Groom, C., & Bodenhausen, G.V. (2003). The reappropriation of stigmatizing labels: Implications for social identity. In J. Polzer (ed.), *Research on managing groups and teams* (Vol. 5, pp. 221–256). Amsterdam, The Netherlands: Elsevier Science.

Gallagher, D.J. (2001). Neutrality as a moral standpoint, conceptual confusion and the full inclusion debate. *Disability and Society, 16*(5), 637–654.

Gallagher, H. (1995). *By trust betrayed: Patients, physicians, and the license to kill in the Third Reich*. Arlington, VA: Vandamere Press.

Gallaudet Research Institute. (2003). Regional and National Summary Report of Data from the 2001–2002 Annual Survey of Deaf and Hard of Hearing Children & Youth [electronic version]. Retrieved August 15, 2006 from http://gri.gallaudet.edu/Demographics/2002_National_Summary.pdf

Garderen, D. van, & Whittaker, C. (2006). Planning differentiated, multicultural instruction for secondary inclusive classrooms. *Teaching Exceptional Children, 38*(3), 12–20.

Gardner, H., & Hatch, T. (1989). Multiple intelligences go to school: Educational implications of the theory of multiple intelligences. *Educational Researcher, 18*(8), 4–9.

Garland, R. (1995). *The eye of the beholder: Deformity and disability in the Greco-Roman world*. Ithaca, NY: Cornell University Press.

Garland Thomson, R. (1997). *Extraordinary bodies: Figuring physical disability in American culture and literature*. New York, NY. Columbia University Press.

Gearheart, B., Mullen, R., & Gearheart, C. (1993). *Exceptional individuals: An introduction*. Belmont, CA: Brooks/Cole Publishing Co.

Gilhool, T.K. (1997). The events, forces and issues that triggered enactment of the Education for All Handicapped Children Act of 1975. In D.K. Lipsky & A. Gartner (eds.), *Inclusion and school reform: Transforming America's classrooms* (pp. 263–273). Baltimore, MD: Paul H. Brookes.

Gill, C.J., & Voss, L.A. (2005). Views of disabled people regarding legalized assisted suicide before and after a balanced informational presentation. *Journal of Disability Policy Studies, 16*(1), 6–15.

Gilligan, V. (Producer). (2008). *Breaking bad* [television series]. New York, NY: AMC Networks.

Gindis, B. (1999). Vygotsky's vision: Reshaping the practice of special education for the 21st century. *Remedial and Special Education, 20*(6), 333–340.

Glass, D.O.N., Meyer, A., & Rose, D.H. (2013). Universal Design for learning and the arts. *Harvard Educational Review, 83*(1), 98–119.

Gliedman, J. (1979, August). The wheelchair rebellion. *Psychology Today*, pp. 59, 60, 63, 64, 99, 101.

Gliedman, J., & Roth, W. (1980). *The unexpected minority: Handicapped children in America*. New York, NY: Harcourt Brace Jovanovich.

Goddard, H. (1912). *The Kallikak family: A study in the heredity of feeble-mindedness*. New York, NY: Macmillan.

Goffman, E. (1963). *Stigma: Notes on the management of spoiled identities*. Englewood Cliffs, NJ: Prentice-Hall.

González, N., Moll, L.C., & Amanti, C. (eds.). (2006). *Funds of knowledge: Theorizing practices in households, communities, and classrooms*. New York, NY: Routledge.

Goodley, D. (2011). *Disability studies: An interdisciplinary introduction*. London: Sage.

Goodley, D. (2014). *Dis/ability studies: Theorising disablism and ableism*. New York, NY: Routledge.

Gordon, B.O., & Rosenblum, K.E. (2001). Bringing disability into the sociological frame: A comparison of disability with race, sex, and sexual orientation statuses. *Disability & Society, 16*(1), 5–19.

Gould, S. (1981). *The mismeasure of man*. New York, NY: W.W. Norton & Company.

Gould, W. (1933). Euthanasia. *Journal of the Institute of Homeopathy, 27*, 82.

Grandin, T. (1995). *Thinking in pictures: And other reports from my life with autism*. New York, NY: Vintage.

Grandin, T. (ed.). (2007). *Livestock handling and transport* (3rd ed.). Wallingford, UK: CAB International.

Grandin, T., & Johnson, C. (2005). *Animals in translation*. New York, NY: Scribner.

Grandin, T., & Scariano, M.M. (1986). *Emergence: Labeled autistic*. New York, NY: Warner Books.

Greene, M. (1971). Curriculum and consciousness. *Teachers College Record, 73*(2), 253–269.

Greene, M. (1977). Toward wide-awakeness: An argument for the arts and humanities in education. *Teachers College Record, 79*(1), 119–125.

Greenstein, A. (2015). *Radical inclusive education: Disability, teaching and struggles for liberation*. New York, NY: Routledge.

Grindler, M., Stratton, B., & McKenna, M. (1997). *The right book, the right time: Helping children cope*. Boston, MA: Allyn & Bacon.

Grob, G. (1994). *The mad among us: A history of the care of America's mentally ill*. New York, NY: The Free Press.

Grolnick, W.S., & Slowiaczek, M.L. (1994). Parents' involvement in children's schooling: A multidimensional conceptualization and motivational model. *Child Development, 65*, 237–252.

Gross, Z. (2014). *Anti-filicide toolkit*. Washington, DC: Autistic Self Advocacy Network.

Guinagh, B. (1980). The social integration of handicapped children. *Phi Delta Kappan, 62*(1), 27–29.

Gutiérrez, K.D., Baquedano-López, P., Alvarez, H.H., & Chiu, M.M. (1999). Building a culture of collaboration through hybrid language practices. *Theory Into Practice, 38*(2), 87–93.

Haddon, M., & Rogers D. Spotswood Collection. (2003). *The curious incident of the dog in the night-time*. New York, NY: Doubleday.

Haggis, P., Rosenberg, T., Ruddy, A. S. (Producers), & Eastwood, C. (Producer/Director). (2004). *Million dollar baby* [motion picture]. Los Angeles, CA: Warner Brothers Pictures.

Hahn, D. (Producer), Trousdale, G., & Wise, K. (Directors). (1996). *The hunchback of Notre Dame* [motion picture]. United States: Walt Disney Pictures, Buena Vista Distribution.

Hahn, H. (1987). Civil rights for disabled Americans: The foundation of a political agenda. In A. Gartner & T. Joe (eds.), *Images of the disabled, disabling images* (pp. 181–203). New York, NY: Praeger Publishers.

Hahn, H. (1988). The politics of physical differences: Disability and discrimination. *Journal of Social Issues, 44*, 39–47. doi:10.1111/j.1540-4560.1988.tb02047.x

Haj, F. (1970). *Disability in antiquity*. New York, NY: Philosophical Library, cited in D. Moores (1996). *Educating the Deaf: Psychology, principles, and practices* (4th ed.). Boston, MA: Houghton Mifflin Co.

Hale, C. (2008). *From exclusivity to exclusion: The LD experience of privileged parents* (Doctoral dissertation). Retrieved from ProQuest Dissertations Publishing. (3325396).

Hall, T.E., Cohen, N., Vue, G., & Ganley, P. (2015). Addressing learning disabilities with UDL and technology: Strategic reader. *Learning Disability Quarterly, 38*(2), 72–83. doi:10.1177/0731948714544375

Hall, T.E., Meyer, A., & Rose, D.H. (eds.). (2012). *Universal design for learning in the classroom: Practical applications*. New York, NY: Guilford Press.

Haller, B. (2000). False positive. *Ragged Edge Online*, January/February. Retrieved April 20, 2002, from http://www.raggededgemagazine.com/0100/c0100media.htm

Haller, B.A. (2010). *Representing disability in an ableist world: Essays on mass media*. Louisville, KY: Advocado Press.

Haller, M. (1963). *Eugenics: Hereditarian attitudes in American thought*. New Brunswick, NJ: Rutgers University Press.

Hardman, M., Drew, C., & Egan, M. (1996). *Human exceptionality: Society, school, and family* (5th ed.). Needham Heights, MA: Allyn & Bacon, Simon & Schuster Company.

Harris, C. (1993). Whiteness as property. *Harvard Law Review, 106*, 1709–1791.

Harry, B. (1994). *The disproportionate representation of minority students in special education: Theories and recommendations*. Alexandria, VA: Project FORUM, National Association of State Directors of Special Education.

Harry, B., & Klingner, J. (2005). *Why are so many minority students in special education? Understanding race and disability in schools*. New York, NY: Teachers College Press.

Harry, B., Klingner, J.K., & Hart, J. (2005). African American families under fire: Ethnographic view of family strengths. *Remedial and Special Education, 26*(2), 101–112.

Hart, S., Dixon, A., Drummond, M.J., & McIntyre, D. (2004). *Learning without limits*. Maidenhead, UK: Open University Press.

Henderson, H., & Bryan, W. (1997). *Psychosocial aspects of disability*. Springfield, IL: Charles C. Thomas.

Herskovitz, M., Solomon, R., Zwick, E. (Producers), & Nelson, J. (Producer/Director). (2001). *I am Sam* [motion picture]. United States: New Line Production.

Heshusius, L. (1989). The Newtonian mechanistic paradigm, special education, and the contours of alternatives: An overview. *Journal of Learning Disabilities, 22*, 402–415.

Hewett, F., & Forness, S. (1977). *Education of exceptional learners* (2nd ed.). Boston, MA: Allyn & Bacon.

Higher Education Opportunity Act of 2008, 20 U.S.C. § 1001 et seq.

Hitler, A. (1971). *Mein Kampf* (R. Manheim, Trans.). Boston, MA: Houghton Mifflin Co. (Original work published 1925)

Hockenberry, J. (1995). *Moving violations: A memoir of war zones, wheelchairs, and declarations of independence*. New York, NY: Hyperion.

Hollander, R. (1989). Euthanasia and mental retardation: Suggesting the unthinkable. *Mental Retardation*, *27*(2), 53–61.

Holt, J. (1964). *How children fail.* New York, NY: Pitman.

Holt, J. (2004). *Instead of education: Ways to help people do things better.* Boulder, CO: Sentient Publications.

Horowitz, S. M., Bility, K. M., Plichta, S. B., Leaf, P. J., & Haynes, N. (1998). Teachers' assessments of behavioral disorders. *American Journal of Orthopsychiatry, 68*(1), 117–125.

Hoversten, P. (August 18, 1995a). Radiation test report: 16,000 were subjects. *USA Today*, p. 1A.

Hoversten, P. (August 18, 1995b). Hunting radiation records—and truth. *USA Today*, p. 3A.

Hugo, V. (1831). *The hunchback of Notre Dame.* New York: Bantam Classics (1986 ed.).

Hull, J. (1990). *Touching the rock: An experience of blindness.* New York, NY: Vintage Press.

Hunt, N., & Marshall, K. (1994). *Exceptional children and youth: An introduction to special education.* Boston, MA: Houghton Mifflin Co.

Hunter, M. (1982). *Mastery teaching.* Thousand Oaks, CA: Corwin Press.

Illich, I. (1971). *Deschooling society.* New York, NY: Harper & Row.

Individuals with Disabilities Education Act (IDEA). P.L. 101–47–642, U.S.C. (1990).

Individuals with Disabilities Education Improvement Act of 2004. Pub. L. No. 108–446, 118 Stat. 2658 (2004).

Ingstad, B., & Whyte, S. (eds.). (1995). *Disability and culture.* Berkeley, CA: University of California Press.

James, H. (1975). *The little victims: How America treats its children.* New York, NY: David McKay Company, Inc.

Jernigan, K. (1983). Blindness: Disability or nuisance. In R. Jones (ed.), *Reflections on growing up disabled* (pp. 58–67). Reston, VA: Council for Exceptional Children.

Jimenez, T.C., Graf, V.L., & Rose, E. (2007). Gaining access to general education: The promise of universal design for learning. *Issues in Teacher Education, 16*(2), 41–54.

Johnson, D.W., & Johnson, R.T. (1999). Making cooperative learning work. *Theory Into Practice, 38*(2), 67–73.

Johnson, E. (January/February, 1987). Life unworthy of life. *Disability Rag, 8*(1), 24–26.

Johnson, H.M. (2003, February 16). Unspeakable conversations. *The New York Times*.

Johnson, H.M. (2005). *Too late to die young: Nearly true tales from a life.* New York, NY: Picador.

Johnson, M. (1994). Communicative action and its utility in disability research. In E. Makas & L. Schlesinger (eds.), *Insights and outlooks: Current trends in disability studies* (pp. 9–16). Portland, ME: The Society for Disability Studies.

Johnson, M. (Producer), & Levinson, B. (Director). (1988). *Rainman* [motion picture]. United States: MGM.

Johnson, R., & Johnson, D. (1980). The social integration of handicapped students into the mainstream. In M. Reynolds (ed.), *Social environment of the schools* (pp. 9–37). Reston, VA: The Council for Exceptional Children.

Johnson, W. (1956). An open letter to the mother of a stuttering child. In W. Johnson, S. Brown, J. Curtis, C. Edney, & S. Keaster (1959 ed.), *Speech handicapped school children* (pp. 443–449). New York: Harper & Bros. Reprinted by the National Society for Crippled Children and Adults.

Jorgensen, C.M. (1996). Designing inclusive curricula right from the start: Practical strategies and examples for the high school classroom. In S. Stainback & W. Stainback (eds.), *Inclusion: A guide for educators* (pp. 221–236). Baltimore, MD: Paul H. Brookes.

Jorgensen, C.M., McSheehan, M., & Sonnenmeier, R.M. (2007). Presumed competence reflected in the educational programs of students with IDD before and after the Beyond Access professional development intervention. *Journal of Intellectual & Developmental Disability, 32*(4), 248–262.

Jorgensen, C.M., McSheehan, M., & Sonnenmeier, R.M. (2010). *The beyond access model. Promoting membership, participation, and learning for students with disabilities in the general education classroom.* Baltimore, MD: Paul. H. Brookes.

Kaestle, C. (1976). Conflict and consensus revisited: Notes toward a reinterpretation of American educational history. *Harvard Educational Review, 46*(3), 390–396.

Kalyanpur, M., & Harry, B. (1999). *Culture in special education: Building reciprocal family-professional relationships.* Baltimore, MD: Paul H. Brookes.

Kane, H., & Tangdhanakanond, K. (2008). A comparison of discrepancy procedures for learning disabilities: Evidence from the United States. *International Journal of Special Education, 23*(2), 70–77.

Kanner, L. (1964). *A history of the care and study of the mentally retarded.* Springfield, IL: Charles C. Thomas.

Kasa-Hendrickson, C. (2005). 'There's no way this kid's retarded': Teachers' optimistic constructions of students' ability. *International Journal of Inclusive Education, 9*(1), 55–69.

Kater, M. (1989). *Doctors under Hitler*. Chapel Hill, NC: The University of North Carolina Press.

Katz, J. (2013). The Three Block Model of Universal Design for Learning (UDL): Engaging students in inclusive education. *Canadian Journal of Education*, 36(1), 153–194.

Katz, J., & Sugden, R. (2013). The three-block model of universal design for learning implementation in a high school. *Canadian Journal of Educational Administration and Policy*, issue 141, 1–28.

Kavale, K.A. (2002). Mainstreaming to full inclusion: From orthogenesis to pathogenesis of an idea. *International Journal of Disability, Development and Education*, 49(2), 201–214.

Kelley, M.J. (2013). Blindness as physical and moral disorder in the works of Gonzalo de Berceo. *Hispanic Review*, 73(2), 131–155.

Kelsay, D.M.R., & Tyler, R.S. (1996). Advantages and disadvantages expected and realized by pediatric cochlear implant recipients as reported by their parents. *American Journal of Otology*, 17(6), 866–873.

Kennedy, K., Marshall, F., Molen, G.R. (Producers), & Spielberg, S. (Director). (1991). *Hook* [motion picture]. United States: TriStar Pictures.

Kennedy, M.J., Thomas, C.N., Meyer, J.P., Alves, K.D., & Lloyd, J.W. (2014). Using evidence-based multimedia to improve vocabulary performance of adolescents with LD: A UDL approach. *Learning Disability Quarterly*, 37(2), 71–86. doi:10.1177/0731948713507262

Kiger, G. (1989). Disability in film and social life: A dramaturgical perspective. In S. Hey, G. Kiger, & D. Evans (eds.), *The changing world of impaired and disabled people in society* (pp. 149–159). Salem, OR: The Society for Disability Studies and Willamette University.

King-Sears, M.E., Johnson, T.M., Berkeley, S., Weiss, M.P., Peters-Burton, E.E., Evmenova, A.S., . . . Hursh, J.C. (2015). An exploratory study of universal design for teaching chemistry to students with and without disabilities. *Learning Disability Quarterly*, 38(2), 84–96. doi:10.1177/0731948714564575

Kirchner, C. (1996). Looking under the street lamp: Inappropriate uses of measures just because they are there. *Journal of Disability Policy Studies*, 7(1), 77–90.

Kirschner, K.L., Brashler, R., & Savage, T.A. (2007). Ashley X. *American Journal of Physical Medicine & Rehabilitation*, 86(12), 1023–1029.

Kisor, H. (1990). *What's that pig outdoors? A memoir of deafness*. New York: Hill & Wang.

Klift, E.V. d., & Kunc, N. (1994). Beyond benevolence: Friendship and the politics of help. In J.S. Thousand, R.A. Villa, & A.I. Nevin (eds.), *Creativity and collaborative learning: A practical guide to empowering students and teachers*. Baltimore, MD: Paul H. Brookes Publishing Co.

Koegel, L.K., Koegel, R.L., Harrower, J.K., & Carter, C.M. (1999). Pivotal Response Intervention I: Overview of approach. *The Journal of the Association for Persons with Severe Handicaps*, 24(3), 174–185.

Koegel, L.K., Koegel, R.L., Shoshan, Y., & McNerney, E. (1999). Pivotal Response Intervention II: Preliminary long-term outcome data. *The Journal of the Association for Persons with Severe Handicaps*, 24(3), 186–198.

Kokaska, C., & Brolin, D. (1985). *Career education for handicapped individuals* (2nd ed.). New York, NY: Merrill, Macmillan Publishing Co.

Kortering, L.J., McClannon, T.W., & Braziel, P.M. (2008). Universal Design for Learning: A look at what algebra and biology students with and without high incidence conditions are saying. *Remedial & Special Education*, 29(6), 352–363.

Korthagen, F.A.J. (1999). Linking reflection and technical competence: The logbook as an instrument in teacher education. *European Journal of Teacher Education*, 22(2/3), 191–207.

Kozleski, E.B., & Thorius, K.K. (eds.). (2014). *Ability, equity, and culture: Sustaining inclusive urban education reform*. New York, NY: Teachers College Press.

Kozol, J. (1991). *Savage inequalities*. New York, NY: Crown.

Kozol, J. (2005). *The shame of the nation: The restoration of apartheid schooling in America*. New York, NY: Crown.

Kriegel, L. (Fall, 1982). The wolf in the pit in the zoo. *Social Policy*, 13, 16–23.

Kriegel, L. (1991). *Falling into life*. San Francisco, CA: North Point Press.

Kroeger, S.D., Leibold, C.K., & Ryan, B. (1999). Creating a sense of ownership in the IEP process. *Teaching Exceptional Children*, 32(1), 4–9.

Kudlick, C.J. (2003). Disability history: Why we need another "other". Retrieved August 22, 2003, from http://www.historycoop.org/journals/ahr/108.3/kudlick.html

Kuhl, S. (1994). *The Nazi connection: Eugenics, American racism, and German national socialism*. New York, NY: Oxford University Press.

Kumashiro, K.K. (2012). *Bad teacher! How blaming teachers distorts the bigger picture*. New York, NY: Teachers College Press.

Kurtts, S. A., Matthews, C. E., & Smallwood, T. (2009). (Dis)Solving the differences: A physical science lesson using Universal Design. *Intervention in School & Clinic, 44*(3), 151–159.

L'Abate, L., & Curtis, L. (1975). *Teaching the exceptional child.* Philadelphia, PA: W. B. Saunders Co.

Ladson-Billings, G. (1995). Toward a theory of culturally relevant pedagogy. *American Education Research Journal, 32*(3), 465–491.

Ladson-Billings, G. (2009). Race *still* matters: Critical race theory in education. In M. W. Apple, W. Au, & L. A. Gandin (eds.), *Routledge international handbook of critical education* (pp. 110–122). New York, NY: Routledge.

Ladson-Billings, G. (2014). Culturally relevant pedagogy 2.0: aka the remix. *Harvard Educational Review, 84*(1), 74–84.

Ladson-Billings, G., & Tate, W. (1995). Toward a Critical Race Theory of education. *Teachers College Record, 97*(1), 47–68.

Lalvani, P. (2012). Parents' participation in special education in the context of implicit educational ideologies and socioeconomic status. *Education and Training in Autism and Developmental Disabilities, 47*(4), 474–486.

Lareau, A. (1996). Assessing parent involvement in schooling: A critical analysis. In A. Booth & J. F. Dunn (eds.), *Family–school links* (pp. 57–64). Mahwah, NJ: Lawrence Erlbaum Associates.

Lavoie, R. (Writer). (1989). How difficult can this be? The F.A.T. City workshop [DVD]. USA: www.ricklavoie.com.

Lederer, J. M. (2000). Reciprocal teaching of social studies in inclusive elementary classrooms. *Journal of Learning Disabilities, 33*(1), 91–106.

Lee, C. D. (2007). *Culture, literacy, and learning: Taking bloom in the midst of the whirlwind.* New York, NY: Teachers College Press.

Lee, S., Everett, B., & Rosen, S. (1964). "The origin of Daredevil." *Daredevil* #1. New York, NY: Marvel Comics.

Leonardo, Z. (2009). *Race, whiteness, and education.* New York, NY: Routledge.

Leroux, G. (1910). *The phantom of the opera.* Paris: Pierre Lafitte and Cie.

Lessen, E. (1994). *Exceptional persons in society.* Needham Heights, MA: Simon & Schuster.

Lieberman, L. J., Lytle, R. K., & Clarcq, J. A. (2008). Getting it right from the start: Employing the Universal Design for Learning approach to your curriculum. *JOPERD: The Journal of Physical Education, Recreation & Dance, 79*(2), 32–39.

Lifton, R. (1986). *The Nazi doctors: Medical killing and the psychology of genocide.* New York, NY: Basic Books.

Lifton, R. (1990). Sterilization and euthanasia. In M. Berenbaum, (ed.), *A mosaic of victims: Non-Jews persecuted and murdered by the Nazis* (pp. 222–228). New York, NY: New York University Press.

Linton, S. (1998). *Claiming disability: Knowledge and identity.* New York, NY: New York University Press.

Linton, S. (2007). *My body politic: A memoir.* Ann Arbor, MI: University of Michigan Press.

Linton, S. (2008). Simi Linton: Disability/Arts [website]. Accessed March 13, 2008, at http://www.similinton.com/dac.htm

Lo, L. (2008). Interactions between Chinese parents and special education professionals in IEP meetings: Implications for the education of Chinese immigrant children with disabilities. In G. Li & L. Wang (eds.), *Model minority myth revisited: An interdisciplinary approach to demystifying Asian American educational experiences* (pp. 195–212). Charlotte, NC: Information Age Publishing.

Long, E. (1985/1990). Riding the iron worm. In A. Brightman (ed.), *Ordinary moments: The disabled experience* (pp. 79–98). Syracuse, NY: Human Policy Press.

Longmore, P. (1987). Screening stereotypes: Images of disabled people in television and motion pictures. In A. Gartner & T. Joe (eds.), *Images of the disabled, disabling images* (pp. 65–78). New York, NY: Praeger.

Longmore, P. (2005). The cultural framing of disability: Telethons as a case study. *Publications of the Modern Language Association of America, 120*(2), 502–517.

Longmore, P. K., & Umansky, L. (eds.). (2001). *The new disability history: American perspectives.* New York, NY: New York University Press.

Losen, D. J., & Orfield, G. (eds.). (2002). *Racial inequity in special education.* Boston, MA: Harvard Educational Publishing Group.

Luke, C., & Gore, J. (1992). *Feminisms and critical pedagogy.* New York, NY: Routledge.

Lynch, S. A., & Warner, L. (2008). Creating lesson plans for all learners. *Kappa Delta Pi Record, 45*(1), 10–15.

Mace, R. L., Hardie, G. J., & Place, J. P. (1990). *Accessible environments: Toward universal design.* Raleigh, NC: Center for Accessible Housing, North Carolina State University.

MacFarlane, S. (Producer). (1999). *Family guy* [television series]. Los Angeles, CA: Fox Broadcasting Company.

Mackelprang, R., & Salsgiver, O. (Jan., 1996). People with disabilities and social work: Historical and contemporary issues. *Social Work, 41*(1), 7–14.

Maloff, C., & Wood, S. (1988). *Business and social etiquette with disabled people: A guide to getting along with persons who have impairments of mobility, vision, hearing, or speech*. Springfield, IL: Charles C. Thomas.

Margolis, H., & Shapiro, A. (1987). Countering negative images of disability in classical literature. *The English Journal, 76*(3), 18–22.

Mariage, T.V., Paxton-Buursma, D.J., & Bouck, E.C. (2004). Interanimation: Repositioning possibilities in educational contexts. *Journal of Learning Disabilities, 37*(6), 534–549.

Marino, M.T. (2009). Understanding how adolescents with reading difficulties utilize technology-based tools. *Exceptionality, 17*(2), 88–102. doi:10.1080/09362830902805848

Marino, M.T., Black, A.C., Hayes, M.T., & Beecher, C.C. (2010). An analysis of factors that affect struggling readers' achievement during a technology-enhanced STEM astronomy curriculum. *Journal of Special Education Technology, 25*(3), 35–47.

Marino, M.T., Gotch, C.M., Israel, M., Vasquez, E., Basham, J.D., & Becht, K. (2014). UDL in the middle school science classroom: Can video games and alternative text heighten engagement and learning for students with learning disabilities? *Learning Disability Quarterly, 37*(2), 87–99. doi:10.1177/0731948713503963

Martin, G.R.R. (1996). *A game of thrones*. New York, NY: Bantam Spectra.

Martin, J.E., Marshall, L.H., Maxson, L.M., & Jerman, P. (1996). *Self-directed IEP*. Longmont, CO: Sopris West.

Mason, C.Y., McGahee-Kovac, M., & Johnson, L. (2004). How to help students lead their IEP meetings. *Teaching Exceptional Children, 36*(3), 18–25.

McConnell, S.R. (2002). Interventions to facilitate social interaction for young children with autism: Review of available research and recommendations for educational intervention and future research. *Journal of Autism and Developmental Disorders, 32*(5), 351–372.

McCormic, P., Fisher, L., Wick, D. (Producers), & Hogan, P.J., (Director). (2003). *Peter Pan* [motion picture]. United States: Universal Studios, Columbia Pictures.

McDermott, R., & Varenne, H. (1995). Culture "as" disability. *Anthropology and Education Quarterly, 26*(3), 324–348.

McGuire, J.M. (2014). Universally Accessible Instruction: Oxymoron or opportunity? *Journal of Postsecondary Education and Disability, 27*(4), 387–398.

McGuire, J.M., Scott, S.S., & Shaw, S.F. (2006). Universal design and its applications in educational environments. *Remedial and Special Education, 27*(3), 166–175.

McLaren, P. (2003). Critical pedagogy: A look at the major concepts. In A. Darder, M. Baltodano, & R.D. Torres (eds.), *The critical pedagogy reader* (pp. 69–96). New York, NY: RoutledgeFalmer.

McLaughlin, M.W., & Talbert, J.E. (1992). *Social constructions of students: Challenges to policy coherence*. Paper presented at the American Educational Research Association Annual Meeting, Washington, DC.

McNeal Jr, R.B. (2012). Checking in or checking out? Investigating the parent involvement reactive hypothesis. *The Journal of Educational Research, 105*(2), 79–89.

McTighe, J., & Brown, J.L. (2005). Differentiated instruction and educational standards: Is detente possible? *Theory Into Practice, 44*(3), 234–244.

McTighe, J., & Wiggins, G. (2004). *The understanding by design professional development workbook*. Alexandria, VA: ASCD.

Meo, G. (2008). Curriculum planning for all learners: applying Universal Design for Learning (UDL) to a high school reading comprehension program. *Preventing School Failure, 52*(2), 21–30.

Metcalf, U. (1818). The interior of Bethlehem Hospital. In D. Peterson (ed.). (1982), *A mad people's history of madness*. Pittsburgh, PA: University of Pittsburgh Press.

Metz, M.H. (1994). Desegregation as necessity and challenge. *Journal of Negro Education, 63*(1), 64–76.

Meyer, A., Rose, D.H., & Gordon, D. (2014). *Universal design for learning: Theory and practice*. Wakefield, MA: CAST Professional Publishing.

Mezirow, J. (1991). *Transformative dimensions of adult learning*. San Francisco, CA: Jossey-Bass.

Mezirow, J. (1998). On critical reflection. *Adult Education Quarterly, 48*(3), 185–198.

Miller, H.M. (2001). Including "the included". *The Reading Teacher, 54*(8), 820–822.

Mills v. Board of Education of District of Columbia, 348 F. Supp. 866 (D.D.C. 1972).

Miron, G., Urschel, J.L., Mathis, W.J., & Tornquist, E. (2010). Schools without diversity: education management organizations, charter schools, and the demographic stratification of the American school system. Boulder, CO: Education and the Public Interest Center. Retrieved from http://eric.ed.gov/?id=ED509329

Mitchell, D.T., & Snyder, S.L. (Producers/Directors). (1995). *Vital signs: Crip culture talks back* [motion picture]. United States: Fanlight Productions.

Mitchell, D.T., & Snyder, S.L. (2001). *Narrative prosthesis: Disability and the dependencies of discourse.* Ann Arbor, MI: University of Michigan Press.

Mitchell, D.T., Snyder, S.L., & Ware, L. (2014). "[Every] Child Left Behind": Curricular cripistemologies and the crip/queer art of failure. *Journal of Literary & Cultural Disability Studies, 8*(3), 295–313.

Monestier, M. (1987). *Human oddities: A book of nature's anomalies.* Secaucus, NJ: Citadel Press.

Mooney, J. (2007). *The short bus: A journey beyond normal.* New York, NY: Henry Holt.

Moores, D. (1996). *Educating the Deaf: Psychology, principles, and practices.* Boston, MA: Houghton Mifflin Co.

Morgan, S. (1987). *Abuse and neglect of handicapped children.* Boston, MA: Little, Brown and Company.

Morocco, C.C. (2001). Teaching for understanding with students with disabilities: New directions for research on access to the general education curriculum. *Learning Disability Quarterly, 24*(1), 5–13.

Morocco, C.C., & Hindin, A. (2002). The role of conversation in a thematic understanding of literature. *Learning Disabilities Research and Practice, 17*(3), 144–159.

Mr. Snafoo. (1997, December 21). *The New York Times,* Section 6, p. 21.

Mueller, T.G. (2009). IEP facilitation: A promising approach to resolving conflicts between families and schools. *Teaching Exceptional Children, 41*(3), 60–67.

Müller, I. (1991). *Hitler's justice: The courts of the Third Reich.* Cambridge, MA: Harvard University Press.

Murugami, M.W. (2009). Disability and identity. *Disability Studies Quarterly, 29*(4). http://dsq-sds.org/article/view/979/1173

Nario-Redmond, M. (2008, June). *Consensus for disability stereotypes: Maintaining group boundaries and legitimizing the status quo.* Paper presented at the meeting of the Society for Disability Studies, New York, NY.

Narkon, D.E., & Wells, J.C. (2013). Improving reading comprehension for elementary students with learning disabilities: UDL enhanced story mapping. *Preventing School Failure, 57*(4), 231–239. doi:10.1080/1045988X.2012.726286

National Association of the Deaf. (2000). *Cochlear implants: NAD position statement.* Retrieved June 5, 2009, from http://www.nad.org/ciposition

National Center for Education Statistics [NCES]. (2015). Table 204.30: Children 3 to 21 years old served under Individuals with Disabilities Education Act (IDEA), Part B, by type of disability: Selected years, 1976–77 through 2013–14. Retrieved from https://nces.ed.gov/programs/digest/d15/tables/dt15_204.30.asp

National Child Traumatic Stress Network. (2004). Facts on trauma and deaf children [electronic version]. Retrieved August 1, 2008, from www.NCTSNet.org

Nielsen, K.E. (2012). *A disability history of the United States* (Vol. 2). Boston, MA: Beacon Press.

Noddings, N. (1994). An ethic of caring and its implications for instructional arrangements. In L. Stone (ed.), *The education feminism reader* (pp. 171–183). New York, NY: Routledge.

Noguera, P.A. (2008). *The trouble with black boys: And other reflections on race, equity and the future of public education.* Hoboken, NJ: John Wiley & Sons.

Nussbaum, S. (2013). *Good kings, bad kings: A novel.* Chapel Hill, NC: Algonquin Books.

Obermann, C. (1965). *A history of vocational rehabilitation in America.* Minneapolis, MN: T.S. Denison.

Oberti vs. Board of Education of the Borough of Clementon School District (3rd Circuit Court, 1993).

O'Brien, J., Forest, M., Snow, J., Pearpoint, J., & Hasbury, D. (1989). *Action for inclusion: How to improve schools by welcoming children with special needs into regular classrooms.* Toronto: Inclusion Press.

O'Brien, R. (ed.). (2004). *Voices from the edge: Narratives about the Americans with Disabilities Act.* Oxford: Oxford University Press.

Ogle, D. (1986). K-W-L: A teaching model that develops active reading of expository text. *The Reading Teacher, 39,* 564–570.

Oliver, M. (1983). *Social work with disabled people.* Basingstoke, UK: Macmillan.

Oliver, M. (1990). *The politics of disablement: A sociological approach.* New York, NY: St. Martin's Press.

Oliver, M. (1996). *Understanding disability. From theory to practice.* Basingstoke, UK: Macmillan.

Oliver, M.J. (1999). Capitalism, disability, and ideology: A materialist critique of the normalization principle. In R.J. Flynn & R.A. Lemay (eds.), *A quarter-century of normalization and social role valorization: Evolution and impact* (pp. 163–173). Ottawa: University of Ottawa Press.

Onosko, J.J., & Jorgensen, C.M. (1998). Unit and lesson planning in the inclusive classroom: Maximizing learning opportunities for all students. In C.M. Jorgensen (ed.), *Restructuring high schools for all students* (pp. 71–105). Baltimore, MD: Brookes.

Opp, G. (1994). Historical roots of the field of learning disabilities: Some nineteenth-century German contributions. *Journal of Learning Disabilities, 27*(January), 10–19.

Orkwis, R. & McLane, K. (1998). A curriculum every student can use: Design principles for student access. Reston, VA: ERIC/OSEP Special Project. Retrieved from http://files.eric.ed.gov/fulltext/ED423654.pdf

Owen, A., Rosenfelt, K. (Producers), & Sharrock, T. (Director). (2016). *Me before you* [motion picture]. USA: Metro-Goldwyn-Mayer.

Oyler, C. (2001). Democratic classrooms and accessible instruction. *Democracy & Education, 14*(1), 28–31.

Padden, C., & Humphries, T. (1988). *Deaf in America: Voices from a culture.* Cambridge, MA: Harvard University Press.

Palacio, R.J. (2012). *Wonder.* New York, NY: Random House.

Palincsar, A.S., & Brown, A.L. (1984). Reciprocal teaching of comprehension-fostering and comprehension-monitoring activities. *Cognition and Instruction, 1*(2), 117–175.

Palincsar, A.S. (1998). Social constructivist perspectives on teaching and learning. *Annual Review of Psychology, 49*, 345–375.

Palincsar, A.S., Magnusson, S.J., Collins, K.M., & Cutter, J. (2001). Making science accessible to all: Results of a design experiment in inclusive classrooms. *Learning Disability Quarterly, 24*(1), 15–32.

Paré, A. (1982). *On monsters and marvels* (J. Pallister, Trans.) Chicago, IL: University of Chicago Press. (Original work published 1840).

Parens, E., & Asch, A. (eds.). (2000). *Prenatal testing and disability rights.* Washington, DC: Georgetown University Press.

Paris, D. (2012). Culturally sustaining pedagogy: A needed change in stance, terminology, and practice. *Educational Researcher, 41*(3), 93–97.

Paul, P.V., & Ward, M.E. (1996). Inclusion paradigms in conflict. *Theory Into Practice, 35*(1), 4–11.

Pearson, N. (Producer), & Sheridan, J. (Director). (1989). *My left foot* [motion picture]. Ireland, UK: Granada Films (UK), Miramax Films.

Pedroni, T.C. (2006). Acting neoliberal: Is Black support for vouchers a rejection of progressive educational values? *Educational Studies, 40*(3), 265–278.

Pennsylvania Association for Retarded Children v. Commonwealth of Pennsylvania, 334 F. Supp. 1257 (E.D. Pa. 1971), 343; F. Supp. 279 (E.D. Pa. 1972).

People in motion: Viewers guide. (1995). New York, NY: Thirteen: WNET. Available from: People in Motion, Box 245, Little Falls, NJ 07424–0245.

Pernick, M. (1996). *The black stork: Eugenics and the death of "defective" babies in American medicine and motion pictures since 1915.* New York, NY: Oxford University Press.

Peters, S. (2000). Is there a disability culture? A syncretisation of three possible world views. *Disability & Society, 15*(4), 583–601.

Pisha, B., & Coyne, P. (2001). Smart from the start: The promise of universal design for learning. *Remedial and Special Education, 22*(4), 197–203.

Plessy v. Ferguson, 163 U.S. 537 (1896).

Pope, A., & Tarlov, A. (eds.). (1991). *Disability in America.* Washington, DC: Committee on a National Agenda for the Prevention of Disabilities, Division of Health Promotion and Disease Prevention, Institute of Medicine, National Academy Press.

Preen, B. (1976). *Schooling for the mentally retarded: A historical perspective.* New York, NY: St. Martin's Press.

President's Committee on Employment of the Handicapped. (1977). *Disabled Americans: A history.* Washington, DC: Author.

President's Committee on Mental Retardation. (1975). *Mental retardation: The known and the unknown* (DHEW Publication Nos. [OHD] 76–21008). Washington, DC: U.S. Government Printing Office.

President's Committee on Mental Retardation. (1977). *Mental retardation past and present.* Washington, DC: U.S. Government Printing Office.

Price, C., Goodson, B., & Stewart, G. (2007). *Infant environmental exposure to thimerosal and neuropsychological outcomes at ages 7 to 10 years* (Technical report; Vol. I.). Bethesda, MD: Abt Associates Inc.

Proctor, C.P., Dalton, B., Uccelli, P., Biancarosa, G., Mo, E., Snow, C., & Neugebauer, S. (2011). Improving comprehension online: Effects of deep vocabulary instruction with bilingual and monolingual fifth graders. *Reading and Writing, 24*(5), 517–544. doi: 10.1007/s11145-009-9218-2

Proctor, R. (1988). *Racial hygiene: Medicine under the Nazis.* Cambridge, MA: Harvard University Press.

Proctor, R. (1992). Nazi biomedical policies. In A. Caplan (ed.), *When medicine went mad: Bioethics and the Holocaust* (pp. 23–42). Totowa, NJ: Humana Press.

Pross, C. (1992). Nazi doctors, German medicine, and historical truth. In G. Annas & M. Grodin (eds.), *The Nazi doctors and the Nuremberg code: Human rights in human experimentation* (pp. 32–59). New York, NY: Oxford University Press.

Pugach, M. C., & Warger, C. L. (eds.). (1996). *Curriculum trends, special education, and reform: Refocusing the conversation*. New York, NY: Teachers College Press.

Rappolt-Schlichtmann, G., Daley, S. G., Seoin, L., Lapinski, S., Robinson, K. H., & Johnson, M. (2013). Universal Design for Learning and elementary school science: Exploring the efficacy, use, and perceptions of a web-based science notebook. *Journal of Educational Psychology, 105*(4), 1210–1225. doi:10.1037/a0033217

Raven, J. C. (1958). *The Standard Progressive Matrices*. London: H. K. Lewis.

Rees, J. (2001). Frederick Taylor in the classroom: Standardized testing and scientific management. *Radical Pedagogy, 3*(2), 1–8.

Reid, D. K., & Valle, J. W. (2004). The discursive practice of learning disability: Implications for instruction and parent–school relations. *Journal of Learning Disabilities*, special issue, *37*(6), 466–481.

Reiman, J. W., Beck, L., Coppola, T., & Engiles, A. (2010). *Parents' experiences with the IEP process: Considerations for improving practice*. Report. Eugene, OR: Center for Appropriate Dispute Resolution in Special Education (CADRE). Retrieved from http://eric.ed.gov/?id=ED512611

Reisberg, L. (1998). Facilitating inclusion with integrated curriculum: A multidisciplinary approach. *Intervention and School Clinic, 33*(5), 272–277.

Remak, J. (ed.). (1969). *The Nazi years*. Englewood Cliffs, NJ: Prentice Hall.

Reschly, D. J. (1996). Identification and assessment of children with disabilities. *The Future of Children: Special Education for Children with Disabilities, 6*(1), 40–53.

Retarded school alumni told they consumed radiation with their oatmeal. (1994, January 14). *The Star Ledger*, p. 27.

Rice, N. (2006). "Reining in" special education: Constructions of "Special Education" in *New York Times* editorials, 1975–2004 [electronic version]. *Disability Studies Quarterly, 26*. Retrieved June 30, 2006 from http://www.dsq-sds-archives.org/test4dpubs/2006_spring_toc.html

Rickover, H. G. (1957, November 20, 1956). *The education of our talented children*. Paper presented at the the Seventh Institute of The Thomas Alva Edison Foundation, Hotel Suburban, East Orange, NY.

Rioux, M. (1996). Services and supports in a human rights framework. *Disability Studies Quarterly, 16*(1), 4–10.

Rogasky, B. (1988). *Smoke and ashes: The story of the Holocaust*. New York, NY: Holiday House.

Rogers, B. (October, 1978). Richard III: Shakespeare was quite wrong. *In Britain, 33*, 31–35.

Rogers, C. (2011). Mothering and intellectual disability: partnership rhetoric? *British Journal of Sociology of Education, 32*(4), 563–581.

Rogers, R. (2002). Between contexts: A critical discourse analysis of family literacy, discursive practices, and literate subjectivities. *Reading Research Quarterly, 37*(3), 248–277.

Rose, D., & Meyer, A. (2000). Universal Design for Learning. *Journal of Special Education Technology, 15*(1), 67–70.

Rose, D., & Meyer, A. (2002). *Teaching every student in the digital age: Universal Design for Learning*. Alexandria, VA: ASCD.

Rosen, R. S. (2006). An unintended consequence of IDEA: American Sign Language, the Deaf community, and Deaf culture into mainstream education [electronic version]. *Disability Studies Quarterly, 26*. Retrieved June 5, 2009 from http://www.dsq-sds.org/article/view/685/862

Ross, R. (1978). Civilization's treatment of the handicapped. In G. McDevitt & L. McDevitt (eds.), *The handicapped experience: Some human perspectives* (pp. 7–13). Baltimore, MD: University of Baltimore.

Ross, R., & Freelander, R. (1977). *Handicapped people in society: A curriculum guide*. Burlington, VT: University of Vermont.

Rothman, D. (ed.). (1990). *The discovery of the asylum: Social order and disorder in the new republic*. Boston, MA: Little Brown & Company.

Ruch, F. (1967). *Psychology and life* (7th ed.). Glenview, IL: Scott Foresman.

Russell, M. (1998). *Beyond ramps: Disability at the end of the social contract*. Monroe, ME: Common Courage Press.

Salas, L. (2004). Individualized educational plan (IEP) meetings and Mexican American parents: Let's talk about it. *Journal of Latinos and Education, 3*(3), 181–192.

Salend, S. J. (1994). *Effective mainstreaming: Creating inclusive classrooms* (2nd ed.). New York, NY: Macmillan.

Saltman, K. J. (2007). *Capitalizing on disaster: Taking and breaking public schools.* Herndon, VA: Paradigm Publishers.

Sapon-Shevin, M. (2000/2001). Schools fit for all. *Educational Leadership, 58*(4), 34–39.

Sarason, S., & Doris, J. (1979). *Educational handicap, public policy, and social history: A broadened perspective on mental retardation.* New York, NY: The Free Press.

Saville, V. (Producer), & Fleming, V. (Director). (1941). *Dr. Jekyll and Mr. Hyde* [motion picture]. United States: Metro-Goldwyn-Mayer.

Scheerenberger, R. (1983). *A history of mental retardation.* Baltimore, MD: Paul H. Brookes.

Scholl, G. (ed.). (1986). *Foundations of education for blind and visually handicapped children and youth: Theory and practice.* New York, NY: American Foundation for the Blind.

Schou, S. J. (2006, February 15). Disabled Los Angeles playwright and activist John Belluso dies. *AP Worldstream.* Retrieved from http://www.highbeam.com/doc/1P1–118511159.html

Schramm, D., Fitzpatrick, E., & Seguin, C. (2002). Cochlear implantation for adolescents and adults with prelinguistic deafness. *Otology & Neurotology, 23*(5), 698–703.

Schroedel, J. (ed.). (1979). *Attitudes toward persons with disabilities: A compendium of related literature.* Albertson, NY: National Center on Employment of the Handicapped at the Human Resource Center.

Schultz, B. D. (2008). *Spectacular things happen along the way: Lessons from an urban classroom.* New York, NY: Teachers College Press.

Schwarz, P. (2006). *From disability to possibility: The power of inclusive classrooms.* Portsmouth, NH: Heinemann.

Shakespeare, T. (1994). Cultural representation of disabled people: Dustbins for disavowal. *Disability & Society, 9*(3), 283–299.

Shapiro, A. (1999). *Everybody belongs: Changing negative attitudes toward classmates with disabilities* (Vol. 14). New York, NY: Routledge.

Shapiro, A., & Barton, E. (1991). Changing lives by eliminating handicapism. *New Jersey Journal of Lifelong Learning, Winter,* 2–4.

Shapiro, A., & Margolis, H. (1988). Changing negative peer attitudes toward students with learning disabilities. *Reading & Writing Quarterly, 4*(2), 133–146.

Shapiro, J. (1993). *No pity: People with disabilities forging a new civil rights movement.* New York, NY: Random House.

Shea, T., & Bauer, A. (1997). *An introduction to special education: A social systems perspective.* Madison, WI: Brown & Benchmark Publishers.

Simon, J. B. (2006). Perceptions of the IEP requirement. *Teacher Education and Special Education, 29*(4), 225–235.

Silver, P., Bourke, A., & Strehorn, K. C. (1998). Universal Instructional Design in higher education: An approach for inclusion. *Equity & Excellence, 31*(2), 47–51.

Silveri, S. (Producer). (2016). *Speechless* [television series]. Hollywood, CA: 20th Century Fox Television/ABC Studios.

Skrtic, T. M. (1991). *Behind special education: A critical analysis of professional culture and school organization.* Denver, CO: Love Publishing Company.

Slater, W. H., & Horstman, F. R. (2002). Teaching reading and writing to struggling middle school and high school students: The case for reciprocal teaching. *Preventing School Failure, 46*(4), 163–166.

Slavin, R. (1990). *Cooperative learning: Theory, research and practice.* Boston, MA: Allyn & Bacon.

Slavin, R. E. (1999). Comprehensive approaches to cooperative learning. *Theory Into Practice, 38*(2), 74–79.

Sleeter, C. E. (1987). Why is there learning disabilities? A critical analysis of the birth of the field in its social context. In T. Popkewitz (ed.), *The formation of school subjects: The struggle for creating an American institution* (pp. 210–237). London: Falmer Press.

Sleeter, C. E., & Grant, C. A. (2007). *Making choices for multicultural education: Five approaches to race, class and gender* (6th ed.). Hoboken, NJ: Wiley.

Smart, J. (2001). *Disability, society, and the individual.* Austin, TX: Pro-ed, Inc.

Smith, D., & Luckasson, R. (1995). *Introduction to special education: Teaching in an age of challenge* (2nd ed.). Needham Heights, MA: Allyn & Bacon.

Smith, J. (1985). *Minds made simple: The myth and legacy of the Kallikaks.* Austin, TX: Pro-Ed.

Smith, J. (1994). *Pieces of purgatory: Mental retardation in and out of institutions.* Belmont, CA: Brooks/Cole Publishing, a Division of Wadsworth.

Snow, K. (2001). *Creating new lives for children and their families: Revolutionary common sense for raising successful children with disabilities.* Woodland Park, CO: Brave Heart Press.

Snyder, S.L., & Mitchell, D.T. (Producers/Directors). (2005). *Self preservation: The art of Riva Lehrer* [motion picture]. Chicago, IL: Brace Yourselves Productions.

Snyder, S.L., & Mitchell, D.T. (2006). *Cultural locations of disability.* Chicago, IL: University of Chicago Press.

Spooner, F., Baker, J.N., Harris, A.A., Ahlgrim-Delzell, L., & Browder, D.M. (2007). Effects of training in universal design for learning on lesson plan development. *Remedial and Special Education, 28*(2), 108–116.

Stainback, S., & Stainback, W. (1996). *Inclusion: A guide for educators.* Baltimore, MD: Paul H. Brookes.

Steeves, P. (2006). Sliding doors: Opening our world. *Equity & Excellence in Education, 39*(2), 105–114.

Steinbeck, J. (1937). *Of mice and men.* New York:, NY Triangle Books.

Steinberg, S.R. (ed.). (2009). *Diversity and multiculturalism: A reader.* New York, NY: Peter Lang.

Steinberg, S.R., & Kincheloe, J.L. (2009). Smoke and mirrors: More than one way to be diverse and multicultural. In S.R. Steinberg (ed.), *Diversity and multiculturalism: A reader* (pp. 3–22). New York, NY: Peter Lang.

Stevenson, R.L. (1886). *Strange case of Dr. Jekyll and Mr. Hyde.* London: Longmans, Green & Co.

Stiker, H.-J. (1997). *A history of disability.* Ann Arbor, MI: University of Michigan Press.

Stobie, J., & Cole, J. (Producers). (2004). *Freedom machines* [television program]. USA: Richard Cox Productions/New Day Films.

Stubblefield, A. (2007). "Beyond the pale": Tainted whiteness, cognitive disability, and eugenic sterilization. *Hypatia, 22*(2), 162–181.

Sumara, D., & Davis, B. (1999). Interrupting heteronormativity: Toward a queer curriculum theory. *Curriculum Inquiry, 29*(2), 191–208.

Sutherland, A. (1984). *Disabled we stand.* Bloomington, IN: Indiana University Press.

Sutton v. United Airlines, 527 U.S. 471 (1999).

Szasz, T. (1970). *The manufacture of madness.* New York, NY: Harper & Row.

Taylor, S.J. (1988/2004). Caught in the continuum: A critical analysis of the principle of the least restrictive environment. *Research and Practice for Persons with Severe Disabilities, 29*(4), 218–230.

Thomas, C., & Corker, M. (2002). A journey around the social model. In M. Corker & T. Shakespeare (eds.), *Disability/Postmodernity: Embodying disability theory* (pp. 18–31). London: Continuum.

Thompson, C. (1968). *Giants, dwarfs and other oddities.* New York, NY: Citadel Press.

Thompson, C. (1994). *The mystery and lore of monsters.* New York, NY: Barnes & Nobel Books.

Thompson, D. (1985). Anger. In S. Browne, D. Connors, & N. Stern (eds.), *With the power of each breath: A disabled women's anthology* (pp. 78–85). Pittsburgh, PA: Cleis Press.

Thurer, S. (1980). Disability and monstrosity: A look at literary distortions of handicapping conditions. *Rehabilitation Literature, 41*(1–2), 12–15.

Titchkosky, T. (2001). Disability: A rose by any other name? "People-first" language in Candadian society. *Canadian Review of Sociology and Anthropology, 38*(2), 125–140.

Tomlinson, C.A. (1999). *The differentiated classroom: Responding to the needs of all learners.* Alexandria, WV: ASCD.

Tomlinson, C.A. (2004). The mobius effect: Addressing learner variance in schools. *Journal of Learning Disabilities, 37*(6), 516–524.

Tomlinson, C.A., & Kalbfleisch, M.L. (1998). Teach me, teach my brain. A call for differentiated classrooms. *Educational Leadership, 56*(3), 56–60.

Tomlinson, C.A., & McTighe, J. (2006). *Integrating differentiated instruction and understanding by design.* Alexandria, VA: ASCD.

Toyota Motor Manufacturing v. Williams, 534 U.S. 184 (2002).

Trattner, W. (1994). *From poor laws to welfare state: A history of social welfare in America.* New York, NY: The Free Press, A Division of Simon & Schuster.

Trent, J. (1994). *Inventing the feeble mind: A history of mental retardation in the United States.* Berkeley, CA: University of California Press.

UN Decade of Disabled Persons 1983–1992. (1983). *World Programme of Action Concerning Disabled Persons.* New York: United Nations.

United Nations. (2007). *Convention on the Rights of Persons with Disabilities.* New York, NY: Author.

United Nations General Assembly. (1948). *UN Declaration on Human Rights.*

United Nations Ministry of Educational, Scientific and Education and Science Cultural Organization [UNESCO]. (1994). *The Salamanca statement and framework for action on special needs education.* Salamanca, Spain.

United States Congress. (1973), *Public Law 93–112, Vocational Rehabilitation Act 1973, Section 504.*

United States Congress. (1974), *Public Law 94–142, The Education for All Handicapped Children Act of 1975.*

United States Department of Education. (2001). *To assure the free appropriate public education of all children with disabilities: Individuals with Disabilities Education Act, Section 618.* Twenty-third annual report to congress on the implementation of the Individuals with Disabilities Education Act. Jessup, MD: U.S. Department of Education Publications Center. Retrieved from http://www2.ed.gov/about/reports/annual/osep/2001/index.html

United States Department of Education (2007, September). 27th annual report to congress on the implementation of the Individuals with Disabilities Education Act, 2005. Retrieved from: https://www2.ed.gov/about/reports/annual/osep/2005/parts-b-c/27th-vol-1.pdf

Valente, J.M. (2011). *d/Deaf and d/Dumb: A portrait of a deaf kid as a young superhero.* New York, NY: Peter Lang.

Valle, J.W. (2009). *What mothers say about special education: From the 1960s to the present.* New York, NY: Palgrave Macmillan.

Valle, J.W., & Aponte, E. (2002). IDEA and collaboration: A Bakhtinian perspective on parent and professional discourse. *Journal of Learning Disabilities, 35*(5), 471–481.

Van der Klift, E., & Kunc, N. (1994). Beyond benevolence. In J.S. Thousand, R.A. Villa, & A.I. Nevins (eds.), *Creativity and collaborative learning: A practical guide to empowering students and teachers* (pp. 391–401). Baltimore, MD: Brookes.

Van Riper, C., & Emerick, L. (1984). *Speech correction: An introduction to speech pathology and audiology.* Englewood Cliffs, NJ: Prentice-Hall.

Varenne, H., & McDermott, R. (1998). *Successful failure: The school America builds.* Boulder, CO: Westview.

Vash, C. (1981). *The psychology of disability.* New York, NY: Springer Publishing Company.

Vavrus, F., & Cole, K. (2002). "I didn't do nothin'": The discursive construction of school suspension. *The Urban Review, 34*(2), 87–111.

Virginia Sterilization Act, Va. Acts 569–71. (1924, repealed 1968).

Vygotsky, L.S. (1986). *Thought and language.* A. Kozulin (ed.). Cambridge, MA: The Massachusetts Institute of Technology.

Waitoller, F.R., & Artiles, A.J. (2013). A decade of professional development research for inclusive education: A critical review and notes for a research program. *Review of Education Research, 83*(3), 319–356. doi:10.3102/0034654313483905

Waitoller, F.R., & Kozleski, E.B. (2013). Working in boundary practices: Identity development and learning in partnerships for inclusive education. *Teaching and Teacher Education, 31*, 35–45.

Ware, L. (2001). Writing, identity, and the other: Dare we do disability studies? *Journal of Teacher Education, 52*(2), 107–123.

Watts, W. (1984). Attitude change: Theories and methods. In R. Jones (ed.), *Attitudes and attitude change in special education* (pp. 41–69). Reston, VA: Council for Exceptional Children.

Webber, A.L. (Producer), & Schumacher, J. (Director). (2004). *The phantom of the opera* [motion picture]. United States, United Kingdom: Warner Bros.

Wechsler, D. Kaplan, E., Fein, D., Kramer, J., Morris, R., Delis, D., & Maerlender, A. (2004). *Wechsler Intelligence Scales for Children–integrated* (4th ed.). San Antonio, TX: Harcourt Assessment, Inc.

Wehmeyer, M.L. (2006). Beyond access: Ensuring progress in the general education curriculum for students with severe disabilities. *Research and Practice for Persons with Severe Disabilities, 31*(4), 322–326.

Weindling, P. (1989). *Health, race and German politics between national unification and Nazism, 1870–1945.* Cambridge, UK: Cambridge University Press.

Weisberg, R. (Producer), & Aronson, J. (Director). (2000). *Sound and fury* [motion picture]. United States: Aronson Film Associates.

Welch, A.B. (2000). Responding to student concerns about fairness. *Exceptional Children, 33*(2), 36–40.

Welner, K.G. (April 2013). The dirty dozen: How charter schools influence student enrollment. *Teachers College Record* [online], http://www.tcrecord.org ID Number: 17104. Retrieved from http://nepc.colorado.edu/publication/TCR-Dirty-Dozen

Wendell, S. (1997). Toward a feminist theory of disability. In L. Davis (ed.), *The disability studies reader* (pp. 260–292). New York, NY: Routledge.

Wertham, F. (1980). *The German euthanasia program: Excerpts from "A sign from Cain".* Cincinnati, OH: Hayes Publishing Company, Inc.

Westridge Young Writers Workshop. (1994). *Kids explore the gifts of children with special needs.* Santa Fe, NM: John Muir Publications.

White, G. (1993). *Justice Oliver Wendell Holmes.* New York, NY: Oxford University Press.

Wiggins, G., & McTighe, J. (1998). *Understanding by design.* Alexandria, VA: ASCD.

Wolfensberger, W. (1980). Extermination: Disabled people in Nazi Germany. *Disabled USA, 4*(2), 22–24.

Wolfensberger, W. (1981). The extermination of handicapped people in World War II Germany. *Mental Retardation, 19*(February), 1–7.

Wolfensberger, W., Nirje, B., Olshansky, S., Perske, R., & Roos, P. (1972). *Normalization: The principle of normalization in human services.* Toronto, Canada: National Institute on Mental Retardation.

Wotherspoon, T., & Schissel, B. (2001). The business of placing Canadian children and youth "at-risk". *Canadian Journal of Education, 26*(3), 321–339.

Wright, B. (1983). *Physical disability—A psychosocial approach.* New York, NY: Harper & Row.

Wright, M.H. (1999). *Sounds like home: Growing up Black and Deaf in the south.* Washington, DC: Gallaudet University Press.

Wright, P. (1987). Disabling attitudes. *Contact, XII*(3), 4–9.

Wurzburg, G. (Producer/Director), & Biklen, D. (Co-Producer). (2004). *Autism is a world* [DVD]. United States: State of the Art/CNN Presents.

Yell, M., & Drasgow, E. (1999). A legal analysis of inclusion. *Preventing School Failure, 43*(3), 118–123.

Young, R. (2005). Neurobiology of savant syndrome. In C. Stough (ed.), *Neurobiology of exceptionality* (pp. 199–215). New York, NY: Kluwer Academic/Plenum Publishers.

Yuker, H., & Block, J. (1979). *Challenging barriers to change: Attitudes toward the disabled.* Albertson, NY: National Center on the Employment of the Handicapped at Human Resources Center.

Zola, I. (1982). *Missing pieces: A chronicle of living with a disability.* Philadelphia, PA: Temple University Press.

INDEX

Taylor & Francis eBooks

Helping you to choose the right eBooks for your Library

Add Routledge titles to your library's digital collection today. Taylor and Francis ebooks contains over 50,000 titles in the Humanities, Social Sciences, Behavioural Sciences, Built Environment and Law.

Choose from a range of subject packages or create your own!

Benefits for you

» Free MARC records

» COUNTER-compliant usage statistics

» Flexible purchase and pricing options

» All titles DRM-free.

REQUEST YOUR FREE INSTITUTIONAL TRIAL TODAY

Free Trials Available
We offer free trials to qualifying academic, corporate and government customers.

Benefits for your user

» Off-site, anytime access via Athens or referring URL

» Print or copy pages or chapters

» Full content search

» Bookmark, highlight and annotate text

» Access to thousands of pages of quality research at the click of a button.

eCollections – Choose from over 30 subject eCollections, including:

Archaeology	Language Learning
Architecture	Law
Asian Studies	Literature
Business & Management	Media & Communication
Classical Studies	Middle East Studies
Construction	Music
Creative & Media Arts	Philosophy
Criminology & Criminal Justice	Planning
Economics	Politics
Education	Psychology & Mental Health
Energy	Religion
Engineering	Security
English Language & Linguistics	Social Work
Environment & Sustainability	Sociology
Geography	Sport
Health Studies	Theatre & Performance
History	Tourism, Hospitality & Events

For more information, pricing enquiries or to order a free trial, please contact your local sales team: www.tandfebooks.com/page/sales

 Routledge
Taylor & Francis Group

The home of
Routledge books

www.tandfebooks.com